Håkan Gustavsson & Ludovico

Desert Prelude
Early clashes
June – November 1940

This work is dedicated to our beloved wives Lotta and Eva.

STRATUS

Published in Poland in 2010
by STRATUS s.c.
Po. Box 123,
27-600 Sandomierz 1, Poland.
e-mail: office@mmpbooks.biz

for MMP
3 Gloucester Close, Petersfield
Hampshire GU32 3AX, UK.
e-mail: rogerw@mmpbooks.biz
© 2010 MMP
http://www.mmpbooks.biz

All rights reserved. Apart from any fair dealing for the purpose of private study, research, criticism or review, as permitted under the Copyright, Design and Patents Act, 1988, no part of this publication May be reproduced, stored in a retrieval system, or transmitted in any form or by any means, electronic, electrical, chemical, mechanical, optical, photocopying, recording or otherwise, without prior written permission. All enquiries should be addressed to the publisher.

ISBN
978-83-89450-52-4

Editor in chief
Roger Wallsgrove

Editorial Team
**Bartłomiej Belcarz
Robert Pęczkowski
Artur Juszczak
James Kightly**

Map
Dariusz Karnas

Colour Drawings
**Artur Juszczak
Tedor Liviu Morosanu
Krzysztof Wołowski
Remi Pierlot**

DTP
**Artur Bukowski
Bartłomiej Belcarz**

Printed by
**Drukarnia Diecezjalna,
ul. Żeromskiego 4,
27-600 Sandomierz**
tel. +48 (15) 832 31 92
fax +48 (15) 832 77 87
www.wds.pl
marketing@wds.pl

PRINTED IN POLAND

Table of Contents

Introduction 3
1940 4
Before the storm 4
June 1940 18
    The ground war 18
    Operations 27
July 1940 57
    The ground war 57
    Operations 64
August 1940 93
    Operations 99
September 1940 124
    The ground war 124
    Operations 133
October 1940 155
    The ground war 155
    Operations 160
November 1940 186
    Operations 192
Index 205
Colour profiles 212

Acknowledgments

This work has used a huge number of sources, which will be recorded in the end of part 2.

However, a number of colleague, friends and historians have also kindly helped the authors with support, inspiration and additional material. Our gratitude goes especially to:

Giorgio Apostolo, Andrea Angiolino, Roberto Bassi, Nick Beale, Csaba Becze, Christer Bergström, Vincent Biondi, Gianni Biguzzi, Maria Teresa Bobba, Colleen Bowker, Gabriele Brancaccio, Rob Brown, Gianandrea Bussi, Jean Michel Cala, Massimo Cappone, Alberto Casirati, Matteo Cerofolini, Don Clark, Gordon Clarke, Shawn Cottingham, Alexander Crawford, Ferdinando D'Amico, Francesco D'Amico, Ernest Dean, Peter Dean, Luca Delle Canne, Averil DoRego, Santiago Flores, Marco Gargari, Luigi Gorrini, Chris Goss, Mike Grierson, Russell Guest, Börje Henningsson, Ian Hodkinson, Peter Holloway, Clare Gordon Jones, David LaJuett, Stefano Lazzaro, Enrico Locatelli, Alfredo Logoluso, Petr Lukes, Nicola Malizia, Antonio Maraziti, Giovanni Massimello, Fabio Marzocca, Francesco Mattesini, Ross McNeill, Carlo Minguzzi, Pierluigi Moncalvo, Patricia Molloy, Simon Muggleton, Claudio Narduzzi, Gustavo Ottolenghi, Manlio Palmieri, David Park, Michele Palermo, Antonio Poggi, Tomáš Polák, Ondrej Repka, Giuseppe Riccardi, Vanni Rinaldi, Roberto Scaglioni, Flavio Silvestri, Graham Buxton Smither, Gianmaria Spagnoletti, Andrew Thomas, Gabriele Valentini, Mirek Wawrzynski, Hugh Wheeler, and Paul Whelan.

All the personnel of Ufficio Storico Stato magg. Aeronautica and in particular: m. llo. Pasquale Rubertone, ten. col. Giancarlo Montinaro, ten. col. Massimiliano Barlattani and col. Euro Rossi

The personnel of Fototeca AMI and in particular ten. Gianluca Pasqualini of "Troupe Azzurra".

Another special thanks goes to Ian Acworth, Fulvio Chianese, Patricia Molloy, Vanni Rinaldi and Renato Zavattini, who all provided us with unique images and information for this book, to Enrico Cernuschi for all his help and encouragement and to Many Souffan who kindly shared with us his knowledge and expertise on French Air Force and in particular the operations of FAFL.

We apologize if we have forgotten any names.

Håkan Gustavsson & Ludovico Slongo, Borlänge & Padova January 2010

Introduction

The first North African Campaign was a very interesting one for several reasons. North Africa was Italy's main front in what was later called the "Parallel War", i.e. the period during which Italy tried to fight the Commonwealth autonomously, without the help of the German Armed Forces, and thus a period during which achievements and defeats were due only to Italian merits or mistakes. This period is one of the very few where historians can try to assess the real effectiveness of the Italian war effort, without being confused by the presence of German forces, and this is obviously true also in the field of air warfare.

With the Battle of Britain absorbing practically all the best resources, the Commonwealth forces on the North African front had to rely mostly on second line machines, sometimes already put out of service at home. This, together with the Italian trust in the biplane formula, meant that the Western Desert was (together with Greece and East Africa) the last battlefield in the history of air warfare where biplanes confronted each other. Needless to say, pilots of these archaic aircraft were by no means inferior in determination or skill to their colleagues fighting in Spitfires or Messerschmitts over the English Channel. Many of the most important Italian and Commonwealth pilots of the conflict drew first blood during this campaign, notably amongst them the top Italian and RAF aces of WW II, Teresio Martinoli and Thomas Pattle.

Despite this, the air war during this campaign has been rather neglected by historians, being treated only as a marginal sideshow overshadowed by events of the subsequent periods, after the *Luftwaffe* intervention. This book is an attempt to correct this negligence, and show that these eight months were a period of heavy fighting where large formations of aircraft clashed under the burning North African sun, with heavy losses suffered by both sides in the air.

Maggiore *Ernesto Botto in an aircraft from the 73ª* Squadriglia, *leading a formation from the 9º Gruppo over North Africa during the return from a mission. Identified in the image are fighters from the 96ª* Squadriglia. **[via Fulvio Chianese at Associazione Culturale 4º Stormo di Gorizia]**

1940 Before the storm

Italian forces

When Italy declared war on France and Britain on 10 June 1940, it faced forces from both countries in their North African possessions. The *Regia Aeronautica* forces in the region formed the *Aeronautica della Libia*, which was commanded by *Generale* Felice Porro.

At the start of the conflict there were two fighter *Gruppi* in North Africa; the 8° and the 13° *Gruppi* of the 2° *Stormo C.T.*, soon joined by a third one; the 10° *Gr.* of the 4° *Stormo C.T.*

The 2° *Stormo C.T.* was commanded by *col.* Angelo Federici. The two *Gruppi* (8° and 13°) had their headquarters in Tripoli Castel Benito at the airbase "Enea Silvio Recagno", but on 1 June they received orders to move to their war bases. For the 13° *Gr.* it was the same Tripoli Castel Benito, while the 8° *Gr.* received orders to move to Tobruk T2 starting from 4 June. The 8° *Gr.* was waiting for the first deliveries of CR.42s, and moved to T2 with only the CR.32 *quaters* combat-ready. Only a very small ground echelon followed the pilots because most of the fitters and engineers (among them the best) had to remain in Tripoli to erect the crated CR.42s arriving from Italy. In this quite unsatisfactory situation, the 8° *Gr.* moved to war only to find that T2 was a mere deserted piece of flat land, lacking any form of accommodation for pilots and planes, not to mention the complete absence of AA defences and warning network.

The 8° *Gr.* (92ª, 93ª and 94ª *Squadriglie*) was commanded by *magg.* Vincenzo La Carruba, and started the war based at Tobruk T2 airfield with a full complement of 25 Fiat CR.32 *quaters*.

Pilots in the 92ª *Sq.* on 11 June were: *cap.* Martino "Nino" Zannier (CO), *ten.* Riccardo Marcovich (*Gruppo Adjutant*), *ten.* Ranieri Piccolomini, *ten.* Giorgio Savoia, *serg. magg.* Guglielmo Gorgone, *serg.* Vito Copersino, *serg.* Nadio Monti, *serg.* Ernesto Pavan and *serg.* Bruno Salvi. These pilots had nine CR.32 *quaters* (including *magg.* La Carruba's) and one S.81 (piloted by Savini during the transfer) available on 11 June. On strength, there was also *serg.* Giovanni Sessa, but he hadn't left Tripoli. A number of pilots had been assigned to the *Squadriglia* before the start of the hostilities; *s. ten.* Alfonso Notari (from the 4° *Stormo* on 8 June), *serg.* Augusto Mannu (from 53° *Stormo* on 8 June), *serg.* Guido Piazza (from 53° *Stormo* on 10 June) and *serg.* Clemente Bonfanti (from 53° *Stormo* on 10 June); these pilots however remained at Tripoli.

The 93ª Squadriglia's badge on a Fiat CR.32 before the war, in 1939. [Argenton via Fulvio Chianese – Associazione Culturale 4° Stormo di Gorizia]

Pilots in the 93ª *Sq.* on 11 June were: *cap.* Mario Bacich (CO), *ten.* Alberto Argenton, *ten.* Gioacchino Bissoli, *serg. magg.* Italo Bertinelli, *serg.* Luigi Di Lorenzo, *serg.* Edoardo Azzarone, *serg.* Roberto Lendaro and *serg.* Duilio Bernardi. These pilots had eight CR.32 *quaters* available on 11 June. On strength there were also *ten.* Vincenzo Sansone, *s. ten.* Alberto Radice, *serg.* Orazio Antonicelli and *serg.* Ottorino Lancia, but they hadn't left Tripoli. *serg.* Armando Angelini was assigned from the 53° *Stormo* on 9 June but he also remained in Tripoli.

Pilots in the 94ª *Sq.* on 11 June were: *cap.* Franco Lavelli (CO), *ten.* Giovanni Tadini, *s. ten.* Giacomo Maggi, *s. ten.* Nunzio De Fraia, *serg. magg.* Trento Cecchi, *serg. magg.* Danilo Billi, *serg. magg.* Alessandro Ruzzene and *serg. magg.* Arturo Cardano. These pilots had eight CR.32 *quaters* available on 11 June.

The 13° *Gr.* (77ª, 78ª and 82ª *Squadriglie*) was commanded by *magg. Secondo* Revetria and started the war based at Tripoli Castel Benito airfield, with 25 CR.42s and eleven CR.32s combat-ready on hand (the CR.32s, kept as a reserve, were later passed on to the 50° *Stormo Assalto*) to guard against a possible French attach from the west.

Pilots in the 77ᵃ *Sq.* were: *cap.* Mario Fedele (CO), *ten.* Eduardo Sorvillo (recently arrived from 4° *Stormo*), *ten.* Giulio Torresi, *s. ten.* Gianmario Zuccarini, *s. ten.* Mario Fabbricatore, *serg. magg.* Ernesto Scalet, *serg. magg.* Leone Basso, *serg. magg.* Agostino Fausti, *serg.* Raoul Scodellari, *serg.* Ernesto Paolini, *serg.* Enrico Botti (recently arrived from 53° *Stormo*), *serg.* Amedeo Benati and *serg.* Vincenzo Campolo. These pilots had twelve CR.42s (including *magg.* Revetria's and *col.* Federici's), eight combat-ready and three still under assembly, and four CR.32 *quaters*.

Pilots in the 78ᵃ *Sq.* were: *cap.* Giuseppe Dall'Aglio (CO), *ten.* Ippolito Lalatta, *ten.* Domenico Bevilacqua, *ten.* Giovanni Beduz, *s. ten.* Natale Cima, *s. ten.* Italo Santavacca, *s. ten.* Dario Magnabosco, *serg. magg.* Giuseppe Frigo, *serg. magg.* Salvatore Mechelli, *serg.* Rovero Abbarchi, *serg.* Cassio Poggi, *serg.* Ernesto Taddia, *serg.* Vito Rinaldi, *serg.* Marcello Della Rovere and *serg.* Aldo Loioli. These pilots had twelve CR.42s (some still under assembly) and seven CR.32 *quaters* (five combat-ready and the others already disassembled). The two types were both used at the beginning of the hostilities in patrol missions over Tripolitania (the last flight for the CR.32s was recorded on 17 June).

Pilots in the 82ᵃ *Sq.* were: *cap.* Guglielmo Arrabito (CO), *ten.* Guglielmo Chiarini (arrived from 53° *Stormo* on 9 June), *s. ten.* Giuseppe Bottà, *s. ten.* Virgilio Vanzan, *s. ten.* Giuseppe Timolina,

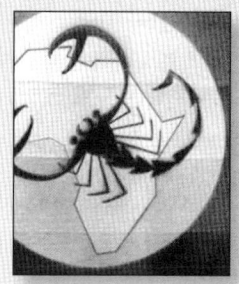

The 93ᵃ Squadriglia's badge on a Fiat CR.32 in North Africa. [Argenton via Fulvio Chianese – Associazione Culturale 4° Stormo di Gorizia]

Alberto Argenton's (93ᵃ Squadriglia, 8° Gruppo) CR.32 after a crash-landing in 1939. [Argenton via Fulvio Chianese – Associazione Culturale 4° Stormo di Gorizia]

A CR.42 from the 93ᵃ Squadriglia, 8° Gruppo is being recovered after a forced landing. [Argenton via Fulvio Chianese – Associazione Culturale 4° Stormo di Gorizia]

Group-photo of the 10° Gruppo at Gorizia before departing for Tobruk. [via Fulvio Chianese]

s. ten. Gilberto Cerofolini, *serg. magg.* Dante Davico, *serg.* Renato Giansante, *serg.* Franco Porta, *serg.* Francesco Nanin, *serg.* Filippo Baldin, *serg.* Riccardo Bonoli and *serg.* Albino Falasco (arrived on 9 June).

Total strength of the *Squadriglia* was twelve CR.42s (three of them still under assembly), six CR.32 *quaters* and one Breda Ba.25 for liaison. The CR.32s were used in patrol missions until 13 June.

On 12 June, the 2° *Stormo*'s fighters were joined by those of the 10° *Gr.* (84ª, 90ª and 91ª *Squadriglie*) of the Gorizia-based 4° *Stormo C.T.* The *Gruppo* was commanded by *ten. col.* Armando Piragino and started the war at Tobruk T2 with 27 CR.42s.

At the beginning of the hostilities the 84ª *Sq. C.T.* was composed of the following pilots: *cap.* Luigi Monti (CO), *cap.* Aldo Lanfranco, *ten.* Vincenzo Vanni, *m. llo.* Emiro Nicola, *m. llo.* Mario Bandini, *serg. magg.* Ugo Corsi, *serg.* Domenico Santonocito, *serg.* Roberto Steppi, *serg.* Giuseppe Scaglioni, *serg.* Corrado Patrizi and *serg.* Narciso Pillepich. The eleven pilots had only eight Fiat CR.42s. It seems that *serg. magg.* Corsi and *serg.* Pillepich didn't take part in the move from Gorizia on 7 June, but were in T2 with the unit from at least 13 June and 15 June.

Specialist from the 90ª Squadriglia starting from Gorizia, Italy, bound for North Africa. [Historical Office Italian Air Force]

A factory photo of a Fiat CR.32 quater. Although outdated at the start of war it soldiered on in some units during the starting months of the war. However, in North Africa, by the end of July, the Fiat CR.42 had replaced it in the fighter role. [via Massimo Cappone]

The 90ª *Sq.* was composed of the following pilots: *cap.* Renzo Maggini (CO), *ten.* Franco Lucchini, *ten.* Giovanni Guiducci, *s. ten.* Neri De Benedetti, *s. ten.* Alessandro Rusconi, *m. llo.* Omero Alesi, *serg. magg.* Angelo Savini, *serg.* Amleto Monterumici, *serg.* Silvio Crociati, *serg.* Giovanni Battista Ceoletta, *serg.* Alfredo Sclavo, *serg.* Bruno Bortoletti, *serg.* Paolo Guillet and *serg.* Ernesto Keller. The last three pilots didn't take part in the move to T2. The *Squadriglia* had nine Fiat CR.42s on strength.

The 91ª *Sq. C.T.* was composed of the following pilots: *cap.* Giuseppe D'Agostinis (CO), *ten.* Enzo Martissa, *s. ten.* Ruggero Caporali, *m. llo.* Raffaele Chianese, *m. llo.* Vittorio Romandini, *serg. magg.* Leonardo Ferrulli, *serg. magg.* Lorenzo Migliorato, *serg. magg.* Natale Fiorito, *serg. magg.* Elio Miotto, *serg.* Aldo Rosa, *serg.* Alessandro Bladelli, *serg.* Guido Scozzoli and *serg.* Luigi Ferrario. They had ten CR.42s on strength (including Piragino's).

The ground attack role was covered by the 50º *Stormo* and its two *Gruppi* (12º and 16º *Gruppi*).

The 50º *Stormo Assalto* was based in Libya from the summer of 1939 and equipped with Breda Ba.65/A80s. The aircraft were worn out even before the beginning of the war, and because of this serviceability was down to very low levels, sometimes only 18% of the flight line. Apart from this, the Bredas were considered unsafe because of a string of accidents (sometimes fatal).

The HQ in Rome took the decision to replace the Bredas of the 50º *Stormo* with a new plane, and the choice fell on the Caproni Ca.310B *Libeccio*.

During the second half of May 1940, the Bredas based in Libya were discharged (83 planes in various degrees of efficiency and not all in charge of the 50º *Stormo*; there were also some Breda Ba.65/K14s which had been left behind by the 2º *Stormo* after an unsuccessful attempt to use them in the dual role of fighter/fighter-bomber).

After a brief period of training in Northern Italy, some pilots of the *Stormo* came back to Libya with the first examples (nine) of the new aircraft.

On 1 June 1940 the *Stormo* was under the command of *col.* Pietro Molino and was comprised of two *Gruppi* with three *Squadriglie*:

The 12º *Gr.* was commanded by *magg.* Bruno Cudugnello and comprised the 159ª *Sq.* (*cap.* Antonio Dell'Oro), the 160ª *Sq.* (*cap.* Aldo Iannaci) and the 165ª *Sq.* (*cap.* Duilio Fanali) at Sorman.

The 16º *Gr.* was commanded by *magg.* Spartaco Sella and comprised the 167ª *Sq.* (*cap.* Alfredo Zanardi), the 168ª *Sq.* (*ten.* Mario Burroni) and the 169ª *Sq.* (*ten.* Luigi Lisardi).

On this date the *Stormo* became a *Bombardamento Leggero* (Light Bomber) unit, and took the two *Squadriglie* structure of the bombing units, the 165ª *Sq.* and the 169ª *Sq.* being disbanded.

The 122ª Squadriglia, 64° O.A., at Tripoli – Mellah in 1939. A number of the unit's IMAM Ro.37bis can be spotted in the photo. [via Italian Air Force]

Caproni Ca.309 Ghibli of Sezione Sahariana Oasi Cufra in 1938. [via Andrea Di Pauli]

Benghazi Benina photographed from a Fiat CR.42. [Gino via Fulvio Chianese – Associazione Culturale 4° Stormo di Gorizia]

In the 16° Gr. Lisardi was promoted *cap.* and took command of the 168ª Sq., while *cap.* Francesco Beccaria replaced *cap.* Alfredo Zanardi as CO of the 167ª Sq. The number of planes of the *Stormo* (theoretical) decreased from 54 to 48. (from two *Gruppi* of three *Squadriglie* of nine, to two *Gruppi* of two *Squadriglie* of twelve). However the real strength of the Italian air units was normally well below the theoretical value.

The new Capronis were a big disappointment, and the new aircraft were even worse than the old Bredas. *Generale* Felice Porro, who ordered the refitting of the surviving planes to give them back to the 50° *Stormo*, stopped the demolition of the Bredas. But the war was impending and a ground attack unit, (theoretically) strong with 54 assault planes and with one year of training in desert conditions, was reduced on 10 June 1940 to nine Capronis (of limited efficiency) and eight (or nine) recovered Breda Ba.65/A80s that constituted an autonomous *Squadriglia* inside the *Stormo*, under command of *cap.* Duilio Fanali (the so called " *Nucleo Fanali*"). All these aircraft were under the 12° Gr. since the 16° Gr. had no aircraft left at all, and was waiting for the first delivery of Capronis.

Bureaucracy at the Air Ministry of Rome reacted slower than the Commander in the field, so assignation of the undesired Capronis went on. The first twenty days of war in June saw the delivery of new Capronis from Italy (in the end around 42 arrived, which were mostly passed to the A.P.C. and reconnaissance *Gruppi*), and of old Bredas refitted by the SRAM of Berka. The number of the remaining Bredas, however, was not sufficient even for the reduced strength of the *Stormo*, so the decision was taken to re-equip two of its four *Squadriglie* with Fiat CR.32s that were leaving the 2° *Stormo*.

The bomber forces of the *Aeronautica della Libia* were split between Tripolitana and Cirenaica with two *Stormi* each. The two *Stormi* in Tripolitana were 15° and 33° *Stormo B.T.* The 15° *Stormo* was based at Tarhuna T18 and commanded by *col.* Silvio Napoli. The *Stormo* consisted of:

Benghazi-Berka airfield in 1938 or spring 1939. In the photo 44 Breda Ba.65/K14s of the 2° Stormo and 6 IMAM Ro.41s can be spotted.
[via Italian Air Force]

- 46º *Gr.* (CO *magg.* Bruno Cerne) with 20ª *Sq.* (CO *ten.* Diego Recagno) and 21ª *Sq.* (CO *cap.* Angelo Lualdi).
- 47º *Gr.* (temporary CO *cap.* Giuseppe Magrì) with 53ª *Sq.* (CO *cap.* Magrì) and 54ª *Sq.* (CO *ten.* Alberto Remorino).

Total strength of the *Stormo* was 36 Savoia SM 79 bombers, of which 35 were combat-ready (nine aircraft in each *Squadriglia*). The 15º *Stormo* also had eight Savoia S.81s (all combat-ready), but these were not used in action and were possibly later passed on to the newly arrived 54º *Gr. Aut. B.T.*

The 33º *Stormo* was based at Bir el Berha and commanded by *col.* Giuseppe Leonardi. The *Stormo* consisted of:
- 35º *Gr.* (CO *ten. col.* Michele Scattaglia) with 43ª *Sq.* (CO *cap.* Silvio Pugnali) and 44ª *Sq.* (CO *cap.* Giuseppe Pagliacci).
- 36º *Gr.* (CO *magg.* Pietro De Mattia) with 45ª *Sq.* (CO *cap.* Calcedonio Baculo) and 46ª *Sq.* (CO *cap.* Riccardo Folinea).

The *Stormo* arrived from Italy on 3 June, and the total strength of the *Stormo* was 33 Savoia SM 79 bombers, of which around 31 were combat-ready.

The two *Stormi* in Cirenaica were 14º and 10º *Stormo B.T.*

The 14º *Stormo* was based at El Adem T3 and commanded by *col.* Giovanni Coppi. The *Stormo* consisted of:
- 44º *Gr.* (CO *ten. col.* Enrico Maramaldo Della Minerva) with 6ª *Sq.* (CO *cap.* Venanzio Brescianini) equipped with six SM 79s and six S.81s, and 7ª *Sq.* (CO *cap.* Maurizio Niggi) equipped with five SM 79s.
- 45º *Gr.* (CO *magg.* Ezio Berni) with 2ª *Sq.* (CO *cap.* Fortunato Profumi) and 22ª *Sq.*

Total strength of the 45º *Gr.* was 15 Savoia S.81 bombers. In total the *Stormo* had eleven SM 79s (five combat-ready) and 21 S.81s (nine combat-ready). The S.81s of the *Stormo* were frequently used in action during the opening phase of the war, until new SM 79s arrived to replace them.

The 10º *Stormo* was based at Benghazi Benina Z1 and commanded by *col.* Giovanni Benedetti. The *Stormo* consisted of:
- 30º *Gr.* (CO *ten. col.* Giuseppe Rossi) with 55ª *Sq.* (CO *cap.* Luigi Bressanelli) and 56ª *Sq.* (CO *cap.* Gerardo Musch).
- 32º *Gr.* (CO *ten. col.* Carlo Unia) with 57ª *Sq.* (CO *cap.* Mayer-Zotti) and 58ª *Sq.* (CO *cap.* Erminio Bertelli).

The *Stormo* arrived from Italy on 9 June and the total strength was 32 Savoia SM 79 bombers, of which around 30 were combat-ready (eight aircraft in each *Squadriglia*).

Total bomber force of *Aeronautica della Libia* was 112 Savoia SM 79s (101 combat-ready) and 29 Savoia S.81s (17 combat-ready).

Opposing the RAF were, however, only 43 SM 79s (35 combat-ready) and 21 S.81s (nine combat-ready). Furthermore, more than half of these aircraft had just arrived from Italy.

The reconnaissance force consisted of four *Gruppi* and four *Squadriglie autonome*.

The 1º *Gr. A.P.C. (Aviazione Presidio Coloniale)* (12ª, 89ª and 104ª *Squadriglie*) was based at Tripoli – Mellaha (12ª and 104ª *Squadriglie*) with the 89ª *Sq.* based at Sirte. The unit was commanded by ten. col. Aristide Bagatta, temporarily replaced by Capitano Mario Pozzati that was also CO of the 104ª *Sq.* An additional unit, the 99ª *Sq.* operated autonomously, having its HQ at Hon and sections temporarily detached in Ubari, Mirda and Murzuk. The 12ª *Sq.* was commanded by *ten.* Mario Gulli and the 89ª *Sq.* was commanded by *cap.* Massimiliano Erasi. It had 22 Ca.309s, one Ca.308, one Z.1012, one Z.506, one Z.509, one S.75 and one SM 79 on strength.

The 2º *Gr. A.P.C.* (16ª and 23ª *Squadriglie*), temporarily commanded by Capitano Mario Musumeci, had its headquarter at El Adem while the aircraft (nine Ca.309s, eight of them combat ready) were also detached to Apollonia and Menastir. *Aviazione Presidio Coloniale* was then completed by the 26ª *Sq.* based at Cufra for armed reconnaissance duties and the *Squadriglia*

Hawker Hart K4901 was still in RAF service in the Middle East in 1941. [via Eleonor Collins]

Allenamento Aviazione Sahariana (a training unit with five Ca.309s). According with some sources the *A.P.C.* had around 43 Capronis on strength.

The 64° *Gr. O.A.* (122ª and 136ª *Squadriglie*), with around seven IMAM Ro.37*bis*, was at Mellaha for armed reconnaissance duties.

The 73° *Gr. O.A.* was commanded by *magg.* Adolfo Domenici and was equipped with IMAM Ro.37*bis* for armed reconnaissance duties, with the 137ª *Sq.* at El Adem with four aircraft under *cap.* Giovanni Civale and the 127ª *Sq.* with three aircraft at Tobruk T2.

20 other Ro.37bis were on strength in the two *O.A. Gruppi* but they were not combat ready, in fact the wood and fabric built IMAM biplanes suffered badly from the heat excursions while their Piaggio engines were affected by the sand thus reducing to less then 50% the combat strength of the unit equipped with the plane.

The 143ª *Sq. R.M.* commanded by *magg.* Mario Bellotto and with six Cant Z.501s was based at Menelao station west of Tobruk for armed reconnaissance and air-sea rescue duties.

Two transport units were based in Libya at the beginning of the conflict, both based at Benghazi: the 604ª *Sq. Autonoma T (Trasporto* – transport) commanded by *cap.* Bruno Trocca and equipped with six S.75s and the 610ª *Sq. Autonoma T*, equipped with eight Savoia Marchetti S 75s and commanded by *magg.* Barbieri.

A line-up of 80 Sqn Gladiators in the Middle East. F/L Pattle claimed two CR.42s with K7971 on 8 August. In December 1940, this aircraft was passed on to the Royal Hellenic Air Force. [via Stratus]

Both units had been hastly formed at the very beginning of the hostilities using planes and pilots coming from the civil airline company *Ala Littoria*. The two units were later joined by a third one the 600ª *Sq. T* and formed the 145° *Gr. T*.

A rescue unit was also based in North Africa and this was the 614ª *Sq. Soccorso*, which was equipped with six Cant Z.506Cs and commanded by *cap*. Enzo Cocchia. The unit was based at Tripoli with sections of two planes detached at Benghazi and Menelao. At the beginning of the conflict it also worked on transport duties and in fact it is known that in July alone, Cocchia was able to perform a record 21 flights between Cirenaica and Sicily.

The two most important airbases of Cirenaica (eastern Libya) were El Adem and Berka, near Benghasi. El Adem was built in 1936, 25 km south of Tobruk inside the Libyan desert, and was equipped with many hangars, big fuel and ammunition stores, and had a SRAM (*Squadra Riparazione Aeromobile e Motori* – maintenance team for aircraft and engines). The other SRAM in Cirenaica was at Berka, together with the only available team able to do the general repair of engines.

The Italian units of II *Squadra Aerea* based in Sicily, and those of *Aeronautica della Sardegna* (Sardinian air force) based in Sardinia, would also take part in operations over North Africa (especially against the French).

Gladiator K8009 after its one-wheel landing in the hands of F/O Pattle from 80 Sqn. Very little damaged was caused to the aircraft and it was flying again in a couple of days. [via Stratus]

An 80 Sqn Gladiator K7971/YK-X on a desert patrol. The lack of fin stripes suggests this is a pre-June 1940 photo. Note also the Vokes air-filter under the engine cowling. [via Dave Williams]

Commonwealth forces

In the Middle East, the first line strength of a squadron consisted of a number of initial equipment (I.E.) aircraft. An immediate reserve (I.R.) of up to 50 % of the I.E. was usually (but not always) held by each squadron. Further reserves were kept at air stores parks and maintenance units. An example of the established strengths of squadrons in the Middle East soon after the fall of France was:

Fighter Sqn	I.E. 16 aircraft	I.R. 8 aircraft
Bomber Sqn	I.E. 16 aircraft	I.R. 8 aircraft
Flying-Boat Sqn	I.E. 6 aircraft	I.R. 2 aircraft
Army Co-operation Sqn	I.E. 12 aircraft	I.R. 6 aircraft

The bulk of the Royal Air Force units in Egypt formed 202 Group under the command of Air Commodore Raymond Collishaw. In total, he had 6 squadrons under his command:

- 33 (Fighter) Sqn based at Mersa Matruh.
- 45 (Bomber) Sqn based at Fuka.
- 55 (Bomber) Sqn based at Fuka.
- 113 (Bomber) Sqn based at Ma'aten Bagush (arrived from Heliopolis on 10 June).
- 211 (Bomber) Sqn based at El Daba.
- 208 (Army Co-operation) Sqn based at Qasaba.

33 Sqn was commanded by S/Ldr D. V. Johnson and equipped with 21 Gloster Gladiators (mainly Mk.IIs) (on 11 June), and six Gloster Gauntlets Mk.IIs (K5273, K5286, K5399, K5316, K7793 and K7844) kept in reserve. It had 22 pilots in three flights:

'A' Flight included F/Sgt Leonard Cottingham, Sgt Roy Leslie Green, F/O Monk, P/O Eric Woods, P/O Brown, P/O Preston, P/O Perry St. Quintin and F/Lt G. E. Hawkins.

'B' Flight included F/O Ernest Dean, Sgt Shaw, P/O Vernon Woodward, Sgt J. Craig, F/O Couchman, F/O John Littler and P/O Alfred Costello.

'C' Flight included F/Lt Bolingbroke, Sgt William Vale, P/O E. K. Leveille, F/Sgt Harry Goodchild, F/O Henry Starrett and P/O Boulton.

45 Sqn was commanded by S/Ldr J. W. Dallamore and was equipped with a dozen Bristol Blenheim Mk.Is.

55 Sqn was led by S/Ldr R. A. T. Stowell and was equipped with 13 Bristol Blenheims Mk.Is.

211 Sqn, commanded by S/Ldr J. W. B. Judge, was equipped with twelve Bristol Blenheim Mk.Is.

113 Sqn was the only unit equipped with the more modern Bristol Blenheim Mk.IV (but the conversion to the type was not completed), it however had around twelve machines on hand.

Joseph Fraser of 112 Sqn in the cockpit of a Gloster Gladiator.
[via Patricia Molloy]

More Blenheims (all Mk.Is) were kept as reserve. It is known for example that, apart from the first line complement of twelve planes, 211 Sqn had taken on charge at least six more Blenheims before the end of May 1940. The situation was most likely similar in the other units equipped with the Bristol bomber.

202 Group was completed by 208 Sqn commanded by S/Ldr R. A. Sprague and equipped with twelve Westland Lysanders divided among its three flights. The unit was under operational command of the 6th Infantry Division.

Other RAF units in Egypt were 252 (Fighter) Wing, with its HQ at Helwan and in charge of the defence of Cairo, the naval base of Alexandria and the Canal Zone. Two RAF and one REAF (Royal Egyptian Air Force) squadrons composed the wing.

80 Sqn was commanded by S/Ldr R. C. Jonas and based at Amriya. It had 22 Gladiators (mainly Mk.Is) and one Hurricane Mk.I (L1669 – nicknamed *Collie's Battleship*) on hand. Its main role was the defence of Alexandria. The pilots were divided into three Flights.

'A' Flight included S/Ldr R. C. Jonas (CO), F/Lt Edward Jones, F/O George Kettlewell, P/O Anthony Hugh Cholmeley, P/O Ernest Mason, P/O Arthur Weller, P/O Johnny Lancaster, P/O P. T. Dowding, Sgt Donald Gregory, F/Sgt T. C. Morris and Sgt J. C. Hulbert.

'B' Flight included F/Lt Thomas 'Pat' Pattle, F/O Greg Graham, F/O John Lapsley, P/O Sidney Linnard, P/O Vincent 'Heimar' Stuckey, F/Sgt Sidney Richens, F/Sgt Trevor Martin Vaughan and F/Sgt Charles Casbolt.

'C' Flight included F/Lt Ralph Evers-Swindell, F/O Peter Wykeham-Barnes, P/O Harold Sykes, P/O Frankie Stubbs, P/O Wanklyn Flower, Sgt George Barker, Sgt J. H. Clarke, Sgt Edward Hewett and Sgt Kenneth Russell Rew.

112 Sqn was commanded by S/Ldr D. M. Somerville. It was based at Helwan 15 miles south of Cairo and solely responsible for the defence of Egypt's capital. It probably had between 13 to 21 Gladiators and five Gauntlet Mk.IIs (among these were K5292, just received from 6 Sqn) left in Egypt. When the unit reached Egypt at the end of May 1939 for a *"6 months temporary duty"*, it had 24 Gloster Gladiator Mk.Is (all used machines coming from 72 Sqn). F/O Joseph Fraser remembered a slightly superior number, around 30. Since then only one machine was known to have been lost before the beginning of the war. This was the CO's Gladiator, whose engine caught fire on 15 March 1940 during a training flight. Somerville was badly hurt in the accident and S/Ldr A. R. G. Bax temporarily took command of the squadron. The squadron was organised in three flights:

- 'A' Flight was commanded by F/Lt W. C. Williams and included F/O H. C. Worcester, F/O W. B. Price-Owen, P/O Ross, P/O Richard Acworth, P/O Davison, P/O Smither, P/O Anthony Gray-Worcester, P/O Harrison, P/O Peter Wickham, P/O Peter Strahan and P/O Van der Heijden.
- 'B' Flight was commanded by F/Lt Savage, but this unit had been ordered to Sudan on 2 June (with 10 Gladiators – 8 aircraft according to the memories of the Adjutant, F/O Fraser) to act as a detached unit, subsequently known as 'K' Flight. This flight was finally detached from 112 Sqn on 31 August 1940.
- 'C' Flight was commanded by F/Lt Charles Fry and included F/O R. H. Smith, F/O Joseph Fraser (Adjutant of 112 Sqn), P/O Clarke, P/O Chapman, P/O Duff, P/O de la Hoyde, P/O R. J. Bennett, P/O Homer Cochrane, P/O Butcher and Sgt George Millar Donaldson.

This fighter force was backed by one squadron of the Royal Egyptian Air Force (no. 5) that, although Egypt was neutral, helped to defend the Suez Canal zone and formed a reserve of aircraft that the Commonwealth forces could use to made good their own losses. Another Egyptian fighter squadron (no. 2) was still independent. The two Egyptian squadrons were equipped with around 36 Gloster Gladiators, mainly Mark IIs.

201 Group, with its HQ in Alexandria, completed the RAF complement in Egypt. Among its units were one flying-boat squadron, 230 Sqn equipped with Short Sunderlands. The squadron was commanded by the newly promoted Wing Commander G. Francis and equipped with seven aircraft: L5804/S, L2164/Z, L5803/T, L2160/X, L2166/U, N9029/V and L2161/Y. Then there was 30

Sqn led by S/Ldr U. Y. Shannon and equipped with 15 Blenheim Mk.Is kept as a reserve in Ismailia. 70 Bomber/Transport Squadron was based at Helwan under Wing Commander E. B. Webb. It was equipped with at least 14 Vickers Valentias biplanes (K1313, K2793, K2796, K2800, K2803, K3160, K3602, K3610, K3614, K3624, K8848, K8849, K8851 and J8921). 216 Bomber/Transport Sqn was based at Heliopolis and equipped with 21 Bristol Bombays (mainly) and (a few) Vickers Valentias. Of 216 Sqn's aircraft, the first type was used in the dual role of night bomber-transport, while the other was used only as transports. Out of the 21 aircraft on strength 17 were serviceable and four unserviceable. Total personnel strength was 27 pilots (out of an establishment of 33) and 35 crewmembers (out of an establishment of 39). On 10 June, it was decided to strengthen the Sunderland component with an additional unit, and 228 Sqn started to move from Pembroke Dock. The first machines to take off were Sunderlands L5806/Q, L5807/R and N9025/Y. Wing Commander G. E. Nicholetts, AFC, commanded the unit's detachment. The Sunderlands arrived on 11 June.

Four additional Sea Gladiator Mk.IIs of 813 Sqn (based on the carrier HMS *Eagle* since 28 May 1940) were stationed ashore and joined with 252 Wing in the defence of Cairo, while other Sea Gladiators were kept in reserve at Alexandria.

French forces

In 1940 French territories in Africa and Middle East were the Madagascar, the so-called French Somaliland (in fact not more than a small patch of land around the coastal town of Djibouti), Syria, Lebanon, and finally the three big areas of AFN, AOF and AÉF, which constituted roughly the north-western part of the African continent.

The AFN (*Afrique Française du Nord*) – French North Africa – included the three important areas of Tunisia, Algeria and Morocco, and bordered to the east with the Italian-owned Tripolitania (the Tripoli region of Libya).

The AOF (*Afrique Occidentale Française*) – French Western Africa – included Mauritania, Senegal, Guinea, Upper Volta (now Burkina) , Ivory Coast, Togo, Dahomey (now Benin), Niger, and Mali. At the top of the northern territory of Niger, it bordered with the southern Saharan region of Tripolitania. Its most important city was the harbour of Dakar in Senegal.

AÉF (*Afrique Équatorial Française*) – French Western Africa – included Cameron, Chad, Oubangui-Chari (now Central African Republic), Gabon and Congo (the so-called Moyen-Congo, not the Belgian Congo). AÉF bordered with Southern Cirenaica through the northern territory of Chad.

In all these territories there was no more than a handful of military aircraft on 10 June 1940, with AOF and AÉF particularly lacking in this aspect.

The only modern fighters in the AFN were stationed in the Tunis-Bizerta area in Tunisia. They were:
- GC III/5, which was formed in May 1940 with two *Escadrilles* of second-hand Morane Saulnier MS.406s.
- GC I/9, which was commanded by *Commandant* Rousseauu-Dumarcet and arrived in Tunisia in May with 28 Morane Saulnier MS.406s, two transport Bloch MB.220s and six Potez 630s heavy fighters. Its second *Escadrille* was based near Tunis, while the first was at El Hamma near Gabes in the south of Tunisia.
- GC I/10, which was commanded by *Commandant* Legrix de La Salle and equipped with only three *Patrouilles* of Morane Saulnier MS.406s (nine fighters, roughly the strength of a single *Escadrille*) since most of its pilots were sent to metropolitan France to strengthen the fighter units stationed there.

In Morocco, GC III/4 was stationed. This unit was formed in May 1940 from the *Escadrilles Regional de Chasse* based there, and equipped with a handful of old fixed landing-gear Dewoitine D.510s and two even older Morane Saulnier MS.230s on strength. The unit was based in Casablanca under command of *Capitaine* Davy.

The situation of the AFN's bomber force was slightly better, and at the beginning of hostilities with Germany many bomber *Groupes* were based in Tunisia and Algeria but were gradually redeployed to metropolitan France, so on June 1940 only four *Groupes* remained; GR I/61, GB II/25, GB I/32, GB II/32.

GR I/61 was equipped with Glenn-Martin GM 167Fs employed in the reconnaissance-bomber roles and based at Youks-les-Bains in Algeria.

GB II/25 was based at Bougie in Algeria with around fifteen Lioré et Olivier LeO H 257*bis* seaplanes.

GB I/32 was equipped with Glenn-Martin GM 167Fs based at Mediouna in Morocco from 14 June.

GB II/32 was equipped with Douglas DB7s.

Apart from these units, there were many independent *Groupes* and *Escadrilles d'Observation Aerienne* (around fifteen) based in Tunisia, Algeria and Morocco, and equipped almost exclusively with elderly Potez 25 TOE biplanes.

The *Armée de l'Air* was complemented with the *Aeronavale*, which in AFN had the following units: HB1, HB2, T1, 4S1, 4S2, E7, 11E and E3.

HB1 was equipped with Latécoère 298 seaplanes and commanded by Lieutenant de Vaisseau Georges Baron. On 10 June, it was based at Bizerta-Karouba, Tunisia.

HB2 was equipped with ten Latécoère 298 seaplanes and commanded by Lieutenant de Vaisseau Veyre de Soras. On 10 June, it was based at Bizerta-Karouba, Tunisia.

HB1 and HB2 were formerly the air complement of the seaplane tender *Commandant Teste* and constituted a *Flotille*.

T1 was equipped with Latécoère 298 and commanded by *Lieutenant de Vaisseau* Cambon. On 10 June, it was based at Bizerta-Karouba.

4S1 was equipped with CAMS 55 seaplanes and commanded by *Lieutenant de Vaisseau* Renè Durand. On 10 June, it was based at Bizerta-Karouba, Tunisia.

4S2 was equipped with three CAMS 55 and four Lioré et Olivier 258 and commanded by *Lieutenant de Vaisseau* Luthereau. On 10 June, it was based at Bizerta-Karouba, Tunisia.

E7 was equipped with six Loire 70 and commanded by *Lieutenant de Vaisseau* Lacoste. On 10 June, it was based at Bizerta-Karouba, Tunisia.

11E (anomalous name for E11) was equipped with four LeO H-470 ex civil seaplane airliners of Air France, and commanded by *Lieutenant de Vaisseau* Bellando. On 10 June, it was based at Bizerta-Karouba, Tunisia.

E3 was equipped with six Bréguet Bizerte seaplanes and commanded by *Lieutenant de Vaisseau* Mouliérac. On 10 June, it was based at Bizerta-Karouba, Tunisia, with a section of two detached to Arzew near Mers-el-Kébir, Algeria.

In AOF and AÉF the aerial forces were very weak.

In AOF there were only seven *Escadrilles* based around Dakar (Thiès and Ouakam airbases) and in the localities of Gao and Bamako in Mali. The only fighter *Escadrille* (*Escadrille* n°6 d'AOF) was based at Ouakam with around ten Dewoitines D.501-510, and was commanded by *Commandant* Labit. The other six *Escadrilles*, were equipped with a motley collection of monoplanes and biplanes of various types, notably among them were Potez 542 bombers, and Potez 25 spotters. Then there were Potez Salmson, Potez 29, Farman 222.2, Bloch 120, in all no more than forty aircraft.

L'Aeronavale had its own aircraft based in AOF.

E4 at Dakar-Bel Air commanded by *Lieutenant de Vaisseau* Durand Couppel de Saint-Front. In 1939, it was equipped with three Latécoère 302 and one Latécoère 301, but in June 1940 it had no more than two operational seaplanes.

8S3 was formed in February 1940 with three Loire 130 to protect Dakar harbour.

In AÉF the situation was, if possible, even worse. Only one *Escadrille* was based there, a multi-role group of Potez 25s, Potez 29, Potez 540, Caudron Pélican and Bloch 120, for a total of twelve aircraft in all.

This and opposite page: The Base Aerienne *at Blida, Algeria, May 1940, during a ceremony at the School of Air Gunners. Bloch 200s and Potez 25s can be seen in front of the hangars.*
[via CBW Warsaw]

June 1940

The ground war

On 14 June, British patrols probing the Italian defences attacked and captured the forts of Capuzzo and Maddalena.

On 16 June, an Italian contingent with infantry units coming from the Marmarica Division and the 1ª *Divisione Libica* (1st Libyan division) and some L3/35 tankettes, which was marching through Capuzzo, was intercepted by elements of the 11th Hussars reinforced by some cruiser tanks from the 4th Armoured Brigade. The Italians were annihilated, losing also their commander *ten. col.* D'Avanzo.

On 24 June, the Franco-Italian armistice was signed, with effect from 00:35 on 25 June.

Later in the month, the British patrols retreated behind the border, and Capuzzo and Maddalena returned to Italian hands.

Regia Aeronautica

On the Italian airbases on 14 June, work started to modify the national insignias of the aircraft. In particular, the red-white-green stripes (Italian national colours) on the tail fin were replaced by a white cross of the coat of arms of the Savoia dynasty then reigning over Italy. The operation was performed by maintaining the central white stripe, covering the red and green stripes with camouflage, and then drawing a second transverse white stripe.

Around 19 June, the fighters and assault aircraft of *Aeronautica Della Libia* were formed together into a new unit, *Brigata Mista di Formazione* (Compound Air Brigade). On 24 July, the unit changed name to the 14º *Brigata Aerea* (Air Brigade) *"Rex"*. Command of the *Brigata* was given to *Generale di Brigata Aerea* Guglielmo Cassinelli.

Fighters

On 12 June, the first fighter of the 10º *Gr.* to arrive at Tobruk T2 was that of *cap.* Luigi Monti, who landed in the morning. His comrades arrived later, obliged to turn back by bad weather. Then the other *Squadriglie* followed.

Capitano *Aldo Iannaci* of the 160ª Squadriglia in front of a Fiat CR.32 at Tobruk T2 during the summer of 1940.
[via Przemek Skulski]

The *Gruppo* received six additional CR.42s on 17 June.

The CR.42s were devoid of any protective devices, and thus suffered heavily from wear due to the sand. They were continuously required to perform protective cruises over the Italian infantry, but these useless patrols involved many flying hours, and the low-level attacks against enemy troops put the aircraft in a sandy environment that affected guns and engines. The engines of the CR.42s were worn out after only around ten hours, oil consumption increased alarmingly and breakdowns too. This problem had never emerged before, mainly because the Fiat A 30 R.A. engines of the CR.32s had the carburettor air intake on the upper part of the nose and thus were less prone to ingest sand than the Fiat A 74 of the CR.42s, which had its inlet under the nose and closer to the ground.

On 20 June, an aircraft of the 90ª *Sq.* caught fire during maintenance, while two other fighters of the *Gruppo* suffered breakdowns to their oil pumps. Because of the total lack of any spare parts, the three fighters remained unserviceable. The efficiency of the line decreased steadily.

On 30 June, in fact, after only twenty days of war, the 10º *Gr.* received the order to return to Benghazi Berka K airfield to start the general overhaul of its fighters.

The 90ª *Sq.* managed to muster only six flyable CR.42s, which with the unit's Caproni Ca.133 flew back to Benghazi. *serg.* Giovanni Battista Ceoletta was forced to make an emergency landing near Barce airfield, caused by the total loss of the engine's oil. The aircraft was not recovered; the other five aircraft also arrived at Berka without oil in their engines.

Two more CR.42s suffered accidents during the move (*serg.* Roberto Steppi of the 84ª *Sq.* and *serg. magg.* Lorenzo Migliorato of the 91ª *Sq.*

Finally, on 4 July, all the aircraft of the *Gruppo* met in Benghazi.

On 21 June, the first nine CR.42s arrived from Tripoli to replace the CR.32s of the 8º *Gr.*; they were assigned to the 94ª *Sq.* During the day, *cap.* Mario Bacich, *ten.* Alberto Argenton, *ten.* Gioacchino Bissoli, *serg. magg.* Italo Bertinelli and *serg.* Roberto Lendaro of the 93ª *Sq.* went to Castel Benito in an S.81 to collect the first six CR.42s for the *Squadriglia*. In the meantime, the CR.32s were passed on to the 50º *Stormo*. *serg. magg.* Trento Cecchi, *serg. magg.* Alessandro Ruzzene and *serg. magg.* Danilo Billi of the 94ª *Sq.* went with them, taking off at 12:30.

At 08:30 on 26 June, the first three CR.42s of the 93ª *Sq.* arrived. On 27 June, eight pilots of the 92ª *Sq.* left their nine CR.32s to the pilots of 12º *Gr.* at T2, and then flew to Tripoli Castel Benito in a transport SM 82 to collect the first CR.42s. They returned with ten machines at 11:30 on 4 July. At 06:20 on 28 June, the last two CR.42s of the 93ª *Sq.* arrived at T2 together with three aircraft of the 94ª *Sq.*

The general lack of spare parts and means of transport, combined with the distance between T2 and the Tripoli area (where the *Stormo* depots were located), meant that serviceability of the 8º and 13º *Gruppi* steadily decreased.

On 18 June, the 13º *Gr.* rejoined its sister *Gruppo* on T2 airfield minus one *Squadriglia* (78ª) that remained in Berka to protect Benghazi.

On 29 June, *ten.* Guglielmo Chiarini of the 82ª *Sq.* scrambled in a 77ª *Sq.* fighter, and while testing the guns, pierced one propeller blade (a common problem with the synchronisation). During the last mission of the day, *serg.* Ernesto Paolini's aircraft suffered from overheating, and thus at the end of the day only six of the 77ª *Sq.*'s nine fighters remained serviceable.

Bombers

Following the heavy losses suffered on the ground at El Adem by the 45º *Gr.* (which was already suffering from lack of aircraft), it was retired to Benghazi Berka on 19 June and momentarily classified as "not operational". The pilots returned to Italy, where on 29 June they collected the first six factory-fresh SM 79s that were assigned to the 2ª *Sq.*

The 14º *Stormo* was back on operations as a whole only on 22 July, now equipped entirely with SM 79s and based at Benghazi Benina.

On 30 June, the *Aeronautica della Libia* had 82 combat-ready SM 79s.

Ground attack forces

On 12 June, the 50º *Stormo* moved to Tobruk T2.

On 14 June, the Bredas of the 165ª *Sq.* were passed to 159ª *Sq.*, 12º *Gr.*, 50º *Stormo*.

On 20 June, *ten.* Adriano Visconti was assigned from the 2º *Gr. A.P.C.* to the 159ª *Sq.*, 12º *Gr. Assalto*.

With the French threat less dangerous, the 16º *Gr. Assalto* was transferred from Sorman, Tripolitania, to El Adem T3.

The *Gruppo* was still without aircraft and started to take on charge the Capronis of the 12º *Gr.* This *Gruppo* in the meantime received nine Fiat CR.32s at T2 from the 8º *Gr.* (those from the 93ª *Sq.* plus probably one aircraft from the 94ª *Sq.*) and equipped *cap.* Duilio Fanali's 160ª *Sq.* with these. On 14 June, *cap.* Fanali had left the command of the autonomous *Squadriglia* of Bredas (which had been disbanded, passing its Bredas to the 159ª *Sq.*, 12º *Gr.*) and took command of the unit on 21 June. Part of the Fiats remained in T2, occupying the south-west side of the airfield, while others went to Benghazi-Benina airfield to be modified with a belly rack for two 15kg bombs.

Until 24 June the 160ª *Sq.* underwent a training period on their "new" CR.32s. During this period, *serg. magg.* Angelo Cirillo died in a landing accident.

At the very end of June, the 167ª *Sq.* of the 16º *Gr.* also took charge of its Fiat CR.32s.

Reconaissance forces

After the heavy losses suffered the first day of war, the 136ª *Sq.* of the 64° *Gr.* under *cap.* Nicola Nicolai was moved from Tripolitania to Tobruk T5 on 21 June to operate under control of 73° *Gr.* In the meantime, the 127ª *Sq.* had given its planes to the 137ª *Sq.* to make good its losses.

Colonial forces

The 2º *Gr. A.P.C.* received five S.81s modified as ambulance aircraft in June. The 16ª *Sq.* used these.

Royal Air Force

The French in Syria operated the most modern fighters in the area and following the Italian declaration of war, the RAF ME Command requested assistance from them. After a meeting in Beirut on 20 June between French and British Officers, the French GOC in the Orient, *Général* Mittelhauser, authorised GC I/7 based at Estabel south of Rayak in the Lebanon to move to Egypt. At 08:30 on 23 June, a vanguard of three Morane Saulnier MS.406s arrived at Ismailia. The pilots were *Lieutenant* Antoine Péronne of 1ère *Escadrille*, who badly damaged his aircraft (No. 833 and with no. 3 in Arabic letter on the fin) on landing, *Adjutant-Chef* Christian Coudray of 1ère *Escadrille* (No. 826 with no. 4 in Arabic letter on the fin. This aircraft later received the British serial AX674) and *Adjutant-Chef* André Ballatore of 2ème *Escadrille* (No. 827 and with no. 2 in French letter on the fin. This aircraft later received the British serial AX675). Ground crews consisted of five mechanics (*Adjudant-Chef* Th. Epery radio, *Sergents-chefs* R. Geiger and L. Couturier and *Caporal-Chef* J-B Calorbe mechanics and *Sergent* L. Chaïla armourer), which arrived aboard two Fokker trimotor F.VIIs.

Following the armistice between Italy and France, some of the French wanted to continue fight beside the RAF while others wanted to return to Syria including the two pilots on the two Fokker F.VIIs. On 27 June, *Capitaine* Paul Jacquier of GAO 1/583 based at Qoussair in Syria, landed at Ismailia in a twin-engine Potez 63.11 reconnaissance aircraft (No. 799. Later with the British serial AX672). The day after, *Lieutenant* Peronne and *Adjutant-Chef* Coudray landed with their Morane Saulnier MS.406s to try to understand the situation. Despite pleas of French officers who were sent (in a Potez 540) from Beirut to persuade them to return to Estabel, the two pilots were pleased to meet Paul Jacquier, this latter explained them the situation and asked them to continue fight the war with the RAF. The Frenchmen decided unanimously to enrol in the RAF.

On 30 June, some other pilots joined them with two Caudron Simouns (no. 110 and no. 158, which later received the British serial AX676) and a Bloch 81 (no. 4, which later received the British serial AX677).

Both sides suffered from problems with the dust, and I. S. O. Playfair recorded in the official history that:

"...there was no air filter that would satisfactorily resist the all-pervading sand and dust, with the result that day-to-day serviceability was seriously affected, while the change to coarse pitch of the variable pitch air screw was often made impracticable. Instruments, too, were so badly affected that it was necessary, soon after war began, to form a special mobile section to service the instruments in the Sqn aircraft. Another serious inconvenient was the blowing-out and cracking of the Perspex panels of the Blenheim aircraft due to distortion from the heat of the sun. All these difficulties and many others, involved so much additional maintenance work that it was found necessary, soon after the war began, to form an advanced repair and salvage section in the Western Desert and to augment the maintenance organization in the Canal Zone".

Fighters

When the war started, 33 Sqn went to the front line to confront the *Regia Aeronautica*.

The squadron was based at Qasaba, an airstrip around 40 kilometres south-east of Mersa Matruh, with sections based further west at Sidi Barrani. Periodically pilots of the other two squadrons joined 33 Sqn to gain combat experience.

On 13 June, the 'B' Flight of 33 Sqn (six or seven Gladiators) moved from Mersa Matruh to Sidi Barrani to be within range to escort bombers the next day.

To counter the increased Italian bombers activity, a section composed of two Blenheim Mk IFs of 30 Sqn and a Hurricane of 80 Sqn was formed, and attached to 33 Sqn from 16 June.

On 17 June, the squadron moved from Mersa Matruh to Qasaba. The unit was to remain there for a very short period until a satellite aerodrome was prepared at Ma'aten Gerawla. The unit was at Gerawla on 22 June.

On 13 June, three Hawker Hurricane Mk.Is arrived in Egypt and were taken on charge by 80 Sqn. S/Ldr Charles Ryley, F/Lt T. M. Lockyer and P/O D. T. Saville flew them.

On 24 June, three more Hawker Hurricanes arrived: P2544 flown by P/O Carter, P 2651 flown by P/O Glen and P 2641 flown by P/O Collins. They all came via Malta and landed at Mersa Matruh before reaching Amryia.

80 Sqn Gladiator L8010/YK-V on a desert patrol. This aircraft was lost on 8 August 1940 after being involved in combat with Italian CR.42s. F/L Evers-Swindell force-landed but not before he had shot down two of the enemy biplanes. He set the aircraft on fire and started walking towards his own lines. Armoured cars recovered him the next day. [via Dave Williams]

Known serial numbers of the Hurricanes in the Middle East up to that moment were L1669, N2624, N2499, P2544, P2627, P2639, P2641, P2651, P2687, P2695 and P2864. This meant that at the beginning of July RAF had at least eleven Hurricanes on hand in Egypt.

On 25 June, F/Lt 'Pat' Pattle with one of the new Hurricanes relieved F/O Peter Wykeham-Barnes at 33 Sqn's landing ground.

On 28 June, the 80 Sqn formed a complete flight armed with seven Hawker Hurricanes and its command was taken by F/Lt Edward 'Tap' Jones.

On 24 June, S/Ldr A. R. G. Bax ceased to be attached to 112 Sqn on the return of S/Ldr D. M. Somerville.

Bombers

On 11 June, 55 Sqn moved from Ismailia to its war base at Fuka, with 13 combat-ready Blenheims.

During June, daily small-scale raids against Italian Army bases and airfields in Libya were made in rotation by aircraft of the four Egyptian-based Blenheim squadrons – 113 with its Mk.IVs at Ma'aten Bagush, together with the Mk.Is of 45 and 55 at Fuka and 211 at El Daba –so that each squadron operated only every fourth day. However, 45 Sqn soon ceased operations and from 15 June was released from active service and placed in reserve at Helwan, as a measure of the severity of the losses suffered by the squadron during the first four days of war (three complete crews). The Blenheims of all the squadrons had been dispersed to satellite landing grounds to avoid the frequent bombing of their main airfields by the Italians. It was not possible to launch any larger-scale raids, as fewer serviceable aircraft remained available. At the end of the month, 45 Sqn send a flight of four aircraft to 211 Sqn at El Daba and three aircrews to 113 Sqn at Ma'aten Bagush.

On the first day of the war 30 Sqn began fitting packs containing four forward-firing Brownings under the fuselage of half their Blenheims, converting the aircraft into Blenheim Mk.IF fighters. On 15 June, the 'B' and 'C' Flights finished the conversion of their nine Bristol Blenheims Mk.I to Mk.IF standard. These fighter Blenheims had in the meantime been joined by one Mk.IF coming from 211 Sqn and two coming from 11 Sqn (three machines not produced directly by Bristol but coming from a shadow factory), so that the strength of the squadron at this date was twelve Mk.IFs and six standard Mk.Is.

Several detachments were temporarily sent to Amiriya, Helwan, Qasaba, Gerawla and Mersa Matruh during the first weeks of the war, but no action was recorded. One of the first duties assigned to 30 Sqn was that of "*Shadow Patrols*", a kind of mission where the Blenheims had to take off and shadow the Italian bombers after they had bombed Amriya and Helwan and to follow them to their home bases to discover where these airstrips were. This type of mission was very dangerous and of dubious utility, and thus was quickly cancelled.

The Blenheim forces in the Mediterranean area suffered a heavy blow on 18 June, when seven Blenheim Mk.IVs (L9263, L9314, L9315, L9317, L9318, L9334 and L935) were lost, mostly due to bad weather, during delivery flights from the U.K. Aboard these aircraft, no less than 18 pilots and crewmembers lost their life.

On 10 June, 70 Sqn reached Heliopolis from Helwan with eleven aircraft. The squadron received a fifteenth machine (Valentia J8062) on 12 June, while a detachment of the squadron (force unknown) remained at Habbaniya in Iraq. Activity during the months of June, July and August was transport duties. However, a three-aircraft detachment, left in Dekheila under command of S/Ldr C. G. Hohler, carried out some operational flying with general sea reconnaissance missions to a maximum of 100 miles from land, convoy protection and anti-submarine patrols. No losses were suffered during the period.

A Royal Egyptian Air Force Lysander on roll-out at Yeovil.
[via Westland Archives]

Reconnaissance forces

On 11 June, 'B' Flight of 208 Sqn under F/Lt Black moved from Qasaba to Sidi Barrani with four Lysanders, to work with 7th Armoured Division. P/O Webber flew F/O Finch of 45 Sqn back to Fuka during the day.

'B' Flight moved its four Lysanders from Sidi Barrani to Buq-Buq on 13 June. In the next weeks, their comrades from Qasaba would periodically relieve pilots of the Flight.

The squadron's diarist reported the arrival of four reserve Blenheims of 113 Sqn at Qasaba together with 40 men of a maintenance party and a workshop party on 15 June. They were attached to the squadron. 'B' Flight in the meantime returned to Sidi Barrani from Buq-Buq.

On 20 June, the squadron started to disperse to the new airstrip of Bir Kenayis, south of Mersa Matruh, to avoid the Italian bombing attacks. squadron strength was 14 aircraft, five still at Qasaba, five at Bir Kenayis and four at Sidi Barrani.

L8017 was one of 18 Gladiators supplied of the Royal Egyptian Air Force in 1939. They were given the Egyptian serials K1331-1348, although it is not known if these were ever worn. This aircraft appears to be in overall aluminum. No machine-guns are carried and the port outer wheel covers looks to be darker than the rest of the airframe, although this may be a flight color.
[via Tim Kershaw]

23

228 Sqn was reinforced by the arrival of Sunderland N9020/W, which arrived from Mount Batten piloted by S/Ldr Menzies.

Sunderlands P9621 and P9622 completed 228 Sqn's complement, on 30 June flying from Pembroke Dock to Gibraltar piloted by F/Lt Brooks and F/Lt Craven DFC. The flying-boats however remained at "The Rock" on attachment to 202 Sqn.

Royal Egyptian Air Force

After the first raid on Alexandria during the night of 21-22 June both REAF Gladiator squadrons were placed under the command of 252 Fighter Wing RAF. 2 Sqn was based at Helwan under command of S/Ldr Muhammed Ibrahim Abu Rabia, while 5 Sqn was based at Dekhalia.

Armée de l'Air

Fighters

GC I/10 was sent to Djedeida airstrip (close to Tunis) on 11 June, and two days later the first *Escadrille* of GC III/5 joined it. It never saw action against the Italians.

On 13 June, *Capitaine* De Place replaced *Capitaine* Davy as commander of GC III/4.

On 17 June, the French fighters in Tunisia were reorganized with the formation *of Sous-Groupement* n° 45 that included GC I/9 (which went to El Hamma in the south), and the *2ème Escadrille* of GC III/5 (at Bir Guénich), together with the only *Escadrille* of GC I/10 (at Djedeida near Tunis).

GC III/5 was reunited at Bir Guénich some days later.

All the units remained equipped with their old Morane Saulnier MS.406s

On 17 June, the French opened negotiations for the surrender. From this moment onwards, the maximum possible numbers of air units were to retreat to AFN. For some units heavily committed against the Germans the retreat was impossible, as it was for units equipped with short range aircraft (Bloch 151 and 152 fighters and the Morane Saulnier MS.406s) but many other units, among them some of the best up to that moment, were able to reach Algeria at full strength. However, apart from the bombers of *Groupements* n°1 and n°2, and GB II/11, none of these aircraft saw further action during the closing stages of the war. Most fighter units, in particular, arrived without their ground echelons, and obviously without any form of spare part or maintenance equipment.

On 18 June, GC III/2, GC I/3 and GC I/4 reached Oran. GC III/2 had 24 Curtiss H75s and 26 pilots, and was credited with 33 victories against the *Luftwaffe*. GC I/3 had 28 Dewoitine D.520s, 31 pilots, and had claimed 55 confirmed victories against the Germans; among its pilots was seven-victories ace *Sous-Lieutenant* Michel Madon. GC I/4 had 17 Curtiss H75s and in the peri-

Curtiss fighters of GC II/5 at Saint-Denis-du-Sig at the end of June 1940. Nearest the camera are n°153 and H-751 (H 75 A4) n°8 of the 3rd Escadrille.
[via G.Botquin]

od September 1939 – June 1940 its pilots had claimed 36 victories; among its pilots was the seven victory ace *Lieutenant* Edmond Guillaume.

On the same day, GC III/6 left Le Luc en Provence for AFN with its Dewoitine D.520s after its successful encounters with the *Regia Aeronautica* on 13 and 15 June. The newly promoted *Sous Lieutenant* Pierre Le Gloan, who joined the Vichy Air forces with his comrades, had scored eleven of the 18 victories claimed by the unit.

The two *Escadrilles* of GC I/9 reunited at El Hamma around 19 June. Up to that moment, only the *2ème Escadrille* had had opportunities to engage the Italians near Tunis.

On 19 and 20 June, GC III/3 reached Algiers in two groups. After some flight problems, which resulted in one destroyed aircraft and one killed pilot, the *Groupe* reunited at Relizane.

On 20 June, GC II/3 (15 Dewoitine D.520s), GC II/4 (22 Curtiss H75s and 22 pilots), GC I/5 (24 Curtiss H75s and 30 pilots) and GC II/5 (34 Curtiss H75s, some of them of the latest A4 model, and 34 pilots) reached Algiers.

GC II/5 went on to St-Denis-du-Sig after the stop in Algiers. The *Groupe* was credited with 48 confirmed victories up to that time.

On the same day, GC II/7 went to Bone with 25 Dewoitine D.520s and 22 pilots, while GC I/3 regrouped at Oudna.

The day after the Franco-Italian armistice, on 25 June, GC III/3 had 22 Dewoitines and 35 pilots. The unit had claimed 33 victories against the *Luftwaffe* and had among its pilots one of the highest scoring of the Campaign, *Sous-Lieutenant* Edouard Le Nigen, credited with twelve victories (tragically he was to die of peritonitis in July).

GC I/4 was at Meknès with 25 fighters and 24 pilots.

GC II/3 was at Relizane with 20 Dewoitines and 27 pilots. The unit was credited with 35 victories against the *Luftwaffe*.

GC II/4 was at Meknès. It was credited with 52 victories against the *Luftwaffe*; among its pilots there were 14 victories-ace *Sous-Lieutenant* Camille Plumbeau and nine victory ace *Sous-Lieutenant* Georges Baptizet.

GC I/5 went to St-Denis-du-Sig. This unit was the highest scoring French unit from the May-June Campaign, with 84 confirmed victories. Among its pilots retreating to North Africa were the triple ace (16 "*homologuées victories*") *Lieutenant* Edmond Marin La Meslée, top scorer of the campaign for *Armèe de l'Air* and 14 victory ace *Lieutenant* Michel Dorance. Many other aces also still served with the unit.

GC II/7 was at Oudna. It had 29 victories to its credit.

GC III/2 moved on to Rouiba during the day.

French Martin 167 in North Africa in 1941.
[via B. Belcarz]

Bombers

GB II/32 went to Aïn Beda in Algeria on 17 June but never saw action against Italy.

A few days after the declaration of war, the French bomber forces were joined by *Groupements* n°1 and n°2 from France, which just had re-equipped with the latest American Douglas and Martin bombers. These saw frequent action before the end of the campaign against Italy.

GB I/62, GB II/62, GBI/63, GB II/63, forming *Groupement* n°1, arrived from France on 19 June. The *Escadre* 62 went to Canrobert and the *Escadre* 63 to Aïn Beda in northern and southern Algeria respectively. The Glenn-Martins of the Groupement operated frequently against Italy from their new bases, from 22 June to 25 June.

GB I/19, GB II/19, GB II/61, forming *Groupement* n°2, arrived from France with twenty aircraft, and on 22 June went to the airfield of Souk-el-Arba in Algeria. The Douglas DB 7s of the *Groupement* operated against Italy on 24 June.

GB II/11 took off at 14:00 in the afternoon on 18 June from Avignon, and reached Blida in Algeria four hours later with 14 Lioré et Olivier LeO 451s. The LeO no. 387 suffered a fire in the engine during landing, but the crew escaped unhurt.

Groupement n°7, formed by GB II/23 and GB I/11 on Lioré et Olivier LeO 451s, started to reach Blida on 19 June, its redeployment was completed on 24 June.

During the day on 20 June, *Groupement* n°9 (composed of GB I/21, GB II/21, GB I/34 and GB II/34) reached Blida. It was equipped with a collection of types - Amiot A 351/354, Amiot A 143 and Bloch MB 210. The movement was completed the day after.

On 21 June GB I/32 went to Sidi-Rahal near Marrakech. It never saw action against the Italians.

Reconnaissance forces

Around 20 June reconnaissance units also reached ANF; twelve GAOs went to Algeria and four to Tunisia. These were mainly equipped with Potez 63.11s.

On 20 June, GR I/33, GR II/33 (the French writer Antoine de Saint-Exupéry's unit and to which he dedicated his novel "Flight to Arras"), GR I/35, GR I/36, GR II/36, GR II/52, GR I/55, went to Algeria with 17 Bloch MB 174s, 12 MB 175s, 22 Potez 63.11s, 5 Leo 45s plus one Glenn Martin GM 167F, one Bréguet 693 and one Farman 222.

GR I/22 and GR I/52 went to Tunisia with 18 Potez 63.11s, two Bloch MB 174 and four Bréguet 693s.

Aeronavale

On 10 June *Groupement* HS7 was created, and equipped with six Loire 130 unloaded from the fleet and based at Arzew for the defence of Mers-el-Kébir.

HB1 and HB2 moved to Oubeïra, Algeria, from 19 June.

On 21 June, T2 arrived from France equipped with nine Latécoère 298s, to be based at Bougie, Algeria. The unit was commanded by *Lieutenant de Vaisseau* Lamiot and had seen action against the German army, employing its Laté as dive-bombers, suffering heavy losses in May.

Many aircraft of the *Aeronavale* received the order to retreat to AFN during 24 June.

B3 returned to Morocco with its Glenn-Martin GM 167Fs on 24 June.

Four Bloch MB.151s of AC3 succeeded in reaching Bone after a stop in Corsica on the evening on 24 June, with almost empty tanks.

The Loire-Nieuport 411 dive bombers of AB2 and AB4 arrived at Bone in the morning of 25 June. Three planes failed to arrive because of mechanical breakdowns. Two of them (from AB 4) crash-landed on Sardinia where the pilots were interned (Maitre Méheut and Second-Maitre Le Moal). The last planes of AB4 landed at Bone on 28 June. During these last attempts to reach AFN, another LN dive-bomber crash-landed on Sardinia (*Second-Maitre* Méhault P.O.W.).

AB3 with its last three Vought 156Fs arrived at Bone on 25 June. The ten Dewoitine D.520 fighters of AC1 and AC2 (*Flotille de Chasse* of the carrier *Bearn*) arrived at Bone with three North American NAA-57 trainers and a Potez 631, on the evening of 25 June.

Operations

10 June 1940 - British-Italian Front

It has often been reported that during the night of 10 and 11 June, Air Commodore Collishaw undertook an unofficial bombing mission accompanied by a volunteer crew in a Vickers Valentia nicknamed 'Bessie'. They took off from Ma'aten Bagush with a crate of hand-grenades stowed on board, with which they attacked an Italian camp. Collishaw's second pilot was F/O Harvey. After the 'attack' the aircraft returned to Ma'aten Bagush.

The authors haven't so far been able to find corroboration of this action in the official documents of 70 and 216 Sqns, the two units that operated the Valentia in Egypt.

11 June 1940- British-Italian Front

The *Regia Aeronautica* was in readiness from 00:00 (throughout this book the times will be reported as found in the original sources, so typically Italian time in the description of Italian activities and British time for the Commonwealth ones), and a standing patrol of three Fiat CR.32s of the 8° *Gr.* was maintained over Tobruk T2 airfield and Tobruk harbour. This was not possible over El Adem T3, because there were no fighter units based there.

At 05:00, seven Fiats of the 93ª *Sq.*, 8° *Gr.*, scrambled to meet a formation of seven British bombers sighted by the observation post at Bardia, flying in an eastward direction. The fighters climbed to 2000 metres, and the British formation was seen as if it was coming back from an incursion over T3. The CR.32s started in pursuit, but were unable to catch them, and the bombers disappeared in the dawn mist.

Two hours later, at around 07:00, seven more CR.32s scrambled to meet another attack directed on El Adem. Six of the aircraft were from the 94ª *Sq.* (*cap.* Franco Lavelli, *ten.* Giovanni Tadini, *serg. magg.* Alessandro Ruzzene, *serg. magg.* Danilo Billi, *serg. magg.* Arturo Cardano and *serg. magg.* Trento Cecchi) while the seventh was from the 92ª *Sq.* (CO Martino Zannier). The Italian pilots had a slight height advantage over the seven Blenheims, and this made it possible to intercept. The Fiat pilots claimed two bombers shot down (one into the sea and one from which the crew was seen to bale out) and four damaged, all shared among the seven pilots. Zannier returned at 07:40

Technical personnel working with a Fiat CR.32 of 160ª Squadriglia, Libya.
[via Przemek Skulski]

Photo from June 1940 showing one of the first Blenheims shot down that fell within the Italian lines. Possibly, it is the Blenheim of 113 Sqn shot down in the afternoon of 11 June. The pilot on top of it is unknown but it is most likely one from the 8° Gruppo; perhaps Tenente Gioacchino Bissoli, who claimed a Blenheim during the combat.
[via Istituto Luce]

with the engine on his fighter damaged and having expended 500 rounds of ammunition. The pilots of the 94ª *Sq.* landed five minutes later, having expended 3770 rounds of ammunition.

At 11:20, *ten.* Alberto Argenton of the 93ª *Sq.* together with *ten.* Riccardo Marcovich of the 92ª *Sq.*, carried out a visual reconnaissance over the British airstrip of Tishididda. They landed at 12:50 reporting the absence of enemy planes.

At 15:00, a patrol of five CR.32s of the 93ª *Sq.*, led by *ten.* Gioacchino Bissoli and including *ten.* Alberto Argenton, *serg. magg.* Italo Bertinelli, *serg. magg.* Duilio Bernardi and *serg. magg.* Luigi Di Lorenzo, intercepted another formation of six bombers. With a swift attack Bissoli shot down a Blenheim that fell down close to T3 (nobody was seen to jump from the aircraft), while his wingmen claimed damage to two others before the bombers were able to escape. The *Squadriglia* diary reported that all the surviving enemy bombers were damaged, with the use of 1050 rounds.

In total the 25 Fiat CR.32s of the 8° *Gr.* made 96 sorties during the day.

The Italian fighters had clashed with Blenheims from 202 Group (45, 55, 113, and 211 Sqns). A few minutes after midnight six Bristol Blenheim Mk.I crews of 211 Sqn were briefed to carry out an armed reconnaissance at dawn on targets in Libya. Their target was El Adem, photographing from Derna to Giarabub as they went. During a reconnaissance flight over the Giarabub-Capuzzo areas a Blenheim Mk.I of 211 Sqn piloted by P/O Eric Bevington-Smith was obliged to force-land with engine trouble. It is possible that the Blenheims from 211 Sqn were the ones the 8° *Gr.* tried in vain to intercept at 05:40.

These were followed by eight Bristol Blenheim Mk.Is of 45 Sqn, that took off from Fuka at 04:15 and attacked the airfield of El Adem T3. Initially the raid was to be against Tobruk harbour, but the reconnaissance of 211 Sqn showed it had no significant target. The British formation was composed of S/Ldr Dallamore (L8478), F/O Williams (L8469), Sgt Thurlow (L8519), F/Lt Troughton Smith (L8481), P/O Gibbs (L4923), Sgt Bower (L8476), F/O Rixson (L8524) and F/O Finch (L8466). The British pilots returned from T3 claiming that they had attacked at 05:40 with 40lb, 20lb and 4lb incendiary bombs and also had strafed in subsequent passes with front and rear guns. Although no enemy aircraft were encountered, the ground defences had been in action immediately. These were described as "not heavy", and in fact it is known that at the beginning of the conflict that, for

the defence of all the 35 air strips of Cirenaica, the Italians had only 17 ex-Austrian Schwarzlose 8mm gun of WW I vintage, armed with standard ammunition and with a maximum range of 600 meters. Later more details embellished the description of this first attack, reporting that the returning crews had claimed that the entire manpower of the Italian base had been assembled on parade, as if the commanding officer had been reading a signal from Marshal Italo Balbo (Italian Commander-in-Chief) announcing the declaration of war. The Blenheims had hit two hangars, burning them, then had strafed and bombed the Italian aircraft that were parked in rows as in peacetime and not dispersed, destroying several of them. Three Blenheims failed to return and two more were damaged. Blenheim Mk.I L8476 was reportedly hit by light flak shortly after the last attack, caught fire and crashed into the sea killing the crew - Sgt Peter Bower (RAF no. 524415), Sgt Stanley George Fox (RAF no. 747815) and Aircraftman 1st Class John William Allison (RAF no. 543233). Blenheim Mk.I L8519 was damaged during the raid and crash-landed at Sidi Barrani, where it burst into flames killing its crew - Sgt Maurice Cresswell Thurlow (RAF no. 565808), Sgt Bernard Alfred Feldman (RAF no. 747967) and Aircraftman 1st Class Henry Robinson (RAF no. 548048). Blenheim Mk.I L8466 suffered an engine failure over the target (possibly hit by Italian fire), the other engine failed after 100 miles during the return journey eastwards and the aircraft made a wheels-up forced landing near Buq-Buq. The crew (F/O A. Finch, Sgt R. Dodsworth and Leading Aircraftman Fisher) was rescued by the British Army, while the aircraft was later recovered and repaired. It seems possible that these Blenheims were in fact claimed by the pilots of the 92ª and 94ª *Squadriglie*.

The first raid of the war brought also one of the first "mysteries" of the campaign, as it is not sure, from the comparison of the Italian and British documents, which were the opponents of the 8º Gr. during this early morning raid. It seems here right to explain that the time in Italy (and presumably also in Libya) at the beginning of the war was Greenwich Mean Time (G.M.T.) +1h. On the other hand from available documents it transpires that in Egypt it was G.M.T. + 2h, (it seems that only after 15 July did Egypt adopted daylight saving time, which is G.M.T +3h). Thus, even if exceptions to this rule had been noted in the documents consulted, it seems that on 11 June 1940 the British time recorded was one hour in advance of that recorded by the Italians. This is the strongest clue to assume that 45 Sqn was in fact the unit that the 8º *Gr.* failed to intercept during its first morning pursuit, because the RAF recorded this raid at 05:40, which was 04:40 in "Italian" time, quite close to the 05:00 of the first inconclusive scramble of the 93ª *Sq.*

If we accept this, however, the opponents of the 8º *Gr.*, against which 4270 rounds of ammunition were expanded and which damaged Zannier's Fiat, remained undisclosed because no other British raids were reportedly performed in the morning. Additionally it is known that Balbo himself, commenting on the day's actions, credited all three victories claimed by the Italians to the fighters and none to AA, that was explicitly termed as "non existent". As a point of interest, it is also worth noting that Italy adopted daylight saving time (G.M.T. +2h) on 15 June 1940 and kept it for the rest of the war. Thus from 15 June until 15 July, Italians and British recorded the same time (G.M.T + 2h), then after that date the British time returned to one hour in advance of the Italian one.

In the afternoon, 55 and 113 Sqns were transferred from Ismailia to Fuka, and nine planes from each squadron were bombed up and attacked El Adem T3 once again, starting at 14:15. 'A' Flight from 55 Sqn included Blenheim Mk.Is L8530 (Flight Lieutenant Cox (acting S/Ldr), Sgt Wagstaff and Corporal Bennett), L8391 (P/O Walker, Sgt Kavanagh and Leading Aircraftman Noble) and L8667 (Sgt Day, Sgt Browning and Leading Aircraftman McGarry). 'B' Flight included Blenheim Mk.Is L1538 (Flight Lieutenant H. R. Goodman, Sgt Wiles and Leading Aircraftman Jone), L4818 (P/O M. S. Ferguson, P/O H. A. W. How and Leading Aircraftman Cherry) and L8398 (P/O R. H. Nicolson, Leading Aircraftman Bartram and Leading Aircraftman Davison). 'C' Flight included Blenheim Mk.Is L4820 (F/O F. H. Fox, Sgt Nicholas and Leading Aircraftman Klines), L6672 (P/O Godrich, P/O Redfern and Leading Aircraftman Thompson) and L8390 (P/O Smith, Sgt Clarke and Leading Aircraftman Dews).

The returning pilots reported that the aircraft at the base were still not dispersed, and claimed the damage or destruction on the ground of eighteen of them, together with additional damage to the hangars of the base. This time enemy aircraft were encountered, and one Blenheim Mk.IV of 113 Sqn was admitted lost to them when L4823 was shot down (most probably by *ten*. Bissoli) 7 km east of El Adem. The crew of F/Lt D. Beauclair, Warrant Officer H. J. Owen and Sgt J. Dobson were all badly burned, but walked for eight hours before being captured by an Italian Marine post east of Tobruk. Two Blenheims from 55 Sqn were badly damaged, but were able to regain British territory. They had encountered some accurate AA fire and reported that, although CR.32 fighters were seen, they didn't engage. L1538 received five hits on the starboard engine cowling, the engine stopped through lack of petrol and the aircraft made an emergency landing at Mersa Matruh, while L8398 received a bullet in the undercarriage that collapsed on landing at Mersa Matruh. The two aircraft were left there. The starboard engine of L4820, which had been followed by two Fiat fighters that reportedly scored no hits on it, seized when over Mersa Matruh. The bomber was however able to successfully land at Fuka. In all 26 bombers attacked T3 during the day, hitting it with 416 forty pound bombs, 524 twenty pound bombs and 2080 four pound incendiary bombs.

The Italians reported three different raids against El Adem (made by a reported six-nine-six enemy bombers). The 44° *Gr.* lost one completely burnt out SM 79, two more lightly damaged (RS) and two more seriously damaged (they had to be repaired in the local S.R.A.M.). The *Gruppo* also suffered three dead and twenty-four wounded.

Three Ro.37s of the 137ª *Sq.* were also destroyed and two Ca.309s were also heavily damaged and two Ro.37s and six S.81s were more lightly damaged. Ten more soldiers were wounded.

The Italian Air Force had a three levels system to classify damage suffered. The aircraft so badly damaged that they couldn't be repaired where classified "*Fuori Uso*" (FU). Aircraft so heavily damaged that they required to be repaired in special workshops or to be sent back to the manufacturer's workshops were classified "*Riparabile in Ditta*" (RD). Finally, aircraft lightly damaged were classified "*Riparabile in Squadriglia*" (RS). The classification of damage (and in particular the choice between FU and RD was highly dependent on the capability of the available maintenance structure, so aircraft, which in Italy would had been classified RD where FU in Libya and, sometimes, aircraft initially declared FU where later repaired.

Sunderlands N9029/V (between 04:45 and 11:50) and L2164/Z (04:45-16:50) of 230 Sqn flew an anti-submarine and a general reconnaissance patrol between 04:45 and 11:50 to provide a forward screen for a British cruiser force steaming westward from Alexandria.

This patrol was followed by two more Sunderlands L5804/S (between 10:35 and 23:00) and L5803/T (10:55-22:40), which continued to provide the forward screen. Both aircraft made a night alighting in Alexandria's Eastern Harbour without difficulty.

Sunderland L2161/Y from the same unit flew from Alexandria to Mersa Matruh between 14:30 and 16:20 to stand by for operations the following day.

P/O Benson, starting from Qasaba, carried out the first operational sortie of 208 Sqn, an uneventful early morning tactical reconnaissance from Sollum to Fort Maddalena. The Lysanders of 208 continued with daily reconnaissance missions of the border area, the vulnerability to enemy fighters meant that the missions very rarely were carried out more deeply than a few miles into Libyan territory.

Seven aircraft of 30 Sqn were loaded with 250lbs general purpose bombs and moved to El Daba, in preparation for carrying out strategic reconnaissance duties in the Western Desert. At 08:00, the order was cancelled by 202 Group HQ and the Blenheims returned to Ismailia, landing at 10:30.

During the day, 33 Sqn flew three patrols and scrambled twice, but no contact with enemy aircraft was made.

The squadron dispersed its Gladiators, with five from 'C' Flight moving to the satellite field in the morning followed by six from 'B' Flight at midday. Five aircraft from 'C' Flight moved to Matruh.

80 Sqn flew four patrols but no enemy aircraft were encountered.

112 Sqn carried out seven patrols during the day, five of them by 'C' Flight and two by 'A' Flight. No interceptions were made and visibility was poor, with sand haze up to 15,000 feet all day.

Ten Bombays from 216 Sqn, each carrying eight 250lb bombs, reached El Daba for a night raid on Tobruk, which was cancelled. One of the Bombays was badly damaged by a Blenheim taxiing into it (possibly a 211 Sqn machine).

11 June 1940 - Franco-Italian Front

In general, the attitude of *Regia Aeronautica* and *Armée de l'Air* in the opening phase was of cautious waiting.

Three SM 79s of the 15° *Stormo* made a photographic reconnaissance in the areas of Sfax, Ben Gardane and the border with Tunisia. A Ro.37*bis* of the 64° *Gr. O.A.* went over Ben Gardane to control eventual French troop movements towards the border zone.

Two Z.501s of the 188ª *Sq.* made a reconnaissance along the Elmas – Capo Bergut – La Galite island – Elmas route.

Two SM 79s of the 228ª *Sq.*, 89° *Gr.*, 32° *Stormo* from Decimomannu reconnoitred over Bizerta, Karouba and Sidi Ahmed, two Z.506s of the 196ª *Sq.* from Elmas reconnoitred over Oran, while two Z.506s of the 197ª *Sq.* from Elmas reconnoitred over Algiers.

GR I/61 made some reconnaissance sorties from Voulas-les-Bains.

12 June 1940 - British-Italian Front

Reconnaissance sorties by 113 Sqn had revealed Tobruk harbour to be crowded, and a combined action by the RAF and the Royal Navy was planned at dawn against the shipping in the harbour.

The light cruiser HMS *Gloucester* and the Australian cruiser HMAS *Sydney* were to carry out a sweep against Tobruk, while the RAF bombed the harbour to drive shipping out of it and into the guns of the waiting fleet, and to destroy at their moorings those vessels that did not flee.

29 Blenheims from four squadrons were briefed to be over Tobruk at sunrise.

Six Blenheim Mk.Is from 45 Sqn, led by F/Lt Mills, took off but Sgt Grant in L6664 aborted with port engine failure, and F/O Woodroffe never joined the formation. F/O Rixson (L8524) suffered engine troubles before taking off, touched the ground with one propeller, and then lost touch

Alexandria seen from a SM 79 of the R.S.T. [via Italian Air Force]

with the formation. He bombed some troops near Bardia but had to force-land at Mersa Matruh during the return journey owing to lack of fuel. All the other aircraft failed to find the target and returned with the bombs still aboard.

Only two of the five from 55 Sqn reached Tobruk since many aircraft were still unserviceable after damage suffered the previous day – an engine on L8394 would not start, the observer Sgt Lulan on L8390 was struck by a propeller so it too did not take off, while L8664 had to turn back with engine trouble. Over the target, they met a reported 50 CR.42s, which did not attack, so they returned to base unharmed.

Two of the nine from 211 Sqn crashed on take-off while a third suffered a ground collision with a Bombay; the remaining six were engaged by (reportedly) Fiat CR.42s defending Tobruk and claimed to have shot down two of them (first claims by the Royal Air Force in the desert).

Finally nine Blenheim Mk.IVs of 113 Sqn did manage to find and bomb the harbour, and reporting hits on the old cruiser *San Giorgio*.

There were no CR.42s operational over Tobruk on the morning of 12 June, only the CR.32s of the 8° *Gr*. The *Gruppo* reported that two different formations of British bombers were intercepted before they were able to reach their target, and obliged to jettison their bombs and turn back, suffering heavy damage. The intercepting fighters were from three sections drawn from the three *Squadriglie* of the *Gruppo*. The section of the 92ª *Sq*. was commanded by *ten*. Ranieri Piccolomini, the 93ª *Sq*. section was commanded by *serg. magg.* Italo Bertinelli and the 94ª *Sq*. section was commanded by *s. ten.* Giacomo Maggi. The Italian fighters didn't claim any victories (only damage) and didn't suffer any losses.

It seems that some bombs fell on T2 but didn't cause any damage. The air attack on the harbour was similarly devoid of concrete results.

According to the war diary of the cruiser *San Giorgio*, at dawn two British cruisers with their escort of destroyers shelled the base, sinking the minesweeper *Giovanni Berta*, which was caught 3.5 miles out of the harbour. In the meantime, between 04:52 and 05:02, the Navy base was under air attacks that didn't cause damage; *San Giorgio* was not damaged.

Three SM 79s from the 10° *Stormo* took off at 09.00 to carry out *Aeronautica della Libia*'s first strategic reconnaissance missions. They were flown by *cap*. Musch from the 56ª *Sq*., *ten*. Cabassi from the 58ª *Sq*. and *ten*. Spadaccini from the 55ª *Sq*. They checked the Nile Delta area, Port Said and Alexandria harbour.

During the day *ten*. Adriano Visconti, CO of the 23ª *Sq*., succeeded in freeing an Italian infantry platoon from an attack by three British armoured cars in an area between the air strips of Sidi Azeiz and Amseat A3.

Many reconnaissance and escort mission were flown by the 10° *Gr*. pilots during the day. No more enemy aircraft were encountered, however.

British reconnaissance again found Tobruk harbour crowded, and also revealed large naval oil reserves on the wharves. There were army and air forces headquarters in the town, and thirty-four aircraft on the airfields at El Adem and El Gubbi, on its outskirts (El Gubbi is most probably the name the British gave to T2).

Air Chief Marshal Sir Arthur Longmore decided to place one Bombay of 216 Sqn under Air Commodore Raymond Collishaw's control for a week at each moon period, effective immediately. It was to arrive at Mersa Matruh at dusk every day and take off at dawn to return to Heliopolis, to avoid damage if the forward landing grounds were bombed.

12 June 1940 - Franco-Italian Front

On the front towards the French, the *Regia Aeronautica* was busy with reconnaissance missions from 07:05 to 14:50.

A Ro.37*bis* of the 64° *Gr. O.A.* flew a reconnaissance mission over Ben Gardane, while an SM 79 of the 33° *Stormo* piloted by *ten*. Gregagnin of the 45ª *Sq*. made a reconnaissance over Gabés – Ben Gardane – Medenine, the Sparviero encountering AA fire.

An SM 79 from the 256ª *Sq.*, 36º *Stormo*, flown by *cap.* Arduino Buri (later a torpedo bomber ace) made a photographic reconnaissance of Bizerta, discovering a seaplane tender, four destroyers and two scout ships. Three fighters that were unable to catch it pursued the SM 79. They were probably Morane MS.406s of GC III/5, of which only the fighter flown by *Adjutant Chef* Buisson was able to open fire at its intended target before it escaped.

The mission ended badly for the French fighters, because one of them had to crash-land without fuel while coming back to base.

Two more SM 79s from the same *Stormo* took off to reconnoitre the airfields in the areas of Tunis and Sousse. Bad weather prevented them from accomplishing the mission over Sousse, which was later reconnoitred by a 30º *Stormo* machine piloted by *ten.* Martinelli. In the meantime *cap.* Crosara of the 193ª *Sq.* made a photographic reconnaissance of the Tunis area.

After the reconnaissance missions, 21 SM 79s of the 32º *Stormo*, commanded by the young *Generale di Brigata Aerea* Stefano Cagna (formerly co-pilot in the seaplane piloted by Italo Balbo during the air crossing of northern and southern Atlantic) took off from Decimomannu at 14:10. They attacked the harbour and the nearby airbase of Bizerta-Karouba. Seven bombers returned damaged by the heavy AA.

The French base suffered heavy damage. *Escadrille* E7 was destroyed on the ground, losing four aircraft burnt out or written off and one damaged out of its six Loire 70s. A week later its pilots were put at the disposal of GB II/25 based at Bougie, and took part in some missions flying its old Lioré et Olivier LeO H 257*bis* seaplanes.

At the conclusion of hostilities an Italian commission checked the French documents detailing the damage suffered in Bizerta area on 12 June. In this way it was found that, apart from the already recorded hits on E7, the merchant ship *Finisterre* was sunk in Ponty bay and the minelayer *Castor* was slightly damaged, together with some submarines, and the railway near Bizerta was damaged. On Sidi Ahmed airport a Caudron Goeland liaison aircraft was pulverized by a direct hit while another was heavily damaged and a Bloch slightly so, two hundred 200 litres drums of fuel went up in flames and an AA battery (the number three) was hit, while in the nearby Sebra two captive balloons were destroyed on the ground. Twelve bombs hit short of the intended targets, on the town of Bizerta itself.

French fighters from GC III/5 (six Moranes) tried to intercept but arrived too late. They remained on standing patrol, however.

Strangely enough *Generale* Francesco Pricolo (Commander in chief of the *Regia Aeronautica*) blamed Cagna for the attack: "*risk high, results few*" was his comment after the highly successful attack.

One Bréguet Bizerte of E3 (serial number no.7, coded E.3.3) went up flames at Arzew, reason unknown.

13 June 1940 - British-Italian Front

The 50º *Stormo Assalto* flew their first combat mission during the day when they attacked British vehicles near the border at Esc Scegga.

The Capronis of the 2º *Gr. A.P.C.* also saw action. In particular, a section of the 23ª *Sq.*, commanded by *ten.* Adriano Visconti, attacked British troops near the border.

The British flew some reconnaissance missions over Fort Capuzzo and other frontier posts with their Blenheims.

An SM 79 from the 44º *Gr.*, flown by *cap.* Brescianini, flew over Alexandria for the usual daily reconnaissance.

13 June 1940 - Franco-Italian Front

On Italy's western front a Z.506 of the 197ª *Sq.* 31º *Stormo*, piloted by *ten.* Barioglio, flew over Algiers but was unable to take photos because of bad weather. They had a narrow escape after icing on the wings, which caused the aircraft to fall into a spin from 5000 metres.

Teresio Martinoli of the 384ª Squadriglia, who claimed his first victory on 13 June 1940 when he claimed a French aircraft over Tunis. Martinoli was later to become Regia Aeronautica's most successful pilots with 22 and 3 shared victories before being killed in a training accident on 25 August 1944. [via D'Amico-Valentini]

For the third consecutive day a Ro.37*bis* of the 64º *Gr. O.A.* went over Ben Gardane to monitor French Army movements.

Two aircraft from the 36º *Stormo* monitored northern Tunisia, while a 33º *Stormo* machine from Bir el Bhera, piloted by *ten.* Gregagnin, checked the border zone with Libya.

Bombers from the 30º and 36º *Stormi* attacked the airfields in the Tunis area, escorted by the 1º *Stormo*'s fighters. The SM 79s of the 108º and 109º *Gruppi* under command of *Generale* Giuseppe Barba and *col.* Carlo Drago took off from Castelvetrano at 07:05 in two formations. In the meantime 15 SM 79s of the 30º *Stormo* (five each from the 193ª, 194ª, and 195ª *Squadriglie*) took off from Sciacca and joined with the 36º *Stormo*'s formation. On take-off, *ten.* Arrighi's bomber crashed but the crew was unhurt. The bombers then met 15 CR.42s from the 157º *Gr.*, which had taken off from the island of Pantelleria on seeing the bombers passing overhead. The Italian fighters had taken off from Trapani at 04:40 and had landed at Pantelleria at 05:10. They were three fighters from the 385ª *Sq.* (*cap.* Aldo Li Greci (CO), *s. ten.* Giacomo Cremona and *m. llo.* Marcello Baccara), six fighters from the 386ª *Sq.* (*cap.* Gustavo Garretto (CO), *s. ten.* Angelo Carminati, *serg.* Fausto Fiorani, *s. ten.* Andrea Dalla Pasqua, *serg. magg.* Giuseppe Tomasi, *serg.* Giuseppe Gullà) and six from the 384ª *Sq.* (the war diary of the *Squadriglia* isn't available, but it seems that *serg.* Teresio Martinoli was part of the formation together with five other pilots).

At around 08:35 when the fighters were flying towards Tunis, *s. ten.* Carminati was suddenly taken ill and collided with *serg.* Fiorani, both planes crashing from 6000 metres. The 386ª *Sq.*'s formation became totally uncoordinated with Dalla Pasqua, Tomasi and Gulla returning to Pantelleria after searching for wreckage of their comrades' aircraft, while Garretto went on, lost contact with the bombers and flew alone over Tunis at 6000 metres, finally returning at 09:50.

Over the target, the 36º *Stormo* pilots reported being attacked by French fighters, tentatively identified as Curtisses that were immediately attacked and dispersed by the escorting CR.42s. Only the SM 79 of *ten.* Poggi of the 259ª *Sq.* was slightly damaged in the tail and in a fuel tank.

Teresio Martinoli claimed a French twin-engined aircraft over Tunis during this mission (it seems that the claim was only made in his personal logbook), while the 385ª *Sq.*'s fighters returned with nothing to report, so it seems that only the 384ª *Sq.* made contact with the French interceptors.

The 36º *Stormo* attacked Ksar-Said and Menzel-Temime airstrips with 50 and 100 kilo bombs, while the 30º *Stormo* hit El Aouina from 4000 metres with 120 x 50 kilo and 40 x 100 kilo bombs. *col.* Serra's SM 79 was hit and damaged by AA.

All bombers were back at around 10:00, but on landing at Sciacca the Savoia of *ten.* Mazzotti ('194 – 5') ran into a grove of olive trees and was written off.

The French fighters were almost certainly Morane Saulnier MS.406s and Potez 630s (perhaps the twin-engined aircraft engaged by Martinoli) from *2ème escadrille* GC I/9, but no other detail regarding this combat is known from French sources (and no losses or claims were recorded). It is also possible that first *Escadrille* of GC III/5 took part in the action.

A Caproni Ca.309 Ghibli. [via Italian Air Force]

The Loire 130s seaplanes from the cruisers *Jean de Vienne* and *La Galissonière* were engaged against Italian submarines in the morning. The seaplanes, piloted by *Lieutenant de Vaisseau* Saleun (Jean de Vienne) and *Lieutenant de Vaisseau* Yoyotte-Husson (La Galissonière) discovered an Italian submarine attacking the French fleet that was moving towards Gibraltar, and gave the alarm that permitted the French ships to avoid the torpedoes aimed at them. The Loire 130s continued to attack the submarine, but to avail.

Two Z.501s of the 183ª *Sq.* from Elmas attacked a submarine, claiming it sunk.

An SM 79 of the 33º *Stormo* made a reconnaissance over the Gabes – Medenine – Ben Gardane route.

The 2º *Stormo* performed numerous patrols and scrambles, taking off from Tripoli Castel Benito and from the advanced landing ground at Bir El Bhera.

After an afternoon scramble by the 82ª *Sq.*'s alarm patrol at Bir El Bhera, *serg.* Filippo Baldin experienced engine problems and overturned on landing at the emergency strip at El Assab. Baldin was unhurt, but the fighter was heavily damaged (RD).

At 20:10, the two remaining pilots from the 82ª *Sq.*'s alarm patrol at Bir El Bhera (*s. ten.* Giuseppe Bottà and *serg.* Renato Giansante), took off to return to Tripoli. Immediately after take-off, Giansante experienced engine problems and tried to force land. A few metres above the ground his fighter suddenly crashed into the ground and burst into flames, killing the pilot.

Giuseppe Bottà returned alone at 20:20.

14 June 1940 - British-Italian Front

This day saw the first combats between opposing RAF and *Regia Aeronautica* fighters over North Africa. This followed the 11th Hussars (Prince Albert's Own), joined by elements of 4th Armoured Brigade and 1st Battalion, King's Royal Rifle Corps, assaulting Fort Capuzzo and Fort Maddalena (the two most important Italian frontier posts). The offensive was supported by attacks by Blenheims from 45, 55, 113 and 211 Sqns.

During early morning, the 4º *Stormo* recorded its first victory, and maybe this was the first clash between fighters from the *Regia Aeronautica* and the RAF.

At 08:50, a patrol of four aircraft of the 90ª *Sq.* (*cap.* Renzo Maggini, *ten.* Giovanni Guiducci, *ten.* Franco Lucchini and *serg.* Giovanni Battista Ceoletta) was up, heading for the border when, at 10:00 and at a height of 4000 metres over Buq-Buq, Lucchini, famous for his exceptional eyesight, saw in the distance some small dots going eastwards.

Slowly, one of the dots remained behind his colleagues and revealed itself as a Gladiator.

Maggini, Guiducci and Lucchini, flying in a "vic" formation, started to pursue the British fighter. Maggini and Lucchini on the flanks denied him any evasive manoeuvre until he was left with the only option, to dive. Guiducci, who occupied the central position in the formation, followed the Gloster in the dive, opening fire from a distance of 200 metres at a height of 1500 metres.

The British fighter caught fire and fell in the sea off Sollum; the pilot was not seen to bale out. Initially the victory was assigned to the four pilots as "shared". In fact it was a victory by Guiducci. The pilots had together spent 500 rounds of ammunition.

To protect both bombers and ground forces, 33 Sqn flew offensive sweeps as far as Bardia, meeting the *Regia Aeronautica* twice in the morning.

At 07:35 F/O Ernest Dean, F/O R. A. Couchman, P/O Vernon Woodward and P/O Alfred Costello of 33 Sqn took off from Sidi Barrani to provided indirect escort to Blenheims from 45 Sqn. Two Blenheims (L4923 piloted by F/Lt Troughton-Smith and L8469 piloted by P/O Collins) were out at 07:00 to attack the nearby airstrip of Sidi Azeiz, three bombers led by the commanding officer S/Ldr Dallamore were out for Fort Maddalena (that the Italians had already abandoned) while a sixth bomber (L8524) was out to attack Giarabub. According to the 11th Hussars (charged with the capture of Fort Maddalena), the initial bombing of the RAF completely missed the fort. It was then taken practically without fighting (in fact it was already half abandoned), and when the *"Cherry Pickers"* were retreating with (a few) prisoners and booty from the abandoned fort, the RAF tried again. Inside Maddalena there was a single British troop filling up with

*Ernest Dean of 33 Sqn, who claimed one CR.32 in combat with the 8° Gruppo on 14 June 1940. Dean was to claim four fighters shot down during 1940 before his unit was posted to Greece, where he claimed one additional victory.
[via Peter Dean]*

water that had a narrow escape when the RAF scored some direct hits. These were by three machines of 45 Sqn, led by F/Lt Millis in a second raid, which confirmed the reports of the Army, claiming a direct hit into the fort and British armoured fighting vehicles in the vicinity . The attack on Giarabub caused damage to two hangars but L8524 was shot down by light AA fire, killing the crew; F/O John Scott Davies, Sgt Geoffrey Edward Negus and Leading Aircraftman John King Copeland. Later during the day, P/O Gibbs in L4923, probably after the afternoon attack on Maddalena, flew over Giarabub and reported damage to the base's hangars and a burnt out aircraft at the edge of the aerodrome, that might have been that of F/O Davies.

The fighters of 33 Sqn returned at 09:25 and reported a successful low flying attack carried out on a Ghibli bomber on the ground at Sidi Aziez. Advancing British troops later captured the disabled bomber.

It seems that they had run into a Caproni Ca.309 Ghibli of the 2° Gr. A.P.C. That morning *ten*. Adriano Visconti was based at Menastir M airstrip with a section of Ca.309s of the 2° Gr. A.P.C. The Section received the order to send a plane over Sidi Azeiz, which was being attacked by many armoured cars, to report what was happening. Visconti took off immediately (crew: *s. ten*. Osservatore Regio Esercito Umberto Zolesi, an Army officer, and *Primo Aviere Montatore* Luigi Moroso). Over Sidi Azeiz, reached in a few minutes, he was attacked by three Gloster Gladiators that hit one of the engines and wounded Moroso. Visconti didn't lose control of the plane and force landed on Sidi Azeiz, that was already surrounded by enemy troops. There Visconti dismounted the front gun of the Caproni and with it defended the plane for more than one hour. In the meantime, at Menastir, *serg. magg.* Oreste Speranza, not seeing his commanding officer coming back, took off with the other Caproni of the section. He discovered Visconti on the ground, landed near him and saved him together with Moroso and Zolesi. The enemy captured Visconti's aircraft (MM11216). For this mission Visconti was awarded the *Medaglia di bronzo al Valor Militare* for bravery and left the A.P.C. to be assigned to 50° *Assalto*, where he became a Breda pilot. The official citation of the award to Visconti stated that *"during a mission he was attacked by three enemy aircraft that seriously damaged his plane. With skilful manoeuvre he landed it and immediately organized the defence of his crew displaying courage and great determination."*

An early morning raid by Blenheim Mk.Is from 211 Sqn supported the attack on Capuzzo. Eight of them attacked at low level, dropping four 250 pound bombs each. The bombs had 11-second-delay-fuses that mostly failed, so most of the attackers suffered splinter damage from their own bombs or those dropped by their companions. It was possibly after this action that L1539, piloted by Sgt Watkins, with Leading Aircraftman John Gerard Sharrat as Wireless Operator/Air Gunner, force-landed at Mersa Matruh as reported in Sharrat's Flight Log.

The 7th Hussars' Diary (7th Hussars was the unit of 4th Armoured charged with the capture of Fort Capuzzo together with the 1st King's Royal Rifle Corps) remarked that the air attack, done at 08:15, undoubtedly scared the enemy, although the nearest bomb was 100 yards away.

At 09:45, S/Ldr D.V. Johnson and Sgt Shaw took off. During the patrol, Johnson engaged reportedly three CR.32s, over Bardia, possibly the 10° Gr. formation. However details of the engagement aren't available and no losses were noted.

At 10:00, after refuelling the Gladiators, Dean (N5782) and Woodward (N5783) were off again, followed a few minutes later by Sgt J. Craig (N5768). Near Fort Capuzzo they intercepted two Caproni Ca.310Bs escorted by CR.32s. Dean shot down one of the CR.32s while Woodward and Craig jointly attacked one Caproni, setting one of the engines on fire. The Italian bomber crash-landed among British tanks near Fort Capuzzo. Woodward also attacked and claimed a second CR.32 (this claim is unconfirmed, and no more Italian losses have been possible to verify) before returning to base with a single bullet hole in one of the wings. Dean later said:

"Soon after being promoted to F/O , I was posted to No 33 Sqn at Mersa Matruh. I had a good flight with Verne Woodward, Peter Wickham and Sergeant Craig. It wasn't long after Italy declared war that we were moved to Sidi Barrani. We had no warning system at all of aircraft movement by the enemy, and only very sketchy and vague locations of both ours and their positions from the Army. We carried

Savoia SM 79s of the 53ª Squadriglia, 47º Gruppo, 15º Stormo, attacking Sollum from 3500 meters altitude. The photo was probably taken in June 1940. [via Italian Air Force]

out the old traditions of patrolling along and over the border in the beginning in "vics" and pairs. Later, we flew bigger sweeps with more aircraft. The combat of 14 June near Fort Capuzzo was our very first encounter with the enemy. An inoffensive-looking light bomber was seen, and I detached Woodward and Sergeant Craig to attack, whilst I stayed aloft to cover. Within a short spell I saw six aircraft in line astern heading from the west. I recognised them as CR 32s. I remember being quite calm, and wondering what the heck to do. I flew towards them, keeping them well to my right – with the thought of getting behind them (and shooting them down one by one – silly boy!).

Before I got close enough to them, they split in all directions and formed a ring around me – the sitting duck! I remembered somewhere about flying extraordinarily badly to present a very bad target. I throttled back, yawed and waffled up and down and around, and could hear the thump of their half-inch cannon at each pass, and as each came into my sights having a rapid squirt at them. This seemed to go on for ages, and eventually one of them dropped away and suddenly the remainder disappeared, and I was thankfully alone in the sky and flew back.

I heard upon my return to base that one CR 32 had been destroyed, apparently by me, whilst Woodward and Craig had shared the bomber. I did hear later that the pilot of the CR 32 had been struck by a single bullet through the heart."

They had clashed with six CR.32s from the 8° *Gr.* flown by *cap.* Martino Zannier (CO 92ª *Sq.*), *ten.* Ranieri Piccolomini (92ª *Sq.*), *ten.* Gioacchino Bissoli (93ª *Sq.*), *serg.* Ernesto Pavan (92ª *Sq.*), *serg.* Edoardo Azzarone (92ª *Sq.*) and *serg.* Roberto Lendaro (93ª *Sq.*), which had been escorting three Caproni Ca.310s of the 159ª *Sq.*, 12° *Gr.*, 50° *Stormo* that had taken off at 09:30 to attack British armoured cars that were surrounding Amseat (Fort Capuzzo). The Italian fighters reported that they had chased seven (or nine) Gladiators and three of them were claimed shot down by Piccolomini, Pavan and Azzarone before Azzarone was shot down and killed (probably by Dean) over the British lines (according to some sources the Italian fighters only claimed two victories; one by Piccolomini and the second shared between Pavan and Azzarone). The Caproni shot down was flown by *serg. magg.* Stefano Garrisi, who parachuted together with *Primo Aviere Montatore* Alfio Ubaldi, while gunner *Aviere Scelto Armiere* Giuseppe Pascali jumped too low and was killed (his body was recovered near Amseat on 26 December 1940). 130 rounds hit the Caproni of *ten.* Mario Virgilio Corda, and *serg. magg.* Giovanbattista Trevisan was wounded. This was the second mission during the war for the 12° *Gr.* and it revealed the unreliability of Ca.310s in this role. Breda Ba.65s soon replaced them.

In the afternoon, seven CR.32s of the 92ª, 93ª and 94ª *Sq.* took off to escort two S.81s of the 14° *Stormo* attacking in the Amseat area. All the aircraft were back without loss at 18:40.

For the first time since the beginning of hostilities, *Aeronautica della Libia* mounted some bombing sorties against targets in Egypt, when Sollum was attacked twice. During the morning twelve SM 79s of the 15° *Stormo* under command of *col.* Napoli attacked Sollum, and after the raid the SM 79s strafed enemy troops which were discovered near Sidi Azeiz and Amseat (Amseat was the airstrip of Fort Capuzzo). During this raid, the Italian destroyers *Turbine*, *Nembo* and *Aquilone* shelled the same target from 03:49 to 04:05, but in conditions of thick mist little damage was caused.

In the afternoon 17 SM 79s of the 10° *Stormo* under command of *col.* Benedetti again attacked Sollum. This raid was indirectly escorted by CR.42s from the 10° *Gr.*

A lone Bombay from 216 Sqn started from Heliopolis, reached Mersa Matruh and then proceeded to Tobruk for the first 216 Sqn raid of the war. The bomber, piloted by P/O Osborne and P/O Archbell, dropped eight 250lb bombs from 10000 ft. Due to slight haze, the results of the attack were difficult to observe. Later photographs confirmed direct hits on a small craft and a warship, but no bombs on the oil storage that was among the primary targets.

14 June 1940 - Franco-Italian Front

Two Z.506s from the 196ª *Sq.* made a reconnaissance over Algiers.

15 June 1940 - British-Italian Front

In the afternoon the 50° *Stormo*'s Breda Ba.65/A80s carried out their first mission, when they attacked British targets near Sollum; six 10° *Gr.* CR.42s escorted them.

The CR.42s of the 10° *Gr.* continued their patrols and escort missions during the day. The wear caused by sand began to be felt by the engines. Some aircraft had to come back before the end of the missions and, after only two days of war, the front line strength of the *Gruppo* decreased to 24 planes, notwithstanding the strenuous efforts of the mechanics.

Bombay (?)5822 from 216 Sqn, flown by S/Ldr Simmons, attacked Tobruk where oil tanks and barracks were claimed possibly hit from high level

15 June 1940 - Franco-Italian Front

Two Z.501s of the 183ª *Sq.* were attacked by four French fighters and shot at by AA fire during a mission near Le Galite. They returned without suffering damage.

Six French Glenn Martin GM 167s of GB I/61 attacked Tripoli harbour causing slight damage (the city was hit by one bomb) and suffering no losses.

16 June 1940 - British-Italian Front

Nine aircraft from both 113 and 55 Sqns were briefed to attack the airfields of El Adem and El Gubbi at dawn. Three Blenheims (L8664, L8397 and L8390) of the latter squadron failed to reach the target due to engine problems (a penalty of operating from desert airstrips). Reportedly, 25 Italian fighters, which spoiled their aim, heavily engaged those that bombed, and although bombs were seen to fall among the parked aircraft, damage was estimate as slight. All bombers returned to base.

It seems that four aircraft (probably fighters) were slightly damaged at T2 and that *ten*. Vincenzo Vanni of the 84ª *Sq*. was wounded.

During the attack on T2, four pilots (*ten*. Enzo Martissa, *m. llo*. Vittorio Romandini, *serg*. Alessandro Bladelli and *serg*. Elio Miotto) of the 91ª *Sq*. were scrambled. They intercepted three of the Blenheims and claimed two of them shot down. The victories were credited as shared by the four pilots, as was common for the 4° *Stormo* at this stage of the war. In fact, because of this combat, Martissa was awarded the *Medaglia d'argento al Valor Militare* for bravery, and the official citation of this award stated that he had shot down one of the British bombers individually.

M. llo. Mario Bandini, *serg*. Giuseppe Scaglioni and *serg*. Corrado Patrizi (all of the 84ª *Sq*.) went to T3 on alarm duty, and met six bombers coming back from that airfield. Bandini single-handedly attacked the British planes, claiming one of them. During the attack, he was wounded in the left arm by return fire, but succeeded in returning to T2, and displaying great calm, made a perfect landing and a complete debriefing before being carried to Tobruk hospital. Bandini was also awarded a *Medaglia d'Argento al Valor Militare* for bravery for this mission.

Scaglioni and Patrizi meanwhile attacked two Blenheims, emptying their guns on them without seeing their opponents going down.

The only reported intercepted British bomber was Blenheim Mk.I L8531 from 55 Sqn flown by F/O M. F. H. Fox (Observer Sgt Nicholas and Wireless Operator/Air Gunner Leading Aircraftman Klines), which reported being attacked by a fighter that followed it opening fire and hitting both spars of the mainplane, the radio set and the stern frame. The plane was however able to return to Fuka without difficulty. Nothing is known about 113 and 211 Sqns because of the total lack of records of these units for the period.

At El Adem, the 57ª *Sq*. was taking off for a morning raid when the Blenheims arrived. The Italian pilots shut off their engines and remained in place until the end of the bombing, then took off again, less the Savoia of *ten*. Organo, which was slightly damaged. *Regia Aeronautica* retaliated with raids against Sollum and Sidi Barrani by SM 79s and S.81s of 10° and 14° *Stormi*.

208 Sqn's detachment in Sidi Barrani reported that one of their vehicles was damaged during the raids and that during the day "*at one time conditions became very uncomfortable indeed*".

Regia Aeronautica's daily reconnaissance mission over Alexandria was accomplished during the morning by an SM 79 of the 6ª *Sq*., 44° *Gr*., flown by *s. ten*. Melchiorri with *ten*. *Osservatore* Chessa aboard (the army observer officer). The crew chief reported an attempted interception by a group of four Glosters that were left behind. This was the only mission over Alexandria during the day.

During the morning, 30 Sqn sent a two aircraft detachment to Qasaba to operate in conjunction with the fighters of 202 Group.

Later, at dusk, three Blenheims of 113 Sqn made single attacks on hangars and dispersed aircraft at El Adem, surprising the defences by gliding in, with engines shut down, from height over the sea.

In total Italian records show two raids on El Adem with four Savoia S.81s of 14° *Stormo B.T.* destroyed on the ground (plus one SM 79 damaged), one dead and twelve wounded, and one raid on T2 with four aircraft (probably fighters) slightly damaged and *ten*. Vincenzo Vanni wounded. It is not known if the S.81 losses of T3 were suffered during the morning or the evening attack.

During the day 33 Sqn suffered its first loss when six planes were detailed to fly patrols near Sidi Barrani. Thick mist over their destination forced them to return to base. Three pilots lost their way and the leader, 29-year-old F/Lt Hale Winter Bolingbroke DFC, crashed into the sea and was killed.

During the first five days of the war, the Blenheims flew 106 bombing sorties, and only four of them were reported lost through enemy action, although several more were severely damaged and at least three were lost or severely damaged in accidents.

Bombay (?)5850 from 216 Sqn, flown by F/O Cullimore, attacked Tobruk on the night of 16 and 17 June. Heavy AA was met and no damage claimed.

16 June 1940 - Franco-Italian Front

Two SM 79s of 36° *Stormo* from Sicily attacked the French airstrips of Menzel Temime, Ksar-Said, Depienne, Gasr Zit and Bab Ficha. They found only five aircraft on the ground and dropped nine 50-kilo bombs.

An SM 79 from the 194ª *Sq.*, 30° *Stormo* at Sicily, flown by *cap.* Valerio Scarabellotto, made a solo armed reconnaissance over El Aouina, attacking the base with twelve 50-kilo bombs.

Caproni Ca.309s and Savoias of the 15° and 33° *Stormi* from Libya patrolled the Tunisian border area.

During a mission at 11:15, the 33° *Stormo* SM 79 of *ten.* Franco was pursued by three fighters.

Six Glenn-Martin GM 167Fs of GR I/61 attacked Elmas airbase near Cagliari, Sardinia, in the afternoon. A bomb hit a hangar where seven Z.501s were assembled to repaint the national insignias. Six aircraft went up in flames, four from the 183ª *Sq.* (MM32254, MM32269, MM32282 and MM32197) and two from the 188ª *Sq.* (MM35174 and MM35226) while the seventh (MM35271) was heavily damaged. Six personnel and a pilot died and the airbase was heavily damaged.

The 85° *Gr. R.M.* of the *Regia Aeronautica* remained out of action for the duration of the campaign. An SM 79 of the 32° *Stormo* was surprised on the base and heavily damaged, while *serg.* Luigi Moretti of the 50ª *Sq.* was killed.

At 22:50, five SM 79s of the 27° *Gr.*, 8° *Stormo* from Sardinia, under *Generale* Cagna and five Z.506 of the 196ª *Sq.* attacked Bizerta. The returning crews (one of which suffered slight damage to its plane) estimated hits on the submarine moorings.

A Z.501 from the 188ª *Sq.* discovered a submarine surfacing and attacked it without gaining hits.

During the night the Farman 10 E.2 nicknamed "L'Actarus" took off from Oran and made a raid over Rossignano.

17 June 1940 - British-Italian Front

Eight SM 79s of the 10° *Stormo* led by the *Stormo* commander *col.* Benedetti attacked Buq-Buq during the afternoon. F/O Webber from 208 Sqn had just force-landed his Lysander on the airstrip owing to an engine failure when the Italian bombers arrived. No damage was done to personnel or aircraft, but the airfield was "*badly damaged*".

17 June 1940 - Franco-Italian Front

Savoias from Castelvetrano, Sicily, flew over northern Tunisia.

An SM 79 of 36° *Stormo* attacked El Djen airstrip near Tunis and dropped some bombs, claiming damage on two-engines planes on ground (it seem that they were one RAF Hudson and three Hurricanes en-route for Egypt, which didn't suffered any damage). Enemy fighters attacked it.

Another SM 79 from the same unit made a reconnaissance mission over Bizerta, and GC III/5 tried to intercept the Italian shadower over the target without success.

However, the *2ème escadrille* of GC II/9, which just had arrived at Oudna, was more lucky. At 11:00, a *Patrouille* of Czech pilots intercepted an SM 79 from the 36° *Stormo*. *Lieutenant* Vezely fired eight cannon rounds and eighty machine-gun rounds at it before receiving orders over the radio to disengage and go after another Italian machine (which he was unable to find). The SM 79 was credited to him as a probable victory. The Italian plane in fact returned unharmed.

A Z.501 from the 146ª *Sq.* from Elmas (MM35218/'146-2') was forced to ditch after engine problems and was lost. The crew was able to reach the Sardinian coast after 30 hours in their rubber dinghy.

The only war missions by GC III/4 was flown on 17 June, when an Italian aircraft was noted by land observers, but the two formations of Dewoitines that took off to intercept it failed to make contact.

During the night, many aircraft passed over Tripoli, fired at by the AA.

18 June 1940 - Franco-Italian Front

SM 79s from the 36° *Stormo* continued the mission to control the Bizerta area.

A Z.506 of the 196ª *Sq.* flew over Algiers and was pursued, without success, by three enemy fighters.

A CR.32 of the 154ª *Sq.*, 3° *Gr. Aut. C.T.*, piloted by *ten.* Vittorio Broganelli, intercepted a French plane at 4500 metres over Sardinia, hitting it with many rounds before it made good its escape. Broganelli identified his opponent as a Potez 63.11 but in fact it was a Glenn-Martin GM 167F of GR I/61.

19 June 1940 - British-Italian Front

At 07:45, four Gladiators from 33 Sqn flown by S/Ldr D. V. Johnson (N5782), F/Lt G. E. Hawkins (N5765), F/O A. H. Lynch (N5764), and Sgt Roy Leslie Green (L9043), accompanied by F/O Peter Wykeham-Barnes (Hurricane Mk.I P2639) of 80 Sqn and two Blenheim IFs from 30 Sqn, took off from Mersa Matruh to patrol between Buq-Buq and Sollum.

At 09:40, they sighted a formation of nine Fiat CR.42s (in other sources it is stated that it was five CR.42s and either seven CR.32s or Ro.37s). The Fiats were slightly below and to port of the British fighters, who were in an ideal position to make an attack.

Wykeham-Barnes shot down the leader of the Italian fighters whilst he was doing a vertical turn, with a short burst at full deflection. The Gladiators claimed two more CR.42s, but lost 24-year-old Sgt Green when he was shot down despite some violent aerobatics.

The returning RAF pilots reported that, although the enemy was superior in numbers, they lacked the aggression of the Gladiator pilots and gradually retreated towards the Libyan border. Wykeham-Barnes found it difficult to get his sights on the Fiats, because they were so very manoeuvrable, but eventually one of them made a mistake and he was able to get in a good burst of shells, which caused the CR.42 to dive away with smoke trailing behind it. He did not actually see it crash, but it was later confirmed as being destroyed by the ground forces. The Gladiators and the Hurricane were then forced to break off combat by lack of petrol and ammunition. On their way back to Mersa Matruh they had to land at Sidi Barrani to refuel and rearm. The Gladiators were back at 10:10 and Wykeham-Barnes at 10:30. The Blenheims, which reported being out with "*six Gladiators*", in the meantime were patrolling over the sea and arrived too late to participate in the engagement. They however reported that "*five enemy aircraft were encountered and four shot down by the Gladiators (…).*"

The Italian aircraft had been from the Tobruk T2 based 10° *Gr. C.T.* At 08:40, five aircraft of the 84ª *Sq.* took off to escort a formation of five Breda Ba.65/A80s of the 159ª *Sq.*, 12° *Gr. Assalto*, and nine CR.32s from the 8° *Gr.* heading off to attack enemy vehicles between Sollum and Sidi Barrani. The Bredas took off at 07:20, commanded by *cap.* Duilio Fanali. The Italian fighters of the 84ª *Sq.* were flown by *ten. col.* Armando Piragino, *cap.* Luigi Monti, *serg. magg.* Ugo Corsi, *serg.* Giuseppe Scaglioni and *serg.* Narciso Pillepich (almost certainly in MM5552). Monti, who was the pilot with the longest war experience (he was a Spanish Civil war ace with five victories already to his credit), argued with his commander to increase the number of aircraft participating in the escort, but to no avail. The assault planes were out in a search-and-destroy mission, and firstly they had to find targets. In doing so they started with a pass between Amseat and Bardia, then a second one going beyond Sollum, then a third one. In this way, a lot of time was lost and the RAF could scramble its aircraft. The Fiats were over the Bredas, turning at 2000 metres, when a number of Glosters and Hurricanes (the Blenheims were not seen at all while the Hurricane was, as the Italian pilots often did, misidentified as a Spitfire) suddenly attacked them. After a sharp engagement, three pilots came back to T2. The missing pilots were Corsi and Piragino. A CR.42 (Corsi, who was killed) was clearly seen to fall into the sea after being hit by a Hurricane, while nothing was known of the second CR.42. The Ba.65s came back safely, without seeing enemy planes that were obviously too busy with the 4° *Stormo* planes and didn't

Capitano Luigi Monti, CO of the 84ª Squadriglia, 10° Gruppo, in North Africa, 1940. Monti ended the war with 8 and 14 shared victories. Five of his victories were claimed during his service in the Spanish Civil War. [via Bernardo Monti]

engage them. However, returning to T2, the Breda flown by *serg. magg.* Pietro Scaramucci suffered an engine breakdown and crash-landed, being written-off as a consequence.

Serg. Giuseppe Scaglioni returned claiming a Gladiator (probably Green) and a damage to a Spitfire, *serg.* Pillepich claimed two damaged Gladiators and *cap.* Monti claimed a damaged Gladiator. The same evening a *"British communiqué"* advised that six (!) British fighters were lost in exchange for two Italians. So all participating pilots in this combat were credited with six shared victories, because this was the only combat of the day for Italian units. Some days after, a British message dropped on Bardia informed them that Piragino was wounded in the leg after crashing at Sollum, and was a prisoner. Scaglioni described the combat:

"Over Bir el Gib we were surprised by a number of Glosters and a Hurricane that attacked with height advantage giving us a lot of trouble. I saw the commander doing a violent overturning while I was doing a break on the left, this manoeuvre put me behind a Gloster that I shot down with my 12.7 mm guns.

I lost sight of the commander immediately and after landing I knew he was missing. In the same combat we lost serg. magg. Corsi shot down by a Hurricane that I attacked trying to distract it from its action but in vain. For sure Corsi was taken by surprise because he was considered a pilot of exceptional skill and the very best aerobatic pilot of the Stormo."

The nine CR.32s from the 8° *Gr.* had taken off at 08:25. The formation included six CR.32s of the 92ª *Sq.* (*cap.* Martino Zannier, *ten.* Ranieri Piccolomini, *ten.* Giorgio Savoia, *serg. magg.* Guglielmo Gorgone, *serg.* Nadio Monti and *serg.* Ernesto Pavan) and three from the 94ª *Sq.* (*cap.* Franco Lavelli, *s. ten.* Giacomo Maggi and *s. ten.* Nunzio De Fraia), which took off loaded with two-kilo bombs with the dual role of escorting the Bredas from the 159ª *Sq.* and ground attack.

The formation of 92ª *Sq.* was back at 10:35, claiming the destructions of many trucks (left in flames) with the use of 2765 rounds of ammunition and 96 two-kilo bombs. *ten.* Savoia's aircraft was damaged by AA fire, but no enemy planes were noted. Lavelli's group was back at 10:55 without suffering losses. They claimed the destruction of Sollum's electrical station by the use of 36 two-kilo bombs, but noted enemy fighters that had attacked them. It seems that they also had been engaged by the Gladiators from 33 Sqn, the 80 Sqn Hurricane and the two Blenheims from 30 Sqn.

This was 80 Sqn's first action of the war.

After Piragino's capture, *cap.* Giuseppe D'Agostinis took over the command of the 10° *Gr.* and held it until 11 July, when he passed it to the new CO, *magg.* Carlo Romagnoli.

Two Bombays from 216 Sqn left Heliopolis for night operations over Tobruk. That bound for el Gubbi (T2) failed to find the target, while the other targeting El Adem (Flight Lieutenant Wallace-Tarry and P/O Whitaker) firstly bombed from 8000 ft and then came back to attack the dispersed aircraft from 2000 ft. The bombers landed back at Ma'aten Bagush at 04:40.

19 June 1940 - Franco-Italian Front

French bombers attacked Zuara and Bir El Bhera without inflicting damage, while the *Aeronautica della Libia* contented itself with the usual reconnaissance missions.

During the night two sections of three bombers from the 36° *Stormo* attacked Bizerta, encountering heavy AA fire. The first section had to turn back while the second was able to release its bombs but without being able to check their effect.

20 June 1940 - British-Italian Front

At dawn three fighters of the 84ª *Sq.* went to T3 for alarm duty, while during the whole day the 10° *Gr.* flew standing fighter patrols over the 1st Libyan Infantry Division, which was moving in the Bardia area. This use of the CR 42s, although strongly requested by the Army, was a waste of resources being of their dubious utility (apart from the psychological effect on the native troops), and accumulated many flying hours on the engines of the Fiats.

Two Breda Ba.65 A80s of the 159ª *Sq.* 12º *Gr.*, piloted by *cap.* Antonio Dell'Oro and *serg. magg.* Francesco De Vivo, took off from T2 at 13:10 and attacked enemy vehicles in the Sidi Azeiz area.

It is reported that a Ro.37bis of the 137ª *Sq.* piloted by *serg.* Gallina and with observer *s. ten.* Umberto Zolesi was attacked during a reconnaissance by three Gladiators, which disengaged after 15 minutes.

Two Bombays from 216 Sqn proceeded to Ma'aten Bagush for night operations. Bombay L5815 flown by Sgt Ford and P/O Archbell took off at 23:00 and landed back at 03:50 on 21 June, after having attacked El Adem with small calibre and incendiary bombs. Hits were observed among the dispersed aircraft.

The second aircraft (Bombay L5850) flown by F/Lt John Basil Wentworth-Smith and Sgt Benjamin Thomas Morgan Baker with the crew of Corporal William Charles Royle, Leading Aircraftman Alfred Francis Crohill and Leading Aircraftman N. P. Donelly was last seen at 9000 ft over El Gubbi (T2) but didn't return. Only Donelly survived to become a POW. All the squadron operations were cancelled for the rest of the month.

The 90ª *Sq.* diary recorded a first raid against T2 by a four-engine seaplane at 20:15. The British aircraft arrived very low over the harbour (500 metres) and dropped a single bomb without causing any damage. The aircraft disappeared out over open sea and the Navy AA started to fire on it only when it was already a kilometre away. *ten.* Giovanni Guiducci witnessed the aircraft doing some sharp manoeuvres and guessed that some shots could have hit it. During the night the air alarm sounded five times with many bombs (some incendiary) hitting T2 without causing damage; the Navy hospital was hit by a single bomb that caused one death.

Guiducci reported that one of the incursions was recognized to having been by the same seaplane (now he called it Short Sunderland) as from the evening.

20 June 1940 - Franco-Italian Front

An SM 79 from the 36º *Stormo* flown by *cap.* Buri made a photographic reconnaissance mission over Bizerta.

190ª *Sq.* B.M., 86º *Gr.* B.M., arrived at Stagnone from Brindisi with its CANT Z.506s, and started operations with a raid on Bizerta with all its six combat-ready aircraft.

AA was extremely severe, the bomber of *magg.* Marini, the *Gruppo* commander, was hit while Z.506 MM45254 went down for unknown reasons. *ten. Flotard* De Lauzières de Themines and his four crewmembers were killed.

A Z.506 from the 196ª *Sq.* flew a reconnaissance mission over Algiers.

Marshal Italo Balbo on the captured British Morris, armoured car on 22 June. [via Italian Air Force]

Franco Lucchini of the 90ª Squadriglia, who claimed his first victory of the Second World War on 21 June 1940. Lucchini was later to become one of Regia Aeronautica's most successful pilots with 22 victories (including one from the Spanish Civil War) before he was killed in action on 5 July 1943. [via D'Amico-Valentini]

Six SM 79s from the 36° *Stormo* attacked Bizerta during the night. AA seriously damaged *ten*. Sacchetti's bomber.

21 June 1940 - British-Italian Front

At dawn, a Short Sunderland appeared over Tobruk harbour. *serg.* Roberto Steppi of the 84ª *Sq.* took off immediately and intercepted the seaplane 20 kilometres north of Tobruk, where it was already under attack by two CR.32s flown by *ten*. Ranieri Piccolomini and *ten*. Giorgio Savoia of the 92ª *Sq.*, which had scrambled from Tobruk T2 at 04:30. Diving on the Sunderland, Steppi opened fire aiming at the cockpit, but after two bursts of fire his guns jammed and he was obliged to leave the pursuit.

Ten. Franco Lucchini of the 90ª *Sq.* took off after Steppi and joined the fight, following the Sunderland far out over open sea and leaving it off the coast with two engines smoking.

Neither Lucchini nor Steppi claimed any victory but, two days later, on 23 June, news arrived from the Navy base at Bardia that the Sunderland, heavily damaged, had been forced to ditch in the sea off the coast, and had been captured with all the crew dead except the pilot, who was wounded. The victory was assigned to the four pilots collectively, although it should be attributed to Lucchini.

This was the first reported Italian meeting with the lumbering Sunderland, and its overall dimensions made a strong impression on them. Asked about his feelings during the combat, the *"Archduke"*, as Piccolomini was playfully nicknamed by his comrades, stated graphically – *"That was not a plane, that was a tram"*.

According to British records, the intruder on the evening of 20 June was a 228 Sqn Sunderland (N9025/Y), piloted by Acting F/Lt T. M. W. Smith DFC and F/O D. R. S. Bevan-John. The British crew reported heavy AA during an evening reconnaissance of Tobruk's harbour, and landed at Alexandria by night, undamaged.

Then the attack of the Bombay followed, and finally at 02:20 Sunderland L2160/X of 230 Sqn, piloted by Wing Commander G. Francis and F/Lt Garside, took off from Alexandria for a reconnaissance of Tobruk's harbour. Over Tobruk they were intercepted by reportedly four CR.32s or CR.42s, claiming one of them shot down while the others broke off after a 15 minute engagement. L2160 was however heavily damaged by explosive bullets, principal damage being a large hole

The crew of the armoured car in the shadow of Marshal Italo Balbo's SM 79 on 22 June. [via Italian Air Force]

in the hull (6" x 8"). The fuel tanks were also extensively holed, but these were plugged in flight with plasticize.

From Alexandria L2166/U took off at 08:05, piloted by F/Lt Alington, to escort L2160 as a safety aircraft in case it was unable to make it back. It was however unable to join with "X", which in turn landed in Alexandria at 08:30 and was immediately put on the slipway of Imperial Airways for repairs (the aircraft was back in action on 9 July).

L2160 was undoubtedly the plane attacked by Piccolomini, Savoia, Steppi and Lucchini while there is the strong possibility that the aircraft ditched off Bardia was in fact the 216 Sqn Bombay (perhaps previously hit by AA fire since the AA defences of Tobruk was credited with a victory during the day), that was incorrectly reported as a Sunderland and led to the Italian fighter's claim.

In the early morning, from 05:48 to 06:10, a British fleet composed of the cruisers HMS *Orion*, HMS *Neptune* and HMAS *Sidney*, the French battleship *Lorriane* and four destroyers under command of Vice-Admiral Tovey, bombarded Bardia, while a flight from 33 Sqn protected them.

HMAS *Sydney*'s Seagull Mk.V amphibian, A2-21 (Flight Lieutenant T. MacBride, RAAF, and Lieutenant J. C. Bacon, RN) was erroneously attacked by Gladiators during the bombardment. The badly damaged aircraft reached Mersa Matruh safely, but its port undercarriage collapsed on landing and the aircraft was damaged beyond repair.

33 Sqn reported that at 04:45, Blenheims and a Hurricane had left Qasaba to patrol over Bardia and to protect three Seafoxes and one French naval spotter during the naval bombardment. At 05:15, six 'B' Flight Gladiators took off to patrol between the border and Bardia. Pilots known to have taking part were F/O Ernest Dean (Gladiator N5774), Sgt Shaw (N5783), P/O Vernon Woodward (L9046), P/O Preston (N5761) and Sgt J. Craig (N5768). They returned at 07:00 with nothing to report.

As preparation for the bombardment, 113 Sqn had photographed the harbour. Nine Blenheims of 55 Sqn under F/Lt Cox, set out at 04:30 to bomb the warships in the port, but only seven reached the target (L8393 and L8664 aborted). Over Tobruk they met a heavy anti-aircraft barrage and were chased by two CR.42s or CR.32s, which did not attack. They reported that three bombs straddled a ship in the harbour, and reported seeing smoke pouring from the middle of a ship after their attack.

The bombers from 'A' and 'C' Flights arrived about ten minutes after 'B' Flight over the target, where they were attacked by a CR.42, which was flying with another. This aircraft attacked from the starboard beam and at the same height as the formation. The Blenheim's gunners opened fire and it fell away dropping behind, the gunners claimed it hit.

It seems likely that the 55 Sqn Blenheims had run into *serg.* Corrado Patrizi and *serg.* Giuseppe Scaglioni of the 84ª *Sq.*, who scrambled from Tobruk T2 and intercepted a Blenheim that seemed directed to attack the airfield. Patrizi, with his guns jammed, had to disengage almost immediately, while Scaglioni, hit by return fire coming from the bomber, was forced to land back at base.

Between 05:35 and 06:55, three Gladiators from 'C' Flight of 33 Sqn flew a patrol in the Matruh area. Pilots involved were P/O Alfred Costello (N5766), F/O R. A. Couchman (N5756) and Sgt William Vale (N5769). They returned with nothing to report.

Six CR.32s of the 92ª *Sq.* (*cap.* Martino Zannier, *ten.* Ranieri Piccolomini, *serg. magg.* Guglielmo Gorgone, *serg.* Vito Copersino, *serg.* Nadio Monti and *serg.* Ernesto Pavan) and three from the 93ª *Sq.* (*ten.* Alberto Argenton, *serg.* Italo Bertinelli and *serg.* Roberto Lendaro) took off at 09:40 and attacked enemy vehicles south of Bir El Gobi, escorted by CR.42s from the 13° *Gr.* The fire from the CR.32s, which attacked in single file, stopped an enemy armoured car and forced two other armoured cars of the same formation, less seriously damaged, to flee.

They were back at base at 11:00, where Copersino's fighter was found damaged in the fuel tank by AA. The 92ª *Sq.* formation expended 1756 rounds and 96 two-kilo bombs.

Eleven Blenheims of 113 Sqn set out to attack troop concentrations at Bir El Gobi during the day.

At 12.30, Marshal Italo Balbo arrived at Bir el Gobi with his personal SM 79 a few minutes after a RAF raid that had killed fifteen soldiers of the resident 2nd Libyan Division (probably 113

Sqn's raid). While approaching to land, Balbo discovered a British armoured car only six hundred metres away from the airstrip. Not scared at all Balbo performed a kind of "touch and go" landing, remaining on Bir el Gobi barely the time necessary to dismount from his plane. While his second pilot took off again he ran for the 2nd Libyan camp, and ordered the soldiers to attack the British armoured car.

The initial scepticism of the Libyan soldiers quickly changed to surprise when it was discovered that the armoured car was in fact so close to their base, and finally turned to enthusiasm when it was discovered that the British vehicle, already damaged, was unable to defend itself, and was captured with its four man crew. It was the armoured car of T. S. M. Howarth, commander of N°2 Troop of "B" Sqn, 11th Hussars. Balbo mounted the turret of the armoured car (a Morris CS9/LAC) and made a spirited and galvanizing speech to the Libyan soldiers that at the end forgot in high spirits the losses previously suffered.

The armoured car was obviously that damaged by the planes of 8° *Gr.* and was one of the very first captured by the Italian Army in Libya. At the end, Balbo returned to Tobruk, landing with the four British prisoners, while the armoured car was towed by the Libyans inside their camp.

El Adem T3 was attacked during the day by reportedly five British bombers, which killed one person, wounded five, and lightly damaged two Caproni Ca.309 Ghiblis (presumably of the 2° *Gr. A.P.C.*).

The attacking aircraft were possibly from 211 and 45 Sqns.

At 16:20 in the afternoon five Bredas of the 159ª *Sq.* flew a ground-attack mission in the Bir El Gobi area. This was the last mission with the type for *cap.* Duilio Fanali, and with him were *ten.* Roberto Pastorelli, *serg. magg.* Simonini, *serg. magg.* Corrado Sarti and *serg.* Molteni.

It seems that fighters of the 10° *Gr.* escorted the Bredas and 45-years-old *col.* Marziale Cerutti, the sixth best Italian ace from the First World War with 17 victories to his credit, flew with them in what was probably his last war action. The mission was uneventful.

21 June 1940 - Franco-Italian Front

At 10:10, an SM 79 from the 36° *Stormo* on a reconnaissance mission over Bizerte was intercepted by an enemy fighter. It was a Morane MS.406 from GC III/5 flown by Lieutenant Moran, who had managed to scramble in time and pursued the Italian aircraft as far as Dog's Island, where he had to abandon the chase due to lack of fuel. The bomber was credited to Moran as a probable victory.

The SM79, a 259ª *Sq.* machine flown by *ten.* Atti, had the central engine put out of action but was able to returned to base at 12:25 using the wing engines. Four members of the crew were wounded (*ten. di Vascello Ossevatore* Dadone, *serg. Motorista* Masserini, *Primo Aviere Fotografo* Canè and *Aviere Scelto* Foschi). One the ground, four gun rounds were found lodged in the pilot's parachute pack.

Six Z.506s from the 197ª and 198ª *Squadriglie* discovered a group of French ships and tried to attack, but without luck due to the bad weather.

In the afternoon nine SM 79s of the 8° *Stormo* under *Generale* Cagna attacked a group of four warships near the Balearic Islands, but bad weather prevented accurate bombing.

Z.501 MM35199 of the 146ª *Sq.* was obliged to ditch due to an engine breakdown, and was towed to Cagliari harbour by a submarine.

In the afternoon, nine SM 79s from the 30° *Stormo* (four from the 194ª and five from the 195ª *Sq.*) followed up the 36° *Stormo*'s night attack on Bizerta, claiming three hits on a cruiser, and damage to three seaplanes. AA was reported as heavy but not accurate.

Before night, the 36° *Stormo* was back again over Bizerta with five SM 79s from the 259ª *Sq.*

During the move of T2 from Berre to Bougie its seaplanes attacked one submarine.

22 June 1940 - British-Italian Front

During the night a formation of twelve Savoia S.81 bombers of the 39° *Stormo B.T.*, based at Rodi (Rhodes) in the Aegean Islands, took off and attacked Alexandria in clear moonlight during the early hours of 22 June.

Five aircraft of 80 Sqn took off from Amriya, but failed to intercept and were fired on by their own anti-aircraft defences. The pilots involved were F/Lt Pattle, F/Lt Evers-Swindell, F/O Stuckey, F/O Lapsley and P/O Flower.

On the return flight one of the Italian bombers exhausted all its fuel and was forced to ditch. It went down 45 miles south of Rhodes, and the crew was rescued five hours later by an Italian flying boat.

Twelve SM 79s of the 15° *Stormo* flew the first night raid of the *Aeronautica della Libia* when they attacked Mersa Matruh.

Over the target the very intense AA fire hit an SM 79 of the 21ª *Sq.*, 46° *Gr.* flown by *m. llo.* Giovanni Lampugnani (co-pilot *serg. magg.* Francesco Carlone, *Aviere Scelto motorista* Umberto Costa, *Primo Aviere Radiotelegrafista* Ottorino Bruschi and *Primo Aviere Armiere* Bruno Lovato). Lampugnani lost control of the aircraft and they collided with that of his leader, *cap.* Zelè (co-pilot *ten.* Regoli, *Primo Aviere* Bradde, *Primo Aviere* Fallavena and *Primo Aviere* Capellini), which was forced to crash-land near the coast in Egyptian territory. Lampugnani and his crew were killed, while Zelè and his crew became POWs.

The aircraft of the 10° *Gr.* continued standing patrols over the 1st Libyan Division and the strafing missions against British armoured patrols in the border zone.

The 2° *Stormo* also continued to fly patrols and strafing missions, and consequently their CR.42s began to suffer wear from sand. The records of the *Stormo* show that after fifteen hours of flying their Fiat A 74 RC 38 engines began to use up more oil than petrol, and the fabric covers of the aft fuselage and wings suffered too.

22 June 1940 - Franco-Italian Front

SM 79s from Libya made strategic reconnaissance as far as Ben Gardane.

In the morning's reconnaissance over Bizerta, AA damaged an SM 79 from the 30° *Stormo*.

At around 15:00, twelve bombers from the 36° *Stormo* and ten bombers from the 30° *Stormo*, escorted by ten CR.42s from the 157° *Gr.* from Trapani, attacked Bizerta and bombed the docks, warehouses, submarine moorings and Karouba airbase, claiming heavy damage and hits on two ships.

Martin 167 of GB I/63 on an unknown airfield. [via Polish Aviation Museum Cracow]

Later an SM 79 from the 30° *Stormo* checked the damage inflicted upon the French base, the bomber returning damaged by AA fire. According to French sources, this time the damage suffered was light.

The Z.506s from the 31° *Stormo* flew antisubmarine missions, while six SM 79s from the 89° *Gr.* attacked a freighter and a destroyer.

French bombers retaliated by attacking Trapani, where military installations didn't suffer any damage but twenty civilians were killed.

The attack was conducted with 10 and 50 kilo bombs dropped by 27 Martin GM 167Fs from *Groupement* n°1 (one from the *Groupement* HQ, six from GB I/62, five from GB II/62, six from GB I/63 and nine from GB II/63), in its first mission after the redeployment to AFN. Italian fighters, identified as CR.42s, were seen but were unable to intercept.

Maitre Chauby in a Laté from T2 attacked an Italian submarine, placing his bomb less than one metre from its conning tower, but the bomb failed to explode.

LeO H-470 E11.1 from 11E under *Lieutenant de Vaisseau* Guilloux attacked an Italian submarine together with a CANT seaplane, which was taking off, close to it. No damage was inflicted.

At 12:25, a patrol composed of two planes from 4S1, 4S1.1 (*Enseigne de Vaisseau* Gardanne) and 4S1.5 (*Lieutenant de Vaisseau* Blain), was attacked by a fighter over the sea near Cap Zébib, east of Bizerta.

The fire from the fighter heavily damaged 4S1.1 and with two men of the crew wounded, it was forced to crash-land when returning to Karouba.

Initially French authorities declared that an Italian fighter attacked the seaplane, but later it transpired that the interception of the CAMS was a case of friendly fire, the French fighter responsible was a Morane MS.406 of GC III/5.

23 June 1940 - Franco-Italian Front

Ten SM 79s from the 34° *Stormo* at Catania attacked shipping heading for Bizerta for the last time. Bad weather forced them to turn back with their bomb load intact.

The 36° *Stormo* continued with its reconnaissance missions. Two Z.506s from the 188ª *Sq. R.M.* at Elmas met three French seaplanes, which escaped into the clouds.

Additional Z.506s from the 197ª *Sq.* went out for patrols without meeting the enemy.

French shadowers were discovered over Cagliari, but the CR.32s were unable to intercept them.

The French again bombed Zuara, this time by nine Glenn-Martin GM 167Fs from GB II/62, GB I/63 and GB II/63. No damage was suffered, even though the French pilots claimed the destruction of a fuel storage tank.

In a last-minute attempt to transfer the maximum possible amount of troops and materials from metropolitan France to ANF, the French fleet began to operate frequently west of Sardinia.

The Italian fleet countered this by moving the 7th Naval Division, with four cruisers (*Eugenio di Savoia*, *Montecuccoli*, *Attendolo* and *Duca D'Aosta*), to Cagliari and on this day tried to intercept the French traffic. The French ships weren't encountered, but French seaplanes took off from Karouba to search for the Italians.

Ten Laté 298s of HB1 under *Lieutenant de Vaisseau* Georges Baron searched for the Italian cruisers, together with three Latés of T1 and other aircraft from HB 2. In the bad weather, T1 and HB2 were unable to find the enemy fleet, and only Baron was able to bomb through the clouds but without claiming damage.

In the afternoon Palermo was bombed by four Glenn-Martin GM 167Fs from GB I/62 and three from GB II/62. The French bombers aimed at the harbour but many bombs fell in the city itself, killing 25 civilians and wounding 125 more.

The returning French crews didn't report any presence of Italian fighters but one Glenn crashed before coming back to base and another crash-landed at Canrobert without losses among the crews, reportedly suffering mechanical breakdowns.

Another bombing of Palermo was made by five LeO 451s from GB II/11, which had taken off in the late afternoon from Youks-les-Bains (aircraft n° 200 commanded by *Colonel* Chopin, n° 201 commanded by *Lieutenant* Calmel, n° 213 commanded by *Lieutenant* Zimmermann, n° 144 commanded by *Lieutenant* Drougue and n° 3005 commanded by *Capitaine* Bouyer). In fact, only Zimmermann and Calmel hit the intended target from an altitude of 5000 metres; Chopin returned early because of a breakdown, Bouyer attacked Marsala, while nothing was heard of Drougue's aircraft that, forced to take off late, became immediately separated. In fact it seems that LeO 451 n° 144 returned at night, probably short of fuel and trying to force-land on a beach near Cap Bon it exploded, killing the crew.

From the Italian records we know that at 18:25, seven *"enemy bombers"* were discovered over Palermo at approximately 4000 metres, they attacked the harbour diving with the engines shutdown and achieved complete surprise. The CR.32s of the 17° *Gr.* tried in vain to intercept because of the late discovery and the height of their opponents. In the meantime, alarm was given also to the CR.42s of the 157° *Gr.* and the CR.32s of the 80ª *Sq.*, 17° *Gr.*, then detached to Trapani, in the hope of catching the raiders during the return leg of their mission. The fighters from the 157° *Gr.* scrambled at around 18:40 and returned one hour later without having seen any enemy while, flying north, two CR.32s of the 80ª *Sq.*, piloted by *ten.* Clizio Nioi and *ten.* De Tecini discovered an alone aircraft off Capo Gallo (slightly west of Palermo's harbour). The aircraft was identified as a *"Potez 63"* and attacked by Nioi, who could benefit of a slight height advantage over his target. Nioi hit it, observing the French raider that nose-dived engulfed in a thick cloud of smoke. Later ground observers reported that the aircraft had fallen into the sea and Nioi was credited with his first aerial victory (he ended the war as an ace with seven individual victories to his credit). Finally, at 19:30, a last attack on Mazara del Vallo (an harbour very close to Marsala) was reported.

It seems probable that one of the French bombers, possibly the lone LeO 451 of *Lieutenant* Drogue was the machine attacked by Nioi.

24 June 1940 - British-Italian Front

The *Ghibli* wind, blowing strongly in the Tobruk area, reduced visibility and flying activities of the 10° *Gr.* for the following days.

Eight bombers from 55 Sqn took off at 07:15 to attack Italian troops at Bir El Gobi under S/Ldr R. A. T. Stowell (L6672 aborted due to engine trouble during the take off). The attack was a complete surprise, and even if some bombs were seen to fall short of the target, the majority fell inside the target area.

Later two Blenheims carried out a reconnaissance of the desert area around Bir El Gobi. One of them had to abort suffering engine trouble.

At 07:45 three Ba.65s of the 159ª *Sq.* and three CR.32s of the 160ª *Sq.* (one of them piloted by *magg.* Bruno Cudugnello) took off to attack the usual armoured cars in the Esc. Scegga- Uadi Dalema area. They hit four of them, in exchange for a damaged Breda.

This was the first combat action for the assault CR.32s of the 50° *Stormo*.

On instruction from HQ 202 Group, F/Lt Black of 208 Sqn flew over Bardia and dropped by parachute messages from Italian prisoners shot down over Egypt. In this way news of *ten. col.* Armando Piragino, *serg. magg.* Ugo Corsi and the crews of the two Savoia SM 79s of the 15° *Stormo* that had collided during the night bombing mission on Mersa Matruh were received.

24 June 1940 - Franco-Italian Front

With hostilities near to an end, the *Regia Aeronautica* contented itself with reconnaissance missions, while the French attacked Cagliari in Sardinia (minor damage suffered after a raid by 13 Douglas DB 7s from *Groupement* n°2) and Olivetti Village in Tripolitania (three GM 167Fs from GB II/63). Italian fighters, although scrambled immediately, were unable to intercept.

A Loire 130 of *Groupement* HS7 based at Arzew crashed with the loss of the crew (*Lieutenant de Vaisseau* Roux, *Second-Maitre* Lacampagne and *Quartier-Maitre* Beluche) for unknown reasons.

At 18:00, LeO H-470 E11.2 from 11E under *Enseigne de Vaisseau* Le Saint exchanged fire with a Cant Z.506 from the 199ª *Sq.* without suffering or inflicting damage.

This was the last encounter of the campaign.

25 June 1940

At 06:15, four CR.32s of the 160ª *Sq.* bombed the enemy in the Amseat area with good results.

During the same day Tobruk was bombed but no damage was recorded.

26 June 1940

Four CR.42s from the 82ª *Sq.* and one from the 78ª *Sq.* took off at 08:45 to make a standing patrol over the 2nd Libyan Infantry division. The formation flew as far as Sollum, but at 09:45 during the return flight, *s. ten.* Italo Santavacca (78ª *Sq.*) was forced to make an emergency landing at Sidi Azeiz due to the compete loss of engine oil. *ten.* Guglielmo Chiarini landed near him but when

A burnt out Fiat CR.42 from the 90ª Squadriglia at Tobruk T2 after 55 Sqn's attack on 28 June.
[Historical Office Italian Air Force]

returning to T2, he was obliged to force-land at Gambut for the same reason at 10:05. At 10:20, *serg.* Filippo Baldin also had the same problem. *cap.* Guglielmo Arrabito landed at Gambut to see what had happened to his pilots, but when he taking off again he had to force-land at Sidi Bu Amud for the usual lack of oil, at 10:40. There he found *s. ten.* Gilberto Cerofolini, who had already force-landed at 10:35. The formation completely failed to return! Adding insult to injury, N° 5 Troop of "B" Sqn 11th Hussars led by 2/Lt. Dier that was observing Fort Capuzzo, once Chiarini had flown away, attacked the plane of Santavacca, burning it and taking the pilot prisoner. Later Santavacca told his captors about the capture of T. S. M. Howarth and his armoured car by *Marshal* Italo Balbo.

Two Savoia SM 82s of the 149° *Gr. Trasporti*, which just had arrived in Derna from Italy, were sent to Cufra oasis in the deep Libyan Desert to deliver urgent materials.

During the return journey one of the pilots lost his way and disappeared in the desert. *cap.* Carlo Ludrini, *s. ten.* Vittorio De Barbieri, *m. llo. marconista* Mario Borello, and *serg. magg. motorista* Ludovico Martinelli were never seen again. They were the first losses of Italian transport units during the war.

An SM 79 of the 55ª *Sq.*, 30° *Gr.* flown by *ten.* Spadaccini and *ten.* Rivoli, flew over Cairo and dropped 100 kg of leaflets inviting the British to surrender.

27 June 1940

SM 79s from the 30° *Gr.*, 10° *Stormo*, starting from Derna, attacked British positions in the Sollum area.

A couple of Breda Ba.65s of the 50° *Stormo* (*ten.* Roberto Pastorelli and *m. llo.* Enio Sagliaschi) attacked enemy vehicles in the Sidi Omar area.

20 bombers from the 10° *Stormo* attacked Sidi Barrani and Buq-Buq in subsequent waves during the morning. 208 Sqn reported that no damage was suffered by the unit.

28 June 1940

At 06:30, three CR.32s of the 160ª *Sq.* took off from Tobruk T2 heading for Ponticelli, an airstrip inside the fortified area of Bardia. During the take-off *serg.* Vittorio Macchetti broke the left landing gear and consequently the left wing on his aircraft.

At 10:30, the CR.32s attacked armoured cars in the Amseat area and claimed one in flames.

At 15:30, another attack was made, this time in the nearby Sidi Azeiz area and another armoured car was claimed.

During the morning, *cap.* Luigi Monti flew over Sollum and dropped three messages with information regarding RAF prisoners. This action was an answer to F/Lt Black's mission the day before.

At 10:15, a Short Sunderland (L5804/S) of 230 Sqn from Aboukir, piloted by F/Lt "Willy" Campbell and F/O King, discovered the Italian submarine *Argonauta* sailing from Tobruk towards Taranto at periscope depth. Unseen by the Italian sailors the flying-boat attacked in two passes, releasing four 112kg bombs each time. The *Argonauta* sank immediately with the loss of the *Commander ten. di Vascello* Cavicchia Scalamonti and the whole crew.

Back at Aboukir, the claim of the British crew was treated with some scepticism, because the intelligence service judged it quite unlikely that an Italian submarine would be in the reported area.

A few hours later another Sunderland, this time L5806 of 228 Sqn piloted by Wing Commander G. E. Nicholetts, attacked one large submarine with three bombs from low level. Nicholetts reported that bombs fell over the target and that it was unlikely that submarine was sunk. In fact, he had damaged the submarine *Anfitrite* sufficiently to force it to return to base.

Cap. Giuseppe D'Agostinis of the 91ª *Sq.*, *cap.* Aldo Lanfranco of the 84ª *Sq.* and *ten.* Enzo Martissa of the 91ª *Sq.*, 10° *Gr.*, took off to attack enemy armoured vehicles in the Sidi Azeiz area.

Lanfranco suffered a mechanical breakdown and landed in Bu Amud. D'Agostinis and Martissa in the meantime discovered twelve enemy armoured cars hidden near the landing ground of Sidi

Burnt out fuel drums at Tobruk T2 after 55 Sqn's attack on 28 June. [Historical Office Italian Air Force].

Azeiz, recently recaptured by the Italian Army, and attacked, destroying two of them; the other ten vehicles retired in the Sidi Omar direction.

At 17:12, a formation of fifteen Blenheims, consisting of nine from 55 Sqn (led by F/Lt R. B. Cox) and probably six from 211 Sqn, made a surprise attack on Tobruk T2 with very good results. The aircraft of the 90ª *Sq.* suffered worst and even if only one CR.42 was burnt out completely, not a single plane of the *Squadriglia* escaped unscathed. Two aircraft of the 84ª *Sq.* and some of the 91ª *Sq.* were damaged too (RS). It seems that six Ro.37bis of the 136ª and 137ª Squadriglie were put out of service as well in this attack and many fuel drums burned. In fact, 55 Sqn's returning crews reported that one or more bombs had hit what was probably a bulk petrol store, as dense smoke rose to a height of 1000 feet.

A 90ª *Sq.* trio of pilots (*cap.* Renzo Maggini, *serg.* Amleto Monterumici and *serg.* Silvio Crociati) was on alarm duty and, notwithstanding the bombing, tried to take off. The three pilots were showered by a rain of splinters. Maggini was seriously wounded in the leg while he was trying to jump into his aircraft, and wounded with him was *Aviere Scelto* Francesco Macina, who was following his commander with the compressed air bottle necessary to start the Fiat A.74 RC38 engine of the CR 42. Crociati was wounded by a splinter and sprayed with burning fuel. Taken to Tobruk hospital in critical condition, he died during the night. Together with him five personnel of the 90ª *Sq.* died (*Primo Aviere* Martino Cardascia, *Aviere Scelto* Rocco Madri, *Aviere* Giuseppe Bassanini, *Aviere* Pietro Cappelletti, *Aviere* Nando Fuini) and six soldiers of the Army. Monterumici was also wounded and didn't succeed in taking off. Together with him two personnel of the 90ª *Sq.* were wounded (*Primo Aviere di Governo* Ugo Nante and *Aviere* Alessandro Balistro) and one from the 84ª *Sq.* (*Aviere Armiere* Fausto Mainardis).

Cap. Renzo Maggini was replaced by *ten.* Giovanni Guiducci as CO of the 90ª *Sq.*

This bombing attack represented the end of operations for the 10° *Gr.* because, together with the destruction of the 90ª *Sq.*, the Blenheims also destroyed all the spare parts for the CR.42s of the *Gruppo* that just had arrived in T2. With aircraft already worn out by the first twenty days of operations and no spare parts at all left, the *Gruppo* had to withdraw.

To make a bad situation even worse, the personal aircraft of Air Marshal Italo Balbo, Commander in Chief of the Italian armed forces in Libya, arrived over T2 with Felice Porro, CO of Aeronautica Della Libia, flying in another SM 79 close to it when the last British bombers were just leaving the area.

While approaching the T2 airstrip at low speed the two SM 79s were misidentified as British aircraft by the insufficiently trained Navy personnel of the flak defences of Tobruk, and a heavy barrage was aimed at them. Porro had a narrow escape, fleeing out to sea followed by bursts of AA fire, while Balbo's aircraft was shot down in flames with the death of all the crew inside. The loss of Balbo was a hard blow. Balbo, apart from being one of the most famous aviators of his times, was an aggressive leader (he fought in an elite "*Arditi*" company of the "*Alpini*" troops, the Italian Mountain Sturmtruppen, during the First World War), had been against the war with Great Britain (he was a great admirer of this country), but believed in an all-out attack strategy as the best way of defence. Considering the numerical superiority that the Italian Army attained in the following months, a quick attack in the direction of Egypt with all the forces available was probably the best thing that the Italian Army could do. His successor, Marshal Rodolfo Graziani, was far more cautious, and left the British all the time they need to reinforce and hit back. Balbo was subsequently awarded with a posthumous *Medaglia d'Oro al Valor Militare*.

The British reported that an Italian bombing attack damaged Mersa Matruh airfield and put it out of action until the evening. The 46° *Gr.*, 15° *Stormo*, led by *magg.* Cerne, made the attack.

29 June 1940

At dawn, Blenheims again bombed the airfield of Tobruk T2. Ten fighters from the alarm patrol of the 2° *Stormo* took off at 06:40, following the air alarm given by the Navy with two cannon shots, and intercepted the Blenheims over the airfield. The intercepting fighters were four CR.42s from the 94ª *Sq.* (*cap.* Franco Lavelli, *s. ten.* Nunzio De Fraia, *serg. magg.* Alessandro Ruzzene and *serg. magg.* Arturo Cardano), two CR.42s from the 92ª *Sq.* (*magg.* Vincenzo La Carruba and *ten.* Riccardo Marcovich, who possibly was using a borrowed aircraft from the 93ª *Sq.* together with one of the pilots from the 94ª *Sq.*) and four CR.42s of the 77ª *Sq.* (*cap.* Mario Fedele, *s. ten.* Giulio Torresi, *s. ten.* Gianmario Zuccarini, *serg. magg.* Agostino Fausti). Fedele was slow in taking off because of engine problems and arrived when the combat was already finished, but the others attacked the British formation, which was estimated to consist of nine Blenheims.

S. ten. Torresi reached the bombers and attacked the last Blenheim, which, after three strafes, caught fire and fell. Then, avoiding defensive fire, he attacked another bomber and shot it down. In the meantime, *s. ten.* Zuccarini claimed a bomber with a second as a probable, while *serg. magg.* Fausti continued to attack two stragglers that he finally caught over the open sea, shooting down both. Zuccarini, wounded in the knee and with the aircraft damaged in the oil tank by return fire, managed to return and force landed at the top of a cliff close to the sea, 25 kilometres from Tobruk, damaging the landing gear in the process. *s. ten.* De Fraia claimed a sixth bomber. In total, the pilots from the 77ª *Sq.* used 2200 rounds of ammunition while those of 94ª *Sq.* used 500 rounds.

It seems that they had been involved in combat with Blenheims from 113 Sqn, which lost three aircraft. Blenheim Mk.IV L8436 flown by P/O D. Pike was reportedly damaged by flak and ditched; Pike, Sgt R. Lidstone and Sgt J. Taylor were rescued and taken PoWs. Blenheim Mk.I L8447, flown

Sottotenente *Gianmario Zuccarini of the 77ª Squadriglia next to the wheel cover of a CR.42 with the unit's badge. [via Giorgio Apostolo]*

by 31-year-old F/O Walter Ronald Price Knight Mason, was shot down in flames by fighters and Mason, 28-year-old Sgt James George Juggins and 21-year-old Sgt George Kenneth Biggins were all killed. Enemy fighters also shot down Blenheim Mk.I L8522 flown by 27-year-old F/Sgt Ralph Harry Knott, and Knott, 22-year-old Sgt James Douglas Barber and Leading Aircraftman James Patrick Toner were all killed.

Torresi, Zuccarini and Fausti (in the 77ª *Sq.*'s and 13º *Gr.*'s Diaries, Fausti is credited with two individual victories while the proposal of the *Medaglia d'argento al Valor Militare* speaks of a first plane shot down in cooperation with two unknown pilots and a second one individual) were all proposed to be awarded with the *Medaglia d'argento al Valor Militare* after this combat.

Zuccarini was recovered from the sea by a Navy team from a minesweeper, but his aircraft was too far from any road and the coast was too high, so it was probably abandoned. In fact it seems likely that the aviation historian Franco Pagliano, then an officer of the Air Force, was charged with the recovery of this particular plane and told the story of this operation inside the short novel *"The Abyss"* in his 1969's book *"In cielo ed in terra"*. According to this novel his mission that day was only to recover the most precious instruments, to assess the damage suffered by the plane and to destroy its guns. The recovery of the complete plane was judged too difficult. Pagliano was astonished by the skill demonstrated by the pilot that was able to land a plane in that position. Without deliberately crashing, the plane would probably have fallen down the escarpment that was only ten metres away, causing the death of its occupant.

At 06:00, three CR.32s of the 160ª *Sq.* took off for Ponticelli , they returned at 12:00, being replaced at Ponticelli by another section of two CR.32s.

At 04:55, in the first light of the morning, six Gladiators from 33 Sqn's 'B' Flight flew to Sidi Barrani for patrols covering Mersa Matruh, and during the day, several sorties (at least three) were flown.

At 11:00, three Gladiators flown by F/O Ernest Dean (Gladiator L9046), Sgt J. Craig (N5783) and P/O Peter Wickham (K8031) took off. These were followed by two more flown by P/O Vernon Woodward (N5774) and P/O Henry Harrison (a 112 Sqn pilot on attachment to 33 Sqn) (N5768), which took off at 11:40.

At 12:30, an enemy aircraft was intercepted and a Ro.37 was forced to land three miles west of Sidi Aziez, after being attacked by P/O Wickham. The rear gunner was apparently hit and the aircraft landed in enemy territory.

Three CR.32s were encountered at 12:40 by one formation of three Gladiators in the Ridotta Capuzzo area. A dogfight ensued, and P/O Woodward forced one of the aircraft down 2-3 miles north of Fort Capuzzo, near the road between Capuzzo and Bardia. He then pursued another aircraft of the enemy formation, which he shot down after a long dogfight. Both aircraft were shot down over Italian territory.

During this patrol, P/O Harrison claimed a damaged CR.32 in the Capuzzo-Sidi Aziez area.

The 33 Sqn pilots seem to have been spilt up and Craig landed at 12:30, Dean at 13:15 and the three other pilots at 13:20.

The IMAM Ro.37*bis* claimed by Wickham possibly belonged to the 137ª *Sq. Osservazione Aerea* that during the period was operating its last section of IMAM biplanes from Ponticelli "D" airstrip, no losses were recorded, however. It is also possible that this claim in fact relates to the combat Wickham was involved in the next day (30 June).

According with Italian records, the Army Officer *col. R.E. Osservatore* De Cosa, on seeing British aircraft over Ponticelli, immediately ordered the two CR 32s of the 160ª Sq. off against the three Gladiators, which were already orbiting over the base. Attacked from a disadvantageous position, the fighter of *s. ten.* Antonio Weiss, Adjutant of the 12º *Gr.* was quickly shot down. The pilot, wounded in the foot, made a forced landing near the *"Litoranea"* road, west of Bardia, while the second Fiat succeeded in disengaging.

Woodward's victim seems to have been *s. ten.* Weiss.

It seems that 33 Sqn claimed three victories during the day, while in fact the Italian losses seem to have been one CR.32 (*s. ten.* Weiss).

At 14:00 *magg.* Bruno Cudugnello of the 12° *Gr.* at the head of a formation of four CR.32s and two Ba.65s (*cap.* Antonio Dell'Oro and *ten.* Adriano Visconti) attacked enemy armoured cars in the Amseat area.

A Sunderland from 230 Sqn, flown by F/Lt "Willy" Campbell and F/O King, spotted a submarine sailing on the surface in the water off Taranto. This was the Italian submarine *Rubino*.

The Italian sailors were coming back to base after a patrol off Alexandria, and had already (at 13:00) discovered an aircraft that hadn't shown any hostile intention and being classified as an Italian patrol aircraft. Subsequently, being very close its base, *Rubino's* Commander, *ten. di Vascello* Trebbi, ordered the submarine to remain on the surface. One hour later the aircraft from 230 Sqn suddenly appeared out of clouds and made an immediate attack, hitting *Rubino* with two bombs on the stern and on the tower. Four Italian sailors fell into the sea while the submarine sank with the rest of the crew. Among the survivors was the second in command, *s. ten. di Vascello* Bracco.

The Sunderland pilot landed, captured the four, and flew back to Malta with clear proof of his success.

Campbell was awarded an immediate DFC for this and the action the previous day.

30 June 1940

At 08:00, three CR.32s of the 160ª *Sq.* were ordered off from Ponticelli by *Colonnello* De Cosa to escort the 137ª *Sq.*'s IMAM Ro.37 piloted by 136ª *Sq.*'s serg. magg. Gregorio Pecoraro with observer Lenzi. While climbing over the base, the Italian aircraft were attacked by Gladiators, which immediately shot down the Ro.37 in flames, killing the crew, and the Fiat of *ten.* Ivano Vanni, who parachuted from his burning aircraft seriously wounded. The other Fiats were able to disengage and landed back at 08:25. Later, at 11:30, *serg.* Aldo Santucci crash-landed his CR.32 close to T5 airfield, west of Tobruk while coming back at base. In doing so, he hit an Army truck, seriously wounding the Army driver and writing off his aircraft.

It seems that the Italian aircraft had run into a patrol from 33 Sqn, which claimed two fighters during an early morning patrol over Bardia. The Italian aircraft were variously identified as CR.42s or CR.32s, one of them shot down in flames. One of the planes was claimed by P/O Peter Wickham while the other fell victim to F/O Ernest Dean. One Gladiator was damaged in this combat.

Dean described the combat:

"Peter Wickham and I were patrolling near Bardia, and spotted two CR 42s. We each took one, and within minutes there were two black plumes on the ground. I got involved with another CR 42, a quite aggressive "Eyetie" (most rare), and I unfortunately got into head-on attacks with him, which are not recommended. We had three passes at one another but with no apparent damage, except that when we reached base together I didn't perform any victory rolls, although Peter was performing perfect flick rolls in formation. Lucky for me, because my riggers reported to me that my centre section was badly damaged, and it was as well I had overcome my exuberance."

Tobruk T2 suffered another bombing attack. This time the high number of unserviceable aircraft of the 2° *Stormo*, which was on alarm duty, meant that not a single fighter was able to take-off. The aircraft suffered no damage, but three personnel of the 2° *Stormo* were wounded, *Primo Aviere* Invernici and *Aviere Scelto* Porta of the 13° *Gr.* and *Aviere Scelto* Antonio Landolfi of the 8° *Gr.*

During the day (on 1 July according to some sources), a British aircraft arrived over Bardia and delivered the following message enveloped in a tri-coloured ribbon: *"The British Royal Air Force expresses its sincere sympathy in the death of Marshal Balbo, a great leader and a gallant aviator, personally known to me, whom fate has placed on the other side. Arthur Longmore, Air Officer Commanding-in-Chief, British Royal Air Force, Middle East."* The message was greatly appreciated by the Italian aviators, who replied with thanks the day after. It was another sign of the efforts that both sides made (during the opening stages of this campaign) to keep the conflict inside the limits of a correct and chivalrous professionalism.

July 1940

The ground war

During July and August, the Italians continued to build up their forces in eastern Cyrenaica, in preparation for an offensive operation across the border into Egypt. Mussolini was keen to take the initiative but Marshal Rodolfo Graziani, who had arrived on 30 June to replace Marshal Italo Balbo as the Commander in Chief of the Italian armed forces, hesitated. He complained that his tanks were inferior to the British and this, together with the intensive summer heat, meant that he waited before launching his offensive, much to Mussolini's annoyance.

Regia Aeronautica

The beginning of July saw the *Regia Aeronautica* trying to reinforce and reorganize its forces in Libya, to be able to better counter the British threat on the eastern border. After the fall of France on 25 June, all the forces previously drawn up on the Tunisian front were gradually pulled back and sent to Cirenaica, notably the fourth bomber *Stormo* deployed in Libya (the 33º *Stormo*). The other three (10º, 14º and 15º *Stormi*) were already in action against the British.

The new Commander in Chief of the Italian armed forces, Marshal Rodolfo Graziani, was immediately asked to go on the offensive against Egypt. As his first move, he asked for immediate reinforcements, that arrived from Italy in the first fifteen days of July.

On 5 July, the name of *Aeronautica della Libia* was changed to the Vª *Squadra Aerea*. All the bomber units were organized into a new Air Division: 13ª *Divisione Aerea "Pegaso"*.

Ground attack forces

On 1 July 1940, after a month of almost complete chaos, all the Capronis were struck off charge, and the 50º *Stormo* became for the second time an assault unit, equipped with Bredas and CR.32s and retaining the two *Squadriglie* structure of its *Gruppi* because of lack of aircraft.

Ironically, the delivery of Capronis continued, and the last six aircraft of the type landed at Tripoli Castel Benito on 16 July to raise further more the "paper strength" of the *Regia Aeronautica* in Libya.

In the meantime, the lack of a proper ground attack unit in the front line obliged all the fighter and bomber units of the *Regia Aeronautica* to go down to ground level to strafe enemy armoured vehicles that the Army was unable to counter (a duty for which they were not well suited), and this

Tenente *Vittorio Pezzè and Giuseppe Oblach of the 73ª* Squadriglia, *9º* Gruppo, *at Goriza pre-war.*
[Oblach via Fulvio Chianese – Associazione Culturale 4° Stormo di Gorizia]

drastically reduced the numbers of airworthy aircraft; the units that suffered the worst were those equipped with the CR.42 fighter.

The 12° *Gr.* was transferred to the new airstrip of T2bis, close to T2 airfield, on 15 July.

Between 16 and 31 July the 159ª *Sq.* had 14 Breda Ba.65/A80s on charge (MM75165, MM75169, MM75199, MM75218, MM75219, MM75244, MM75248, MM75252, MM75256, MM75257, MM75258, MM75259, MM75273 and MM75276). The *Squadriglia* also had four IMAM Ro.41s.

During the same period the 168ª *Sq.* had 9 Breda Ba.65/K14s on charge (MM75127, MM75154, MM75097, MM75148, MM75086, MM75149, MM75130, MM75095 and MM75140).

The 16° *Gr.* transferred to Tobruk T2 on 21 July.

Fighters

On 1 July the 13° *Gr.* moved to El Adem T3 airfield with the 18 CR.42s left and was still there at the end of the month.

On the morning on 4 July the *Gruppi* of the 2° *Stormo* (8° and 13° *Gruppi*) had 42 fighters ready for action. In the beginning of July the *Stormo* was temporarily alone on the front line, since the departure of the 10° *Gr.* to Benghazi-Berka K for the revision and refitting of its fighters. Part of the 8° *Gr.* (total force unknown but comprising of elements of the 93ª and 94ª *Squadriglie*) was detached from T2 to Menastir M airfield (that the British often called Monastir) near the fortified village of Bardia.

The 8° *Gr.* had completed conversion to CR.42s at the beginning of July (the CR.32s ceased operations on 2 July); on 4 July, the 92ª *Sq.* arrived at T2 with ten factory-fresh CR.42s collected at Tripoli-Castel Benito. These aircraft were however totally devoid of any sand filters, and soon wear caused by the desert rendered them unserviceable. Thus flying activity was stopped for all aircraft of the *Gruppo* on 6 July. This brief pause was used for a quick refitting of the surviving Fiats. Also, following the heavy losses suffered in combat on 4 July, the *Gruppo* was retired to Benghazi-Berka K airfield on 22 July, giving its last eight combat worthy CR.42s (one from the 94ª *Sq.*, three from the 92ª *Sq.* and four from the 93ª *Sq.*) to the 13° *Gr.*, which was still based at T3. During the return to Benghazi-Berka K eleven aircraft (not combat worthy) remained, but five of them landed at Derna N1 and proceeded to Berka by truck because of their bad condition.

At the end of July, the *Gruppo* was still in Benghazi repairing its aircraft.

This meant that by the end of July, the 2° *Stormo* had only 18 fighters ready for action (those of 13° *Gr.*).

Between 1 and 3 July, *ten.* Domenico Bevilacqua was transferred to the 94ª *Sq.* from the 78ª *Sq.*, 13° *Gr.* At the beginning of July, *serg. magg.* Agostino Fausti was briefly on loan to the 93ª *Sq.* from the 77ª *Sq.*, 13° *Gr.*

On 7 July, *s. ten.* Orlando Mandolini was posted to the 93ª *Sq.* from the 52° *Stormo*. It seems however that he had arrived earlier since he flew a combat mission with the *Squadriglia* on 3 July.

On 14 July, *cap.* Virginio Teucci replaced *cap.* Franco Lavelli as Commanding Officer of the 94ª *Sq.*

On 12 July 1940, the 9° *Gr. C.T.* arrived at Tripoli from Comiso with thirty-three Fiat CR.42s, under the command of *magg.* Ernesto Botto. The *Gruppo* consisted of 73ª, 96ª and 97ª *Squadriglie*.

A Fiat CR.42 of the 97ª Squadriglia, *9° Gruppo C.T. at Gorizia before this unit's departure to North Africa. The 9° Gruppo arrived at Tripoli on 12 July 1940. [via Italian Air Force]*

From left: Sergente Maggiore Massimo Salvatore, Capitano *Antonio Larsimont and Galvino.* [*Gabriele Brancaccio via Fulvio Chianese – Associazione Culturale 4° Stormo di Gorizia*]

A CR.42, most likely an aircraft from the 9º Gruppo C.T, taxiing after landing on its desert airbase (El Adem). Two ground personnel are helping the pilot to taxi. [*via Istituto Luce*]

The 73ª *Sq.* included *ten.* Vittorio Pezzè (CO), *ten.* Valerio De Campo, *ten.* Giulio Reiner, *ten.* Pietro Bonfatti (assigned at the end of July), *s. ten.* Giuseppe Oblach, *s. ten.* Carlo Battaglia, *s. ten.* Alvaro Querci, *m. llo.* Mario Ruffilli, *m. llo.* Alberto Montanari, *m. llo.* Norino Renzi, *m. llo.* Corrado Ranieri, *serg. magg.* Guglielmo Biffani, *serg. magg.* Enrico Dallari, *serg. magg.* Sergio Stauble, *serg. magg.* Antonio Valle, *serg.* Santo Gino, *serg.* Lido Poli, *serg.* Pasquale Rossi, *serg.* Mario Guerci (still in training) and *serg.* Armando Matacena (still in training).

The 96ª *Sq.* included *cap.* Roberto Fassi (CO), *ten.* Alessandro Viotti, *ten.* Aldo Gon, *ten.* Emanuele Annoni, *s. ten.* Bruno Paolazzi, *s. ten.* Carlo Agnelli, *serg. magg.* Dante Labanti, *serg. magg.* Graziadio Rizzati, *serg. magg.* Giovanni Gallerani, *serg.* Bruno Spitzl, *serg.* Vittorio Pozzati,

Maggiore Ernesto Botto, CO of the 9º Gruppo C.T. in front of a Fiat CR.42, probably at Comiso in July 1940. [Oblach via Fulvio Chianese – Associazione Culturale 4° Stormo di Gorizia.]

serg. Gustavo Minelli, *serg.* Bruno Biagini and *serg.* Luigi Battaini. In fact, the *Squadriglia* moved to Libya with only seven non-commissioned officers (Battani was possibly the one who remained in Italy).

The 97ª *Sq.* included *cap.* Antonio Larsimont Pergameni (CO), *cap.* Giuseppe Mauriello, *ten.* Ezio Viglione Borghese, *s. ten.* Jacopo Frigerio, *s. ten.* Riccardo Vaccari, *s. ten.* Giovanni Barcaro, *m. llo.* Vanni Zuliani, *serg. magg.* Raffaello Novelli, *serg. magg.* Otello Perotti, *serg. magg.* Massimo Salvatore, *serg.* Francesco Putzu, *serg.* Franco Sarasino, *serg.* Alcide Leoni and *serg.* Angelo Golino (assigned on 22 July).

After a period of acclimatization at Benghazi-Berka K airfield, a detachment of the 9º *Gr.* was sent to El Adem on 29 July.

Together with the 10º *Gr.* they formed the 4º *Stormo C.T.* under the command of *col.* Michele Grandinetti. Between 11 July and 15 August, *magg.* Carlo Romagnoli temporarily replaced *col.* Grandinetti as CO of the 4º *Stormo C.T.*

The *Gruppo*'s Fiat CR.42s were wisely retrofitted with tropical kits for guns and engines, to avoid the problems suffered by the other *Gruppi*.

Ten. Giuseppe Aurili returned to the 84ª *Sq.*, 10º *Gr.*, on 7 July after having been temporarily detached to Hungary. *magg.* Carlo Romagnoli replaced *cap.* Giuseppe D'Agostinis as CO of the 10º *Gr.* on 11 July. The *Gruppo* rejoined operations from El Adem on 22 July with 16 Fiats on hand (the others were still under repair).

In July *ten.* Stefano Soprana was assigned to the 90ª *Sq.* Apart from being a pilot, Soprana was also a doctor.

In the end of July 1940, the fighter complement of 5ª *Squadra Aerea* was quite strong on paper with two of the best Italian *Stormi* on hand, but its front line was in fact reduced to two depleted *Gruppi* with a total force of no more than thirty-four fighters serviceable and with the strength of one of them (the 13º *Gr.*) that was rapidly fading (on 9 August it too was retired to Berka to change the engines of its fighters).

El Adem, autumn 1940. Maggiore Ernesto Botto is climbing into his personal mount (a 1939 built Serie I Fiat CR.42 - MM4393 - of the 73ª Squadriglia). He is lifting his artificial leg over the cockpit with the help of the right hand. This is an interesting image showing the insignia of 73ª Squadriglia (the red lightning on the wheel fairings as well as the prancing horse and the Gruppo Commander flag – azure blue with a red stripe inside - on the side of the plane). It is also possible to see the red flying helmet that Botto wore instead of the standard white or leather one. The reason for this was to be better recognizable by his men in the heat of combat. Most likely Botto kept this flying cap since 1936 when he was part of the elite Reparto Alta Velocità, (together with Mario Bacich and Duilio Fanali), the unit that trained the very best Italian pilots in Desenzano sul Garda on the high speed techniques necessary to fly the Macchi seaplane racers. For those stunt pilots the Roman firm Giusti had in fact produced a limited edition of its standard flying helmets made in red leather.
[via Istituto Luce]

Fiat CR.42 of the 96ª Squadriglia, 9º Gruppo C.T. at El Adem in 1940.
[Gon via Fulvio Chianese – Associazione Culturale 4° Stormo di Gorizia]

Fiat CR.42 of the 96ª Squadriglia, *9°* Gruppo *C.T. at El Adem in 1940.* ***[Gon via Fulvio Chianese – Associazione Culturale 4° Stormo di Gorizia]***

Fiat CR.42 of the 96ª Squadriglia, *9°* Gruppo *C.T. at El Adem in 1940.* ***[Gon via Fulvio Chianese – Associazione Culturale 4° Stormo di Gorizia]***

Bombers

On 14 July, the 33° *Gr. B.T.* under the command of *ten. col.* Ferri Forte arrived in Benghazi from Comiso, with 16 SM 79 bombers.

The 54° *Gr. B.T.* under *magg.* Giuseppe Colavolpe arrived at Benghazi at the same time. This unit was equipped with thirteen S.81s for night bombing duties.

Reconnaissance forces

At the end of June, the 73° *Gr.* despite the reinforcements from the 64° *Gr.* was almost without any aircraft left and started to take on charge the Ca.310B, leaving the 50° *Stormo*. The 64° *Gr.* itself had only four IMAM combat ready left.

The 175ª *Sq.* R.S.T. (*Ricognizione Strategica Terrestre*/Strategic Land Reconnaissance) was formed on 15 July. The unit was commanded by *cap.* RaffaeleCantarella, equipped with Savoia SM 79s, and employed specifically in the long distance reconnaissance role, mainly over Alexandria and Suez.

On the same day, the 67° *Gr. O.A.* arrived in Tripoli from Trapani with ten IMAM Ro.37*bis* divided in its two *Squadriglie*, 33ª and 115ª. This last *Gruppo* completed the reinforcements of Vª *Squadra Aerea* as requested by Marshal Graziani.

The 33ª *Sq.* had a difficult transfer with almost half of the planes that were damaged or lost because of problems with the Magnaghi fuel pumps. The aircraft of the *Gruppo* were passed over to the 73° *Gr.* while the unit re-equipped with Caproni Ca.310B, four IMAM went to the 50° *Stormo* that used them also for point defence duties over Tobruk.

Royal Air Force

The early British raids demonstrated clearly the effectiveness of the small but extremely aggressive bomber force of 202 Group's Blenheims, but they were exhausting. On 5 July, in particular, during a low level raid against a concentration of motor transport a pilot from 113 Sqn was wounded and an observer killed. This particular event disturbed and alarmed the Air Officer

Commanding in Chief of Middle East Command, Air Marshal Sir Arthur Longmore, who some days later wrote to Air Commodore Raymond Collishaw, commander of 202 Group:

"While fully appreciating the initiative and spirit shown by the squadrons operating under your command in the Western Desert, I must draw your immediate attention to the urgent necessity of conserving resources; instances are still occurring when Blenheims are being used for low-level machine-gun attacks against defended camps and aerodromes. I consider such operations are unjustified having regard to our limited resources of which you are well aware. I fell therefore that we must consider carefully every air operation we embark upon".

Collishaw excused the infringement of laid-down policy as a deviation from his instructions and assured his C-in-C that he had taken *"suitable action"*.

In fact, the number of aircraft already lost or damaged in action or accidents together with the demonstrable difficulties of obtaining any reinforcements meant that fewer and fewer serviceable aircraft remained available. Better times were promised, the Air Ministry announced the immediate despatch of twelve Hurricanes, twelve Blenheims, and twelve Lysanders, with a further monthly supply of twelve Hurricanes, twelve Blenheims, six Lysanders and spare parts. Also 150 American Glenn Martin 167 bombers that *l'Armée de l'Air* had ordered would be built and delivered to the RAF in the Middle East over the coming six months. On 1 August, Longmore was greatly relieved to be advised that deliveries would increase to thirty six Blenheims and eighteen Hurricanes a month as soon as possible.

On 8 July, the French Flights No 1, 2 and 3 were officially formed with the French aircraft and personnel on hand in Egypt.

Fighters

S/Ldr R. C. Jonas relinquished command of 80 Sqn to S/Ldr Patrick Dunn on 8 July. During 16 to 23 July, Vernon Woodward and four other pilots from 33 Sqn were detached to 80 Sqn. On 29 July, 80 Sqn received the order to deploy one of its Flights to Sidi Barrani, the choice falling on 'B' Flight, commanded by F/Lt 'Pat' Pattle. The next day Pattle and S/Ldr Patrick Dunn flew to Sidi Barrani airfield to arrange for the detachment there. They were to replace 33 Sqn, starting from 1 August.

Joseph Fraser of 112 Sqn, thirsty after a forced landing in a Gloster Gladiator. [via Patricia Molloy]

On 3 July, F/O R. H. Smith and F/O R. J. Bennett of 112 Sqn were sent to 'A' Flight of 33 Sqn at Sidi Barrani to gain battle experience. The next day, F/O Anthony Gray-Worcester and F/O W. B. Price-Owen of the same squadron joined them.

112 Sqn was transferred to Maaten Gerawla airfield (in the Mersa Matruh area) on 17 July, and joined 33 Sqn on front line duty a week later when the move of 'A' and 'C' Flights were completed on 25 July. F/O Anthony Gray-Worcester of 112 Sqn was killed on 18 July. F/O A. M. Ross became temporary Flight Commander until the arrival of F/Lt Lloyd Schwab, who arrived on 23 July.

On 25 July P/O P. R. M. Van der Heijden of 112 Sqn tried to slow roll Gladiator K7895 over Sidi Barrani. The aircraft crashed and he was injured. He did not return to the squadron.

At the end of July, the strength of the fighter component of the RAF along the western border with Libya was that of 33 and 112 Sqns, with an unknown total force but probably between twenty and thirty Gladiators (roughly the same number of aircraft as the *Regia Aeronautica*).

Bombers

In the beginning of July two French Martin 167Fs from GB I/39 (Nos 82 and 102) escaped to Egypt. On 13 July, they were attached to 8 Sqn at Khormaksar (Aden), and flown by their French pilots in RAF uniforms.

30 Sqn received a Blenheim from 211 Sqn for conversion to fighter aircraft at the beginning of July. The squadron moved from Ismailia to Ikingi Maryut on 6 July. Two Blenheims, coming from Abu Sueir, were allotted to the squadron at the end of the month.

On 29 July, 45 Sqn send a detachment ('A' Flight) of six Blenheim Mk.Is under the command of F/Lt Troughton-Smith from Helwan in Egypt to Erkowit in Sudan. They started operations against targets in Italian East Africa with a raid on Kassala railway station on 30 July.

211 Sqn flew from El Daba to Qotaifiya on 17 July. On 18 July, they received two replacement aircraft. S/Ldr A. C. R. Bax took over command of 211 Sqn from S/Ldr J. W. B. Judge on 23 July.

Reconnaissance forces

On 5 July, 208 Sqn's detachment at Sidi Barrani was reached by S/Ldr Sprague, who took over command of operations. On 10 July, 'A' Flight moved from Qasaba to Sidi Barrani to relieve 'B' Flight. F/Lt Legge took over command of 'A' Flight at Sidi Barrani from F/Lt Black on 18 July.

S/Ldr Charles Ryley assumed temporary command of 230 Sqn after the absence of Wing Commander G. Francis.

Operations

1 July 1940

Sgt William Vale of 33 Sqn claimed a CR.32 over Fort Capuzzo.

This claim can't be verified from Italian sources, since the 50° *Stormo*, which was the only unit operating this type, didn't suffer any losses on this day. It is however possible that the victory was claimed during the widespread combats of the end of June, and incorrectly recorded on this day.

An SM 79 of the 6ª *Sq.*, 44° *Gr.*, flown by *s. ten.* Toni, took off from El Adem at 15:45 for a reconnaissance mission over Sollum and Buq-Buq. It was attacked by two Gloster Gladiators and the left engine was put out of action by the fire from the enemy fighters, which forced Toni to land at Menastir M at 17:15. The identity of the intercepting British fighters is unknown.

During the first ten days of July, the 50° *Stormo* continued its ground attack missions against British armoured patrols in the Bir El Gobi, Amseat, Bardia and Sollum areas. These attacks helped the Army to stop the initial penetration of the Western Desert Force, whose attacks were called off at the end of July.

During the ten day period, *s. ten.* Weiss' aircraft was recovered, one Breda Ba.65/A80 was heavily damaged by ground fire, and two CR.32s were lost in accidents. *serg.* Patellani's aircraft overturned during a take off, and that of *serg*. Fattoretto caught fire during a flight for unknown reasons. The pilot parachuted safely and was rescued.

2 July 1940 - Operation *Catapult*

After the armistice with Italy and Germany, the fate of the French Fleet was the greatest concern of Winston Churchill. According to the armistice provisions it had to return to Toulon and demobilise, and the French Minister of Marine Admiral Darlan assured the British that the French Fleet would scuttle itself before allowing the Germans or their Italian allies to take control of it.

Despite these assurances, (made in good faith by the French, whose operative instructions to the Fleet, secretly intercepted by the British, were in complete accordance with this) Churchill insisted on an action to seize or disable and destroy all the accessible French Fleet, in order to deny it to the Axis. The operation was christened "*Catapult*", and planned for 3 July.

The main French Fleet, under Admiral Marcel-Bruno Gensoul, was based in the naval harbour of Mers-El Kebir, three miles west of Oran, Algeria. In port were the modern battlecruisers *Dunkerque* and *Strasbourg*, the older battleships *Provence* and *Bretagne*, the seaplane tender *Commandant Teste* and six heavy destroyers (*Lynx*, *Kersaint*, *Tigre*, *Mogador*, *Terrible* and *Volta*). In Oran itself, there were also ten light destroyers, six submarines and thirteen smaller warships.

Force H from Gibraltar, under Vice-Admiral Somerville, was ordered to Oran to deliver an ultimatum to Gensoul and if this was refused, to disable the French Fleet. Somerville had under his command the battlecruiser HMS *Hood*, the battleships HMS *Resolution* and HMS *Valiant*, the aircraft carrier HMS *Ark Royal* (with a full complement of 30 Swordfishes from 810, 818 and 820 Sqns and 24 Skuas from 800 and 803 Sqns), the light cruisers HMS *Arethusa* and HMS *Enterprise* and eleven destroyers (HMS *Faulknor*, HMS *Foxhound*, HMS *Fearless*, HMS *Forester*, HMS *Foresight*, HMS *Escort*, HMS *Keppel*, HMS *Active*, HMS *Wrestler*, HMS *Vidette* and HMS *Vortigern*).

3 July 1940

Three CR.42s from the 94ª *Sq.* (*ten.* Giovanni Tadini, *serg. magg.* Trento Cecchi and *serg. magg.* Danilo Billi) and three from the 93ª *Sq.* (*ten.* Gioacchino Bissoli, *s. ten.* Orlando Mandolini and *serg.* Roberto Lendaro) scrambled from T2. They intercepted a Short Sunderland, which was heading for Tobruk. The three 93ª *Sq.* pilots returned, claiming to have damaged the aircraft with the use of 650 rounds of ammo, and that the same aircraft was immediately after attacked by one of the three planes of the other *Squadriglia* and shot down off Bardia. *ten.* Tadini on the other hand claimed the destruction of this aircraft in collaboration with the 93ª *Sq.* pilots.

It seems that they had intercepted Sunderland L5807/R from 228 Sqn, piloted by F/Lt D. C. McKinley DFC and P/O J. C. J Lylian, which had taken off at 14:15 for an anti-submarine sortie around Tobruk. The flying-boat returned at 20:15, reporting being attacked by Italian aircraft, one of which was believed hit by return fire. The Sunderland reported no damage at all but the day after, back at Alexandria, it was taken up on the slip for maintenance operations.

During the day, five fighters from the 78ª *Sq.* flew forward to Menastir from T3. They were led by *cap.* Giuseppe Dall'Aglio, and operated from the landing ground during the day to be better able to escort Italian reconnaissance aircraft over the front.

A Potez 63.11 (No 670) arrived at Ismailia piloted by *Sgt-Chef* Marcel Lebois of GR II/39 from Damascus. It was joined shortly after by the Potez 63.11 (No 395) flown by *Adjutant* Albert Lamour-Zevacco. Among the passengers on board these aircraft were *Sous-Lieutenant* Jean Pompéi and *Sous-Lieutenant* Daniel Clostre. These aircraft received RAF serials and formed an ad hoc unit called Free French Flight No 2.

Operation *Catapult*

At 08:05, the destroyer HMS *Foxhound* anchored inside the port of Oran to deliver the ultimatum prepared by Churchill and Admiral Pound to Gensoul. The French could scuttle their fleet, disarm it in the French Indies, or join the British and continue to fight with them.

At 08:35, a shadower from HMS *Ark Royal* signalled that the French ships were starting up their boilers. In the meantime Gensoul tried to stall the negotiations while he signalled for help from Algiers, where six light cruisers of the La Galissonnière class were based, and from the nearby airfields of Relizane and Saint-Denis-du-Sig where the fighters of GC II/3 and III/3 (Relizane), GC I/5 and II/5 (Saint-Denis-du-Sig) were stationed. The problem with the fighters was that since the end of hostilities, the French Commander of the area, *Colonel* Rougevin Bainville, was obliged to order many measures to avoid the departure of his aviators, so many aircraft lacked propellers or had the tanks empty. GC II/5 would be ready for action only at midday. Bombers would be ready only in twenty-four hours.

At 15:25, two Swordfishes of 820 Sqn dropped mines at the entrance of the harbour. For the *Armée de l'Air* this was too soon to intervene, and in fact, it only received German authorization to react against an eventual British attack at 15:30.

At 17:30, the last British ultimatum expired (Somerville had already exceeded the time limits fixed by London), and at 17:45, Gensoul asked for air cover while his ships tried to move towards the entrance of the harbour.

At 17:55, HMS *Hood* led HMS *Resolution* and HMS *Valiant* in line of battle and opened fire from maximum range, with aircraft from 820 Sqn spotting the fall of shot.

The French ships, covered by smoke screens, begun to leave the harbour with *Strasbourg* leading the way, followed by the *Dunkerque*, then *Provence* and *Bretagne*. The Loire 130s of *Dunkerque* and *Strasbourg* took off from the harbour (H2S-1 and H2S-5 reached Arzew, while H2S-4 went to Mostaganem and H2S-3 landed on the open sea).

As both sided had been observing each other for hours and taking the range, and with the French ships almost stationary, the fire was quite accurate. However, the confined waters, the process of getting underway, and the fort of Mers-el-Kebir located on a hill overlooking the harbour, all conspired to make it difficult for the French to return fire accurately. For example, *Provence* aimed its first salvo between *Dunkerque*'s masts. French artillery managed to straddle HMS *Hood* once or twice, and splinters wounded two of its crew, but no other damage was inflicted on the British. The French however suffered much more. The first shells hit the quayside, then *Dunkerque* was hit by three shells of a single salvo on "B" turret, the forward engine room and secondary armament. Gensoul had to order the ship not to proceed but to beach itself. *Bretagne* was to suffer the worst;

Skua L3049/ "L" of 800 Sqn on Ark Royal *at Gibraltar, running up on deck while an officer talks to the pilot and a matelot uses his weight to prevent the tail rising in the propeller wash. The ship appears to be berthed in the harbour and the "Rock" looms over the ship. [via Fleet Air Arm Museum]*

Three Gloster Sea Gladiator of HMS Eagle's *Fighter Flight.*
[via Tim Kershaw]

The deck of HMS Ark Royal, *Gibraltar 1940.*
[via Stratus]

the second salvo aimed at it hit, causing an immense internal explosion throwing up a towering pillar of smoke, which obscured the harbour. It sank in seven minutes, with the loss of 976 French sailors. *Provence* had to wait for *Dunkerque* to pass before it could proceed to sea and therefore, as a stationary target, was also hit several times and had to beach itself. The destroyers proceeded to sea independently and all would make it except *Mogador*, which was hit by a shell that exploded 16 depth charges, sending up a plume of smoke as high as the one from *Bretagne*. Finally it had to anchor. The rest joined *Strasbourg*, which by 18:10 was in the harbour channel.

In the meantime, three *Patrouilles de chasse* from GC II/5 under the command of *Capitaine* Portalis, arrived over the harbour. The French pilots in the first *Patrouille* were *Capitaine* Arnaud, *Sous-Lieutenant* Boudier and *Lieutenant* Fabre, in the second *Lieutenant* Huvet, *Adjutant* Lachaux and *Sergeant* Heme, and in the third *Sous-Lieutenant* Villacèque, *Lieutenant* Dunod and *Adjutant-Chef* Dugoujon. Over the harbour, they met aircraft from HMS *Ark Royal*. Portalis described the action:

"*Immediately after taking off from Saint-Denis-du-Sig, I saw many explosions inside the harbour of Oran and some flak explosions at the height of 2000 metres over the port. At 18:10, I arrived at 2000 metres over the harbour, the situation was the following: three ships burned inside the harbour, one of them was the Dunkerque, the French fleet steamed in eastward direction near the coast. The British fleet, ten miles in north-north-westerly direction was covered by a thick smoke curtain. Twenty miles in northern direction an English Carrier was cruising under escort of three Destroyers. There were no English planes over the harbour (...) I brought my formation between the English fleet and the French fleet, ten miles away I discovered some small British two-seaters (probably Gloster Gladiators)* [sic]. *We attacked immediately, three combats started. Capitaine Arnaud attacked one of the two-seaters that escaped nose diving and twisting towards the Carrier. Arnaud hit it many times and left it only over the Carrier at the height of 500 metres. Me and Sous-Lieutenant Boudier attacked first a two-seater then a section of three biplanes. All the British aircraft escaped at 500 metres of height over the Carrier, we followed them firing. During the pursuit Boudier was attacked by a patrol of English single-seaters, he disengaged and joined me. During the combat, one of the single-seaters - against which we didn't even shot a round - fell in an uncontrolled spin and crashed into the sea. We climbed to 2000 metres going fifteen to twenty miles straight out. At 18:30, no more English planes were seen. We went over the French fleet, its first elements among which the Strasbourg were rounding Cap Aiguille (...)"*

In the meantime (18:50) many more French fighters from GC II/5 were scrambling; *Capitaine* Monraisse leading *Sous-Lieutenant* Hébrard and *Adjutant* De Mongolfier; *Lieutenant* Trémolet leading *Sergeant Chef* Legrand and *Sergeant Chef* Salès, and *Sous-Lieutenant* Ruchoux, leading *Sous-Lieutenant* Le Stum and *Adjutant Chef* Gras. Arriving over Force H, they engaged British aircraft. Monraisse described the action:

"Arriving over the British fleet I saw six Gladiators in two patrols of three. They were protected by three Blackburn Skuas. I closed into them and - without being previously attacked by us - they assaulted one of our Patrouilles. The right Patrouille of Lieutenant Trémolet was attacked frontally by two Skuas. The plane of Trémolet was seriously damaged (hits in the engine and tanks) and he had to disengage and land back immediately. Sergeant Chef Legrand attacked the Skua but was shot at by the second Skua. Adjutant De Montgolfier shot the enemy off the tail of Legrand but his plane was already damaged by many hits. Sergeant Chef Legrand shot down the first Skua after a turning combat. Sergeant Chef Salès mixed with the third Skua but didn't even try to shot it down, instead he waved his wings and didn't open fire. The Skua inverted its course and joined the second Skua in formation heading for the carrier. Capitaine Monraisse and Sous-Lieutenant Hébrard flew around the Gladiators without attacking (...), Capitaine Monraisse was attacked frontally by two Skuas without suffering damage. Capitaine Monraisse and Sous-Lieutenant Hébrard disengaged without returning fire and directed for the coast. All the planes were back after 20:00."

It seems that Portalis' fighters firstly attacked Fairey Swordfishes L2787/A4B (Lieutenant Humpries, Lieutenant Williams and Leading Aircraftman Pendleton) and L2840 (Lieutenant Hunter, Lieutenant Gerrett and Petty Officer Smith) from 820 Sqn, engaged in an artillery spotting mission, misidentifying them as Gladiators. The FAA pilots returned, recording the attack by French fighters identified as Dewoitines, only the machine of Humpries had been slightly damaged. Then the French fighters mixed with a patrol of three Skuas of 803 Sqn (L2927/A piloted by Lieutenant Bruen, L2997/B piloted by Sub Lieutenant Brokensha and L2915/C piloted by Petty Officer Riddler).

Monraisse's fighters encountered the same FAA fighters. During the combat Bruen claimed hits on a Morane (probably Trémolet). Skua L2915 failed to return with the loss of its crew (24-year-old Petty Officer Airman Thomas Frank Riddler and 20-year-old Naval Airman 1st Class Horace Turner Chatterley); it seems almost sure that they were inside the aircraft seen spinning into the sea after having chased *Sous-Lieutenant* Boudier but the possibility remains that their were victim of Legrand (the 8th victory of this pilot that already was, together with *Sergeant Chef* Salès, the top scoring ace of the unit). Later in the day, FAA also lost an additional Skua of 803 Sqn, that was shadowing *Strasbourg*. Swordfish L2817/A7M piloted by P/O Harry Glover, force-landed near HMS *Ark Royal*, reportedly for lack of petrol (the crew was rescued). Back at Mers-El-Kebir, the British ships ceased fire at 18:12, in part because of the increasing accuracy of the shore batteries, but mainly because Gensoul asked Somerville to cease fire. However, at 19:25 the French ships had escaped.

HMS *Ark Royal* launched two air attacks against the fleeing *Strasbourg*, one with six Swordfishes armed with bombs (810 Sqn) and the other with six machines of 810 Sqn armed with torpedoes, 20 minutes after sunset. It was during the first of these attacks that Monraisse engaged the Swordfishes (again misidentified for Gladiators) without attacking them. The FAA pilots (displaying as usual superlative flying skills) dropped down to 1200 metres, covering their approach with the smoke coming from a splinter hole in *Strasbourg*'s funnel! None of the 250 lb bombs hit however, only one came close, exploding 25 metres from the stern of *Strasbourg*. Two Swordfishes were shot down by AA fire but their crews were rescued by the destroyer HMS *Wrestler*. Portails was still over the French ships in this moment and noted:

"*the Strasbourg that was rounding Cap Bon turned to the right as if avoiding a torpedo (…)*".

However, he failed to note the attacking Swordfishes and his fighters were back at 19:40.

In general, the French fighter pilots, most of them battle-hardened veterans of the battles of May-June, were most surprised by the British attack and in fact, some of them in the crucial moment of opening fire were unable to act, leaving their opponents unscathed. The returning British crews confirmed that French fighters did not press home their attacks.

The second torpedo attack by six Swordfishes was quite impressive. They attacked at around 20:55 and flew so as to have the coast behind them as they made their final approach at an altitude of around six metres. They came under light AA fire from a group of destroyers seven miles astern of *Strasbourg*, but none were badly damaged. The attacks were bravely pressed home but the closest torpedo passed 25 metres behind the French battleship, even if a hit on target was claimed.

At 08:10 on 4 July, *Strasbourg* and its group safely reached Toulon.

French planes from the *Aeronavale* tried to strike back. Breguet Bizerte E2-1, piloted by Lieutenant de Vaisseau Duval, took off from Arzew at 18:15 and attacked a destroyer. Lieutenants Bruen and Brokensha forced it to crash-land on a beach. Breguet Bizerte n.521 coded E2-3, piloted by *Lieutenant de Vaisseau* Vieillard, attacked another destroyer at 19:40; damaged by AA, it was also forced to crash-land.

Finally, six Loire 130s of HS 1 took off from Arzew at 18:50. Only three of them attacked British ships (HS1-2 flown by *Ensigne de Vaisseau* Gisbert, HS1-8 flown by *Ensigne de Vaisseau* Jolivet and HS1-9). No hits were achieved during these evening attacks.

At Mers-El-Kebir the naval action was over, tactically it was a British success but was a big strategic mistake. For Vichy France the enemy had changed.

4 July 1940

At 06:00, six fighters from the 94ª *Sq.* (*cap.* Franco Lavelli, *ten.* Giovanni Tadini, *s. ten.* Nunzio De Fraia, *serg. magg.* Trento Cecchi, *serg. magg.* Danilo Billi and *serg. magg.* Arturo Cardano) moved to Menastir landing ground to be better able to escort Italian reconnaissance aircraft over the front. They replaced the 78ª *Sq.*, which had performed this duty the day before.

At 08:00, five CR 42s of the 94ª *Sq.* (*cap.* Franco Lavelli, *ten.* Giovanni Tadini, *serg. magg.* Arturo Cardano, *serg. magg.* Trento Cecchi and *s. ten.* Nunzio De Fraia) took off to escort an IMAM Ro.37*bis* reconnoitring the front line in the Sollum area. The Italian formation was intercepted by a number of Gladiators, which attacked the Ro.37. The Italian fighters intervened and managed to save the reconnaissance aircraft, but almost all of the CR.42s suffered gun-jamming during the combat and two CR.42s were shot down. *ten.* Tadini and *serg. magg.* Cardano were both shot down by the Gladiators. Tadini baled out while Cardano crash-landed; both were taken prisoner.

It seems that they had clashed with Gladiators from 33 Sqn, since a flight of three Gladiators from this unit took off to escort the 208 Sqn Lysander of F/O Webber. They met two CR.42s over Sollum at around 08:30, P/O Eric Woods and F/Sgt Leonard Cottingham each shooting one down. No losses were reported nor the presence of other Fiats or the Ro.37 reconnaissance aircraft.

During this combat the presence of *serg. magg.* Agostino Fausti is often reported, and it is also reported that he claimed two Gladiators during this combat. In fact, existing Italian records do not confirm this information.

At 12:10, three fighters from the 93ª *Sq.* (*col.* Angelo Federici (the *Stormo* CO), *ten.* Domenico Bevilacqua and *serg. magg.* Agostino Fausti) joined the other fighters from the 2° *Stormo* at Menastir.

In the early afternoon, Fiat CR.42 MM5542 of the 94ª *Sq.* section went up in flames during start up and was destroyed. The 94ª *Sq.* section remained with only three fighters.

In the evening, at about 18:00, six 33 Sqn Gladiators flying in two sections escorted a Lysander from 208 Sqn, flown by F/O Brown, over the Capuzzo-Bardia area. Nine CR.42s were seen taking off from Menastir Landing Ground west of Bardia, and the Gladiators dived to attack. The No. 2 section, led by F/O Gray-Worcester and including F/Sgt Cottingham and P/O Eric Woods, attacked just as the enemy fighters left ground, and Gray-Worcester shot down four of them while Cottingham claimed two and Woods claimed one. The remaining two CR.42s made good their escape.

The British pilots reported that the Italians scrambled more fighters, and five CR.42s were attempting to get airborne just as the other three Gladiators, all flown by 112 Sqn pilots (F/O Price-Owen, F/O R. H. Smith and F/O R. J. Bennett), decided to join the fray. Taking the barely flying CR.42s by surprise Smith and Bennett each claimed one shot down.

Price-Owen was forced to leave his aircraft (Gladiator II N5751) after an explosion in the fuselage over Buq-Buq. He parachuted safely and came down 15 miles inside the Egyptian border. Post-war British studies suggested that his aircraft was possibly hit by British anti-aircraft fire, but it seems this was not the case. In fact, F/Lt Joseph Fraser reported:

"*During July 1940, pilots from 112 Sqn, on detachment at Sidi Barrani, were gaining operational experience rapidly and many dogfights resulted around the bay of Sollum between Gladiators and CR 42s, for the CR 42 pilot had not yet learnt to respect the Gladiator – his senior, with its greater manoeuvrability. It was during one of these flights that F/O Price-Owen was badly shot up, though uninjured himself, and then decided to bale out. However, unfortunately, he was wearing a parachute belonging to a friend of far greater stature and on pulling the rip cord, the loose harness gave him a very severe jerk between his legs which almost cost him his manhood – a very serious matter with Price-Owen. He was incapacitated for some time and posted from the squadron.*"

Here it is also interesting to note how the British pilots had quickly learned what were the advantages of their machine over the Italians, they however greatly overestimated the speed of their opponent: "*(We tried) to get to grips with CR 42s who declined a fight with the feared and more manoeuvrable Gladiator which was outpaced at full throttle by a good 50 mph (!)*"

The Italians reported that at 18:05, five CR 42s scrambled against a reported nine Gloster Gladiators that were already orbiting over the airstrip of Menastir. The Italian pilots were *cap.* Franco Lavelli, *s. ten.* Nunzio De Fraia and *serg. magg.* Trento Cecchi from the 94ª *Sq.* and *ten.*

A CR.42 from the 77ª Squadriglia *(with the unit's war badge, the "ace of hearts" on the wheel fairing), sporting the very special insignia (a red star inside an azure blue rectangular flag) that characterize the personal machine of a* Generale di Brigata Aerea. *It is very possibly that this was the personal machine of* Generale Guglielmo Cassinelli, *CO of* Brigata Aerea Rex. *The "ace of hearts" was the personal insignia of the WWI 24-victories ace, Pier Ruggero Piccio.*
[via Istituto Luce]

The wreck of the CR.42 of serg. magg. Agostino Fausti in July 1940. The engine of the fighter is detached from the fuselage because the rescue team that found the plane had to move it to recover the body of the Italian pilot. [Historical Museum of Italian Air Force- Vigna di Valle via t. col. Massimo Mondini]

Domenico Bevilacqua and *serg. magg.* Agostino Fausti from the 93ª *Sq*. The Italian pilots started in a helpless position, considering the height advantage of the Glosters, and the fact that at sea level the Gladiator II had better overall performances than the CR.42, being more manoeuvrable with a top speed (flat) of 346 km/h against the 342 km/h of the Italian fighter and with a slightly higher climb rate (in 1 minute and 25 seconds the Gladiator reached 1,184 metres while in the same time the CR 42 only reached 1,000 metres). In quick succession, Cecchi was shot down and killed and De Fraia was obliged to bale out, wounded, from his burning aircraft. Lavelli was the next to fall and then Bevilacqua, who, although slightly wounded, disengaged and landed a heavily damaged aircraft. Only Fausti remained in flight, fighting against the whole RAF formation. From the ground it was seen that his fire hit two enemy fighters that were obliged to leave the combat area (no victories were claimed but one of them seems highly likely to have been Price-Owen) but the other Gladiators didn't give him a chance, hitting his plane while he (probably already wounded) was trying a last evasive manoeuvre, diving in westward direction towards the fading sun. Fausti died in his burning plane (Fiat CR.42 MM5543). His proposal for an *Medaglia d'argento al Valor Militare* from June was subsequently changed to a posthumous *Medaglia d'Oro al Valor Militare* for bravery. Again it was reported that almost all the fighters of the Italian formation suffered gun-jamming during the fight, in particular the plane of *cap.* Lavelli was observed not to fire even when he reached very favourable positions. After landing back at base, Bevilacqua reported that his guns had ceased to fire almost immediately; he had only managed to fire 57 rounds.

Cap. Lavelli, *s. ten.* De Fraia and *serg. magg.* Cecchi had just escorted a formation of Bredas over the front, landing back at 17:45. Together with a scramble they made at 15:55, this was their fourth mission of the day.

This was the blackest day of the whole war for the 8° *Gr. C.T.*, and in total they lost seven CR.42s destroyed and one more damaged. Three pilots were killed, two were taken prisoner and two wounded.

At 18.45, *ten.* Domenico Bevilacqua returned to T2 in his damaged fighter, escorted by *col.* Federici.

In the evening, 'B' Flight of 80 Sqn was scrambled and chased ten SM 79s north of Alexandria. The bombers quickly withdrew, and only P/O Arthur Weller and F/O Greg Graham managed to engage the right-hand aircraft of the formation. Their speed was insufficient to allow them to keep up, but it was believed that the aircraft they attacked had been shot down and they were credited with a probable.

The Italian unit involved was the 34° *Gr. B.T.* from Rhodes, whose bombers were out on their first mission since their arrival in the theatre. They reported being attacked by enemy fighters which heavily damaged two SM 79s, which however made it back to base. *cap.* Ugo Pozza (CO of the 67ª *Sq.*) was acting as bomb aimer in one of the SM 79s, flown by the *Gruppo* Commander, *ten. col.* Vittorio Cannaviello. The fire from the attacking Gladiators wounded almost all the crew of the Savoia; *serg. magg. Motorista* Dante Zirioli, *Primo Aviere Marconista* Vincenzo Dragone and *serg. magg. Armiere* Armando Di Tullio. Pozza, considering the situation, changed places on one of the side guns with the wounded Di Tullio. While Pozza was trying to repel the assaults of the Gladiators, Di Tullio released the bombs on the target. Pozza was then killed manning the gun, and the already wounded Di Tullio returned to his place on the side gun and claimed one of the British fighters shot down in flames, until another bullet struck his head, killing him instantly. The bomber was nursed back to Rhodes by Cannaviello with the help of the second pilot, *m. llo.* Giuseppe Fugaroli. At base 150 holes of various dimensions were counted in the fuselage. For their bravery Pozza and Di Tullio received the *Medaglia d'Oro al Valor Militare* posthumously. Di Tullio was also credited with one enemy fighter shot down.

Operation Catapult

All French aircraft in North Africa were deployed in the west, leaving their positions in front of the Italians.

GC I/4 and II/4 based at Meknès were reactivated, and the *2ème escadrille* of GC I/4 deployed its Curtiss H75s to Médiouna, to cover Casablanca where the battleship *Jean Bart* was moored.

Two Potez 63.11 of GR I/52 went over Gibraltar on a reconnaissance mission, while at 10:30, off the coast of Oran, three Curtiss H75s of GC I/5 exchanged fire with Sunderland P9621 of 228 Sqn. Back at base, the Sunderland was temporarily repaired and then flew back to England on 8 July.

A LeO H-257bis of GB II/25 attacked a British submarine, which just had sunk the French patrol ship *Rigault de Genouilly*.

Five LeO H-257*bis* of B1 took off from Port-Lyautey at 22:08. Three of them bombed Gibraltar during the night.

5 July 1940

Tobruk T2 suffered an air attack by Blenheims from 211 Sqn (twelve Blenheims including four attached Blenheims from 45 Sqn) during which eight Fiat CR.42s, presumably from the 8° *Gr.*, were slightly damaged (RS). One of the attached crews of 45 Sqn reported the participation of 55 Sqn in the attack but this is not consistent with the unit's ORB.

211 Sqn had taken off from El Daba at 15:15 and landed back at 18:45.

Together with the eight Fiats put out of action momentarily or definitively the day before at Menastir this meant that very few (if any) aircraft remained available for the defence of Tobruk harbour. Another raid was made on Menastir where an SM 79 (probably a machine in transit) was slightly damaged (RS).

During a low-level raid against a concentration of motor transport, a pilot from 113 Sqn was severely wounded in the arms and legs, while the observer (F/Sgt Observer John Frederick Taylor) was killed by AA fire. The gunner of the crippled Blenheim was the 45 Sqn's attached aircrew A. C. Meadows, who crawled to the front of the aircraft and applied first aid to the pilot. He then remained in the navigator's seat and assisted the pilot, who was suffering from the effect of his wounds, in landing the aircraft by manipulating the flaps and undercarriage. Meadows was awarded an immediate DFM for this action.

Following the hard defeat suffered by the 8° *Gr.* the previous day, retaliation attacks against RAF airbases were planned.

The 15° *Stormo*, recently moved from Benghazi Benina to Maraua, was ordered to fly the mission and attacked during the afternoon in full strength with 50 kilo bombs.

Three SM 79s of the 21ª *Sq.* led by *cap.* Masoero attacked Tishdidia airfield, together with six SM 79s of the 54ª *Sq.* led by *ten.* Remorino, two aircraft from the 21ª *Sq.* led by *magg.* Cerne, three SM 79s from the 20ª *Sq.* led by *cap.* Guidorzi and three aircraft from the 20ª *Sq.* led by *ten.* Recagno.

One hour later six aircraft of the 53ª *Sq.* led by *magg.* Angelo Tivegna (the new *Gruppo* commander) attacked Bir Enba airfield.

Sergente Maggiore *Agostino Fausti* of the 93ª *Squadriglia*, 8° Gruppo *(on temporary attachment from the 77ª Squadriglia)*, who was killed on 4 July and posthumously awarded a Medaglia d'Oro al Valor Militare. [Italian Air Force]

All the aircraft were back between 19:00 and 19:30 without encountering the enemy and without suffering losses. They claimed to have hit hangars, fuel storage and to have destroyed six enemy planes on ground.

Tishdidia (or Bir Tishdidia) was a coastal airstrip halfway between Sollum and Buq-Buq, while Bir Enba was an airport situated 35 kilometres south of Sidi Barrani (their name in British documents should be LG 1 for Tishdidia and LG 75, 76 or LG 71 for Bir Enba).

33 Sqn reported that twelve Gladiators of the squadron were refuelling at Buq-Buq when Italian bombers hit the field. 'B' Flight managed to get airborne but was unable to engage the enemies, while members of 'C' Flight took cover. Two Gladiators were damaged by bomb splinters but remained flyable. The experience was described by the squadron as "sobering".

The Italian Army was trying to reinforce their forces in Libya as quickly as possible following the urgent requests of Marshals Balbo and then Graziani. On 27 June a fast convoy, formed by three destroyers (*Espero*, *Ostro* and *Zeffiro*), sailed from Italy to quickly reach Tobruk with a troop of 160 "black shirts" with flak guns, necessary to improve the anti-aircraft defences of the Libyan base.

On 28 June the convoy was intercepted 100 miles north of Tobruk by the VII Squadron of the Royal Navy, composed of the cruisers HMS *Liverpool*, HMS *Gloucester*, HMS *Orion*, HMS *Neptune* and HMS *Sydney*, under the command of Vice-Admiral Tovey. They sank *Espero* with the use of an astonishing 5000 shells, while *Ostro* and *Zeffiro* made good their escape.

Another convoy sailed from Augusta on 30 June. It was composed of six merchant ships (*Manzoni*, *Liguria*, *Piemonte*, *Serenitas*, *Virtus*, *Labor*) full of troops, munitions and fuel, and was escorted by six destroyers and four big torpedo-boats. The Royal Navy failed to intercept this second convoy, which safely reached Tobruk.

On 4 July the ships were however discovered at their moorings by an Alexandria-based Sunderland. Immediately Vice-Admiral Andrew Cunningham ordered a torpedo strike to be carried out by the Fairey Swordfishes from HMS *Eagle*.

On 5 July seven destroyers (*Turbine*, *Nembo*, *Aquilone*, *Zeffiro*, *Euro*, *Ostro* and *Borea*), two minesweepers (*Palmaiola* and *Grazioli Lante*), four torpedo-boats (*Procione*, *Orione*, *Orsa* and *Pegaso*), one gun-boat (*Alula*), one cruiser (*San Giorgio*) and the six freighters were present in Tobruk harbour.

At 20:20, a group of six (nine according to some sources) Fairey Swordfishes of 813 Sqn from HMS *Eagle* reached Tobruk harbour, taking the Italian defences completely off guard. Nobody spotted HMS *Eagle's* aircraft until they arrived over the harbour from a north-western direction. In a copy-book attack, which lasted seven minutes, the Swordfishes sank five Italian ships. *Manzoni* (3955ton) was hit by a torpedo, quickly capsized and sank. The destroyer *Zeffiro* was also hit and sank half an hour later. The destroyer *Euro* was hit, beached and was used as a stationary flakship for the rest of the campaign. The 15354ton liner *Liguria* and the freighter *Serenitas* (5171ton) were also hit and both were beached; they were later recovered by the British. The complete lack of aerial opposition helped the British attackers to suffer no losses. The attack had been supported by the Gladiators from 33 Sqn, which escorted Blenheims from 211 Sqn providing reconnaissance.

From the Italian side the only positive thing was that the freighters were already empty (they had been quickly unloaded on 4 July), but no lessons were learned at all from this attack. The *Regia Marina* contented itself accusing *Regia Aeronautica* for the lack of aerial cover, while nothing was done to improve the warning network around Tobruk or to study effective countermeasures against attacks by torpedo-bombers. At the end the Italian Navy paid dear for this lack of response, losing first the use of Tobruk as a harbour and a logistic base and then, during the infamous night of Taranto, half of its battleship force and the initiative in the Mediterranean war.

Operation Catapult

Five Glenn-Martin GM 167Fs of B3 took off to attack HMS *Ark Royal*. One of the bombers crashed at Bouskara killing the crew (*Ensigne de Vaisseau* Chalandre, *Second Maitre* Lallier and *Second Maitre* Macadre), while the others attacked without success.

6 July 1940

Ten bombers of the 20ª and 54ª *Squadriglie* led by *cap.* Guidorzi attacked Mersa Matruh airfield in the early afternoon with one hundred 50 kg bombs.

Lysander L4785 of 208 Sqn, piloted by P/O Benson, force-landed due to engine failure when being flown from Qasaba to Sidi Barrani.

Operation Lever

Vice-Admiral Somerville did not think that the *Dunkerque* had been completely disabled in the attack on 3 July, consequently an air strike was planned to finish it off. The operation was named *Lever*.

At 05:20, six Swordfishes of 820 Sqn, escorted by six Skuas, arrived up sun at a height of 20 metres over the bay of Mers-El-Kebir. They launched their torpedoes (equipped with Duplex pistols) from a distance of 700-800 metres, and without encountering serious AA fire. The returning crews claimed four hits while reporting that the first torpedo, probably released inside pistol safety range, hit amidships, glanced off and exploded against the jetty. In fact, only one hit was obtained and this on the patrol-ship *Terre Neuve*, anchored on the right side of *Dunkerque*.

American Glenn-Martin bombers in French service.
[via Stratus]

At 07:00, three more Swordfishes from 810 Sqn attacked escorted by six Skuas. This time AA fire was heavy and the first attacker failed to release its torpedo, while two other hits were claimed on *Dunkerque*. In fact, only one torpedo struck home, again hitting the unlucky *Terre Neuve* where all 42 depth charges exploded, cutting the patrol-ship in two and opening a 40 metres long hole in the side of *Dunkerque*.

At 07:10, the last wave of three Swordfishes from 810 Sqn, under Lieutenant Godfroy-Fausset and escorted by the same Skuas, attacked. This time two torpedoes hit. One (failing to explode) was the only effective hit on *Dunkerque*, the other sunk the tug *Esterel*.

At 07:03, three fighters led by *Capitaine* Portalis from GC II/5, which were patrolling over the harbour, intervened. Portalis, together with *Adjutant Chef* Dugoujon and *Sergeant Chef* Gisclon followed an enemy aircraft, which disappeared into clouds (probably Swordfish L2760/'A2C' of 810 Sqn), while the Skuas counter-attacked. The Skuas were six aircraft from 803 Sqn; while red section (L2987/'A7P', L2956/'A7R' and a third unknown Skua) was charged to take photos of the attack, blue section (L2953/'F' flown by Lieutenant Christian, L2996/'H' flown by Sub Lieutenant Easton and L2961/'G' flown by Midshipman Griffith) mixed with the French fighters in a turning battle that lasted ten minutes. Gisclon claimed a plane, which disappeared from his sight after an uncontrolled spin, and Portalis was credited with a probable after his opponent dived into a cloud. In fact, Skua L2956/ 'A7R', damaged in combat, had to force-land on the sea and the destroyer HMS *Vidette* picked up the crew (P/O Peacock and N/A Dearnley). This aircraft had been part of the Skua formation that escorted the third wave of Swordfishes. Again, the FAA pilots reported that although the French fighters easily outmanoeuvred their Skuas, they didn't really press home their attacks.

The action at Mers-El-Kebir was over. The French had lost 1,297 sailors killed and 351 wounded.

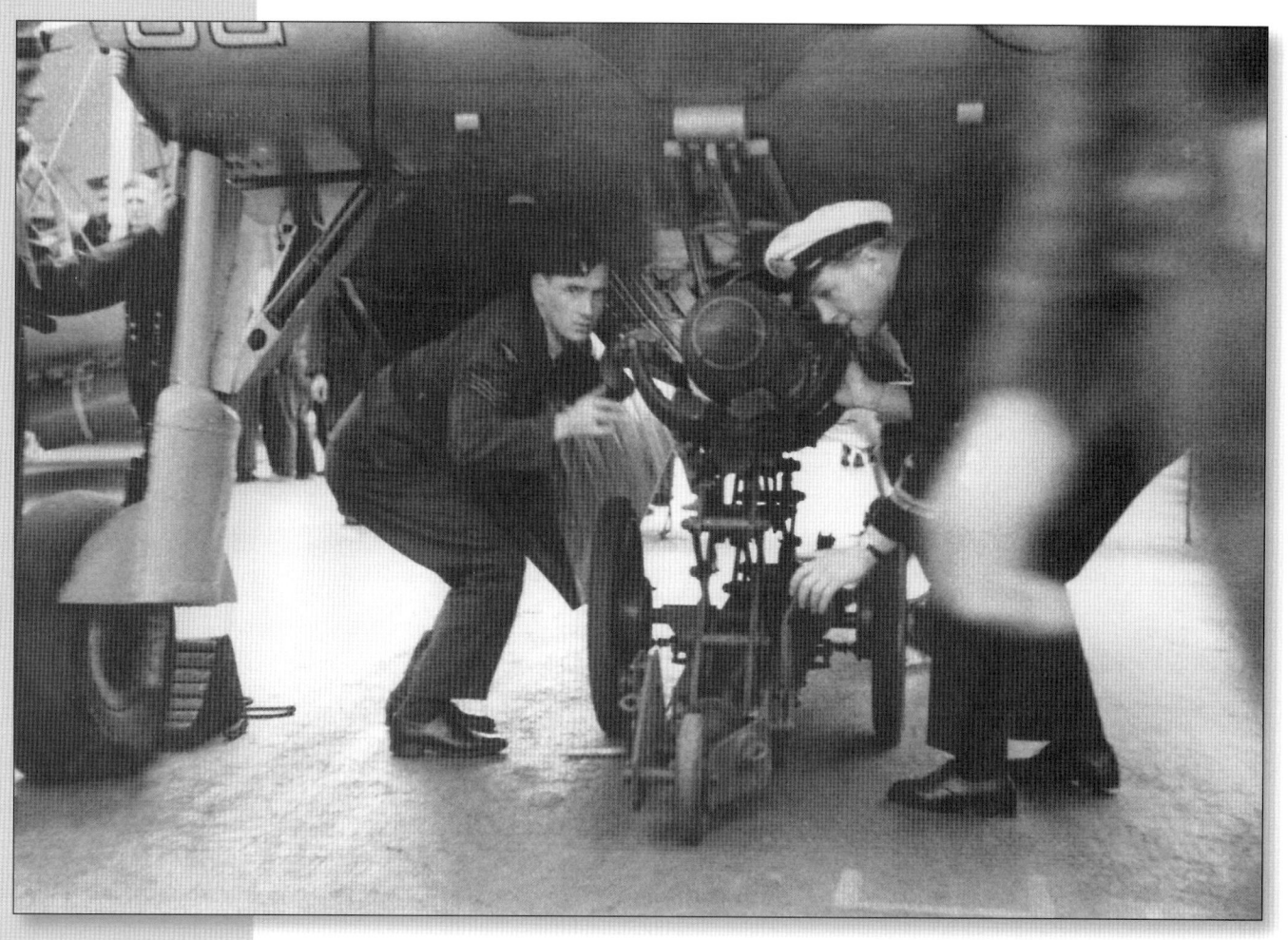

A naval officer and an RAF groundcrew move the weapon, possibly a 500lb SAP, into position. The bomb appears to be a live round, possibly for the attack on the French battleship Richelieu. *[via Fleet Air Arm Museum]*

Dunkerque was effectively out of the war. It reached Toulon in February 1942 but was still under repair when Vichy collapsed under the Germans at the end of 1942.

7 July 1940

Eleven S.81s of the 39° *Stormo* attacked Alexandria during the night. One of the aircraft failed to return, reportedly hit by AA fire over the target.

8 July 1940

During the day, air activity was concentrated in the central Mediterranean, where an important naval action involving major parts of the *Regia Marina* and Royal Navy was developing. The Italian fleet was out from its bases in Taranto and Sicily to escort a convoy carrying supplies and reinforcements for Libya, while Alexandria's fleet (force A, B and C) was out to cover two convoys that were evacuating superfluous personnel and equipment from Malta (operation *M.A. 5*).

The Italians were aware of the presence at sea of the British fleet because of radio interception. It had also been discovered leaving the harbour by a formation of eleven 39° *Stormo* S.81s that had attacked Alexandria during the night of 7-8 July.

Consequently air attacks with all available aircraft were planned for the day by Aegean and Libyan based bombers. Apart from the bomber force available in Libya, the bomber force ready to attack the British fleet was also composed of four Aegean based bomber *Gruppi* of *Comando Aeronautica dell'Egeo* and of the Sicilian based units of II^a *Squadra Aerea*.

In the Aegean there was the complete 39° *Stormo B.T.* composed of the 56° *Gr. B.T.* at Rodi-Gadurrà (Rhodes-Gadurrà) and the 92° *Gr. B.T.* based at Rodi-Marizza (Rhodes-Maritza); this unit was equipped with around 28 S.81s (not all serviceable). Recent reinforcements were the 34° *Gr. B.T.* with twelve SM 79s (previously part of the Sicilian based 11° *Stormo B.T.*) together with the 33° *Gr. B.T.* The 34° *Gr.* had been detached to the Dodecanese on 28 June and had gone to Rodi-

Gadurrà, while the 33° *Gr.* later joined the V^a *Squadra Aerea*), and finally the 41° *Gr. B.T.* with 14 SM 79s (previously part of the Sicilian based 12° *Stormo B.T.* together with the 42° *Gr. B.T.* The 41° *Gr.* arrived at Rodi-Gadurrà on 6 July and was later joined by the 42° *Gr.* on the same airfield).

Alexandria's fleet was discovered at 08:15 by a Cant Z.501 of the 143^a *Sq. R.M.* (*Ricognizione Marittima*) from Menelao (near Tobruk), and shadowed until dusk by the aircraft of this *Squadriglia* and of the Lero based 147^a *Sq.*

The first air attack arrived at 10:00 in the form of three SM 79s from the 34° *Gr. B.T.*, then 68 other bombers followed in twelve different waves. The Libyan based bombers attacked as follows:

10:15; 6 aircraft of the 14° *Stormo*
11:40; 5 aircraft of the 15° *Stormo*
14:20; 6 aircraft of the 32° *Gr.*, 10° *Stormo*, under *cap.* Bertelli and *ten.* Ongaro
17:15; 5 aircraft of the 15° *Stormo*
18:10; 3 aircraft of the 15° *Stormo*
18:20; 5 aircraft of the 14° *Stormo*
18:30; 5 aircraft of the 15° *Stormo*
18:40; 2 aircraft of the 58^a *Sq.*, 32° *Gr.*, 10° *Stormo*

Damaged by the ship's AA, one SM 79 of the Aegean 204^a *Sq.*, 41° *Gr.*, piloted by *ten.* Renato Torelli, force-landed on Crete and was lost (crew interned). The aircraft of *cap.* Meyer was obliged to force-land on the island of Scarpanto, very close to Rhodes where there was a small airstrip (which on 10 June 1940 was still under construction); the crew was rescued the day after.

In total 102 bombs of 250kg and 331 of 100kg fell on the British ships. This rain of bombs only managed one direct hit when, during the last attack, the 58^a *Sq.* hit the command bridge on the cruiser HMS *Gloucester*, killing its commander, Captain Garside, and eighteen men. After this the ship was steered from the auxiliary station in the stern and, even if it didn't turn back, it missed the naval action of 9 July where it should have acted as close escort for the carrier HMS *Eagle*. Additional damage was suffered from the Italian bombers when near misses from 100kg bombs damaged the battleship HMS *Warspite* on the port side abreast No.2 –4inch mounting with other minor damage caused by splinters. A splinter coming from another near miss cut the multi-core cables to the forward H. A. director aboard the battleship HMS *Malaya* causing a temporarily impairment of fighting capacity of the ship.

On the other hand it seems that the last two waves of the 15° *Stormo*'s bombers, both coming from the the 47° *Gr.* and led by *cap.* Giuseppe Magrì and *col.* Silvio Napoli respectively had attacked the Italian fleet in error. This was off the Libyan coast and steaming north to return to Italy. No damage was inflicted on these ships.

The Alexandria's fleet comprised also the aircraft carrier HMS *Eagle* with two squadrons of Fairey Swordfishes and four Gloster Sea Gladiators aboard. Altogether they formed the only air defence for the fleet, but on this day they failed to do any interception at all.

A 45 Sqn Blenheim Mk.I (L8478) piloted by F/O J. Williams suffered a tyre burst on take-off from Helwan and belly-landed. The crew was safe and the plane later repaired.

9 July 1940

In the Mediterranean the two opposing fleets clashed in an inconclusive battle fought off the Calabrian headland of Punta Stilo. Italian bombers attacked all day the British ships and (in error) also the Italians.

The air attacks produced no concrete results. No British or Italian ship was hit, and only an Italian bomber was lost when an SM 79 of the 257^a *Sq.*, 108° *Gr.*, 36° *Stormo*, based in Sicily and piloted by *s. ten.* Luigi Ruggieri, was shot down in error by Italian AA fire.

In total 126 bombers attacked in 17 waves from 16:43 until 21:10, using 8 500kg, 236 250kg and 270 100kg bombs. No Libyan based bombers took part in these attacks, since they were too far north in the Mediterranean.

No interception was made by HMS *Eagle*'s Sea Gladiators, and two torpedo attacks made by formations of nine Swordfishes from HMS *Eagle* at 13:30 and 16:05 failed to score any hits on the Italian fleet.

Sunderland L5803/T from 230 Sqn, flown by F/Lt Woodward and F/O Leatherbarrow and operating from Malta, attacked an Italian submarine at 12:45. The attack was reportedly successful, a direct hit being claimed abaft the conning tower and the submarine was presumed sunk with no survivors. In fact, no Italian submarines at all were lost during July 1940, so the attacked vessel was presumably only damaged.

10 July 1940

Twelve aircraft from the 10° *Stormo*, operating in four groups of three planes, attacked enemy concentrations in the Sidi Barrani area at approximately 09:00. The first two waves attacked undisturbed, and caused considerable damage to 'B' Flight of 208 Sqn. Lysander L4679 was completely destroyed by a direct hit, the tail unit of one of the Tutor liaison aircraft was damaged, the six-wheel vehicle containing all the Flight's equipment and spares was completely destroyed, and a W/T tender was hit by shrapnel and damaged. When the third formation arrived, the RAF had succeeded in scrambling some fighters, and although failing to engage in time to avoid damage they started a running battle during which the SM 79 '56-6' of the 56ª *Sq.*, 30° *Gr.* was forced to crash-land 60 kilometres east of Tobruk, after being heavily damaged by the fire of a reported four Gloster Gladiators. The aircraft was piloted by *s. ten.* Vicoli with the crew of *m. llo.* Cima, *serg.* Piero Angelin, *Aviere scelto* Antonio Camedda, *serg. magg.* Motorista Cucchi and *Primo Aviere* Cibrario.

Angelin and Camedda were killed in their battle positions by the fire from the Gladiators, while Cibrario was wounded. Five other bombers of the 10° *Stormo* returned to Derna with battle damage.

A recovery team reached Vicoli's aircraft on 22 July but found too much damage for it to be salvaged and it was abandoned. This was the first SM 79 shot down by a Gladiator over North Africa, but the claimants are unknown because of the incompleteness of RAF records for the period.

A clue, however, is given by the 112 Sqn pilots F/O Edwin Banks and P/O Richard Acworth. This day, while attached to 33 Sqn, they intercepted a group of three SM 79s that were attacking Sidi Barrani. The British reported that the Italian bombers, when attacked, hurriedly jettisoned their bombs and fled out to the sea. They submitted no claims but obviously other planes of 33 Sqn (to which they were attached) were up and were most probably responsible for the shooting down of *s. ten.* Vicoli.

Ten Blenheims of 211 Sqn under S/Ldr J. W. Judge, with a Flight of three coming from 113 Sqn and other bombers from 55 Sqn, attacked an ammunition dump south of Tobruk at 14:03. No clear results were observed.

At around 21:30, nine Swordfishes of 813 Squadron, which had taken off from the carrier HMS *Eagle* arrived over the Italian base of Augusta. Three of them were armed with torpedoes and attacked the ships in harbour, sinking the destroyer *Leone Pancaldo* with the loss of 16 of the crew.

11 July 1940

After the naval battle off the coast of Calabria, the British ships retreating towards Alexandria were discovered by a reconnoitring Italian flying-boat early in the morning.

Immediately IIª *Squadra Aerea* sent out Sicilian-based SM 79s from the 30°, 34° and 41° *Stormo* and Z.506Bs from the 35° *Stormo* at Brindisi. These attacked from 10:30 to 16:45 in ten separate waves, for a total of eighty-one bombers releasing a total of 175 250-kg and 186 100-kg bombs. One SM 79 of the 195ª *Sq.*, 90° *Gr.*, 30° *Stormo*, claimed hits on a carrier.

The Italian bombers reported interceptions by Fairey Fulmars together with Gladiators, but the defenders were in fact only HMS *Eagle*'s tiny handful of Sea Gladiators, flown by Swordfish pilots. Charles Keighly-Peach in N5517 ('6-A') and Lieutenant (A) Kenneth Keith in N5513 (the latter pilot a Canadian from Calgary) had been on patrol for about twenty minutes at 13,000 feet,

A Ro 37 bis transported by the S.R.A.M. service, El Adem airfield, summer 1940. [via Przemek Skulski]

when at 14:15 they spotted a flight of five SM 79s approaching 2,000 feet below. Keighly-Peach attacked the aircraft on the left of the formation while Keith went for one on the right, both fighters diving vertically from above. Keighly-Peach made three dives, firing from 300 yards to 50 yards. The bomber dropped back and below the formation, emitting black smoke from the port wing. This soon turned to flames and the aircraft spun into the sea, the crew being seen to bale out although they were never found. Return fire hit the Sea Gladiator, one bullet passing through the lower wing longeron to the starboard of the cockpit, going through the diagonal strut immediately above, and then braking up, one fragment entering Keighly-Peach's thigh (it was finally recovered in 1976 when the old wound began to fester). Keith reported hits on his target, but did not see any result before anti-aircraft fire from the Fleet forced the fighters to break away.

The Sea Gladiators had clashed with sixteen SM 79s from the Sicilian 30° *Stormo*, composing the seventh wave of attackers, which reported being attacked by enemy fighters over the fleet at 13:30 and claimed four shot down in exchange for the loss of an SM 79 of the 194ª *Sq.*, 90° *Gr.* flown by *s. ten.* Ciro Floreani and his crew (*serg. magg.* Massimo Boldi, *Primo Aviere Armiere* Raffaele Corbia, *Primo Aviere Montatore* Timo Ranzi, *Aviere Scelto Motorista* Salvo Bacchilega), which all perished when the bomber crashed after having been shot down by Keighly-Peach.

Libyan based aircraft also attacked the British ships, and twelve aircraft of the 33° *Stormo* attacked at 14:35. The aircraft flown by *col.* Giuseppe Leonardi (CO 33° *Stormo*) was shot down, reportedly by AA fire. It appears that its crew was discovered the day after by a Z.501 of the 186ª *Sq. R.M.* from Augusta piloted by *serg.* Mario Spada. Spada tried to land near the wreck of the SM 79 but he failed and the flying boat sank, causing his death. *m. llo. marconista* Antonio Piva, one of the SM 79 crew, tried to reach the men of the Cant to help them but in doing so he drowned. The surviving airmen were later rescued by a Z.506 flying-boat of the 506ª *Sq. R.M.* from Syracuse. It seems that Leonardi was (at least temporarily) replaced by *col.* Attilio Biseo as the CO of the 33° *Stormo*. Biseo was one of the most famous record breakers from the thirties.

At 18:10 twelve aircraft of the 15° *Stormo* attacked the ships.

No hits were recorded on any of the British ships during the day.

12 July 1940

The Libyan bombers continued raids on the Alexandria fleet as follows:

09:00; 18 aircraft of the 30° and 32° *Gruppi* of 10°*Stormo*. This formation was led by the *Stormo* Commander *col.* Giovanni Benedetti and by its *Gruppo* Commanders Rossi and Unia.

09:00; 7 aircraft of the 15° *Stormo*

09:25; 6 aircraft of the 33° *Stormo*

Carlo Romagnoli, who took command over the 10º Gruppo C.T. on 11 July 1940. He was a veteran of the Spanish Civil War and during this conflict, he was CO a reconnaissance and ground attack unit equipped with Ro 37bis. Romagnoli remained in command of the 10º Gruppo until he was killed in combat near Malta on 4 September 1941.
[via Italian Air Force]

09:30; 12 aircraft of the 15º *Stormo*
10:00; 5 aircraft of the 15º *Stormo*
10:35; 6 aircraft of the 15º *Stormo*
10:45; 3 aircraft of the 14º *Stormo*
12:00; 12 aircraft of the 10º *Stormo* led by Capitani Musch and Bressanelli
13:30; 6 aircraft of the 10º *Stormo*
13:50; 10 aircraft of the 15º *Stormo*
14:30; 2 aircraft of the 15º *Stormo*
15:35; 9 aircraft of the 10º *Stormo*

Together with them the Aegean based 34º *Gr.* and 41º *Gr.* attacked at 11:30 and 15:30 respectively, with five and twelve bombers.

The fourteen waves, for a total of 112 SM 79s, expended 197 250 Kg bombs and 110 100 Kg bombs, suffering no losses. Again HMS *Eagle*'s Sea Gladiators were unable to intercept.

S/Ldr Menzies from 228 Sqn (Sunderland N9020/W) claimed an Italian submarine off the Ionian Islands during a patrol from Malta. It seems that he attacked the submarine *Ruggero Settimo*, which was lightly damaged

During the usual reconnaissance of the border, a Lysander of 208 Sqn engaged for the first time Italian troops in the Sidi Azeiz area. P/O Kirton reported strafing personnel intent on digging, claiming four victims. Later during the same sortie, the aircraft was hit in the port wing by AA fire, which also wounded the pilot in the left arm and the air gunner Leading Aircraftman Feldon in both legs. L4690 landed in Sidi Barrani U/S (it needed a new port main plane) and the crew was hospitalized. A replacement machine (L4712) was immediately allotted to 'A' Flight.

216 Sqn restarted night operations over Tobruk when one Bombay attacked, but claiming no hits.

13 July 1940

The skirmishes over the Mediterranean Fleet continued during the next two days, and on 13 July the fleet was again shadowed and six raids followed. Four raids were flown by a total of 20 S.81s from the Aegean-based 39º *Stormo*. SM 79s from the 34º and 41º *Gruppi* made two attacks at 12:15 and 16:05 respectively.

HMS *Eagle*'s Sea Gladiator Flight was up three times. Commander Charles Keighly-Peach in N5517 made first contact at 07:50 when he reported sighting a lone SM 79 ahead of the fleet. Making three diving attacks from out of the sun, he reported that flames issued from the port wing and the aircraft spun into the sea, none of the crew being seen to bale out. This was possibly a Savoia Marchetti S.75 of 604ª *Sq.* T that had been employed temorarily as a reconnaissance aircraft and which was lost during the day. The aircraft coded I-TUFO and with the individual number 604-3 was piloted by *serg.* Mario Ballan and *serg.* Giuliano Giuliani. Aboard the aircraft was also *ten.* di *Vascello Osservatore* Giuseppe Ghidini of the Lero based 145ª *Sq. R.M.* (an officer of the Navy part of the crew to better spot enemy ships).

At 11:15, to the south of Crete, Keighly-Peach (N5517) and Lieutenant (A) Kenneth Keith (N5513), saw three Savoias - identified again as SM 79s - 5,000 feet below, approaching from the direction of Rhodes. Keith attacked first, firing on the left-hand aircraft, and this was then attacked by Keighly-Peach, who made three more attacks on the same bomber, which fell into the sea in flames. Two men baled out, one being picked up by HMS *Hereward*. Keith attacked the other two without obvious result. Keighly-Peach's and Keith's claim was almost surely a wrongly identified S.81, since at 11:20 five S.81s from the 39º *Stormo* attacked and a machine of the 200ª *Sq.*, 92º *Gr.*, flown by *s. ten.* Enrico Carapezza, was shot down by enemy fighters, although defending gunners in the bombers claimed one fighter shot down.

Finally, at 14:50, Keith (again in N5513) saw five SM 79s at 8,000 feet, making a beam attack followed by a stern chase on one. This finally caught fire, turned on its back and spun into the sea, no-one being seen to bale out. This claim was probably made against a group of three

SM 79s of the 15° *Stormo*, which attacked at 14:30 as the only raid of the V^a *Squadra Area* for the day. These Italian pilots were the only ones who reported being attacked by fighters (apart from the 39° *Stormo* at 11:20) and they claimed two shot down by their return fire for no losses. It seems that they shot down a Bristol Blenheim Mk.IF of 30 Sqn (K7181) that was patrolling over the fleet together with two colleagues. The three Blenheims reported that at 14:43 they discovered a formation of three SM 79s at 13,000 feet. One Blenheim was left to guard the fleet while the other two attacked, claiming that the fire from the leader, F/O Le Dieu (Blenheim K7177), silenced the rear gunner of the Italian leader while the combined fire of the two Blenheims hit the number three of the Savoias, which was seen to dive away with smoke pouring from the starboard engine but was not seen to crash. One of the Blenheims was lost. The crew of the Blenheim fighter (22-year old P/O Derryk Austin Lea and 20-year-old Sgt Christopher Frederick Burt) perished. According to the pilot in the third Blenheim, F/Lt Alfred Bocking, P/O Lea was seen to bale out successfully but so great was the submarine menace that the convoy just sailed past him. Credit for the shot down Blenheim went to *Aviere scelto Armiere* Ornani of the 20^a *Sq.*, 46° *Gr*.

During the last two days of bombing, even if no direct hits were achieved, the British ships were badly shaken by several near misses that caused splinter damage on many ships (including HMS *Eagle* and the destroyer HMS *Vampire*), and killed some sailors aboard the cruiser HMS *Liverpool*. In particular, on 12 July, HMS *Warspite* sustained damage from a near miss from an estimated 50kg bomb, which burst abreast of the flying deck on the starboard side and minor damage to structure was again caused by splinters. Back at Alexandria, the ship required two days of dock for permanent repairs.

The 10° *Stormo*'s SM 79s attacked enemy infantry groups near Sidi Barrani.

Six Bombays from 216 Sqn departed Heliopolis for Fuka and then Tobruk. The bombers left Fuka in the early dusk (taking off from 19:35 until 21:20) and bombed the harbour, claiming some damage. All returned reporting heavy but inaccurate AA.

14 July 1940

216 Sqn again attacked Tobruk, but the mission ended in tragedy when two out of the six Bombays failed to return. The Bombays this time had targeted the naval oil tanks in Tobruk harbour and had experienced heavy and very inaccurate AA fire. They also saw a biplane fighter, which came within 500 yards but did not open fire.

A Sea Gladiator picks up a wire on a carrier in the Med. The aircraft appears to have had its camouflage extended all the way down the fuselage, although the engine cowling retains the original scheme.
[via Tim Kershaw]

While returning heavy ground mist was encountered in the desert, and this was reputedly the cause of the loss of the bombers. The lost bombers were those flown by S/Ldr Taylor/P/O Osborne (Bombay L5815) and Sgt Campbell/Sgt Williams (L5819). Campbell and Williams force-landed on the south-west corner of Lake Maryut and were fired on by Egyptian soldiers that mistook them for Italians. Once the situation cleared, they were released and returned to Heliopolis.

Taylor's aircraft was located 25 miles south of Mersa Matruh on 16 July completely burnt out. Of the crew, Taylor and Corporal Hazlitt were badly burnt while P/O Ralph Paul Joseph Osborne, Leading Aircraftman Kenneth Edward Webber and Corporal George Niven were killed.

According to post war British studies a third Bombay from 216 Sqn (L5848 flown by Sgt J. G. Cowlishaw) was lost during the morning in a transport flight.

15 July 1940

During a defensive patrol, Sgt William Vale of 33 Sqn claimed a shared SM 79 near Mersa Matruh. The Italian unit involved is not known but from the available Italian documents only three SM 79 missions were carried out during the day, all reconnaissance missions: one over the border area from Marsa Luch to Giarabub, one up to Sidi El Barrani and the usual strategic reconnaissance of Alexandria with the SM 79 loaded with three 100kg bombs that in the early afternoon attacked a cruiser inside the harbour once completed its checks. No operational losses were explicitly noted while an SM 79 was recorded as lost with the complete crew for non-operational causes.

An air attack on Ain El Gazala airfield caused one dead and two wounded personnel. The attack was made by nine Blenheim Mk.Is of 55 Sqn, which took off at 05:30 to be over the target at 07:25 together with eight bombers from 211 Sqn. During the return flight over Buq-Buq, Blenheim L4820 of the Flight Commander of 'C' Flight, 55 Sqn, when flying at about 300 feet under cloud, suddenly turned in and crashed, the wreckage catching fire killing the crew, 21-year-old F/O Michael Frederick Henry Fox, 26-year-old Sgt Harry Francis Alfred Nicholas and Sgt Maurice Klines. The cause of the loss remains unknown.

The formation from 211 Sqn flew 40 miles over the sea on a course parallel to the coast, overshot the target, and were forced to drop their bombs far from the target in an area south of Apollonia, and then immediately headed towards Egyptian territory. One Blenheim force-landed three kilometres west of Tobruk near T.5 airstrip hit by the Italian AA batteries. It was L1491 (that according to some Italian sources was captured in good condition), and the captured crew was P/O E. Garrand-Cole, Leading Aircraftman W. Smith and AC2 E. Doolin; one of them was wounded (possibly Doolin). Another Blenheim (Sgt Watkins) belly landed short of fuel near Sollum (the crew was helped by the Army), while two machines force-landed at Buq-Buq where the Commanding Officer nosed over in soft sand. In the end, only five machines were able to return to base after refuelling at Buq-Buq and Sidi Barrani.

Three Bombays from 216 Sqn raided Tobruk. One aircraft was lost when L5848, flown by John George Cowlishaw and P/O Thomas Albert Grundy, went missing together with its crew (Leading Aircraftman Thomas Murray, Sgt Peter Douglas Snowden). An Italian night fighter reportedly shot down the Bombay. Encounters with Italian night fighters were sometimes described by the returning crews of 216 Sqn and it is known that around this period some IMAM Ro.41 were used as night fighters by the pilots of the 50° *Stormo* in Tobruk but the incompleteness of Italian records under this aspect doesn't permit to confirm the shooting down and the possibility exists that the Bombay had fallen victim of the improved AA fire.

The body of the gunner, Leading Aircraftman Matthew Hetherington Winship, was washed ashore at Sollum on 18 July.

16 July 1940

A total of 30 SM 79s of the 10°, 14° and 15° *Stormi* attacked Mersa Matruh and Sidi Barrani from medium level in four separate raids, without being intercepted and without suffering losses.

The results obtained by these bombing attacks and those of the previous and following days are not known in detail. British sources are vague on the matter, but the petrol and ammunition dumps of Mersa Matruh after being straddled by the bombing attacks were "duly shifted", and the landing ground of Buq-Buq, being on a dry lake bed where bomb craters had filled with water and could not be repaired, had to be abandoned. By this time, the 202 Group bombers were widely dispersed and using satellite airfields to minimize the risk of bomb damage.

It is also reported that around this day, 33 Sqn Gladiators were taking off when the Italian bombers appeared overhead. As P/O Vernon Woodward skimmed along some 30 feet off the desert a bomb exploded ahead and below his plane, that flipped 90 degrees onto its side!

During the night of 16-17 July, twelve S.81s of the Aegean 39° *Stormo* attacked Alexandria harbour. One of the bombers ditched near the island of Scarpanto during the return journey.

During this period bombing action against Alexandria was carried out only by the Aegean based bombers, while V^a *Squadra Aerea* made only strategic reconnaissance missions with its SM 79s.

Three Bombays from 216 Sqn attacked Tobruk. Operations were then cancelled because of a pending investigation into W/T failures. The squadron didn't carry out any other bombing operations during July, this also because it seems that the Bombays operated only in periods of full moon, i.e. once a month.

18 July 1940

23-years-old F/O Anthony Gray-Worcester, of 112 Sqn, was killed while leading a formation down through cloud. He was probably flying Gladiator K6130, which was lost during the day when it hit a hill obscured by a cloud at Qaret el Naga.

Gray-Worcester was already the rising star of the squadron, and was sorrowfully missed by its colleagues. Joseph Fraser remembered him this way:

"(At the beginning of the war) No.33(F) Sqn were fighting a hard game against greatly superior numbers of Italian fighters at Mersa Matruh during June and July and so sections of 4 were detached from 112 and 80 Sqns for a fortnight at a time to help out 33 Sqn and to give the former squadrons operational experience before they moved to the desert as a whole. The first four pilots to leave 112 Sqn were led by F/O Tony Worcester – a Cranwell graduate of exceptional flying ability. Tony led his section of Gladiators away from Helwan up to Sidi Barani in the early days of July, like a pack of hounds that had been released after months in their kennels. Hardly had they time to refuel at Sidi Barani before they were led over the barbed wire by pilots of 33 Sqn. Now at this stage in the war the landing grounds between Alexandria and Sollum could be counted on two hands with ease and these were frequently visited at night by the Italian bombers, for there was no night fighter organization possible. What success could a Gladiator with H/F have of intercepting a bomber at night without observer screen or RDF

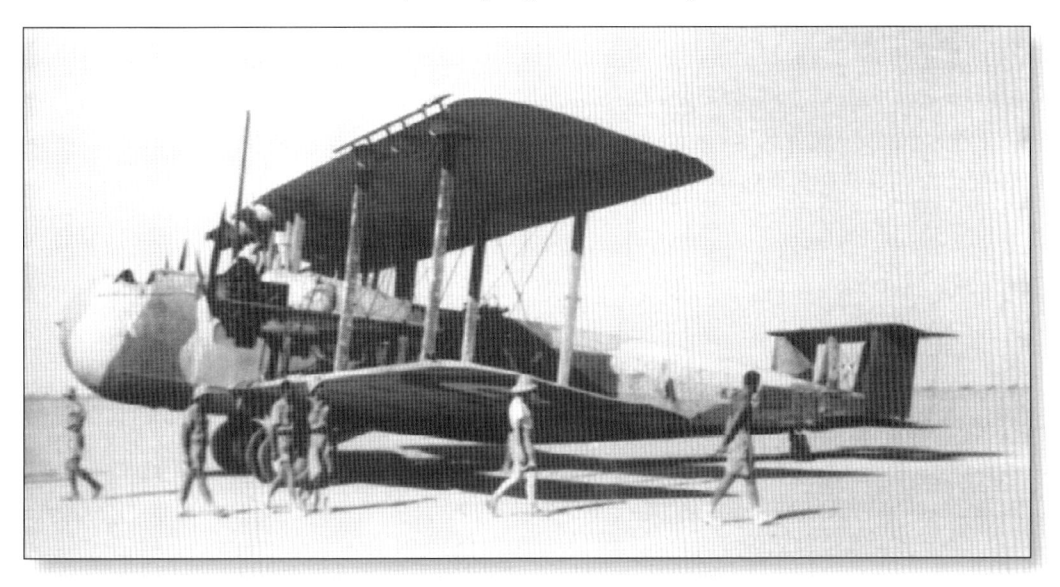

The Vickers Valentia remained in service with 216 Sqn until mid-1941. [via Bouwer/Gibson]

screen? However, it was Tony Worcester who led the first attack onto an enemy occupied aerodrome near Fort Capuzzo [on 4 July]. No one knew then what anti-aircraft defences the Italians had organized, what tactics they would employ or how their fighters compared in speed and manoeuvrability with the already obsolete Gladiator. Out of the clear blue sky came Tony and his three Gladiators in formation, down onto the aerodrome from which the Italian CR 42s were already climbing into battle. Then, for ten minutes, three Gladiators got stuck into an ever- increasing number of Italian fighters. Tony's tactics, manoeuvrability and firing were superb, for in less than 10 minutes four Italian fighters had crashed down onto their own aerodrome from Tony's guns – a mere four .303 machine guns – in full view of the Italians and back came the Gladiators to Sidi Barani almost without a bullet hole in them. The rest of the fortnight was spent chasing Savoia 79s – three engine bombers, which being 40 mph faster than the Gladiator, were able to draw away from them out to sea whenever attacked (....) Back came Tony to Helwan with his Gladiators, the first hero of the Western Desert, having proved correct all his theories of tactics and firing and inspired in all the superiority of British pilots and aircraft over Italian.

Towards the end of July, Tony set out for Sidi Barani with another three pilots and finding his first port of call covered in low cloud, he ordered his section to circle above the cloud while he went down to investigate. He never came up again and his section managed to land by a near-by landing ground; a search found Tony crashed into a sand dune. He had gone down through the cloud to see if it was safe to take his section through but the cloud was lying on the ground and he must have hit the ground and killed himself before he had seen the danger. In this land of clear blue skies, more experienced pilots have killed themselves through feeling their way down through belts of mist over the Delta and coastline than any other reason."

Worcester was leading the vanguard of his squadron to the frontline thus ending the period of the Detachment to 33 Sqn. Fraser remembered:

"The last of these detachments returned to Helwan towards the end of July and nearly all the squadron's pilots had found their Battle Wings, got over the nervousness of meeting their first enemy aircraft and pressed their button, with and without success, at an enemy aircraft. The theoretical tactics of peacetime training were revised by experience in combat to practical tactics; so for all this most valuable fighting experience, only two Gladiators were lost, both pilots having landed safely by parachute and the squadron was credited with 8 confirmed enemy aircraft. The squadron had received orders to relieve 33(F) Sqn at GERAWLA, near Mersa Matruh. The squadron was like a pack of hounds with a dozen tails apiece."

It is just the case of observing that while the eight victories claimed are quite clear (the two of Peter Wickham in the end of June and the six on 4 July) only one of the two losses is known (W. B. Price-Owen on 4 July).

19 July 1940

During the morning the Italian light cruisers *Giovanni dalla Bande Nere* and *Bartolomeo Col* were north of Capo Spada (on the western coast of Crete) searching for British merchant ships when they came upon the cruiser HMS *Sydney*, with four British destroyers (HMS *Hyperion*, HMS *Ilex*, HMS *Hero* and HMS *Hasty*). A sharp battle began during which *Bartolomeo Colleoni* went down and *Giovanni dalle Bande Nere* was damaged and retired to Benghazi, where it arrived during the evening.

One SM 79 of the 7ª *Sq.*, 44° *Gr.* flown by *ten.* Pulzetti took off at 06:20 from T3 and made a reconnaissance mission over the RAF airbase at El Daba. The SM 79 was attacked by two British fighters at 5000 metres and two members of the crew were wounded. The aircraft returned safely to base at 10:50.

At 17:10, six CR.42s scrambled from T2. Three were from the 93ª *Sq.* (*s. ten.* Orlando Mandolini, *serg. magg.* Italo Bertinelli and *serg. magg.* Roberto Lendaro) and the other three were from the 78ª *Sq.* (*ten.* Ippolito Lalatta, *s. ten.* Natale Cima and *serg. magg.* Salvatore Mechelli). They intercepted a formation of four British Blenheims. The three CR.42s from the 78ª *Sq.* claimed damage to one of the Blenheims with the use of 500 rounds of ammunition. The Blenheim was later assessed as shot down over the sea off Marsa Lugh by land observers. *s. ten.* Mandolini claimed damage to a bomber with the use of 150 rounds but it is not clear if it was the same as claimed by *ten.* Lalatta, *s. ten.* Cima and *serg. magg.* Mechelli.

It seems probable that they had intercepted four aircraft of 211 Sqn, since Blenheims from 202 Group were mounting a series of raids aimed at sinking the Italian cruiser *Giovanni Dalle Bande Nere*, which was believed to be in Tobruk. 211 Sqn participated in the day's actions with nine Blenheims that took off in independent flights without being able to discover the Italian cruiser and instead bombed Tobruk harbour from 18:13 to 18:30. After the enemy AA fire had stopped firing on them, the last flight of four aircraft was attacked by three CR.42s, which were 1000 feet above them. Two of the Italian fighters dived at the British leader in wide formation out of the sun from the port quarter and appeared to overshoot. They continued their dive and lost so much height that they could not catch up again. The Italian leader (possibly the Spanish Civil War veteran Lalatta) did a very pretty half roll and dived vertically to the attack. Interestingly, the returning British pilots reported that in their opinion, this half-roll had been not necessary to bring the CR.42 on his target. The Italian leader didn't continue his downward dive but zoomed sharply to a position under the wing of the No.2 machine. The gunner of No.3 Blenheim reported that it would be impossible to shoot down this enemy aircraft without grave risk of shooting down No.2 aircraft, and despite all efforts to dislodge the CR.42, it succeeded in staying in this spot. The face of the Italian pilot could be seen quite plainly. His intention obviously was to tilt the nose of his machine up so as to give the leader of the formation a burst, but the high speed of the Blenheims made this impossible without falling off into the range of the rear gunners. Finally when Bardia was passed, he disengaged.

Another unit participating in attacks over Tobruk at around this hour was 55 Sqn (with eight aircraft), which didn't record losses or interceptions (four or five enemy fighters were seen taking off). It could also be possible that Blenheims from 113 Sqn were present.

During this period, considered the favourable moon conditions, Italian bombers were requested to operate at night against RAF airbases. The aircraft attacked in small groups to be able to cover the whole period between sunset and moonset with raids. The 10º *Stormo* operated during the nights of odd days while the 15º *Stormo* operated during the nights of even days. This day the 10º *Stormo* began attacking the Mersa Matruh area with three aircraft of the 32º *Gr.* In the third and last aircraft, an SM 79 of the 58ª *Sq.* piloted by *ten.* Giulio Cesare Cabassi (crew: *s. ten.* Giuseppe Padovano, *m. llo.* Romano Zannini, *m. llo. motorista* Francesco Ferrero, *Primo Aviere Armiere* Nicola Di Giglio, *Primo Aviere Radiotelegrafista* Fabozzi) was shot down by AA fire guided by searchlights. Fabozzi was the only one who was able to use his parachute and survived, although taken prisoner.

Sunderland L2164 of 230 Sqn, flown by S/Ldr Ryley, force-landed at Aboukir due to engine trouble and was heavily damaged.

20 July 1940

Thinking that the *Giovanni Dalle Bande Nere* might be in Tobruk, Vice Admiral Andrew Cunningham ordered another torpedo attack against this harbour to finish it off.

Six Fairey Swordfishes of HMS Eagle's 824 Sqn had been disembarked on 19 July and moved to a front line airstrip at Sidi Barrani. They attacked the harbour starting from 20:00 on the evening on 19 July, again achieving total surprise. All aircraft launched their torpedoes from a height of around 30 metres and from distances between 300 and 400 metres, practically point-blank range. The attack was another success with three hits on target and three ships sunk. The freighter *Sereno* sank the day after, the destroyer *Nembo* capsized and sank at 01:30 on 20 July and the destroyer *Ostro* was beached the day after near the *Euro*.

British sources reported the loss of at least two Swordfishes, when one aircraft from 700 Sqn was lost during a reconnaissance mission off the Libyan coast and the aircraft of Lieutenant G. R. Browne, Lieutenant K. C. Grieve and Petty Officer Rowland John William Wynn was lost over Tobruk during this particular raid. Grieve and Browne were wounded, while 34-year-old Wynn died. It is also known that between 15 and 20 July, a Fairey Swordfish was captured after an attack on Tobruk harbour, it seems likely that it was one of the above mentioned machines.

After this highly successful attack, future Italian convoys were sent directly to Benghazi, and the use of Tobruk as harbour was greatly reduced. This was a big strategic mistake for the Italian supply system in Libya, that lost more or less a quarter of its (already limited) capacity.

At 08:15, Vickers Wellesley K7789 from 70 OTU dug a wingtip into the ground during a low-level turn while engaged in formation practice and crashed in the south-west corner of Amiriya (LG 29). The 22-year-old pilot P/O Richard John Redfern Powning from 113 Sqn was killed while P/O S. G. Cooper and Corporal R. A. Marden were injured.

An SM 79 of the 6ª Sq., 44º Gr. flown by s. ten. Toni took off at 16:50 from T3 and made a reconnaissance mission over Bir El Gobi, Sidi Omar and Bir Esc Sheferzen. It was intercepted by a Gladiator, whose bursts hit the exit door on the top of the cockpit of the bomber, ripping it off. The bomber, however, escaped and landed back at base at 18:35.

Sunderland L5804 of 230 Sqn, piloted by F/O King, took off from Aboukir to carry out a search for a Swordfish which had force-landed in the sea east of Tobruk, but no trace of the aircraft was found.

22 July 1940

Three Blenheims from 211 Sqn individually attacked El Gubbi, El Adem and the submarine jetty in Tobruk Harbour. Blenheim Mk.I (L6661) took off at 21:00 to attack T3 but failed to return. 26-year-old Sgt George Bartle Smith and 19-year-old Sgt Reginald Alfred Steele perished, while 22-year-old Sgt George Aidan Sewell's body was washed ashore near Ma'aten Bagush.

23 July 1940

At 12:55, *cap.* Mario Fedele of the 77ª *Sq.* scrambled alone from T3 after an alarm. He probably intercepted an enemy aircraft and forced it to flee.

Ten minutes after the scramble while he was coming back to land, his plane was seen to suddenly fall out of the sky and crash without apparent reason, killing the pilot. It was assumed that *cap.* Fedele was probably wounded during the combat or perhaps his plane suffered some sort of hidden damage sufficient to make it crash. However, his loss without apparent reason was officially attributed to a flying accident.

208 Sqn carried out the first bombing attack sortie of the campaign when a Lysander piloted by F/O Aldis dive bombed an Italian column in the vicinity of Sidi Azeiz with eight 20lb HE and eight 25lb incendiary bombs. He returned unharmed, claiming to have caused damage in the target area.

At around 16:20, nine CR.42s from the 13º *Gr.* (*magg.* Secondo Revetria (CO of the 13º *Gr.* in a 77ª *Sq.* CR.42), *ten.* Giulio Torresi and *serg.* Ernesto Paolini (77ª *Sq.*), *cap.* Guglielmo Arrabito, *ten.* Guglielmo Chiarini and *serg.* Franco Porta (82ª *Sq.*), *cap.* Giuseppe Dall'Aglio, *serg. magg.* Salvatore Mechelli and *serg.* Rovero Abbarchi (78ª *Sq.*)) and nine from the 10º *Gr.* (*cap.* Luigi Monti, *ten.* Giuseppe Aurili and *ten.* Vincenzo Vanni (84ª *Sq.*), *ten.* Giovanni Guiducci, *s. ten.* Neri De Benedetti, *serg.* Bruno Bortoletti (90ª *Sq.*),*ten.* Enzo Martissa, *serg.* Elio Miotto, *serg.* Alessandro Bladelli (91ª *Sq.*)) took off from El Adem to make a fighter sweep in the Bir El Gobi – Sollum – Bardia area. At around 17:40, between Sidi Azeiz and Bardia, they intercepted a group of Blenheims escorted by Gladiators.

The 13º *Gr.* attacked the Gladiators with height advantage, and *ten.* Chiarini and the other pilots of the 82ª *Sq.* attacked a group of three Gladiators, which were flying in a wide formation. After ten minutes of combat Chiarini shot down one of these fighters. The enemy plane burned when crashing on the ground while the pilot parachuted near Sidi Azeiz and was seen to be rescued by British armoured cars. *ten.* Torresi in the meantime claimed another Gladiator shot down using 150 rounds of ammunition. Post-war Italian studies claimed that two additional bombers fell burning after the attack by other pilots from the 13º *Gr.*, but the official records do not confirm this.

The 10º *Gr.* formation in the meantime joined combat. While *cap.* Monti with five other pilots remained high to cover the other fighters (and estimating the enemy strength to only three fighters), *ten.* Martissa, *serg.* Miotto and *serg.* Bladelli joined the combat and claimed a single Gloster shared with the 13° *Gr.* pilots.

It looks as if this shared victory was one of the two previously claimed by Torresi and Chiarini because there are no shared victory claims in the records of 2° *Stormo*. An incongruity of this type in the claims of *Regia Aeronautica* during combined actions of different units is not unusual at all.

No Italian aircraft were lost, but four CR.42s of the 13° *Gr.* were damaged, and especially Chiarini's and *cap.* Arrabito's CR.42s were so damaged that they were not flyable when back at base at 18:20. Arrabito's CR.42, in particular, had suffered many hits in the wings and behind the pilot's seat.

Presumably the Gladiator claims were made in combat with Gladiators from 33 Sqn. During the day P/O Preston (Gladiator N5774), flying one of three Gladiators of 33 Sqn, briefed to escort the bomb-carrying Lysander of F/Lt Legge, was shot down by three attacking CR.42s and forced to bale out south of Bardia. Preston suffered a slight concussion and once rescued he was sent to hospital in Alexandria. The 33 Sqn ORB is lacking the times of this combat, but that of 208 Sqn recorded that Legge took off at 18:00 and landed at 19:40 and that one of the escorting fighters was shot down by CR.42s and the pilot escaped by parachute, so it seems highly likely that Preston's Gladiator fell victim to Chiarini.

It seems that the British records are incomplete on this date since there are no claims for the damaged Italian fighters.

24 July 1940

During the day three of the 10° *Stormo*'s SM 79s attacked enemy ships south-west of Crete without obvious results.

At 16:00, a formation of eleven CR.42s from the 10° *Gr.*, backed by six more from the 13° *Gr.* took off to patrol the Bir el Gobi – Sidi Omar – Sollum – Bardia area. Leading the 10° *Gr.* formation was *magg.* Carlo Romagnoli (using an aircraft from the 91ª *Sq.*) and with him were *ten.* Franco Lucchini, *m. llo.* Omero Alesi and and *ten.* Giovanni Guiducci of the 90ª *Sq.*, *cap.* Luigi Monti, *cap.* Aldo Lanfranco, *ten.* Vincenzo Vanni and *ten.* Giuseppe Aurili of the 84ª *Sq.*, *ten.* Enzo Martissa, *serg. magg.* Lorenzo Migliorato and *serg.* Luigi Ferrario of the 91ª *Sq.* Pilots from the 13° *Gr.* were *ten.* Giulio Torresi, *ten.* Eduardo Sorvillo and *serg. magg.* Ernesto Scalet of the 77ª *Sq.*, *serg.* Francesco Nanin of the 82ª *Sq.* and *cap.* Giuseppe Dall'Aglio with *s. ten.* Dario Magnabosco of the 78ª *Sq.*

During the patrol they met a British formation, estimated to be nine Blenheims, which was attacking Bardia escorted by 15 Gladiators. The CR.42s attacked the bombers and were in turn attacked by the British escort. *ten.* Lucchini was the first to enter combat and damaged three of the British bombers by using 510 rounds of ammunition, while the others were dispersed. *ten.* Guiducci claimed a Gladiator using 90 rounds of ammunition. The CR.42s of the 84ª *Sq.* remained manoeuvring in close formation until a 90ª *Sq.* aircraft (Lucchini?) drove them against the enemy

Fiat CR.42s from the 10° Gruppo of the 4° Stormo CT in North Africa. The left aircraft is of 91ª Squadriglia while the right is of the 90ª Squadriglia. The unit emblems were painted on the aircraft at Goriza before departing for North Africa. The photos were taken after 12 June 1940 since the Caproni in the left picture is carrying a white cross on the rudder and this marking was applied on this date. The left photo also shows the tail unit of a third CR.42 from the 9° Gruppo C.T. with a prancing horse. Thus the photo was taken after July 1940 when the 9° Gruppo joined the 10° Gruppo in Africa. Regarding the place only two possibilities exist, El Adem or Bengasi Berka, the only two airbases big enough to have a concrete platform as seen in the photos.
[via Renato Zavattini]

breaking their formation. Three aircraft from the *Squadriglia* returned to base one by one. *ten.* Giuseppe Aurili met three Gladiators and damaged one. *cap.* Lanfranco became isolated and, attacked by a reported three enemy fighters, was shot down and obliged to bale out in the Sidi Azeiz area. A British patrol took him prisoner a little later. Lanfranco was one of the oldest pilots of the 4° and a few days later a British message was thrown down near Tobruk, saying that he was wounded in Alexandria hospital. *ten.* Martissa forced an enemy fighter to force-land then, coming back to base, saw his wingman in difficulties against the determined attack of an enemy fighter and, even with his guns jammed, attacked it, forcing the Gladiator to break away. *serg.* Ferrario returned to base with a damaged fighter. According to some sources *ten.* Lucchini is credited with an additional Gladiator during the day, but this can't be verified from the *Squadriglie*'s Diaries.

Ten. Torresi claimed another Gladiator with 250 rounds of ammunition. No losses were suffered by the 13° *Gr.* formation, which landed back at base between 17:25 and 18:05.

It seems that the Italian formation had been involved in combat with eight Blenheims from 55 Sqn tasked to attack targets in the Bardia area and five Gladiators from 'B' Flight of 33 Sqn, flown by F/O Ernest Dean (Gladiator L9046), P/O Alfred Costello (N5776), P/O Vernon Woodward (N5768), Sgt Ronald Slater (N5783) and Sgt Shaw (N5775), which had taken off from Sidi Barrani at 17:40 and met a reported 18 CR.42s over Sollum at 18:30. In the combat Woodward claimed one of the enemy aircraft shot down and a second as a probable. Slater claimed a second CR.42 destroyed while Costello claimed a third. One more CR.42 was claimed by the other pilots, and since Dean doesn't seems to have claimed anything during the day it is possible that this was claimed by Shaw but it hasn't been possible to verify this. During the return flight Shaw was forced to land east of Buq-Buq with engine trouble probably caused by combat damage (probably the aircraft claimed by Martissa). Enemy bombing the day after destroyed his aircraft on the ground, although he rejoined his unit unharmed after a long walk across the desert. The other pilots from 33 Sqn landed back at base between 18:55 and 19:35.

Returning crews from 55 Sqn reported that, after releasing their bomb load at 18:20, 'A' Flight was attacked by a single CR.42, which was part of a very open formation that didn't attack. The Italian biplane attacked from out of the sun, slightly damaging Blenheim L8667 flown by Sgt Vignaux. The British bomber was hit by two bullets (one explosive), one in each mainplane. At 18:35, 'B' Flight was also attacked by a single CR.42. The attack was made from above and astern twice, but none of the British aircraft were hit. It seems that one or both of these attacks were made by *ten.* Lucchini.

25 July 1940

At 09:15, Derna El Ftàiah N1 suffered a heavy air attack, which destroyed two SM 79s on the ground and damaging two more heavily (RD). Five personnel were killed and thirteen more wounded. The killed personnel were *Aviere* Vincenzo Marinelli, *Aviere* Vincenzo De Fazio, *Aviere* Danilo Bartin, *Aviere* Nicola Fioravante and *Aviere* Paolo Fogliata, who were part of the 30° *Gr.*, 10° *Stormo* as were the destroyed SM 79s.

The attack was carried out by six Bristol Blenheims from 211 Sqn, led by F/Lt Gordon-Finlayson. Originally nine bombers were to take part but two Blenheims didn't take off owing to engine troubles, and one broke the tail wheel on landing at Sidi Barrani, where a refuelling stop was provided. On the return journey L1482, flown by P/O Dundas, lost its port airscrew and reduction gear and was forced to make an emergency landing at Fuka, where the port undercarriage collapsed further damaging the plane.

33 Sqn was detailed to sweep the border area to cover eventual stragglers of 211 Sqn. Five Gladiators from 'B' Flight, flown by F/O Ernest Dean (Gladiator L9046), P/O Alfred Costello (N5761), P/O Vernon Woodward (N5768), Sgt Ronald Slater (N5783) and Sgt Shaw (N5776), encountered a reported seven CR.42s over Bardia. Woodward and Slater each claimed one CR.42, of which Woodward's went down in flames before they shared a third. Slater was then seen spinning down, out of the fight, and Woodward became separated from the remaining Gladiators.

He was attacked for seven or eight minutes at low level by several CR.42s before escaping. Costello claimed one shared CR.42 but who he claimed it with is unknown. A fifth CR.42 was also claimed in the combat by an unknown pilot. Dean didn't claim anything in this combat and whether Shaw claimed anything is unknown. P/O Woodward experienced a very hard combat, probably his hardest against *Regia Aeronautica*, and was very impressed by his opponents, in fact after this combat he once reflected:

"They were clean fighters, those Wops, and quite the equal of any Hun in the skill of combat flying."

A quite rare recognition from a RAF fighter pilot of the period.

It seems that the Gladiators had clashed with CR.42s from the 13° *Gr*. At 09:10, *serg. magg.* Leone Basso of the 77ª *Sq.* scrambled from El Adem following an air alarm. *ten.* Giovanni Beduz of the 78ª *Sq.* joined him ten minutes later. With them were also *serg.* Rovero Abbarchi, *s. ten.* Natale Cima and *serg.* Ernesto Taddia (all of the 78ª *Sq.*). The fighters were directed to an interception course along the probable return route of enemy bombers that had attacked Derna. While cruising over Bardia waiting for the enemy bombers, a formation of British fighters, identified just as "superior in numbers", attacked with height advantage. The Italian fighters (at least part of them because it is not sure that Natale Cima and Ernesto Taddia took part in the combat) turned the tables against their opponents. *serg. magg.* Basso attacked a Gladiator, which was left smoking after using 250 rounds of ammunition while *serg.* Abbarchi followed a Gladiator deep (40 km) inside British territory and finally claimed it shot down. All the planes returned to base between 09:40 and 10:25. In total the 78ª fighters had used 500 rounds of ammunition.

According to many post-war British sources Sgt Slater was shot down in this in combat, even if according to the 33 Sqn's ORB he returned to base at 11:20 together with the other pilots, and took part in another patrol with P/O Costello between 14:00 and 14:40 using Gladiator N5783 again. Some British studies suggested that he was in fact forced down but was able to take off later, regaining his unit.

112 Sqn flew a patrol near Bardia during the day and spotted eight CR.42s. F/O Peter Strahan of 'A' Flight claimed one shot down, although he himself was hit and forced to make an emergency landing on the return flight. He was returned to base by an infantry vehicle.

It is highly likely that 33 and 112 Sqns made a combined operation over Bardia because on the Italian side, the combat of the three 13° *Gr.* pilots is the only recorded combat. This could also explain the claim made by an unknown pilot (F/O Strahan?) reported by 33 Sqn.

Coming back from a patrol over the front in company with *magg.* Carlo Romagnoli, *ten.* Enzo Martissa looked for the aircraft he forced to land the day before. He found it and strafed it to destruction. It seems that this Gladiator was the machine of Sgt Shaw. For this action and the one the day before, Martissa was decorated with a second *Medaglia d'argento al Valor Militare*.

During the night nine S.81s of the 39° *Stormo* from Rhodes attacked Alexandria and returned without losses. According to witnesses aboard the carrier HMS *Eagle* (moored inside the harbour) a freighter, identified as the "*Arrow*", was hit and burned for the whole night before sinking.

26 July 1940

Derna suffered another attack, this time nine British bombers left two SM 79s of the 10° *Stormo* damaged; one from the 58ª *Sq.*, 32° *Gr.*, heavily (RD) and the second lightly (RS).

Considering that 45, 55 and 211 Sqns didn't record any action for the day it seems highly likely that the British unit involved in the raid was 113 Sqn.

The aircraft of the 50° *Stormo* together with the fighters of the 13° (nine aircraft) and the 10° *Gruppi*, stopped a penetration by British armoured forces in the Sidi Rezegh area. Some armoured cars were claimed destroyed, and two of them were subsequently captured by the Italian Army together with a recovery vehicle. Radio intercepts overheard the British tank crews desperately calling for air cover, in vain.

It had in fact been the hardest day since the beginning of the war for the 11th Hussars, with units from "C" Sqn having temporarily seven armoured cars put out of action.

During the attack on Sidi Rezegh, the CR.32 (from the 160ª *Sq.*) of *magg.* Bruno Cudugnello (CO 12° *Gr.*) was hit by anti aircraft fire and he was obliged to force land in the desert. *serg.* Giovacchini landed close to his commander and offered to take him aboard his aircraft, but Cudugnello refused and calmly rejoined the Italian troops on foot.

27 July 1940

P9622, the remaining Sunderland of 228 Sqn's detachment at Gibraltar, was heavily damaged by high seas and was flow back to Pembroke Dock for major repairs. It wasn't back in action until 8 October.

During the night of 27 and 28 July four Rhodes based SM 79s of the 34° *Gr.* attacked Alexandria harbour without losses. Italian pilots noted that the AA defences became more and more accurate, while during the night the fleet tended to disperse out to sea to avoid damage at its mooring.

28 July 1940

Ten. Franco Lucchini and *serg.* Giovanni Battista Ceoletta of the 90ª *Sq.* and Giuseppe Scaglioni of the 84ª *Sq.* took off from El Adem following an air alarm and intercepted three Bristol Blenheims. One bomber was shot down, another so heavily damaged that the Italian pilots claimed it would not make it back, while the third escaped. While landing back at base Scaglioni's aircraft, damaged in the engine and with a wheel pierced by the return fire of the Blenheims, crashed and was written off. The two victories were shared among the three pilots.

They had intercepted Blenheim Mk.IFs of 30 Sqn, which were out to escort Blenheim MK.IVs of 113 Sqn on reconnaissance missions over the border area. A couple of Blenheim Mk.IFs (K7099 piloted by F/Sgt Innes-Smith and K7178) escorted a reconnaissance Blenheim of 113 Sqn taking off at 06:10, while another couple (K7106 piloted by F/O D. R. Walker and K7120 piloted by P/O S. N. Pearce) escorted another reconnaissance Blenheim of 113 Sqn. The first couple immediately became separated in low clouds and while Innes-Smith continued alone trying to rejoin his formation, the other two aircraft were intercepted by a reportedly five CR.32s. One of the 30 Sqn Blenheims (K7178) was shot down, killing the crew (pilot 21-year-old F/Lt Ian Cheesman Swann, observer 32-year-old P/O Herbert Paul Greenwood Fisher and wireless operator/air gunner 23-year-old Sgt John Young). The Blenheim from 113 Sqn returned to base badly damaged, reportedly (incorrectly) by anti-aircraft fire. The other Blenheims became separated too and Walker, who remained with the reconnaissance Blenheim, met another reconnaissance aircraft *"very badly damaged by machine gun and pom-pom fire"* five miles from Bardia. He escorted it as far as 20 miles south of Sidi Barrani, while at 07:40, Pearce encountered a CR.42, which he tried to attack but without success due to the manoeuvrability of his opponent. He was then chased for a short while by three CR.32s or CR.42s, landing finally at Ma'aten Bagush at 09:15.

Magg. Bruno Cudugnello's (CO 12ª *Gr.*) Fiat CR.32 (from the 160ª *Sq.*) was destroyed on the ground by British aircraft, before the Army was able to recover it.

During the same action, the British aircraft shot down an IMAM Ro.37, which they found in the same general area. The Italian pilot, *s. ten.* Dario Brigadue of 136ª *Sq.* was lost.

The 90ª *Sq.*'s Diary recorded:

"The units were informed that during the last hours of the morning a reconnaissance plane type Ro 37 piloted by s. ten. Brigadue was attacked by a Gloster and obliged to land. The crew that was running from the plane was strafed and s. ten. Brigadue was killed. For this reason we decide to throw a message to the English pilots to remind them that the enemy pilots shot down and obliged to bale out were always respected by the Italian pilots. To throw the message however we waited for superior orders."

The British reported that Lysander L4719 (F/O Aldis and Sgt McCue), took off at 08:30 for a morning reconnaissance and in a place described as *"a landing ground a few miles east of El Adem"*, at approximately 09:15, an Italian aircraft that immediately landed was noted. In the airstrip, another aircraft was already parked and Aldis attacked with his front guns the two two-seater aircraft, setting both on fire. The ground attack pilot then strafed the crew of the plane just landed, and noted that the Italian airmen were seen to fall as if killed. Aldis was unopposed during his action and landed safely at 11:00. He had destroyed the IMAM of Brigadue and the Fiat of Cudugnello.

This was a hard day for the Sunderlands of 230 Sqn detached to Malta.

N9029/V piloted by F/O Lywood, was attacked by two Fiat CR.42s for 20 minutes. He returned to Malta without damage, claiming a possible victory over its assailants.

L5804/S was attacked by four Macchi MC.200s (in fact a trio of fighters from the 6° *Gr. C.T.*) at 11:05 when off Syracuse. The engagement lasted a staggering 57 minutes, during which time three gunners received flesh wounds in the legs. Explosive and incendiary bullets of large calibre extensively damaged the Sunderland. The gunners, although wounded, continued to engage the enemy until the combat broke off. Much credit for the safe return of the aircraft was given to Second Fitter Leading Aircraftman D. A. Campbell, who remained in the wing of aircraft, plugging holes in the tanks until rendered unconscious by petrol fumes. He was revived by bullet splinters. Valuable assistance was also given by a special correspondent of Daily Mail, Alex Clifford. The plane landed at 12:15 and was immediately beached in sinking conditions. Back at base, one Macchi was claimed and one badly damaged. The flying-boat was back on operations on 14 October.

L2160/X piloted by F/Lt Garside on patrol from Malta, was intercepted by three Macchi MC.200s from the 6° *Gr.* at 16:40, after an unsuccessful attack on an Italian submarine. After a 15 minute long engagement the Sunderland escaped, landing back at Malta at 17:55. The British crew reported that one Italian fighter was forced to break off the engagement with smoke pouring from the engine after the first attack, while after the third attack another Macchi was shot down. The Italians appeared to be unable to manage with the low height and evasive actions of the flying-boat. On neither occasion did the Italian fighters receive any damage, but the running battle earned the Sunderland the nickname of the "*Flying Porcupine*". In fact, in the light of these and the following engagements the "*Flying turtle*" should have been a more correct nickname.

29 July 1940

An SM 79 was lost north of Sidi Barrani. Together with 40 other bombers of the 10°, 14° and 33° *Stormi* it was trying to attack a British naval group that was shelling Bardia. Its unit is unknown but it was part of the 33° or 14° *Stormi* because the 10° *Stormo* didn't suffer any loss on this occasion.

Between 27 and 29 July the ships were attacked many times by Dodecanese and Libyan based aircraft; HMS *Liverpool* was hit by a bomb which penetrated two decks without exploding, and HMAS *Sydney* suffered bomb splinter damage that wrecked its spotter aircraft and wounded a few of its crew.

HMS *Eagle*'s little band of fighters were again engaged. Lieutenant Kenneth Keith and Lieutenant (A) Patrick Massy were on patrol when two flights of three SM 79s were seen at 15,000 feet. Keith attacked the left-hand aircraft in one flight, which broke formation at once and fled for home, apparently without dropping its bombs. He then attacked that on the right, this jettisoning its cargo and losing height rapidly to disappear in the clouds (Keith was credited with one damaged SM 79). Meanwhile Massy was after the right hand machine of the other flight. After five separate attacks, it caught fire and dived into the sea, an explosion being seen in the rear fuselage just before it went into the water. Two members of the crew baled out and HMS *Capetown* picked up one of them alive. By now, Massy was some way from the convoy and almost out of fuel. He was obliged to ditch near HMAS *Stuart*, one of the escorting destroyers, and was picked up safely.

Massy's victim was most likely the Libyan SM 79 lost this day, even if Italian records claimed it was shot down by AA fire.

The 10° *Gr.* took off at 17:05 for a routine evening patrol over the Bardia-Amseat-Sidi Rezegh area. *magg.* Carlo Romagnoli leading *cap.* D'Agostinis, *m. llo.* Chianese, *ten.* Martissa and *serg.* Rosa of the 91ª *Sq.*, *ten.* Guiducci, *s. ten.* De Benedetti and *serg. magg.* Savini of the 90ª *Sq.* and *cap.*

Monti, *ten.* Vanni and *ten.* Giuseppe Aurili of the 84[a] *Sq.* During the mission, Chianese was seen to suddenly dive towards the ground and was followed by the entire formation assuming that he had discovered some sort of target on ground. In truth, weakened by the insufficient alimentation and the bad hygienic conditions of El Adem, Chianese had lost consciousness, regaining control only when a few metres from the ground. Once at base he was sent back to Gorizia. Chianese was a veteran of the Spanish Civil War (one of the very first Italian pilots to go there) where he had gained at least a couple of individual victories and one of the best aerobatic pilots of the *Stormo*. He never regained active service but his experience was used in the Fighter School of Gorizia. Chianese was almost an ace with four individual and four shared victories confirmed plus a fifth individual unconfirmed during the Spanish Civil War.

A Short Sunderland in Gibraltar harbour in the summer of 1940.
[via Bartłomiej Belcarz]

August 1940

Regia Aeronautica

Fighters

On 1 August, *cap.* Domenico Bevilacqua was transferred to the 77ª *Sq.*, 13° *Gr.* from the 94ª *Sq.*, 8° *Gr.* and took command of this *Sq.*

On 9 August, the 8° *Gr.* had 17 CR.42s on charge at Benghazi Berka.

On 10 August, three fighters from the 93ª *Sq.* went to N2 (Derna - El Ftàiah) on alarm duty and on 18 August they were joined by six more pilots from the 92ª and 93ª *Squadriglie*.

Finally on 28 August, the complete 92ª *Sq.* was moved to Derna with six CR.42s and pilots for the defence of that base, but only three of the fighters were combat-ready.

The 13° *Gr.* had no less then 34 aircraft on hand, but only three were combat-ready (it had taken on charge most of the surviving aircraft of the 8° *Gr.* when this unit retired to Berka on 22 July).

With the arrival at El Adem T3 of the other two *Squadriglie* of the 9° *Gr.*, the 13° *Gr.* was pulled out of line on 9 August and moved to Benghazi Berka for repair and refitting with anti-sand equipment for engines and guns.

On 22 August however, two pilots from the 77ª *Sq.* were ordered back to Tmini where they formed an alarm section. On the same date, three more pilots of the same *Squadriglia* were ordered to Ain el Gazala T4 to form another alarm section. During September, these sections were reinforced with pilots of the other *Squadriglie*.

Reinforcements continued to be flown in from Italy and around 11 August no less than 46 CR.42s where ferried to Castel Benito by the pilots of the 18° *Gr.* 16 of them were taken in charge by the 13° *Gr.* in Berka on 14 August while eight more went to the 93ª and 94ª *Squadriglie* on 26 August.

Fiat CR.42s of the 73ª Squadriglia, 9° Gruppo C.T. at El Adem. [Oblach via Fulvio Chianese – Associazione Culturale 4° Stormo di Gorizia.]

Magg. Ernesto Botto, at the head of the 97ª *Sq.*, 9º *Gr.*, flew back to Benghazi on 5 August, while a section of three fighters commanded by *s. ten.* Riccardo Vaccari landed at Derna and remained there on alarm duty.

Finally, on 7 August the whole 9º *Gr.* was called to front line duty.

The next day the 73ª *Sq.* arrived at El Adem T3 airfield, while Ernesto Botto still was in Benghazi with the rest of the *Gruppo*.

On 15 August *col.* Michele Grandinetti, Commander of the 4º *Stormo*, arrived at El Adem from Gorizia to take command of his unit when he relieved *magg.* Carlo Romagnoli from his temporary command; efficiency was good with 27 aircraft for the 9º *Gr.* and 17 aircraft for the 10º *Gr.*

By 24 August the 9º *Gr.* had 27 fighters operational and the 10º *Gr.* had 21 fighters.

Personnel from the 92ª Squadriglia, 8º Gruppo C.T.
[via Renato Zavattini]

Personnel from the 92ª Squadriglia, 8º Gruppo C.T. testing a dugout. Tenente Ranieri Carlo Piccolomini Clementini Adami holds the mascot of the Squadriglia.
[via Renato Zavattini]

Left: Tenente Ranieri Carlo Piccolomini Clementini Adami of the 92ª Squadriglia, 8º Gruppo C.T. posing. *[via Renato Zavattini]*

Right: Pilot from the 92ª Squadriglia, 8º Gruppo C.T. posing. *[via Renato Zavattini]*

Personnel from the 92ª Squadriglia, 8º Gruppo C.T. during a practise scramble to the air-raid shelter. *[via Renato Zavattini]*

Fiat CR.42s of the 92ª Squadriglia, 8º Gruppo C.T. *[via Renato Zavattini]*

93

On 17 August the 4º *Stormo* received two new pilots when *s. ten.* Paolo Berti was posted to the 84ª *Sq.*, 8º *Gr.*, while *serg. magg.* Giovanni Casero was posted to the 91ª *Sq.*, 10º *Gr.*, around the same time. Casero had served as instructor in the Spanish Air Force until July 1940.

Ground attack forces

On 9 August, 13 twin-engined Breda Ba.88 *Lince* (Lynx) fighter-bombers of the 7º *Gr. Combattimento* arrived at Castle Benito near Tripoli. This was the first unit arriving in North Africa with this eagerly awaited type. The type had however suffered a very disappointing start and was plagued with reliability problems. The problems were well known but decision was nevertheless taken to deploy the Bredas in Libya, hoping to solve them quickly in the new African bases since ground attack aircraft were in great demand.

The unit was commanded by *magg.* Marcello Fossetta and its three *Squadriglie* were commanded by *ten.* Valentino Festa (76ª *Sq.*), *ten.* Bruno Politi (86ª *Sq.*) and *ten.* Saverio Gostini (98ª *Sq.*).

The *Gruppo* had taken off from its home-base of Lonate Pozzolo on 5 August with 20 aircraft. First stop was Capua airfield near Napoli, where only seventeen planes arrived after engine failure on the aircraft flown by *serg. magg.* Gatti, *m. llo.* Giovanni Orofino and *ten.* Sergio Maurer. Luckily, all the crew survived the forced landings almost unhurt. In the afternoon of the same day the *Gruppo* proceeded to Sicily, where it landed at Castelvetrano airfield losing another Breda when *ten.* Elio Martire's Breda was damaged in a landing accident, while *ten.* Bruno Politi succeeded in landing notwithstanding a broken engine. On 9 August the *Gruppo* took off for the last part of the trip to Africa, but at Castel Benito only thirteen aircraft arrived, the Bredas of *m. llo.* Del Zotto and *serg. magg.* Giardini force landing on the island of Pantelleria (engine breakdowns), while *ten.* Maurer destroyed another plane in a landing accident caused by a faulty fuel supply system (Maurer and his gunner were wounded). The damaged aircraft were repaired and four spare Bredas were immediately sent to Africa to raise the strength of the *Gruppo* to twenty planes.

The Ba.88 was destined to never meet the enemy. After a month of acclimatisation, trying to work out their many problems, a desperate attempt to use them in action at least one time was made during the September offensive against Egypt.

On 10 August the 159ª *Sq.* received four IMAM Ro.41s for local day and night defence.

On 12 August *ten. col.* Alberto Moresco took command of the 50º *Stormo* after *col.* Pietro Molino.

At this time the strength of the 50º *Stormo* was 18 Breda Ba.65s, 24 Fiat CR.32s and four IMAM Ro.41s combat-ready.

Between 16 July and 15 August the *Stormo* didn't suffer any losses to its Breda Ba.65s.

From 20 to 30 August, the CR.32 *quater*s of the 160ª *Sq.* intensified training with 15 kilo bombs using real munitions and captured British armoured vehicles as targets. Studying the best angle of impact of their bombs against the enemy's armour plates, Duilio Fanali's men developed an attack system that made the approach at 1500 metres and then, 60 seconds after the target disappeared from the sight of the pilot, the final dive at an angle of sixty degrees.

Bombers

The bomber force of the 5ª *Squadra Aerea*, notwithstanding reinforcements and few losses suffered in the air (only seven aircraft in two months; five of them to AA fire), was down to 71 combat-ready aircraft. The main reason for this was the wear caused by sand, suffered because of the continuous missions almost always done at full strength by all the *Stormi* of the *Squadra*.

During the first months of war, the Vª *Squadra Aerea* was unable to attack Alexandria Harbour because its units were mainly concentrating on tactical support missions over the front and against the British Army main bases at Sidi Barrani and Mersa Matruh. The few Savoia S.81 and SM 79 bombers of *Aeronautica dell'Egeo* mainly carried out the attacks on Alexandria. During August, the Vª *Squadra* also started to take part in small-scale night attacks. From British sources, it is know that during the months of July and August, damage suffered from a reported nine night raids was one mooring vessel sunk (possibly the freighter burned on the night of 25/26 July), splinter damage, which killed one rating on the netlayer HMS *Protector*, and an incendiary bomb hit on an Armament Supply Issuing Ship (ASIS), which acted as floating ammunition depot. This last hit could have developed into a tragedy for the Royal Navy, but luckily the ASIS was empty when hit. Considering the very low number of aircraft used in these attacks, results were not so bad.

Reparto Speciale Aerosilurante landed at Benghazi Berka during the afternoon on 12 August.

This special unit was hastily formed in Gorizia on 25 July, and was intended to be the Italian response to the successful Swordfish raids of the FAA.

Command of the unit was given to *magg.* Vicenzo Dequal, the other crew chiefs were *magg.* Enrico Fusco, *ten.* Carlo Emanuele Buscaglia, *ten.* Franco Melley, *ten.* Carlo Copello, *s. ten.* Guido Robone. They were equipped with five Savoia Marchetti SM 79 bombers modified to carry a Whitehead 450 mm aerial torpedo.

On 12 August the 54º *Gr. Aut. B.T.* (218ª *Sq.* and 219ª *Sq.*), under command of *ten. col.* Colavolpe, became operational. They were based at Ain El Gazala T4, equipped with a mix of Savoia S.81s and SM 79s, and were intended only for night bombing duties.

On 18 August the 175ª *Sq.* had six SM 79 (3 combat-ready), the 10º *Stormo* had 23 (16 combat-ready), the 14º *Stormo* had 27 (22 combat-ready), the 15º *Stormo* had 29 (14 combat-ready) and finaly the 33º *Stormo* (including the 33º *Gr.*) had 45 SM 79s (23 combat-ready).

Royal Air Force

Reinforcements

On 1 August Air Marshal Arthur Longmore was advised of the arrival of new reinforcements for the Middle East Command. Six Wellingtons, coming via Malta, would replace the Bombays, an aircraft carrier, HMS *Argus*, would ferry 24 Hurricanes as soon as possible, and a further twenty-four were being sent to the South African Air Force.

Fighters

On 1 August 80 Sqn's 'B' Flight moved up to Sidi Barrani on the Libyan Front and replaced 33 Sqn's 'B' Flight, which returned to the Suez Canal zone to rest and convert to Hurricanes.

'C' Flight of 80 Sqn arrived at Sidi Barrani on 8 August, while 'A' Flight remained at Amriya.

On 12 August 'A' Flight of 80 Sqn, still at Amriya, protecting Alexandria with its Hurricanes, was joined by the Free French Flight No.2 with two Morane MS.406s and two Potez 63.11s.

S/Ldr William Hickey took command over 80 Sqn on 27 August 1940, replacing S/Ldr Patrick Dunn.

On 3 August, a sub-flight of 'A' Flight, 112 Sqn, was detached to Sidi Barrani.

On 17 August, 'A' and 'C' Flights of 112 Sqn were positioned at 'Z' Landing Ground (Matruh West) and 'Y' Landing Ground, about 11 miles further west. From here they were ordered to patrol over units of the Mediterranean fleet.

On 30 August 'C' Flight of 112 Sqn was posted to Sidi Barrani (East and West satellites).

'B' Flight in Sudan was finally detached from 112 Sqn on 31 August 1940, becoming 'K' Flight and subsequently forming the nucleus of 250 Sqn, formed on 1 April 1941 at Aqir.

On 19 August, Patrick Dunn left 80 Sqn to form 274 Sqn on the first Hurricanes in Egypt, with nine of the pilots from 'A' Flight (the Hurricane Flight) of 80 Sqn. Among these pilots were Peter Wykeham-Barnes, Ralph Evers-Swindell, Arthur Weller and John Lapsley. 'C' Flight from 33 Sqn was also incorporated into this new squadron.

The first six operational Hurricanes were P2544, P2638, P2639, P2641, P2643 and P2651, while L1669 was used mainly for conversion and training duties. One flight of the new squadron

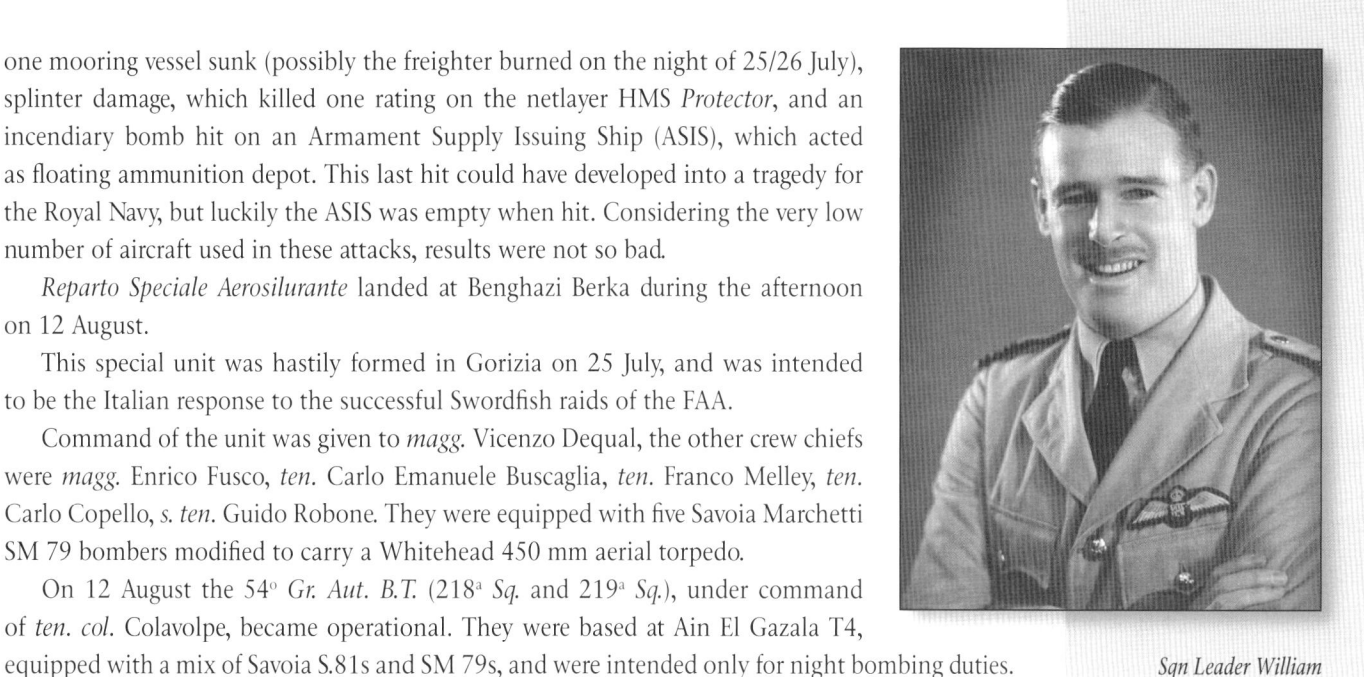

Sqn Leader William Hickey who took command of 80 Sqn on 27 August 1940 replacing Sqn Leader Patrick Dunn. Hickey was an Australian who was seconded from the RAAF to the RAF in 1931. He continued to lead 80 Sqn until 21 December 1940 when he was killed in combat with Fiat CR.42s over Greece.
[via David Park]

remained equipped with Gloster Gladiators, six of them being used mainly for training purposes (N5750, N5756, N5786, N5810, N5819 and N5829).

Since they took over all 80 Sqn's Hurricanes, this latter squadron re-equipped with Gladiators over the next few weeks.

The Moranes and Potez 63.11s of the Free French Flight, now fitted with desert air filters, were also absorbed into 274 Sqn, becoming its 'C' Flight, while the Martins were sent to Aden (where both were subsequently shot down by the Italians) and the light aircraft (the Bloch 81 and two Simouns) joined the Communications Flight as Free French Flight No. 3 at Heliopolis. The French airmen with the various Flights were offered honorary RAF ranks. *Capitaine* Jacquier, the Fighter Flight Commander, become a F/Lt while others received the rank equivalent to their *Armée de l'Air* status. Not all accepted the offer, and these were allowed to retain their French ranks. On learning of the absorption into the RAF of several of his officers, *Général* De Gaulle, the leader of the Free French, angrily declared his intention to denounce them as deserters and thereby liable to arrest and trial for desertion should they enter French-controlled territory, since Prime Minister Churchill had agreed that De Gaulle's volunteers should be recognised as a French force with its own uniforms and discipline! The Prime Minister was forced to intervene and a compromise was reached. However, the French Flight's association with 274 Sqn was soon interrupted when orders were received at the end of the month for it to proceed to Haifa in Palestine. The French pilots were already in action there on 6 September.

Bombers

Between 13 and 16 August, 'A' Flight of 45 Sqn returned from Sudan (with only five aircraft).

On 26 August, 211 Sqn at Qotaifiya welcomed the arrival of a Blenheim Mk.IV, coming directly from England.

Reconnaissance forces

On 10 August, 'C' Flight of 208 Sqn commanded by F/Lt J. R. Wilson relieved 'A' Flight at Sidi Barrani.

On 19 August, S/Ldr Charles Ryley left 230 Sqn and took command of 33 Sqn at Helwan.

On 21 August, Sunderland L2159 was received as reinforcement for 230 Sqn.

The aircraft was soon lost when on 26 August it force landed in neutral territory (St. Nikolo Bay, Kithera), flown by F/Lt Campbell.

112 Sqn line up for an official photo after their arrival in Egypt.
[via Alex Crawford]

Royal Australian Air Force

On 15 July 1940 the 3 Sqn RAAF embarked on RMS *Orontes* at Sydney for service in the Middle East on army co-operation duties. At this time, the unit consisted of the following flying personnel:

S/Ldr Ian McLachlan (CO).

'A' Flight: Flight Lieutenant Gordon Steege (OC), F/O Alan Gatward, F/O Alan Boyd, P/O Peter Turnbull and P/O Wilfred Arthur.

'B' Flight: P/O Charles Gaden (OC), P/O L. E. Knowles, P/O V. East, F/O Alan Rawlinson and F/O B. L. Bracegirdle.

'C' Flight: S/Ldr P. R. Heath (OC), F/Lt Blake Pelly, P/O J. M. Davidson, F/O John Perrin and P/O M D. Ellerton.

In total the squadron had 21 officers and 271 of other ranks on 24 July.

On 7 August RMS *Orontes* arrived at Bombay, and the unit was transhipped the same day to HT *Dilwara*. This ship sailed on 11 August and arrived at Suez on 23 August, where the squadron disembarked at Port Tewfik.

Owing to the fact that the aircraft with which the squadron was to be equipped had not arrived from England, RAF Headquarters Middle East had arranged for the squadron to be divided into three sections, each section being attached to a different station. The squadron was divided into sections to enable the technical personnel to be attached to units at which they would receive the most useful training, pending the arrival of the squadron's aircraft. The headquarters of the squadron was posted to 250 Wing, Ismailia, a section of the squadron to Abu Sueir and the remaining section to Aboukir, pending the receipt of aircraft, when the whole squadron would be located at Ismailia.

On 27 August, the pilots of 3 Sqn RAAF commenced flying practise on Miles Magisters placed at the disposal of the squadron pending the receipt of service type aircraft. The squadron received a Lysander on 31 August on loan for training purposes.

Operations

1 August 1940

Ten. Franco Lucchini, *serg.* Alfredo Sclavo and *serg.* Bruno Bortoletti, all of the 90ª *Sq.*, went to Tmini M2 airfield (around 100km west of Tobruk near the Gulf of Bomba) on alarm duty.

4 August 1940

Sidi Barrani and Mersa Matruh were subject to heavy bombing during the day. The railway station at Mersa Matruh was attacked in the morning by twelve SM 79s from the 10º *Stormo*. The bombers were attacked by a formation of Gladiators, one of which was claimed shot down by the gunners of the SM 79s. No losses were suffered by the Italian formation. The intercepting Gladiators were from 'A' Flight of 112 Sqn, which claimed to have hit one of the Savoias in a reported formation of five Italian bombers.

Sidi Barrani was attacked at 12:00 and at 16:50 from 10,000 feet. The second attack was performed by a formation of the 10º *Stormo* commanded by *ten. col.* Unia. The aerodrome was temporarily rendered unserviceable, and two Lysanders of 208 Sqn were hit. One was slightly damaged, requiring a new petrol tank, and one more seriously, needing a new main plane.

During the morning, 80 Sqn's 'B' Flight received a signal from headquarters to provide four Gladiators to escort a Lysander from 208 Sqn. Flown by P/O Burwell, this was to observe enemy troops movement at Bir Taieb el Esem on the other side of the Libyan border. 'Pat' Pattle (Gladiator Mk.I K7910) decided to lead the escort and took with him F/O Peter Wykeham-Barnes (L8009), P/O Johnny Lancaster (K7923) and Sgt Kenneth George Russell Rew (K7908). They took of at 17:15 and reached the rendezvous point in ten minutes, where they found the Lysander circling at 6000 feet. Wykeham-Barnes and Rew took up a position about 3000 feet above and immediately behind the Lysander, whilst Pattle and Lancaster climbed 1000 feet higher on the starboard flank. The aircraft crossed the border a few miles south of Sidi Omar twenty minutes later, and followed the sand tracks leading to their target.

During the same morning eleven CR.42s of the 97ª *Sq.* went from Benghazi-Berka to El Adem T3, together with twelve other CR.42s from the 96ª *Sq.*, which had arrived the previous day, and nine CR.42s of the 10º *Gr.*, to cover the 2ª *Divisione Libica* of *Regio Esercito*. This Division was marching from Bir el Gobi to Gabr Saleh.

In the meantime, a concentration of British armoured vehicles was discovered in the Bir Sheferzen area, around 30 kilometres south-west of Sollum, near the border where a logistic outpost of the Western Desert Force was located. Consequently an air attack was planned.

At 16:50, a formation of assault aircraft of the 50º *Stormo* took off, together with an escorting group of Fiat CR.42 fighters of the 4º *Stormo*. The assault aircraft took off from Tobruk T2bis and comprised twelve aircraft of the resident 12º *Gr. Assalto*. They included six Breda Ba.65/A80s of the 159ª *Sq.*, armed with 2kg bombs (the Bredas could carry up to 168 of these small calibre bombs), commanded by the *Squadriglia* Commander *cap.* Antonio Dell'Oro and flown by *ten.* Adriano Visconti, *ten.* Fioravante Montanari (who led the second section), *serg. magg.* Giovanni Bianchelli, *serg. magg.* Gianni Pappalepore and *serg. magg.* Paolo Perno. The other six were Fiat CR.32 *quaters* of the 160ª *Sq.*, armed with eight 2kg bombs and divided in two groups of three. The first group led by *cap.* Duilio Fanali (*Sq.* CO) included *s. ten.* Giuseppe Mezzatesta and *serg. magg.* Corrado Sarti as wingmen, while the second group was lead by *s. ten.* Giuseppe Rossi with *s. ten.* Mirko Erzetti and *m. llo.* Romolo Cantelli as wingmen.

The Italian fighter escort took off from El Adem T3 and was composed of 31 CR.42s (ten from the 97ª *Sq.*, eleven from the 96ª *Sq.*, one from the 73ª *Sq.* and nine from the 10º *Gr.*). At the head of the two formations were *magg.* Ernesto Botto (in the aircraft from the 73ª *Sq.*) and *magg.* Carlo Romagnoli. Pilots from the 97ª *Sq.* were *cap.* Antonio Larsimont Pergameni, *s. ten.* Giovanni Barcaro, *serg.* Franco Sarasino, *s. ten.* Riccardo Vaccari, *serg.* Angelo Golino, *s. ten.* Jacopo Frigerio, *serg. magg.* Otello Perotti, *m. llo.* Vanni Zuliani, *serg. magg.* Raffaello Novelli and *serg. magg.* Massimo Salvatore. Pilots from the 10º *Gr.* were apart from *magg.* Romagnoli, *cap.* Giuseppe D'Agostinis, *ten.* Enzo Martissa, *s. ten.* Ruggero Caporali and *serg. magg.* Lorenzo Migliorato from the 91ª *Sq.*, *cap.* Luigi Monti and *ten.* Giuseppe Aurili from the 84ª *Sq.* and *ten.* Franco Lucchini and *serg.* Amleto Monterumici from the 90ª *Sq.*

Fiat CR.42s of the 92ª Squadriglia, 8º Gruppo C.T. in the air. [via Renato Zavattini]

The two Italian formations met at a rendezvous point twenty kilometres east of El Adem and then headed for the target. The 4° *Stormo*'s aircraft flew at heights between 3500 and 4500 meters, the Fiat CR.32s at 1000 meters and the Bredas at 300 meters.

On the way towards the frontline, at 5000 m over Ridotta Capuzzo, they spotted a formation of nine Blenheims heading to El Adem, escorted by many Glosters Gladiators. Aircraft of the 96ª *Sq.* and the 10° *Gr.* attacked the bombers and then chased the fighters. In the fierce combat that followed, *ten.* Lucchini claimed a Gladiator with the use of 385 rounds of ammunition. Pilots from the 91ª *Sq.* claimed two Gladiators and three Blenheims as shared, with two additional Gladiators as shared probables (one of the Glosters was most probably the same claimed by Lucchini). *cap.* Monti and *ten.* Aurili claimed to have damaged two Blenheims each and then reported being credited with the three Blenheims shot down by the *Stormo*'s formation as shared. The pilots from the 90ª *Sq.* claimed the same three Blenheims and a Gladiator jointly with the 96ª *Sq.* and other pilots of the 10° *Gr.* plus the individual victory of Lucchini and recorded "*other Glosters shot down by pilots of 9° and 10° Gruppi*". At the end of the combat, *magg.* Botto, who personally claimed a damaged British bomber with the use of 200 rounds of ammunition, recorded ten enemy aircraft shot down together with other units. Apart from the five confirmed and two probables already detailed, the remaining victories should be those of the 50° *Stormo*. More prudently, the 10° *Gr.*'s Diary claimed only three Blenheims and a single Gloster shot down.

The 97ª *Sq.*, covering at a higher altitude, spotted first six Blenheims, which were attacked by the other *Squadriglie* and then three other Blenheims that were heading towards Egyptian territory, and dived to pursue them. *cap.* Larsimont Pergameni and *serg.* Sarasino chased them for a while, claiming hits.

The fighters from the 97ª *Sq.* had most probably attacked a trio of Blenheim Mk.Is (L8667, L8391 and L8530) from 55 Sqn, which had been ordered at short notice to bomb up and meet two flights from other squadrons over Ma'aten Bagush at 17:00, to attack an Italian M. T. convoy, 13 miles east of Bir El Gobi (obviously the Libyan division). Commanded by P/O T. O. Walker in L8667, they missed the rendezvous with the other squadrons over Ma'aten Bagush and headed alone towards the front. After crossing the frontier, the trio spotted a big formation of about 25 CR.42s (4° *Stormo*'s formation). Twelve of these fighters started in pursuit as the Blenheims turned for home (the 97ª *Sq.* formation). A running engagement lasting seven minutes started, after which the Italian fighters broke off without having caused or suffered any damage. The other RAF squadrons involved in this combat were 211 Sqn and most probably 112 and 113 Sqns. 211 Sqn was up with two Blenheims piloted by S/Ldr Bax (L8533) and F/Lt G. D. Jones (L8532), which were intercepted by a reportedly 40-50 fighters. Sgt J. McIntosh, gunner of L8532, was wounded in the forearm and it seems that the aircraft was badly damaged and forced to land before reaching its base, since it was salvaged by 51 RSU at Sidi Barrani on 10 August but Struck off Charge on 20 September. The total lack of records of 113 Sqn and the high level of incompleteness of those of 112 Sqn makes it quite difficult to reconstruct their contribution to the combat. It seems however probable that at least three Gladiators of 112 Sqn were around this area at the time, because it is known that P/O s R. H. Clarke, Homer Cochrane and B. B. E. Duff left Maaten Gerawla during the day for Sidi Barrani, with the task of patrolling over Sidi Omar (extremely close to the area where the evening combat developed). No encounters with the enemy are however recorded in the fragmentary reconstructed ORB of the unit.

The formation from the 50° *Stormo* continued alone towards the border, arriving over Bir Sheferzen (around thirty kilometres south and slightly east of the position where the escort left it) at 17:20, where they discovered numerous British vehicles, that were immediately attacked by the Bredas and Fanali's trio of CR.32s, while Rossi's stayed at 1000 meters as cover. The Italian aircraft performed two passes over the vehicles and while they were preparing the third the 208 Sqn Lysander and 80 Sqn Gladiators came into the area. The crew of the Lysander spotted the Italians first and alerted the escort with a red Very light before heading due east at low altitude to reach safety. P/O Burwell carried some bombs that he tried to aim at Italian transports that he saw in the vicinity but missed, then he was forced to return by the strong opposition encountered.

Pattle and Lancaster dived down but failed to spot any enemy aircraft. Wykeham-Barnes and Rew had also disappeared but a few seconds later Pattle heard Wykeham-Barnes over the radio ordering Rew to attack. Immediately afterwards Pattle saw a reported seven Breda Ba.65s in two separate flights - one containing three aircraft in vic formation and the other made up of two pairs, heading east hunting the Lysander.

Wykeham-Barnes and Rew attacked the formation of four Bredas before they could reach the Lysander, and Wykeham-Barnes shot down one of them in flames immediately, but at the same time Rew was shot down and killed. Pattle and Lancaster meanwhile attacked the other three Italians from astern. The Bredas dispersed, and all four Gladiators separated as they each selected a different enemy machine as a target. Pattle attacked two aircraft, which kept close together and turned in a complete circle. The Bredas dropped to around 200 feet and each released two bombs. This reduced weight meant that they slowly began to creep away from Pattle's slower Gladiator. Suddenly they however turned north towards the fighter base at El Adem. Pattle quickly cut inside their turn and closed in to 150 yards. He delivered a quarter attack on the nearest Breda but his two port guns almost immediately ceased firing. His aim had been good however, and he had hit one of the Italians who slowed down considerably. He swung in directly astern of it and, after a few more bursts from his remaining two guns, saw a puff of white smoke from the starboard side of the engine. He continued to attack the Breda, which dropped lower and lower and finally force-landed on good ground five miles further on. The second Breda got away. Lancaster had also been having trouble with his guns. After his initial burst, all four guns jammed and he spent the next ten minutes frantically pulling his Constantinescu gear pistons and aiming at various enemy aircraft, but without any further bullets leaving his guns. Eventually he was forced to go on to the defensive and got an explosive bullet in the left arm and shoulder. Because he feared the loss of blood would cause him to lose consciousness, he wriggled out of the fight and with his right thumb pressed tightly against his left radial artery, held the stick between his knees and waggled his way home. In spite of his wounds and the serious damage to his Gladiator, he made quite a smooth landing before losing consciousness. It is reported that the fitter who came to examine the aircraft shortly afterwards pronounced it too damaged to repair in situ, and ordered it to be burned forthwith! However, in fact it seems that even if 80 Sqn didn't fly it any more, Gladiator Mk.I K 7923 was repaired and later in the year passed to the Greek Air Force.

After claiming the Breda, Wykeham-Barnes was attacked by the CR.32s. He claimed one of them before another attacked him, which hit his Gladiator. In his Combat Fighter Report he recorded: *"The left side of the instrument panel and most of the windscreen went and two bullets came through the back of the seat before I could close the throttle, and the CR 32 passed under me. My machine then fell into a dive and I abandoned it, landing by parachute."* He had received a shrapnel wound. He was also to receive a swollen tongue and a pair of very painful blistered feet before being rescued by a detachment of 11th Hussars, who brought him back to Sidi Barrani.

Four of the Bredas were damaged and in particular that of *serg. magg.* Perno, which was hit fifty times and the pilot was slightly wounded in the leg, before Fanali's Fiats were able to intervene. In the meantime, it was the section of *s. ten.* Rossi, which was waiting higher up for its turn to attack, that first fell over the RAF fighters, taking them by surprise. After the sharp initial attack of the Fiats the combat developed into a WW I style dogfight which lasted fifteen minutes. At the end all the Italian aircraft returned to base claiming three of the enemies; one by Fanali (probably Wykeham-Barnes) and two by Cantelli (probably Rew and Lancaster).

One of the damaged Bredas was piloted by *ten.* Adriano Visconti who pressed home his attacks against the enemy armoured vehicles, notwithstanding the enemy's fighter opposition. The behaviour of Visconti in this particular combat deeply impressed his commander *cap.* Dell'Oro who proposed him for a *Medaglia d'argento al Valor Militare*. The citation for this award, which Visconti received "in the field", stated that: *"During a strafing attack against enemy armoured vehicles*

Bombs at the ground at the 92ª Squadriglia, 8º Gruppo's airfield. [via Renato Zavattini]

A mascot of the 92ª Squadriglia, 8º Gruppo C.T. [via Renato Zavattini]

Ground crews from the 90ª Squadriglia at El Adem in August 1940. [Historical Office Italian Air Force]

he pressed home his attacks careless of an enemy fighter that was following him shooting at him from short distance (...) and with its last ammunition he succeeded in burning one of the armoured cars of the enemy(...)".

After Pattle had claimed the Breda he broke away while attempting, without much success, to clear his port fuselage gun. Immediately, he was attacked by five biplanes (identified as CR.42s) diving towards him from the direction of El Adem, which was approximately 10 miles northwest. He flew on, pretending that he had not seen the Italians, until they were almost in position to open fire and then, with a flick of the wrist and a sharp prod of the foot, shot up and away from the Fiats. The Italians split up and attacked him independently from all directions. The Fiats made repeated attacks simultaneously from the quarter and beam, using the speed they gained in the dive to regain altitude. After each attack Pattle was forced on to the defensive and turned away from each attack, occasionally delivering a short attack on the most suitably target as it dived past. One Fiat on completing its attack turned directly in front of his Gladiator, presenting him with an excellent deflection shot at close range. He fired a long burst with his remaining two guns, which caused the Italian fighter to turn slowly onto its back and then spin down towards the desert. Pattle last saw it spinning at 200 feet and didn't claim it for sure, but was later credited with this victory. Soon after his starboard wing gun also jammed, but fortunately at the same time the remaining Italian fighters broke away. He was now 40 miles behind enemy lines with only one gun operational, and he turned for home at 1000 feet altitude.

When some miles north-west of Bir Taieb El Essem, he was again spotted and attacked by twelve CR.42s and three Breda Ba.65s. The Bredas broke away after a few dives, while the CR.42s attacked. They used the same tactics as the five earlier had used, with quarter and beam attacks. Within a few seconds Pattle's remaining gun jammed because of an exploded round in the breach, so he attempted to make the border by evasive tactics and heading east at every opportunity. He soon discovered that one of the Italian pilots was an exceptional shot who made repeated attacks using full deflection with great accuracy. Each time this particular Italian came in, he had to use all his skill and cunning to keep out of the sights of the Fiat. The remainder of the Italians as a whole lacked accuracy and did not press home their attacks to a decisive range. Nevertheless, their presence and the fact that he had to consider each attack made the work of the more determined pilot

Hits on Mersa Matruh railway station during an Italian bombing raid. [via Italian Air Force]

very much easier. He managed to keep this up for fully fifteen minutes before the Italian came out of a loop directly above Pattle's Gladiator and opened fire. Pattle turned away to avoid the bullets, but flew straight into the line of fire from another Fiat. The rudder controls were shot away, so he could no longer turn. He pulled back on the control column, climbed to about 400 feet and jumped. As he fell the parachute caught his foot, but he managed to kick it free and the main chute opened just in time for him to make a safe landing off the first swing. The time was now around 19:00. He started to walk towards what he thought was Egypt during the night, but found out at dawn to his horror that he had actually walked in the opposite direction, deeper into Libya. He turned around and crossed the border at around midday. At 16:00 on 5 August, he was rescued by a detachment from 11th Hussars, which brought him back to Sidi Barrani.

It is possible that Pattle was shot down by *ten.* Franco Lucchini.

6 August 1940

During the morning *ten.* Franco Lucchini and *serg.* Amleto Monterumici scrambled without success against an enemy intruder which they failed to intercept. While landing Lucchini's aircraft overturned and was heavily damaged. He thus missed the actions of the subsequent days.

In the afternoon, *cap.* Luigi Monti, *m. llo.* Emiro Nicola (84ª *Sq.*) and *serg.* Alessandro Bladelli (91ª *Sq.*) scrambled from T3 and intercepted a Short Sunderland 30 kilometres north west of Tobruk. Nicola was obliged to turn back when his guns jammed while Monti and Bladelli attacked the flying-boat.

The British aircraft was Sunderland N9025/OO-Y of 228 Sqn from Aboukir, flown by F/Lt T. M. W. Smith DFC (crew; F/O D. R. S. Bevan-John, P/O I. T. G. Stewart, Sgt H. J. Baxter, Leading Aircraftsman P. F. O. Davies, Leading Aircraftsman W. J. Pitt, AC1 W. D. Price, Leading Aircraftsman A. McWhinnie and Leading Aircraftsman Colin James Cambell Jones). They had replaced another Sunderland of 228 Sqn flown by S/Ldr Menzies, which had shadowed a small Italian convoy from the early morning.

Attacking from out of the sun the Italian fighters firstly put the rear turret out of action, and then with two separate attacks they disabled the right and left flank guns. Inside the Sunderland, the situation was very difficult - Baxter was wounded three times, Jones was hit in the stomach and died one hour later, while the flank gunner Davies was severely wounded in the stomach and the left eye. Two other members of the crew – Price and Pitt – were less severely wounded. One of the engines on the right wing was put out of action and the right fuel tank started to burn. The attack lasted fifteen minutes and Smith was forced to ditch at 16:20 near Tobruk (position 32° 19' N 23° 42' E).

Monti ordered Bladelli to return to T3, and he directed the Italian torpedo-boat *Rosolino Pilo* to the Sunderland before returning to Tobruk T2bis. Here he immediately took off in a CR.32 to continue to guide the Italian ship toward the British aircraft, which was reached at 19:00. The Sunderland had maintained w/t contact with base, and this only ceased when the Italian ship came alongside.

A CR.32 of the 160ª *Sq.*, flown by *serg.* Giovacchini, witnessed the whole action and continued to signal the position of the sinking Sunderland to *Rosolino Pilo's* crew while Monti was away.

The British crew was captured, except for Jones who had succumbed to his wounds and thus was left inside the Sunderland, which sank while the Italian sailors were trying to take it in tow. This was the first Sunderland admitted lost to the Italians in North Africa, and was shared between Monti and Bladelli.

A formation of 19 Fiats CR.42s of the 96ª and 73ª *Squadriglie*, commanded by *cap.* Roberto Fassi and *ten.* Vittorio Pezzè, together with five aircraft of the 10ª *Gr.*, commanded by *cap.* Giuseppe D'Agostinis, escorted a formation of bombers over Sollum without meeting any enemies. When they returned, the aircraft of *serg. magg.* Graziadio Rizzati of the 96ª *Sq.* was heavily damaged after a crash-landing due to engine failure.

8 August 1940

At 17:00, *magg.* Carlo Romagnoli (CO of the 10° *Gr.*) took off from El Adem T3 airfield with 15 other aircraft from the 9° and 10° *Gruppi* to patrol along the Egyptian border and to give indirect cover to five SM 79 bombers and a single reconnaissance Ro.37, which were out to patrol the same area. The five SM 79s were a formation from the 44ª *Sq.*, 35° *Gr.*, led by *cap.* Giuseppe Pagliacci, which were out to bomb enemy vehicles and aircraft in the Bir El Chreigat area.

Participating pilots were Romagnoli, *cap.* Giuseppe D'Agostinis (CO 91ª *Sq.*), *ten.* Enzo Martissa (91ª *Sq.*), *serg.* Aldo Rosa (91ª *Sq.*), *ten.* Giovanni Guiducci (CO 90ª *Sq.*), *serg. magg.* Angelo Savini (90ª *Sq.*), *cap.* Luigi Monti (CO 84ª*Sq.*), *ten.* Vittorio Pezzè (CO 73ª *Sq.*), *ten.* Valerio De Campo (73ª *Sq.*), *s. ten.* Carlo Battaglia (73ª *Sq.*), *s. ten.* Alvaro Querci (73ª *Sq.*), *m. llo.* Norino Renzi (73ª *Sq.*), *serg. magg.* Enrico Dallari (73ª *Sq.*), *serg. magg.* Antonio Valle (73ª *Sq.*), *serg.* Santo Gino (73ª *Sq.*) and *serg.* Lido Poli (73ª *Sq.*).

Immediately after take-off, Romagnoli started to climb, keeping the sun at his back. At 2500 meters over Gabr Saleh (around 65 kilometres south-east of El Adem and 35 kilometres east of Bir El Gobi, well inside the Italian territory) when the Italian formation was still climbing, *ten.* Pezzè saw two formations of Gloster Gladiators higher, and after giving the alarm to the *Gruppo* commander, tried to attack the enemy fighters frontally and from below.

Then, completely unseen by Pezzè and the other Italian pilots, a third formation of Glosters attacked the 73ª *Sq.* formation from above (the surviving Italian pilots estimated that each British formation was nine planes strong so, after the combat, they assessed that they fought against 27 enemy fighters for fifteen minutes).

The Gladiators were from 80 Sqn ('C' Flight had arrived at Sidi Barrani during the day, led by the commanding officer, S/Ldr 'Paddy' Dunn). At 17:40, 14 Gladiators from the squadron flew an offensive patrol in the neighbourhood of El Gobi, since it had been reported by observers that large formations of CR.42s had been patrolling a triangle between El Adem, Sidi Omar and El Gobi fairly regularly twice a day at about 07:00 and 18:15. It was decided to attempt to destroy a portion of this patrol. The mission had been suggested by S/Ldr Dunn as a reprisal and to re-establish *"the moral superiority already gained previously by other squadrons"* after the gruelling engagement on 4 August. Tactics had been carefully discussed by Dunn and his Flight Commanders, on the agreed assumption that if the engagement could be controlled for the initial two minutes, a decided advantage would be with the side in control. To do this, it was arranged that a Sub-Flight of the formation (Sub-Flight one) should fly low (at 8,000 feet) and slightly in front to act as bait. These three Gladiators were flown (after lots had been drawn) by Dunn (leader) (Gladiator K8009), F/O Peter Wykeham-Barnes (K7916) and P/O 'Heimar' Stuckey (K8022). The rest of the formation,

Tenente *Enzo Martissa's* Fiat CR.42 in August 1940.
[via Przemek Skulski]

Sqn Leader Dunn was the CO of 80 Sqn during their early actions against the Italians. He scored two victories on 8 August. Note the rear view mirror on the upper wing. [IWM neg. no. CM.42]

divided in three Sub-Flights of three fighters with an independent aircraft between the lower Sub-Flights, would be stepped at 10,000, 12,000 and 14,000 feet. The independent machine was that of F/Sgt Trevor Martin Vaughan (K7903), who attacked with Sub-Flight one. It seems that P/O Anthony Hugh Cholmeley flew a fourteenth Gladiator, but that he was forced to turn back early, probably with engine problems.

Sub-Flight two included F/Lt Ralph Evers-Swindell (leader) (L8010), F/O Wanklyn Flower (K8011) and F/O P. T. Dowding (K7912). Sub-Flight three included P/O Harold Sykes (leader) (K8003), Sgt Donald Gregory (K8051) and F/O Sidney Linnard (K8017). Sub-Flight four at 14,000 feet included F/Lt 'Pat' Pattle (leader) (K7971), F/O Greg Graham (L8008) and F/Sgt Sidney Richens (K7892). The plan was for Sub-Flight one to engage (or be engaged by) the Italians, do what it could until Sub-Flights two, three and four would be ordered to enter the combat on seeing the trend, the overall control being given to Sub-Flight four. All formations flew in a broad vic, and it was the first time that the 80 Sqn operated at full operational strength.

Just after 18:00, the squadron crossed the frontier south of Sidi Omar, and immediately changed course to head north towards Bir Taieb el Esem. At 18:25, as they were approaching Bir el Gobi, a formation of CR.42 flying in echelons was spotted by F/Lt Pattle. The Fiats were flying approximately parallel but reciprocal to the course of the British formation, and they were at 2 o'clock and slightly (500 feet) below the lower Sub-Flight. With a careful turn to the right, ordered by radio, Pattle put the 80 Sqn formation behind the Italian one, up-sun and between it and its base at El Adem, then a full boost and throttle stern chase began to catch up with the fast cruising (in fact climbing) Italian fighters. Pilots in the lower Sub-Flights now began to see their opponents, dead ahead and lower. The ideal attack position! S/Ldr Dunn counted 18 of them in four formations of seven, five, three and three; he was very close to the truth, but later Sub-Flight four reported that an additional Italian formation of nine planes was present and it was incorrectly assessed that the Italians were 27 in number, flying in nine sections of three aircraft. After an unobserved astern chase Sub-Flight one engaged the starboard flank of three aircraft and shot down all of them (they were probably part of the 73[a] *Sq.*). S/Ldr Dunn later reported:

"(...) I followed my first target down, who rolled over slowly on to his back with smoke coming out: Observed P/O. Stuckey's (No. 3 on my left) quarry in much the same condition and gave him a burst of my own, then pulled up and across the rear of the formation of 18 that was beginning to peel-off."

F/O Stuckey experienced a very successful combat:

Maresciallo Norino Renzi was born on 22 January 1912 in Russi (Ravenna). He joined the Regia Aeronautica *in 1929. He was assigned to the 4° Stormo and received his military pilot's license on 25 December 1930. He served with this unit until his death on 8 August 1940. Pre-war he was part of 4°* Stormo's *aerobatics group.*
[Romandini via Fulvio Chianese – Associazione Culturale 4° Stormo di Gorizia]

"(…) our C.O. led the first Flight and attacked the right hand enemy flight.

I was No. 3 of the C.O.'s Flight and managed to get in a long burst with full deflection as my opposite aircraft stall turned out of his formation. (later the C.O. said that he followed this aircraft down giving it bursts and saw it crash.

Immediately after I attacked No. 3 aircraft of the farthest flight and gave it a short burst before that flight broke up as well."

The third CR.42 of the section probably fell victim to F/Sgt Trevor Martin Vaughan. F/O Peter Wykeham-Barnes confirmed the shooting down of all three Italian CR.42s of the section. Wykeham-Barnes seems to have claimed the first Italian aircraft, witnessed by F/Lt Evers-Swindell.

After the attack by this Sub-Flight, the Italian fighters started to break, and Pattle ordered down the other two sections, while a wild low-altitude dogfight was beginning. S/Ldr Dunn continued his report:

"(…) A C.R.42 did a steep diving turn away from his formation and I was easily able to give him a full deflection shot for about 8 seconds, he continued in a dive with smoke issuing from him but as the formation of 18 was approaching around about me with advantage of number and height, it was impossible to pursue him. I claimed it definitely shot down and consider it to be one of the five observed on the ground by Sub 4 before entering. Then followed a long period of loose play in which numerous targets offered themselves.

At the same time large numbers of enemy aircraft attacked me, chiefly from straight ahead and beam but not driving home determinedly. In one of them I throttled back and stall turned on the attacker's tail before he was quite past me, he then rolled on to his back and dived down in the second half of a loop. I followed and gave this aircraft what I thought was an effective burst with the result that he did not recover and continued down with bluish smoke issuing from him.

The other flights had by now entered and attacked their opponents, and the number of enemy aircraft thinned down. Two or three enemy aircraft were still about ; I pulled up steeply to avoid one in particular who was dangerously near to my tail, having chased me down in the dive from the port quarter. In the ensuing black-out I have little knowledge of what he did but at the top of what was the first half of something like a rocket loop, I found myself going in the opposite direction with the aircraft climbing rapidly past me on my left and below, he then appeared ahead of me and did a slow roll, unfortunately, I was too surprised and failed to get him in my sight, whereupon he half rolled and dived out; another stall turn brought me on his tail, but he did a rapid dive, turned to the left and streamed off like a homing rabbit - next stop El Adem.

I engaged one more enemy aircraft but my guns failed to fire (after 300 rounds approx.) I tried to clear them but was only able to get one more short burst. I left the fight, gained height at 12,000 feet and returned to witness a dog-fight between three aircraft two of which were Gladiators. I then set off home and picked up two other Gladiators."

In the end, Dunn was credited with two confirmed victories and 1 probable, and reported that the Sub-Flight gained five confirmed victories and two unconfirmed.

P/O Stuckey was now in the middle of a whirling dogfight:

"I was then attacked from about 2 o'clock by the two flights that had already broken; I pulled away and down from them, and as I came up in a climbing turn saw a CR 42 following one of our Gladiators in a loop. While it was going up I gave it a long burst and saw it fall away and dive, the pilot jumped almost as soon as I attacked him. Another 42 came straight towards me while I was circling the parachute but I made a quick turn in the opposite direction and he passed just under my port wings. I then saw a 42 with a Gladiator on its tail and as I flew in on a beam attack the 42 flick rolled two or three times and continued doing so in a dive. I followed it all the way in a steep turn and dive giving a lot of short bursts and saw it crash. I was then at only about 3,000' and when I had climbed to about 5,000' joined in a dog-fight that ended when the 42 dived away and headed for Bir El Essem."

Form 541 of 80 Sqn ORB credited Stuckey only with a single confirmed victory, probably his first victim was credited to his Commanding Officer who finished it off, while of the last biplane he saw hitting the ground he wrote "(...) *seen to crash but believed hit before I attacked it*". However, it seems that he later was credited with two destroyed and one probable.

F/Sgt Trevor Martin Vaughan overshot and was cut to pieces by the fire from a couple of CR.42s and killed. Form 541 credited him with a confirmed individual victory, obviously the third CR.42 of the first section.

The second and third Sub-Flights were in the meantime joining combat. Finding the Italians already alerted they fared slightly less well than the first Sub-Flight. F/Lt Evers-Swindell led his Sub-Flight into the centre formation of nine Italian aircraft, which were already scattered all over the sky:

"(...) *I saw the leading formation attack the right hand formation of 9 E.A: so I put my sub flight into line astern expecting the E.A. to break up which they did as soon the first machine was shot down by No.2 of the leading formation. I led my sub flight into the centre formation of nine E.A. which by then were scattered all over the sky. I did a diving quarter attack on an E.A. up to about 50 feet, it turned over on its back and went down in a steep spiral. I was then attacked head on by another E.A. after this I looked down and saw the first one crash in flames. The pilot still in the cockpit. I managed to manoeuvre myself on to the tail of a third and after having given him a longish burst, saw him go down in the same way as the first, but was unable to follow him down as an explosive bullet took away one of my port flying wires and another burst on the starboard side of the instrument panel. I got in two more quick burst on two different E.A. but don't think I did any damage. My engine then started to pour out smoke and soon afterwards cut out. I glided down in a series of steep turns and found no E.A. following. I looked round and saw nine a/c burning on the ground and one pilot coming down by parachute. I glided for about three miles and at about 200 feet the engine seized up I did not have time to inspect the engine so set the aircraft on fire (...).*"

Evers-Swindell was credited with two unconfirmed victories. F/O Wanklyn Flower was able to claim a probable, he reported:

"(...) *I picked out a CR 42 flying in left hand turn ahead of me. I dropped in behind and fired three long bursts at close range – I last saw the aircraft diving vertically downwards. At this moment another C.R 42 fired a burst into my machine damaging the engine. I got away from him and, as there were no more enemy machines in sight, made for home (...)*"

F/O Dowding also claimed a probable:

"(...) *Before we had reached them they had already been broken up before we joined amongst them. I then saw a CR.42 coming towards me on port beam, it pulled its nose up and did a half roll to the left. I got my sights on to it, as it started to pull its nose up, and followed it round as it did*

MM4306, flown by Tenente Enzo Martissa on 8 August. After repair, this plane was given the individual number 84-4 by El Adem SRAM but never saw service with the 84ª Sq. In fact it was assigned to another unit (most likely of the 2° Stormo) shortly after this photo was taken.
[via Fulvio Chianese]

Sergente Lido Poli *of the 73ª* Squadriglia, *who on 8 August was severely wounded in the left arm during combat. Despite this, he continued to fight, claiming to have shot down one Gladiator before force-landing close to the T3 airfield. His arm was amputated but for this courageous display, he was awarded the* Medaglia d'Oro al Valor Militare.
[Italian Air Force]

the half roll, giving it a longish burst. It went into a spin, and went down a long way until I lost sight of it.

When I looked again there was an aircraft burning on the ground at approximately the position where the one went down, but I cannot say for certain whether it was the same as the one I saw go down.

I also saw at least four other aircraft burning on the ground, and three people descending by parachutes (…)"

P/O Sykes led his Sub-Flight into the right flank of the Italian formation:

"(…) I was leading sub 3 flight and putting the flight into echelon right turned on to their right flank. The enemy aircraft suddenly reeled off from their echelon formation probably owing to the fact that the leading flight had come into firing range and had opened fire. A general dog fight then commenced, I engaged a CR.42 which commenced a steep climbing turn, I commenced firing at the beginning of the climb and continued until I saw him fall and commence a flay spiral. I saw fragments or splinters falling from the centre section or the cockpit and saw the aircraft drop about 4-5000 feet and then engaged another which I followed in a steep turn firing all the time. This enemy aircraft went into a spin suddenly and saw one of our own aircraft follow it down. There were no more enemy aircraft in sight. During the action I saw several parachute open and several aircraft burning. I landed back on our aerodrome at 1915. One aircraft in my flight was forced to return just before the action because all its guns stopped."

Sykes was credited with two unconfirmed victories. The returning aircraft was flown by Sgt Gregory, who had had tested his gun before the attack, but found them all jammed and had been forced to withdraw. F/O Linnard was more successful:

"(…) We were given R/T instructions by the top flight to enter the fight.

I slipped under my leader to the left and found myself in a mass of milling aircraft. I went to attack a CR.42 which was on a Gladiator's tail when another CR.42 passed in front of me. I gave him deflection burst and got on to his tail – he pulled up in a loop. I followed him around giving him bursts and when he was upside down in the loop he baled out dropping past me, his parachute opening just below me. My range would be about 50 yards or less. I got on to another CR.42 and practically the same thing happened as before except that I did not get him and my engine cut as I was following him in the loop when I was in the vertical position. I saw the enemy aircraft diving past me but I was so close to him that he could not fire at me. I pushed my nose down and got my engine started and then saw a CR.42 diving down on me from vertically above but he did not hit me. I then saw a CR.42 practically head-on. I gave him a burst at very close range. The enemy aircraft turned over to the right on its back and went into a flat spin. I was at about 4,000 feet at this time. I watched the aircraft spin for about 1000 feet and then heard gunfire which I thought was from behind but there were no enemy aircraft within range of me. I then looked for the spinning aircraft but all I saw was an aircraft in flames on the ground beneath me. Another CR.42 dived past going very fast. I gave him a quick burst and saw some black smoke coming from him, but he kept straight on diving as fast as he could go towards Bir-el-Gobi. I did not follow him down. I then turned back towards where the fight had been but saw only one aircraft a Gladiator (P/O. Stuckey). We hung around a bit and then made for home. I caught up with F/Lt. Pattle and F/O. Graham and returned with them. I landed at 1910. I sustained no damage to self or aircraft except for one Fabric panel torn out.

I saw altogether 6 aircraft burning on ground and 4 parachutes dropping."

Linnard was credited with two confirmed victories.

Finally, F/Lt Pattle, after having masterfully conducted the action, joined the fray:

"(…) I saw no's 2 and 3 sections engage and before I brought my section into the fight I saw five crashed aircraft on the ground , three of which were in flames.

My own section then engaged those E.A. who were attempting to reach their own base and immediately became engaged in separate combats.

I engaged a CR 42 and, after a short skirmish, got into position immediately behind him. On firing two short bursts at about 50 yards range the E.A. fell into a spin and burst into flames on striking the ground. The pilot did not abandon his aircraft.

I then attacked 3 E.A. immediately below me. This action was indecisive as after a few minutes they broke away by diving vertically for the ground and pulling out at very low altitude.

Whilst searching for other E.A. I saw two more aircraft crash and burst into flames. Owing to the widespread area and the number of aircraft engaged it was impossible to confirm what types of aircraft were involved in these crashes or who shot them down.

The sky seemed clear of 42s although several Gladiators were still in the vicinity. I was about to turn for our base when a 42 attacked me from below. With the advantage of height I dived astern of him and after a short burst he spun into the ground into flames. As before the pilot didn't abandon his aircraft. F/O Graham confirms both my combats which ended decisively.

Seeing no further sign of Enemy Aircraft over the area, I turned towards our base. On my way home F/O Graham and P/O Linnard joined me in formation and my section landed at 19.10 hrs."

Pattle's two claims were confirmed by F/O Graham, who claimed one victory (later downgraded to a probable). F/Sgt Richens claimed one probable while confirming Graham's claim.

The British pilots returned with a multitude of claims. Because the large number of aircraft involved there is some confusion regarding these claims but it seems that they claimed 13 to 16 confirmed victories and 1 to 7 probables. Victories were claimed by Dunn (who also claimed one of the probables), Stuckey (who also claimed one of the probables), Evers-Swindell, Pattle, Linnard and Sykes, all six pilots claiming two destroyed each, while Wykeham-Barnes and Vaughan claimed one destroyed each. Additional probables were claimed by Dowding, Flower, Graham and Richens. This giving a total of 14 victories and 7 probables. All in exchange for two Gladiators shot down with F/Sgt Trevor Martin Vaughan, who was killed, and Fight Lieutenant Evers-Swindell, who reported:

"(…) set the aircraft on fire. First removing the water bottle and Very pistol. I walked for three hours away from the sun and then lay down to sleep. I slept till about 01.00 hours finding dense fog and myself wet through. I then dug a hole in some soft sand and buried my self. There I stayed till daylight. At about 06.30 next morning when the fog started to lift I started to walk into the sun until 15.00hrs. when I saw three armoured cars on the horizon. I fired three very light cartridges, the next thing I remember I was lying in the shade of the armoured car the crew told me I was about five miles from the wire."

He had been picked up by three armoured cars of the 11th Hussars.

The port wheel cover of Tenente Enzo Martissa's Fiat CR.42 MM4306 of the 91ª Squadriglia containing his "last message" carved with a knife. [Alcide Leoni via Gianandrea Bussi

It seems that the 73ª *Sq.* suffered most from the surprise attack, losing five aircraft when *serg.* Enrico Dallari and *serg.* Antonio Valle baled out (possibly shot down by Sykes and Linnard), *s. ten.* Querci and *serg.* Santo Gino force-landed and *m. llo.* Norino Renzi failed to return. *serg.* Lido Poli was hit early in the fight, being severely wounded in the left arm. Despite this, he continued to fight, claiming to have shot down one Gladiator before force-landing close to an infantry unit at the outskirts of T3 airfield. A patrol from the army immediately took him back to El Adem. Then he was send to the navy hospital of Tobruk where his arm was amputated. For this courageous display, he was awarded the *Medaglia d'Oro al Valor Militare*. The official citation of his award stated that he *"shared in the destruction of five enemy fighters"*. His aircraft was recovered lightly damaged as also stated in the same citation: *"he succeeded in landing his plane without damage"*, forced only by the loss of blood caused by his wound.

Serg. Dallari and *serg.* Valle were recovered by the 2ª Divisione Libica (Libyan Division) and were back at base on the following days, while Querci's and Gino's fighters were recovered and sent to the SRAM of El Adem on 15 August. *serg.* Rosa was slightly wounded and baled out while *ten.* Martissa force-landed wounded.

Martissa, who was initially missing, had force-landed his CR.42 with a hundred bullet holes in it, only 15 kilometres from El Adem. The wounded pilot claimed the individual destruction of two Gladiators (not confirmed in the official documents of his unit but later credited to him by post-war studies). In fact, Martissa was awarded with a third *Medaglia d'argento al Valor Militare* (in as many months) for this action. The official citation of the award stated that he: *"shared in the destruction of five enemy planes together with other pilots"*. He survived his ordeal by drinking dewdrops at dawn, but after two days he was coming to expect the worst. One of the bullets which had hit his aircraft had pierced the griffin's head of *Squadriglia*'s badge on the port wheel cover, and Martissa wrote with a knife on the white background disc of the badge:

"You, little griffin, have been struck in the head. I would have suffered less if I had been likewise! I'm not mortally wounded, but I shall pass away, since I can't walk for 10-20 km to reach a track. And it will be by hunger and thirst."

Martissa was found on 10 August by the XXII *Compagnia Bersaglieri Motociclisti*, led by *ten.* Domenico Raspini, which was patrolling 80 km south of Tobruk. Raspini recalled:

"We saw an aircraft in the desert. We approached and found ten. Martissa under a wing, with a leg almost torn off by an explosive bullet from a British fighter. We rescued him. He told us that if we didn't come [to save him], he'd shoot himself in the head with his gun, because he was dying of thirst. We rescued the pilot and left the aircraft."

The Fiat CR.42 flown by Martissa (MM4306) was recovered and, in September 1940, assigned to the 84ª *Sq.* of the 10° *Gr.* as "84-4".

Ten. Guiducci was also awarded with a *Medaglia d'argento al Valor Militare* for this combat.

The Italians in total lost four aircraft, while four more force-landed (it seems that all were later recovered). In return the Italian pilots claimed five Gladiators (three shared amongst the pilots of 10° *Gr.* and two shared by the surviving 73ª *Sq.* pilots) and two probables (the 90ª *Sq.*'s Diary reported six victories). Remembering the combat for the press, the Italian leader (obviously *magg.* Romagnoli) recalled that even if the attack by the Gladiators was possibly the deadliest he had ever seen, the reaction of his pilots was *"miraculously immediate"*. He had just heard the first bullets whistling around him when his right wingman already was breaking with a zoom. Then he saw in his gunsight, the belly of a Gladiator and shot this down (most likely F/Sgt Vaughan, who had overshot during the first bounce).

For this exploit, 80 Sqn received Press honours as well as written congratulations from the RAF HQ Middle East. Dunn and his pilots had exploited the strong points of the Gladiator over the CR.42 to the maximum extent, especially the radio equipment, which had permitted a coordinated attack, being also crucial for obtaining the initial surprise, and the Gladiators' superior low altitude overall performance.

F/O Harold Sykes of 80 Sqn, who claimed two CR.42s on 8 August 1940. Sykes was killed in combat with Italian fighters over Greece on 28 November 1940.
[via Averil Dorego]

During the combat, the Gladiator demonstrated another interesting characteristic: a markedly superior horizontal manoeuvrability over its opponent. On regard of this point, it is interesting to report the impressions of F/O Stuckey and F/O Linnard.

"With trimming gear slightly back, found I could easily out manoeuvre a/c attacking from rear. No blacking out."

"No difficulty in keeping astern of enemy aircraft. Enemy invariably looped for evasive action."

After this combat, morale, particularly among the 9° *Gr.*'s pilots suffering their first African experiences, fell considerably. The 73ª *Sq.* was considered the top gun unit of 4° *Stormo*, its pilots (notably among them Enrico Dallari, Renzi, Valerio De Campo and Vittorio Pezzè) were mostly part of the last Italian aerobatic team, which had performed with great success in Berlin Staaken on 23 June 1939, in honour of the returning Condor Legion pilots. However, this air battle demonstrated clearly, even in a pure biplane dogfight, that good tactics and sound flight discipline, enhanced by R/T communications, were better than the pure aerobatic skill. However, despite this heavy beating, operations for the 9° *Gr.* restarted the next day.

9 August 1940

During the day, the 4° *Stormo* pilots flew a lot of reconnaissance missions looking for the missing Norino Renzi and Enzo Martissa. *magg.* Ernesto Botto personally led a 23 strong CR.42 formation from the 9° *Gr.* in a free sweep in the Bir El Gobi-Sidi Omar area, taking off at 16:50 and landing back at 18:15.

211 Sqn bombed Tobruk harbour with nine Blenheims during the evening.

12 August 1940

While taking off from Benghazi Benina, an SM 79 of the 33° *Gr.* flown by *ten.* Gregorio Gregnanin, (co-pilot *s. ten.* Raffaele Arragona, *serg magg. montatore* Paolo D'Orazio, *Primo Aviere Motorista* Pietro Basoli, *Primo Aviere* Armiere Nunzio Di Donna, *Primo Aviere Radiotelegrafista* Sante Coppola, *Aviere Scelto* Motorista Ferruccio Ronzan) crashed with the loss of the entire crew.

During the evening, 211 Sqn under S/Ldr Bax again bombed Tobruk harbour. No particular results were observed.

15 August 1940

At 16:00, 30 Sqn accompanied eleven Blenheims from 55 Sqn led by the CO, S/Ldr Stowell, to strafe the seaplane base in the Gulf of Bomba. Two Blenheims from 55 Sqn had to abort due to engine problems, but the other Blenheims pressed home. En route they meet a reconnaissance machine of 113 Sqn that had already checked the target and which led them to Bomba. 55 Sqn bombed first and 30 Sqn then strafed with all front guns, firing until the ammunition was exhausted. All moored seaplanes were claimed damaged and a Cant Z.506B was reported to tip up onto its nose and sunk. The six Blenheims of 30 Sqn were led by S/Ldr Shannon and landed back at 18:00. Only a single machine had suffered a single bullet hole in a main plane. The 113 Sqn machine confirmed the four seaplanes lying in damaged conditions on or under the water.

Italian records show a raid by 10 bombers that damaged slightly five Z.501s and two Z.506Bs (RS).

The recently arrived *Reparto Speciale Aerosiluranti* was immediately requested to go into action, and a night attack on the British fleet in Alexandria harbour was planned for the night. Participating pilots were Dequal, Fusco, Buscaglia, Robone and Copello, using all the five torpedo bombers available. The plan was to attack in two different waves, the first of three (Dequal, Buscaglia, Robone) at 21:30 and the second of two (Fusco, Copello) at 21:45. In the meantime, between 20:55 and 22:10, six night bombers from the 10° *Stormo* under the command of *col.* Benedetti would make a nuisance raid from high altitude.

The first wave of torpedo bombers, composed of only two aircraft (Robone suffered engine problem and immediately became separated), took off from El Adem and arrived over the harbour at around 21:37. The presence of thick clouds at very low level and the strong AA reaction driven by searchlights didn't stop them releasing their torpedoes against an unidentified ship.

The ship was probably the cruiser HMS *Gloucester*, which was not hit because the two torpedoes most likely ran into a sand bank inside the shallow waters of Alexandria harbour. The Italian pilots were not able to observe the results of their action and flew back to El Adem T3, where the right landing gear of Buscaglia's SM 79, which had been damaged, refused to work and the Italian torpedo ace had to land on a single wheel, causing very slightly damage to his aircraft in the process.

The other three planes, disturbed by clouds and enemy reaction, didn't even succeed in identifying their targets. Robone remained over Alexandria for 35 minutes, doing two torpedo runs without success. Eventually he tried to fly back home with his precious torpedo intact, but low on fuel, he had to release his torpedo in the desert during the return journey, landing near the Balbia road. With his plane refuelled he arrived at El Adem the day after.

Copello didn't succeed in attacking either, and had to release his torpedo in the open sea before force landing (without damage) on a beach inside Italian territory. He too returned the day after with his SM 79 intact.

Magg. Fusco was less fortunate. After failing in his attack he had to force land short of fuel inside British territory. The crew destroyed the aircraft and then were taken POW at dawn on 16 August (crew; *serg. magg.* Attilio Ferrandi, *s. ten. di Vascello* Giovanni Bertoli, *Motorista* Guido Franco and *Marconista* Renato Vanelli). They were brought into camp at Sidi Barrani and interrogated by the Intelligence Officer, P/O J. E. Helfield. Later the Army transferred them to Mersa Matruh.

The attack was a complete failure, and showed that even if the British defences were not sufficient to stop it (eleven Italian planes remained over Alexandria at different heights, unchallenged, for almost two hours) such actions needed carefully preparation and good intelligence support, as too often courage alone was not enough.

One Bombay from 216 Sqn attacked Tobruk harbour, reportedly claiming little or no damage.

16 August 1940

30 SM 79s of the 15° and 33° *Stormi* attacked one British cruiser and three destroyers north of the Egyptian coast without claiming any hits.

A strong formation of fighters from the 4° *Stormo* (20 two from the 9° *Gr.* and 17 from the 10° *Gr.*) escorted an IMAM Ro.37*bis* spotting artillery fire in the Sollum area. No enemies were encountered but on landing back the aircraft of *s. ten.* Bruno Paolazzi of the 96ª *Sq.* crashed after an engine breakdown and was written off, while the pilot went to Tobruk hospital suffering serious fractures.

One Bombay from 216 Sqn attacked Tobruk harbour, reportedly claiming little or no damage.

17 August 1940

During the morning, the Mediterranean Fleet was out for a raid in support of the Army. The battleships HMS *Warspite*, HMS *Ramilles* and HMS *Malaya*, supported by the cruiser HMS *Kent* and three flotillas of destroyers, bombarded Bardia harbour and Fort Capuzzo, starting at 06:45 and continuing for 22 minutes. As the vessels headed back towards Alexandria a series of bombing attacks were launched against them by the *Regia Aeronautica*.

The RAF and the FAA provided escort for the fleet. HMS *Eagle*'s Fighter Flight of three Sea Gladiators had been flown to Sidi Barrani airfield in Libya, and from here patrolled over the Fleet. 'B' and 'C' Flights of 80 Sqn provided air support with flights of four Gladiators over the ships from dawn to dusk. 'A' Flight of 112 Sqn was positioned at Z Landing Ground (Matruh West) while 'C' Flight of 112 Sqn was based at Y LG about 18 kilometres further west, and they also took part in the covering missions.

At 08:20, F/O Peter Wykeham-Barnes and his three-aircraft section (P/O Frankie Stubbs as no.2 and P/O P. T. Dowding as no. 3) from 'B' flight of 80 Sqn took off on patrol over the fleet and climbed to 16,000 feet . At 09:10, they spotted a Cant Z.501 flying boat over Tobruk. The British pilots formed line astern and attacked from above and behind, using No. 1 Fighter attack. Wykeham-Barnes dived down through the clouds to attack it. As he was about to open fire his starboard gun came unmounted and ripped through the fuselage, severing a strut and damaging the leading edge of the tailplane. The Gladiator started to roll but he reacted quickly, put on full aileron to hold the mainplane and then continued the attack. It seems that Wykeham-Barnes had killed the gunner on the Italian flying boat since no more return fire was experienced. The three pilots made two passes each and the flying boat eventually fell in flames, crashed into the sea and sank immediately. The pilots returned to base at 10:00.

The Italian flying boat was a 143ª *Sq.* Z.501 from Menalao, flown by *s. ten.* Cesare Como with *s. ten. di Vascello* Renzo Monselesan as observer, that was shot down; the crew perished.

Fiat CR.42 of the 96ª Squadriglia *damaged during landing by Sottotenente Bruno Paolazzi on 16 August 1940 at El Adem airfield.* [via Przemek Skulski]

Two hours later the attacks on the Royal Navy began, when at 10:40 five SM 79s were seen at 12,000 feet, heading in from the north-east. Over the fleet there were, on standing patrol, the Gladiators of 'A' Flight 112 Sqn (probably six of them), the three Sea Gladiators of HMS *Eagle*'s Fighter Flight, and a single Hurricane from 'A' Flight of 80 Sqn, flown by F/O John Lapsley (P2641). They intercepted the Italian bombers and altogether claimed six of them; one by F/Lt Lloyd Schwab, one by P/O Peter Wickham, (both from 112 Sqn) and three by Lapsley. Two Sea Gladiators flown by Lieutenant (A) Kenneth Keith (N5513) and Lieutenant Anthony Young (N5567) attacked several formations. Young attacked one in company with a 112 Sqn Gladiator flown by an unknown pilot. Keith joined the attack and the port wing of the bomber burst into flames, two members of the crew bailing out before the Savoia crashed into the sea. Commander Charles Keighly-Peach (N5517) became separated, and realizing the futility of chasing the fleeing bombers alone, headed back over the Fleet in time to see two more formations attacking (25 SM 79s were counted). He made three attacks on one bomber, seeing numerous pieces fall off, and it went into a shallow dive. One man baled out, but as the aircraft lost height rapidly, it disappeared into cloud. He attacked another twice but without result.

The Italians lost four bombers and claimed seven Gladiators shot down in return (it seems that all the seven claims were submitted by the gunners aboard the Savoia bombers, two of them by 10° *Stormo* gunners). In fact only the Gladiator of P/O Richard Acworth was seriously damaged when he attacked an SM 79, but although wounded himself Acworth was able to fly back to base where he crash-landed and the aircraft was written-off.

In 1942, Joseph Fraser remembered:

"During August, the squadron's C.O. Slim Somerville was still non-operational, recovering from extensive burns which he had received getting out of a Gladiator on fire while practicing aerobatics at Helwan. The Flights were commanded by F/Lt C. H. Fry and Algy Schwab, the latter had just been posted in Wally Williams' place as O.C. "A" Flight. A number of patrols were carried out during August between Sollum and Mersa Matruh and a couple more victories were credited to the squadron. F/O Acworth was badly injured by shrapnel in the leg during a dog-fight off Sidi Barrani but he managed to get his aircraft back to Gerawla, landing downwind and finishing up at the opening of the medical tent. The medical officer was infuriated at this demonstration, until he realized Acky was unable to get out of the cockpit and that it had saved him carrying Acky some hundreds of yards. A dozen or more splinters were taken out of Acky's leg, two weeks sick leave in Alex. and he was back in the cockpit again."

John Lapsley told a newspaper about this combat:

"I arrived just as five S 79s had dropped their bombs, all well astern of the fleet, and were making off. One immediately went down in flames – evidently hit by anti-aircraft fire from the battleships. I picked on the leader and gave him about eight short bursts. He fell away, obviously in difficulties. Actually he landed his aircraft in our lines – there were six hundred bullet holes in it [probably '56-9' flown by ten. Lauchard of the 56ª Sq.].

Then I picked on another and had just got a second burst into him he went up in flames. I was about one hundred yards away and the planes were much too close for comfort so I swerved away just as the crew of the S 79 'baled out'.

The third remaining S 79 by this time was quite close to the coast and he was diving like mad for a cloud. I gave him three or four long bursts, and with one engine smoking he disappeared. I think he went into 'the drink'.

These Italian aircraft seem to be built of ply-wood. At any rate you have to dodge the pieces that come flying back at you when you fire your guns.

There didn't seem to be much more doing, so I came home. Even then I had some ammunition left."

Italian units participating in the attack were the 10° *Stormo* with ten aircraft and the 15° and the 33° *Stormi* with another 16 aircraft. The Italians arrived over the target in consecutive waves. There is a lack of details of the attack by the 15° and the 33° *Stormi* but they suffered no losses, even if it seems that the bombers from the 15° *Stormo* were intercepted by the British fighters. Primo *Aviere* Antonio Trevigni of the 53ª *Sq.*, 47° *Gr.*, although seriously wounded in both legs, kept firing against them until his aircraft was able to escape, claiming two victories in the process. Trevigni was awarded with a *Medaglia d'Oro al Valor Militare* but was never able to recover and finally died in an Italian hospital on 23 October 1942.

The 10° *Stormo* aircraft were a first group of five Savoias of the 58ª *Sq.* and a second group under the command of *cap.* Musch and composed of four aircraft of the 56ª *Sq.* and one of the 57ª *Sq.* The 58ª *Sq.* took off from Derna N1 at 07:55 and arrived over the Royal Navy ships at around

10:00 where they unloaded forty 100 kg bombs. A group of seven Gladiators tried to intercept after the bombing, but were left behind, while AA was reported as extremely intense and precise.

The second group led by *cap.* Musch arrived over the fleet to find all the enemy fighters already alerted and ready for the interception. Attacked by the Gladiators and Lapsley's Hurricane, the first to go down was aircraft '57-7' flown by *ten.* Visentin and *s. ten.* Sartore (crew; *m. llo.* Fasce, *Primo Aviere* Radiotelegrafista Pian, *Aviere* Armiere Vitolo, *Aviere* Scelto *Motorista* Innocenti). The crew were all killed. The second aircraft to go down was the aircraft of *s. ten.* Mussi of the 56ª *Sq.*, with the loss of the crew. The third to be shot down was '56-9' flown by *ten.* Arturo Lauchard of the 56ª *Sq.*, which was seriously damaged. With all the crew dead inside, the second pilot *ten.* Vittorio Cèard (Lauchard was wounded) made a forced landing on a beach. The beach was in Egyptian territory and the two pilots were taken prisoners. The plane of Lauchard was later recovered and, taken to Alexandria, was exposed as a war prize on Ismailia Square. Lauchard reported of his capture that he was transported to the airport of Sidi Barrani where he was taken to the Officer's Mess, where an Intelligence Officer examined him. Lauchard told him only his name and rank and the amused British Officer showed him a chart where all the units of *Regia Aeronautica* were recorded with airbase, number of planes and names of the crew chiefs. There his name already was, written on a tag that the Intelligence Officer removed. Later the RAF officers offered him a drink, and he met a young F/Lt that around ten days before had been shot down by Italian fighters and obliged to bale out. The British pilot told Lauchard that while descending in his parachute an Italian fighter pointed on him but instead of opening fire he passed near him weaving with his arm. It seems that the pilot was almost surely F/Lt 'Pat' Pattle.

The two surviving Savoias ran for home but only *cap.* Musch arrived back at Derna, with the aircraft damaged and a wounded crewman (*Primo Aviere Motorista* Falzoni). The other SM 79 flown by *s. ten.* Venosta and *Marsciallo* Breda was almost shot down by the fighters when a cloud saved them. They were however obliged to force land at T3, where the plane was written off as a consequence of the damage suffered. The 10° *Stormo*'s records reported that three of their number were shot down by a single Hurricane that, hidden inside the Gladiator formation, attacked but always remaining out of range of the Italian return fire.

The two Moranes of the Free French Flight No. 2, temporarily attached to 80 Sqn, also flew operational patrols over the Fleet, but failed to encounter any of the Italian raiders. The same

Members of 3 RAAF Sqn inspect a captured Italian SM 79 at the Abbassia Barracks, Cario on 24 November 1940. The SM 79 is probably 56-9 of the 56ª Squadriglia, 30° Gruppo flown by Tenente Lauchard, which made an emergency landing after combat on Egyptian territory on 17 August 1940. The bomber was later recovered and, taken to Alexandria, was displayed as a war prize on Ismailia Square. [via Australian War Memorial]

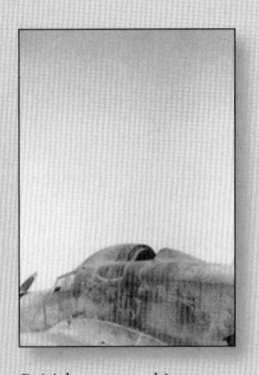

British personnel inspect a captured Italian SM 79. This SM 79 is also probably 56-9 of the 56ª Squadriglia, 30° Gruppo. [via Australian War Memorial]

happened to 33 Sqn, which was resting and refitting in Helwan when it was suddenly moved to Maaten Gerawla on 16 August, and the day after took part in covering patrols over the fleet between Sidi Barrani and Fuka. However they were not engaged in combat and by the next evening they were back at Helwan.

The 4° *Stormo* was up in the morning to escort the bombers attacking the British ships, but the Italian pilots didn't record any encounters with the enemy.

Finally, a formation of four Breda Ba.65s and eleven Fiat CR.32s took off from T2 to attack the enemy ships. Luckily for the Italians they were unable to find the Mediterranean Fleet, that was already on its way back home. The assault planes landed back having avoided useless slaughter since their 50 and 15 kg bombs would have had little effect upon the Royal Navy ships.

In the end very little damage was suffered by the Italian targets, and in fact the greatest loss was suffered in the air by the bombing units opposing the naval bombardment. When the British air reconnaissance reports, showing little damage, arrived in Alexandria, Andrew Cunningham concluded that the Italians skill in dispersing stores and transport over wide areas meant future bombardments would bear little fruit.

One Bombay from 216 Sqn was out to raid Derna but the attack was aborted.

18 August 1940

The 9° *Gr.* made numerous scrambles from T3, and the 10° *Gr.* from Ain El Gazala T4, where it had deployed an alarm section.

The 2° *Stormo*, the bulk of its fighters still being serviced at Benghazi Berka, deployed two alarm sections of four planes each to Derna N1 and to T4. However, lacking an effective warning network, they failed to make any interceptions.

In the late morning, five aircraft of the 15° *Stormo* led by *cap.* Guidozzi attacked enemy vehicles in the border area, and then the landing ground of Sidi Barrani, where the Ford W/T van of 208 Sqn was destroyed, a Crossley Fire tender six-wheeler was damaged and Aircraftman S. Oakley was wounded by splinters. *cap.* Magrì's SM 79 was damaged during the action and force-landed near Tobruk T5; the co-pilot, *serg. magg.* Soffiantino, was slightly wounded.

An SM 79 of the 60ª *Sq.*, 33° *Gr.*, flown by *s. ten.* Giglioli, was intercepted by a Hurricane at 5600 meters over Alexandria harbour during the daily reconnaissance mission. For unknown reasons the Hurricane broke off the attack when in a good position to open fire.

19 August 1940

S. ten. Giglioli was again intercepted over Alexandria by a Hurricane that broke off the attack. One Bombay from 216 Sqn attacked Derna harbour, reportedly claiming little or no damage.

20 August 1940

A raid by British bombers over El Adem was recorded but no losses were suffered.

Ten. Giovanni Guiducci, *serg. magg.* Angelo Savini and *serg.* Amleto Monterumici (all from the 90ª *Sq.*) scrambled against enemy intruders over Tobruk, but they failed to make contact. They were, however, almost shot down by the Italian AA defences, in particular the batteries of the cruiser *San Giorgio*.

One Bombay from 216 Sqn attacked Derna harbour, while a second attacked Tobruk harbour. Little or no damage were claimed.

21 August 1940

A raid by five British bombers was recorded over Menelao, together with a raid by eight British bombers on Tmini M2. No losses were suffered at Menelao, but at Tmini two SM 79s were destroyed. These were possibly from the 33° *Stormo* and/or 33° *Gr.*

It seems that the bombers were Blenheims of 55 Sqn, which at around 13:00 attacked the airfield of Tmini M2 and the relatively close seaplane base of Menelao on the west bank of the Gulf of Bomba. While returning from the attack three of the Blenheims observed a group of three Italian ships on the eastern side of the Gulf.

The Italian ships were the submarine *Iride*, the torpedo boat *Calipso* and the tender *Monte Gargano*. They were there as the first move of Operation G. A., an attack on Alexandria to be carried out by eight frogmen of the 1ª *Flottiglia* MAS driving four SLCs (*Siluro Lenta Corsa* – human torpedo - the assault submarine vehicle that the British later called Chariot). *Iride* was to carry the SLC teams close to the Egyptian base.

The information from the bomber Blenheims was later confirmed by a reconnaissance aircraft from 113 Sqn. The presence of Italian ships in the usually deserted Gulf attracted the attention of Air Commodore Collishaw, who believed that the area was becoming an Italian submarine base and consequently an attack was planned for the next day.

The 10° *Stormo* recorded a raid on Derna N1 resulting in five dead among the personnel.

During an attack on Tobruk two SM 79s were destroyed on the ground. These aircraft were possibly from the 14° *Stormo* and/or 175ª *Sq*.

22 August 1940

At 06:30 an additional reconnaissance mission against the Italian ships in Gulf of Bomba was carried out by 113 Sqn.

At 10:30 three Fairey Swordfishes of 824 Sqn, armed with torpedoes, took off from Sidi Barrani (recently crated by an Italian attack) and headed towards Bomba. The three aircraft were flown by Lieutenant Commander Oliver Patch (RM), Lieutenant J.W.G. Wellham and Lieutenant N.A.F. Cheesman.

The attack was carried out from 12:02 to 12:04. Patch sank the submarine *Iride* and Wellham, although seriously damaged by the fire coming from *Calipso*, sank *Monte Gargano* (1,976 tons), while the torpedo from Cheedman's Swordfish, aimed at *Calipso*, was lost, probably hitting a sand bank.

The three torpedo bombers landed back at 15:00. They were all damaged but only Wellham's aircraft, hit in the engine and in the main tank and with a broken spar, was written off.

The sinking of *Monte Gargano* didn't cause any loss of life, while 27 sailors trapped inside *Iride* drowned and a sailor and the Second Commander of *Calipso* were killed by splinters from *Monte Gargano*.

The British pilots claimed the sinking of four ships with their three torpedoes, but even if they didn't obtain such an astonishing result they perhaps achieved more, since their attack effectively put an end to the first Italian attempt to attack the harbour of Alexandria with the SLCs. Not until December 1941 did the Italian frogmen finally succeed in breaking into the British base.

A raid by nine British bombers over Derna was recorded, but no losses were suffered. The attacking force came from 211 Sqn, and was composed of eight Blenheims under S/Ldr Bax, two of which were obliged to force land at Sidi Barrani and one at Mersa Matruh due to lack of fuel during the return journey.

One Bombay from 216 Sqn attacked Bomba, reportedly claiming little or no damage.

23 August 1940

During the night a single SM 79 of the *Reparto Speciale Arosilurante* again was out over Alexandria harbour. The plane, no. 1, flown by *s. ten*. Robone, remained over Alexandria from 01:30 until 02:20 without finding the occasion to attack. They landed back at El Adem 04:45 with the torpedo still onboard.

In the meantime, from 00:12 to 00:30, two SM 79s of the 32° *Gr.*, flown by *ten. col.* Carlo Unia and *ten.* Organo, attacked from medium level with 100 kg bombs to distract the British AA. Both returned without problems.

Menelao was again raided but no losses were suffered.

The seaplane base at the Gulf of Bomba was shelled during the night by the destroyers HMAS *Stuart*, *Diamond*, *Juno* and *Ilex* together with the cruiser HMAS *Sydney*, but they failed to inflict serious damage. The gunboat *Ladybird* and the destroyer HMAS *Waterhen* shelled Bardia; *Ladybird* entering the harbour to hit the shore installations at point blank range, safe from the Italian coastal batteries which faced seaward.

A night raid on El Adem caused slight damage to two CR.42s of the 9° *Gr.*

German Junkers Ju88s were in Libya for tropical tests during this period. One of them was obliged to force land in Gadames during the afternoon of 23 August because of hydraulic problems.

One Bombay from 216 Sqn attacked Tobruk harbour, reportedly claiming little or no damage.

24 August 1940

A night raid on El Adem caused slight damage to two CR.42s of the 84ª *Sq.*

One Bombay from 216 Sqn attacked Bardia and El Adem. The returning bomber claimed one hangar demolished.

25 August 1940

A Z.501 of the 139ª *Sq.*, temporarily based at Menelao, was lost to enemy fighters over Ras El Tin, near Bomba, during the day. The crew, including the observer *Guardiamarina* Mariuccio Pozzo, was lost. The British unit involved remains unknown.

A raid by a single British bomber over El Adem was recorded, six CR.42s were slightly damaged (RS).

26 August 1940

Nine S.81s of the 39° *Stormo* attacked Alexandria during the night. All aircraft returned to Rhodes.

Lysander L4719, piloted by P/O J. H. Kirton from Qasaba, crashed at Bir Kenayis in a landing accident. Lysander L4722 was allotted as replacement.

27 August 1940

At 06:58 SM 79 no. 2 of *Reparto Speciale Aerosilurante*, flown by *ten.* Emanuele Buscaglia, attacked a British London type cruiser off the coast of Sidi Barrani. The identity of the British ship remains unknown, but it seems that no damage was suffered. Buscaglia, who attacked without the help of any kind of torpedo sight, thought he hit the target but couldn't claim any certain success.

This was the first attack in open water made by an Italian torpedo bomber, and a probable victory was officially assigned to him for Bulletin purposes.

211 Sqn recorded a successful raid against Derna harbour, made by nine Blenheims. Many near misses and at least two direct hits were claimed. On the return journey, F/Lt Gordon-Finlayson had to force-land at Sidi Barrani owing to engine trouble.

According to post-war British studies, Bombay L5849 of 216 Sqn was lost during the day for unknown causes.

28 August 1940

During the night eight S.81s of the 39° *Stormo* attacked El Qantara railway station in the Suez Canal Zone and the fuel storage at Port Said. This was the only attack made by the *Regia Aeronautica* in this area during 1940.

29 August 1940

30 SM 79s (15 from the 15° *Stormo* and 15 from 10° *Stormo*) attacked Mersa Matruh in the afternoon. The attack was made by the two formations simultaneously, and was widely publicized in the Italian War Bulletin. In fact, this was the first time since the beginning of the war that an

Italian formation of this size hit a ground target in Egypt almost simultaneously, and not in waves as was usual practice.

S/Ldr Sprague of 208 Sqn force-landed Lysander L4685 due to engine failure after an afternoon reconnaissance in the Capuzzo-Bardia area. The aircraft was damaged but the crew was unhurt.

30 August 1940

The reinforcements that Cunningham requested after Punta Stilo finally arrived and prepared to cross the Mediterranean to reach Alexandria. They were the carrier HMS *Illustrious*, the battleship HMS *Valiant* and the AA cruisers HMS *Coventry* and HMS *Calcutta*. Two heavy cruisers - HMS *Ajax* and HMS *York* - would also join the fleet off Alexandria, but they would reach Egypt passing through the longer route around the Cape and escorting merchant vessels with badly needed reinforcements for the Army in the process. The Royal Navy also took the opportunity to move a four ship convoy (three merchant ships and a tanker) from Alexandria to reinforce Malta. All these movements were known at Operation 'Hats'

On 30 August the reinforcement ships, consisting of HMS *Illustrious* (with two squadrons of Swordfishes, 815 and 819 Sqns, each with twelve aircraft, and a squadron of fighters, 806 Sqn, equipped with the new eight gun Fairey Fulmar and commanded by Lieutenant Commander Charles Evans), HMS *Valiant*, HMS *Calcutta* and HMS *Coventry* left Gibraltar under the name of Force F. They were escorted by the resident Force H consisting of the carrier HMS *Ark Royal*, the battle cruiser HMS *Renown*, the light cruiser HMS *Sheffield* and twelve destroyers, under the command of Vice Admiral Somerville. From Alexandria the four ship convoy bound for Malta sailed together with the Mediterranean Fleet (the carrier HMS *Eagle*, the battleships HMS *Warspite* and HMS *Malaya*, five cruisers and 13 destroyers).

31 August 1940

Lieutenant Commander Charles Keighly-Peach (Gladiator N5517) was scrambled from HMS *Eagle* together with Lieutenant (A) R. H. H. L. Oliphant (a member of HMS *Eagle's* Air Staff flying Gladiator N5567), to intercept a 'shadower'. They found a Z.506B at 6,000 feet flying in the direction of Kythera Island. Keighly-Peach continues:

"Again off Crete I came across a Cant Z.506B - I think the crew must have been asleep as I was offered no opposition and felt almost committing murder - it was too easy. The Cant ditched off the coast of Crete and I saw the crew descending via parachutes and they must have landed close enough to land to be able to swim ashore."

It is possible that this combat was witnessed by Telegraphist/Air Gunner "Ginger" Tyler of 813 FAA Sqn, who recalled on an unknown date:

"...On the following morning I went off with my usual pilot and observer, Leatham and Grieve. As we climbed through a thin layer of early morning haze, there, right on our starboard beam, about three miles aways was a huge Cant reconnaissance seaplane. Pointing out the target to the observer, I immediately rattled off a brief sighting report on the radio. This completed, I stood up an readied my gun for possible action. We were heading at top speed for the Cant, but within what appeared to be just a few seconds, one of Eagle's Gladiators streaked by and immediately tore into action. The Italians didn't know what hit them, and soon they were spiralling down into the sea trailing a great black plume of smoke.

Keighly-Peach had done it again, and hopefully the shadower had been downed before he had time to signal our position back to his base. But it was wishful thinking on our part, for, from about eleven o'clock in the forenoon until about six in the evening the fleet was subjected to ten more bombing attacks, again without suffering any damage or casualties."

Three 'shadowers' of the *Regia Aeronautica* were lost on this date: a Z.506B of the 287ª *Sq.* from Elmas, Sardinia (*s. ten.* Antonio Di Trapani, *ten. di Vascello Osservatore* Ugo Simonazzi all KIA), a Z.501 of the 188ª *Sq.* from Elmas (*ten.* Giovanni Riosa, *ten. di Vascello Osservatore* Alfredo Manfroi KIA) and a Z.501 of the 148ª *Sq.* (Observer *ten. di Vascello Osservatore* Corrado Silvestri).

It seems that the first two fell victim to Skuas from HMS *Ark Royal* and the sections commanded by Lieutenant Spurway and Lieutenant Bruen. It is however possible that the third was the victim of Keighly-Peach and was misidentified as a Z.506, but it is necessary to note that the 148ª *Sq.* was based in central Italy and usually operated in the Tirreno Sea, not in the Aegean area.

In the meantime in the eastern Mediterranean a group of ten SM 79s from the 34° *Gr.* found and bombed the British ships, hitting the freighter *Cornwall* (11,290 tons) with a bomb on the stern that left it stationary with a broken rudder. The bomb also started a small fire. According to Andrew Cunningham:

"(…) the convoy was heavily bombed south of Crete, and the largest ship, the Federal Steam Navigation Company's Cornwall, Captain F. C. Perry, was hit and set on fire aft. She was also holed below the waterline, while her steering gear, wireless and two guns were put completely out of action. The master and the crew acted with great determination. The magazine blew up and the fire spread to one of the holds; but she was eventually got under control. Captain Perry signalled that he could steer his ship with the propellers, maintained his speed and station in the convoy and arrived safely at Malta two days afterwards (…)".

Around this time the Italian fleet was at sea and only 120 miles from the Mediterranean Fleet that, apart from the problems with *Cornwall*, was heavily outgunned, having only two battleships and five cruisers against the four battleships and thirteen cruisers of the Italians. Amazingly, the Italian ships were called back to Taranto, and one of the greatest possibilities of obtaining a decisive victory in the Mediterranean war at sea was lost.

55 Sqn flew "nuisance" high-level raids over the Italian airfields, together with bombers from 113 and 211 Sqns. Fighters from 80 and 112 Sqns covered the bombers.

Three Blenheims flew the eighth and last raid of the day by 55 Sqn. Shortly after take off Blenheim L6657 (pilot Sgt Coughlan) aborted after suffering engine problem. Off Sidi Barrani,

A Cant Z.501 off Sollum.
[via Italian Air Force]

Blenheim Mk.I L8397 turned back and afterwards crashed on landing at Mersa Matruh. It seems that the aircraft suffered engine problems and, after the bombs were jettisoned, control was lost in a turn when an engine cut and the aircraft crashed, killing the crew; 21-year-old P/O Robert Alwyn Smith, 24-year-old Sgt John Leonard Sugden and Wireless Operator/Air Gunner 20-year-old Aircraftman 1st Class Leslie Lowe.

The remaining Blenheim (L8667 flown by P/O E. M. Metcalfe) continued towards the target but encountered one enemy fighter before reaching its objective. The engagement lasted five minutes, and the attack was made from astern. The bomber didn't suffer any damage, but one good burst from the rear gunner (Leading Aircraftman G. W. Harrison) is believed to have hit the enemy aircraft, which broke off the engagement. The target was reached at 16:48 (about five minutes after breaking off the engagement). The Blenheim landed back home at 18:35.

211 Sqn carried out ten missions by two Blenheims each for a total of 20 sorties against Ain El Gazala, Tobruk T4, T2 and Bardia. Many hits were claimed and no losses were recorded.

10º *Stormo* recorded a morning air raid on Derna N1 made by Bristol Blenheims that damaged two SM 79s and killed seven personnel of the 58ª *Sq.*: Egisto Colli, Narciso Gherardelli, Ernesto Paolini, Matteo Coco, Pierino Borgonovo, Mario Bernardiello, Giuseppe Di Nardo, while many others were wounded.

F/Sgt John Roy Marshall of 211 Sqn recorded in his logbook a raid on Gazala, flying Blenheim I L1482 together with Sgt Alcock.

September 1940

The ground war

On 13 September, the Italian attack on Egypt began.

The Italian forces reached Sid Barrani on 17 September, where they halted and began to construct a line of fortified camps extending from Sidi Barrani on the coast to 50 miles inland. The plan was to consolidate and improve the supply lines until cooler weather arrived, before continuing the push eastwards.

Regia Aeronautica

Fighters

Ten. Stefano Soprana (from the 90ª *Sq*.) was assigned to command the Fighter School and Alarm Section of Castel Benito, Tripoli, on 3 September when the previous commander, *cap*. Eduardo Travaglini, returned to Italy.

The school was equipped with a number of Fiat CR.32s, Fiat CR.42s and Fiat CR.30 two-seaters and had around fifteen cadets.

The school was later closed following a request from Soprana to *Generale* Francesco Pricolo (Commander in Chief of the Air Force), since Soprana thought that the pilots could be better trained in Italy without all the logistic problems of Castel Benito. The school closed and Soprana concentrated only on the Alarm Section, whose command he retained until the end of the year.

By the beginning of September, the 2º *Stormo* was fully back on operations.

The 8º *Gr*.'s headquarters moved from Berka to Gambut G on 10 September, but on the same day the *Gruppo* moved on to El Adem T3 because of the complete lack of equipment and accommodation at Gambut G. The strength of the *Gruppo* (re-joined by the 92ª *Sq*. the day before) was 24 CR.42s, a couple more fighters arrived in the following days for the 94ª *Sq*. Finally, on 19 September, the *Gruppo* moved to its final destination at Menastir M with 26 CR.42s.

On 12 September, the bulk of 13º *Gr*. moved from Benghazi K to Gambut. Sections of the *Gruppo* were still detached at Tmini M2, Derna and Ain El Gazala T4 for local defence duties. In total 20

Aircraft of the 73ª Squadriglia *of the 9º* Gruppo, *4º* Stormo C.T., *undergoing maintenance works. The photo was most probably taken when the 73ª* Squadriglia *shared an airfield with the 92ª* Squadriglia, *probably at El Adem T3.*
[via Renato Zavattini]

122

CR.42s moved from Benghazi K to Gambut G, while around eight fighters remained in the detached alarm sections.

On 7 September, eleven CR.42s from the 157° *Gr.* arrived from Comiso to Castel Benito and nine of the pilots were posted to the 2° *Stormo*. Posted to the 77ª *Sq.* were *s. ten.* Mario Nicoloso, *s. ten.* Carmelo Catania and *serg.* Renato Gori. Posted to the 78ª *Sq.* were *s. ten.* Luigi Cannepele, *serg.* Teresio Martinoli and *serg.* Francesco Morana. Posted to the 82ª *Sq.* were *ten.* Gianfranco Perversi and *serg.* Nino Campanini (from 385ª *Sq.*) while *ten.* Vittorio Gnudi was posted to the 94ª *Sq.*

On 9 September *serg.* Onorino Crestani, from the 53° *Stormo*, went to the 84ª *Sq.*, 10° *Gr.*, while *s. ten.* Luigi Prati and *serg.* Luigi Contarini went to 90ª *Sq.*

In the middle of September, *s. ten.* Carlo Albertini of the 366ª *Sq.*, 151° *Gr.*, and *m. llo.* Giorgio Di Giulio were assigned to the 91ª *Sq.*, 10° *Gr.*, while *serg.* Giuseppe Tomasi was assigned to the 96ª *Sq.*, 9° *Gr.*

When the operations for the capture of Sidi Barrani ended, the 10° *Gr.* was down to a very low efficiency, and for the second time since the beginning of the war the unit was forced to return to Benghazi Berka's SRAM on 24 September for a general overhaul of its fighters and engines.

With the bulk of its aircraft at Berka, sections of fighters on readiness remained at Ain El Gazala T4 (91ª *Sq.*) and Derna N1 (84ª *Sq.*).

The 10° *Gr.* returned to front line duty at the beginning of December.

The 9° *Gr.* suffered more or less the same problems as the 10° *Gr.* but the overhaul of its aircraft would be done directly at the SRAM of El Adem.

On the last day of August the 151° *Gr. C.T.* (366ª, 367ª and 368ª *Squadriglie*) was ordered to move to Libya with 30 CR.42s as a reinforcement for the attack against Sidi Barrani. The unit, under the command of *magg.* Carlo Calosso, was one of the first equipped with CR.42s in 1939 and was based in Caselle Torinese near Turin, with sections and *Squadriglie* detached to different airbases in North Italy for local defence duties. They departed Caselle Torinese on the morning of 6 September and at 18:20 on 8 September the whole *Gruppo* landed in Tripoli Castel Benito.

The 366ª *Sq.* formation was composed of ten aircraft, flown by *cap.* Bernardino Serafini (CO), *ten.* Mario Ferrero (the *Gruppo* Adjutant), *s. ten.* Amedeo Guidi, *m. llo.* Giulio Cesare, *serg. magg.* Fiorenzo Milella, *serg. magg.* Dino Carta, *serg. magg.* Roberto Marchi, *serg. magg.* Cesare Chiarmetta,

Another photo of aircraft from the 73ª Squadriglia of the 9° Gruppo, 4° Stormo C.T., undergoing maintenance works. [via Renato Zavattini]

Aircraft from the 73ª Squadriglia of the 9º Gruppo, 4º Stormo C.T. [via Renato Zavattini]

serg. Antonio Camerini, *serg.* Eugenio Cicognani. *ten.* Piero Veneziani and *m. llo.* Giovanni Accorsi followed in the unit's hack Caproni Ca.133 together with five ground personnel.

The 367ª *Sq.* formation comprised the *Gruppo* Commander *magg.* Carlo Calosso, the 368ª *Sq.* pilot *serg.* Piero Hosquet, and nine other pilots. Among them were *cap.* Simeone Marsan (the CO), *ten.* Irzio Bozzolan, *ten.* Aldo Bonuti, *serg. magg.* Gino Bogoni and *serg.* Tolmino Zanarini. The *Squadriglia*'s six other pilots were *ten.* Giuseppe Costantini, *m. llo.* Bruno Castellani, *serg. magg.* Rodolfo Benco, *serg. magg.* Bruno Celotto, *serg.* Renato Mingozzi and *serg.* Maggiorino Soldati.

The 368ª *Sq.* formation was composed of nine aircraft: *cap.* Bruno Locatelli (CO), *ten.* Giuseppe Zuffi, *s. ten.* Furio Lauri, *serg. magg.* Davide Colauzzi, *serg. magg.* Annibale Ricotti, *serg. magg.* Alvise Andrich, *serg.* Stefano Fiore, *serg.* Ottorino Ambrosi, *serg.* Mario Turchi. *ten.* Orfeo Paroli and *m. llo.* Guido Paparatti followed in the Ca.133 of the *Squadriglia* (Paroli and Fiore were just transferred from 367ª *Sq.*).

On 25 September the 151º *Gr.* transferred from Benghazi to El Adem where it replaced the 9º *Gr. C.T.*

Fiat CR.42s, which had just taken off from Tmini in September 1940. [via Italian Air Force]

Bombers

In the beginning of September and following the recent movements, the bomber strength of the 5ª *Squadra Aerea* was raised to 130 combat-ready Savoia SM 79s, the highest number attained since the beginning of the war.

On 4 September the 10° *Stormo*, the bomber unit that had suffered most losses (in the air and on the ground), was ordered back on Italy. They flew their last mission on 5 September (against Mersa Matruh) and its operational record for the period June-September 1940 listed 320 sorties, three SM 79s shot down by enemy fighters, one SM 79 shot down by AA, six SM 79s hit by enemy action during combat and eight aircraft hit on the ground.

Only four planes destroyed in the air doesn't seem to be a big loss, considering the 32 aircraft of the initial complement of the *Stormo*, but it is necessary to bear in mind that two of the six planes hit by enemy fighters were subsequently written off, while many of the eight planes hit on ground were classified RD. That meant that the big tri-motors had to be sent back in Italy for major repairs in the SIAI workshops, and considering that they couldn't reach Italy in flight the only option they had was to arrive there by ship; on the other hand the large SM 79 wing was made in a single piece and this required special equipment to disassemble the damaged planes and to transport them to the already overburdened harbours of Libya. In other words the planes classified RD were virtually lost. Also losses among the personnel were high: 36 dead, 15 wounded and two prisoners.

The retreat of the unit was completed during the first ten days of the month.

The *Stormo* left its remaining "combat-ready" SM 79s in North Africa; three to the 14° *Stormo*, one to the 15° *Stormo* and five to the 33° *Stormo*.

They were replaced by the 9° *Stormo B.T.* from Viterbo (the so called "*Iron Stormo*"). This *Stormo* arrived at Tripoli Castel Benito under the command of *col.* Mario Aramu and was composed of:

26° Gr. (CO *ten. col.* Italo Napoleoni) with 11ª Sq. (CO *ten.* Giovanni Ruggiero) and 13ª Sq. (CO *cap.* Edvige Pucci).

Close escort of CR.42s (possibly of the 2° Stormo) for Italian SM 79s coming back after a raid against Sidi Barrani in the summer of 1940.
[via Istituto Luce]

29º *Gr.* (CO *ten. col.* Guglielmo Grandjacquet) with 62ª *Sq.* (CO *cap.* Vincenzo Tedeschi) and 63ª *Sq.* (CO *cap.* Victor Hugo Girolami).

Total strength of the *Stormo* was 32 Savoia SM 79 bombers, all combat-ready.

On 3 September the *Reparto Speciale Aerosiluranti* changed name and became the 278ª *Sq. Autonoma Aerosiluranti*.

On 8 September the 33º *Gr.* transferred from Tmini to Z1 with its 13 combat-ready SM 79s.

Land operations ended successfully with the conquest of Sidi Barrani on 17 September, and the SM 79s started a period of recovery. Losses on the ground and in the air, together with the wear caused by the intense operations, meant that the number of combat-ready SM 79s was down to 80. Problems of serviceability on the SM 79s were due to the sand wear that affected the lining of the fuselage and the wooden, together with the constant lack of spare parts of whatever kind; compared to the CR.42s the engines never gave particular problems. A young *Aviere motorista* of 10º *Stormo* had the opinion:

"That engines (the Alfa Romeo 126), even in the desert, always run well and never gave problems without particular cares. We never used anti-sand filters that, however, we never had, it was sufficient to close the shutter of the carburettor and to move the engine deflectors, those things we learned when we discovered them on the wreck of a shot down RAF Blenheim, a plane equipped with the same engines as the S79 although built by the Bristol".

In fact, the Blenheim was equipped with Bristol Mercury engines while the Alfa Romeo 126 was a licence built Bristol Pegasus. However, the Mercury and Pegasus were more or less the same design with a different piston stroke.

The 54º *Gr. B.T.*, one of the very few units of the RA active over the front (together with the usual reconnaissance planes), transferred from Ain El Gazala to Benina on 27 September.

Ten. Rinaldo Galimberti joined the 278ª *Sq.* at T3 on 10 September, coming from the 50º *Stormo*.

Ground attack forces

At the end of the period of frequent action in support of the Italian Army the 50º *Stormo* only had eighteen combat-ready CR.32s and ten Ba.65s, out of a total force of forty attack aircraft.

A Fiat CR.42 taking off.
[Italian Air Force]

Reconaissance forces

The 137ª and 127ª *Squadriglie* of the 73° *Gr.* rejoined front line operations with their Ro.37bis. During this period the *Gruppo* also had a section of SM 79s from the 175ª *Sq.* that operated under its control. On the end of the month the SM 79 left the unit.

Colonial forces

On 29 September, a Fiesler Fi156C-1 was in use by Italian units in Libya. It is believed that the plane was the former personal aircraft of Marshal Italo Balbo (with the civil marking I-ULIA), who received it from Hermann Göring in January 1939 in exchange for a statue of Venus found in the archaeological area of Leptis Magna, which Balbo had presented to the Nazi leader. Only later (in July 1941), the *Regia Aeronautica* officially bought the aircraft from Balbo's family and assigned it to 104ª *Sq.*, 1° *Gr. A.P.C.* with the serial number MM56631.

Five Ca.309s of the 23ª *Sq.*, 2° *Gr. A.P.C.* took part in the advance on Sidi Barrani.

Royal Air Force

Reinforcements

Up to now the situation for the Desert Air Force reinforcements was the following, apart from the few Hurricanes and Blenheims that had reached Egypt by air before the French collapse: 24 Hurricanes shipped via the Cape were approaching the end of their long voyage; 36 more were nearing Takoradi. 24 Blenheim Mk.IVs had reached Egypt by air via Malta, 24 were at sea bound either for Takoradi or for Egypt round the Cape.

The development of the Takoradi air route was a direct consequence of the fact that the air route across France could no longer be used for aircraft of short endurance. So a combined sea and air route from England to the Gold Coast port of Takoradi and from there to Egypt via Khartoum was developed. Briefly the planes were shipped in crates to Takoradi, erected there and flew across Africa to Abu Sueir (in the Suez Canal zone) via Lagos (378 miles) – Kano (525 miles) – Maiduguri (325 miles) – Geneina (689 miles) – Khartoum (754 miles) – Abu Sueir (1,026 miles) for a total distance of 3,697 miles. Except for a distance of 600 miles when it crossed the Chad province

Air route from England to the Gold Coast port of Takoradi and from there to Egypt via Khartoum.
[via Robert Gretzyngier]

of French Equatorial Africa, the route passed over British-controlled territory. The planes once erected needed around a week to reach Egypt.

On 26 September the first reinforcements using the Takoradi route arrived at Abu Suerir in Egypt, in the form of five Hurricanes and a Blenheim Mk.IV, which were part of a batch of six Hurricanes and six Blenheims that arrived crated at Takoradi on 5 September. They were erected and six of the fighters with a Blenheim for navigational aid left for Egypt on 18 September. One of the Hurricanes was lost en route.

In the following days the other Blenheims would follow, together with 30 fighters disembarked at Takoradi by the carrier HMS *Argus*. The first Blenheims went to 14 Sqn in East Africa to replace this unit's Wellesleys.

At the end of August, four Valentias of 70 Sqn were transferred to the South African Air Force while S/Ldr Hohler, S/Ldr B. J. McGinn with four officers and five Sgt Pilots left for the UK, to bring back the new Wellingtons with which the squadron was to be equipped.

The first delivery of six Wellingtons arrived at Heliopolis at 13:30 on 1 September. The six bombers (T2730, T2731, T2732, T2733, T2734 and T2735) were led by S/Ldr R. J. Wells and they had left England at 21:15 on 29 August.

On 9 September, the squadron moved from Heliopolis to Kabrit.

Another French Potez 63.11 no. 395, which had landed badly on 30 May during a liaison flight between Ismaïlia and Damascus was repaired in September with some pieces from Potez 63.11 no. 799/AX673, which had had a landing accident on 16 September. The pilot, Paul Jacquier, had been slightly wounded in his back. The Potez 63.11 n°395 was later assigned the British serial AX680 and joined the Free French Flight No. 2. *Sous-Lieutenant* Jean Pompeï arrived in Egypt in September after leaving Liban by feet to Palestine. Perhaps another French pilot, *Lieutenant* Daniel Closter, arrived around this date but we have little info about him. Before the war, he worked for the French company of the Canal de Suez. He took part of the Battle of France. After the Armistice, he was authorized to come back to Cairo, but it seems that he came at the 2 FFF at the end of 1940 and was shot down on 16 May 1941 in the Tobruk area while flying Hurricane W9302 of the 'C' Flight of 274 Sqn.

Fighters

On 31 August 'B' Flight of 80 Sqn prepared to transfer from Sidi Barrani to Sidi Haneish, which was reached on 1 September. There it would join the rest of the squadron. The order to retreat arrived because increasing concentrations of enemy forces were noticed at the border.

'B' Flight of 80 Sqn was replaced by 'A' Flight of 112 Sqn at Sidi Barrani on 3 September.

The rest of 80 Sqn moved to Sidi Haneish on 13 September.

On 7 September, 112 Sqn moved to Sidi Haneish because of the foreseen offensive by the Italian Army.

On 14 September, 'C' Flight of 112 Sqn moved to 'Z' LG. On 29 September, S/Ldr Harry Brown took command of 112 Sqn from S/Ldr D. M. Somerville. During the same month, 'C' Flight of 112 Sqn became 'B' Flight of the same squadron.

On 13 September, word came that 33 Sqn was to be re-equipped with Hurricanes, while its Gladiators would be handed over to 3 Sqn RAAF. 'A' Flight was first to convert to the Hurricane. 'B' Flight of 33 Sqn was moved forward to Fuka on 22 September without waiting for re-equipment with Hurricanes. Ten Gladiators arrived this day, while 'A' Flight was still at Helwan rushing the conversion to Hurricanes.

In the evening of 28 September, the Free French Flight attached to 274 Sqn was posted Haifa, Palestine, to convert to Hurricanes.

L1669 (*Collie's Battleship*), the only operational Hurricane at the start of the Desert War, was written off following a forced landing at Amiriya on 30 September while serving with 274 Sqn.

Flight Lieutenant Alfred Bocking took his Flight of fighter Blenheims from 30 Sqn to Haifa, Palestine, in September to protect the harbour from SM 79s from the Dodecanese Islands.

Bombers

70 Sqn was completely re-equipped before the end of September. On 25 September, two more Wellingtons (T2826 and T2832) arrived at Kabrit and were allotted to the squadron, while the third machine of the reinforcement party (T2817) had crashed on Malta. Finally, on 30 September, three more machines (T2813, T2814 and T2816) arrived from England and were allotted to the squadron.

During the month, another Valentia was passed to SAAF. At the end of the month, 70 Sqn had ten Wellingtons serviceable, one unserviceable but repairable, seven Valentias serviceable and one unserviceable but repairable, plus a Magister.

The arrival of the Wellingtons made it possible for a British unit to attack the Benghazi area with sufficient bombload for the first time.

At the end of August, 45 Sqn received orders to move to Sudan as a whole and prepared to do so. A gap in 45's records don't permit us to see exactly how it was deployed, but it seems that a contingent of at least four bombers under F/Lt Troughton-Smith was in action over Italian East Africa on 11 September. The rest of the squadron, under command of S/Ldr Dallamore (where F/Lt Dudgeon also had been promoted to S/Ldr), arrived from Helwan to Wadi Gazouza around 25 September. It is supposed that the move of the squadron was delayed by the Italian offensive. However, no details are known of the eventual activity of the squadron over Egypt from 9 September to 24 September.

On 27 September, 113 Sqn moved from Ma'aten Bagush to 'Waterloo' aerodrome, the move being completed the next day.

Reconnaissance forces

On 17 September, the RAF policy regarding fighter escort for tactical reconnaissance was discussed and it was laid down by 202 Group that "*no such escorts could be given under the present circumstances*".

At the start of the Italian offensive on 13 September, 'C' flight of 6 Sqn was called in from Palestine, arriving at Qasaba on 19 September on attachment to 208 Sqn. 6 Sqn was based at Ramleh, with sections detached to Gaza since the beginning of the war. The unit was commanded by S/Ldr R. E. Weld from 24 September, who arrived to temporarily replace S/Ldr W. N. McKechnie, who had been wounded during an Italian bombing of Tel Aviv on 19 September. S/Ldr Weld later took permanent command of the unit.

The first detachment was commanded by F/Lt D. J. H. Lay DFC, and was composed of four Westland Lysander Mk.IIs (L6875, L6876, L6877 and L6879), with five additional pilots. The rest of the squadron with seven Lysanders remained in Palestine.

On 30 September, Lysander L6879 left Quasaba piloted by F/O F. E. G. Hayter for Siwa, where it went to reinforce 'A' Flight of 208 Sqn.

'B' Flight of 208 Sqn was ordered to relieve 'C' Flight at Sidi Barrani on 10 September. On 14 September, 'C' Flight received orders to move from Sidi Barrani to landing Ground 'Z' in the Matruh-Sollum road, due to the advance of the Italian Army.

'C' Flight flew to Bir Kenayis, close to the HQ of 7th Armoured Division, on 15 September. On 17 September, it was notified that one Flight of the squadron was to be rearmed with Hurricanes.

Two Lysanders and a small ground party from 'A' Flight were moved to Siwa oasis on 20 September to operate against the Italian base Giarabub.

'B' Flight moved to the ALG of Bir Qa'aim on 21 September to operate over the new front line extending from Sofafi to Sidi Barrani.

On 23 September, 'B' Flight moved to a new and better landing ground at Min'Qar Qa'aim.

Royal Australian Air Force

On 1 September the 3 Sqn RAAF pilots commenced flying instruction and training on the Lysander, but the amount of training each pilot received was strictly limited owing to the fact that only one aircraft was held by the unit on loan.

On 3 September the 3 Sqn RAAF commenced work on unpacking and erection of Lysanders received from overseas. Due to the fact that it was found that no propellers or air cleaners had arrived with the aircraft, they couldn't be completed, and training had to continue with the borrowed aircraft.

3 Sqn RAAF received a second Lysander on loan for training purposes on 5 September. This aircraft was received from 102 MU, Abu Sueir.

On 7 September all personnel of 3 Sqn RAAF joined the unit at Ismailia.

A third Lysander was received by 3 Sqn RAAF on 12 September. This aircraft was also on loan from 102 MU, Abu Sueir.

On 13 September a number of promotions of 3 Sqn RAAF officers were notified by signal from Air Board. Charles Gaden was promoted to F/Lt (Temporary) as of 1 September, while Wilfred Arthur and Alan Boyd were promoted to F/O s as off 9 September.

On 14 September Air Chief Marshal Longmore, the Air Officer commanding-in-Chief, RAF Middle East, visited 3 Sqn RAAF at Ismailia, and addressed the members of the squadron on parade.

3 Sqn RAAF received a signal from HQME on 16 September advising that it had been decided to re-arm the squadron with two flights of Gladiators and one flight of Lysanders.

In order to carry out this re-arming, the unit was to move from Ismailia to Helwan on 23 September, where the Gladiators were to be taken over from 33 Sqn.

In view of the fact that the propellers and air cleaners had still not been received for the Lysanders, and that stores from overseas were still being received at Ismailia, it was decided that the main portion of the unit would proceed to Helwan on 23 September, whilst the remainder of the unit would

(Left to right) Flying Officer Alan Rawlinson, Flight Lieutenant Blake Pelly and Flying Officer Alan Boyd of 3 RAAF Sqn on 24 November 1940 during a photo session following the "successful" combat on 19 November. [via Australian War Memorial]

remain at Ismailia to complete the erection of six Lysanders and for the sorting of stores. These last remainders moved to Helwan on 9 October.

On 18 September an advance party from 3 Sqn RAAF proceeded to Helwan by road to commence taking over Gladiator aircraft and other equipment from 33 Sqn. The party consisted of S/Ldr P. R. Heath, F/Lt Charles Gaden, F/O s John Perrin, Alan Boyd, B. L. Bracegirdle, M. D. Ellerton and Alan Gatward and 14 other ranks.

During 21 to 23 September the advanced party took over four Gladiators from 33 Sqn and the pilots were put on daily stand-by for operational duty, which was defence of Cairo against air attack. Eleven more personnel followed on to Helwan on 20 September, while the rest of the squadron prepared for the move which was made on 23 September.

On 19 September, 3 Sqn RAAF received instructions from HQME that four pilots with nine ground crew were to be attached to 208 Sqn in the Western Desert for operational duties. The pilots detailed for this duty were F/Lt Blake Pelly and F/O s Alan Rawlinson, Peter Turnbull and L. E. Knowles.

The pilots collected Gloster Gauntlets from 102 MU at Abu Sueir the same day, and proceeded to 208 Sqn the following day, while the ground crew followed in a Bombay.

3 Sqn RAAF's stand-by duty was discontinued on 24 September and the pilots were able to carry out flying training. An intensive period of training followed, and the training was complemented with exercises with 6th division AIF and air fighting tactics with Blenheims from 84 Sqn. The pilots also visited Haskard range for artillery co-operation training on 4 October. This training period continued up until 31 October.

Operations

1 September 1940

Force F approached the Sicilian Narrows under constant fighter cover, while the three ship convoy from Alexandria continued to steam towards Malta harbour. During the night HMS *Ark Royal's* Swordfishes made a diversionary strike against Cagliari, losing one aircraft in a crash-landing.

Sunderland L5806/Q from 228 Sqn flown by F/Lt Ware was followed by a CR.42 at 17:45 during a patrol from Malta off Sicily. The Italian plane didn't press home any attack.

2 September 1940

The three ship convoy reached Malta safely, while Force F met the Mediterranean fleet south of Malta. A shadower appeared over the fleet, but a patrol of three Fulmars from 806 Sqn flown by Lieutenant Commander Evans, Lieutenant Commander Robin Kilroy and Sub Lieutenant Lowe intercepted and jointly shot it down into the sea. This was possibly a Cant Z.501 of the 182^a *Sq. R.M.*, *s. ten.* Ottavio De Martis and *s. ten. di Vascello* Fortunato Campione becoming MIA. This loss caused by enemy fighters is actually reported on 3 September, but this is probably incorrect.

The shadower was, however, able to signal the presence of the enemy fleet, which was then attacked by Sicilian-based SM 79s from the 36° and 41° *Stormi*. The attacks were intercepted by the Fulmars, which claimed three SM 79s of the 41° *Stormo*. For the first time since the beginning of the war the Mediterranean fleet was successfully protected by its fighters.

Also the newly-arrived Junkers Ju87B-2 and R-2 *Stukas* of the 96° *Gr. B.T.* under *cap.* Ercolano Ercolani (formerly one of the three pilots in the Italian aerobatic team that had taken part in the Berlin Olympic Games in 1936) saw their first action during the day, when they attacked twice claiming hits on two cruisers, a large vessel and HMS *Illustrious* (however they reported that the bomb that hit the aircraft carrier failed to explode). However it seems that they actually didn't score any hits, but they didn't suffer any losses.

Force H, coming back to Gibraltar, was subjected to an air attack and the Polish destroyer *Garland* was hit by a bomb.

4 September 1940

During the day, the 92ª *Sq.*, 8º *Gr. C.T.* flew four protective patrols and made four scrambles over and around Derna. Twice they met British bombers, which attacked Derna six times with formations of two aircraft without causing casualties among the personnel but were able to hit and damage some aircraft of the 10º *Stormo*.

The first engagement happened at around 09:20, when a covering patrol of *s. ten.* Alfonso Notari and *serg.* Nadio Monti intercepted two British bombers coming back from a raid on Derna. The two bombers were followed 30 kilometres inside their own lines and finally left in a cloudbank.

S. ten. Notari claimed one Blenheim probably shot down and one heavily damaged with the use of 1000 rounds of ammunition. One the British bomber was reported as having one engine on fire.

Even if records of 113 Sqn for this day are completely lost, it is known that the squadron was ordered to raid Derna with four pairs of bombers and an Mk.I nicknamed "*the old un*" was hit by fighters that killed the pilot, 24-year-old P/O John Harry Reynolds. With the aircraft in a shallow dive and its wings rocking, the two Leading Aircraftmen that made up the rest of the crew hauled the dead pilot out of his seat, and took command of the aircraft. They were Leading Aircraftman Hutchinson and Leading Aircraftman Ian "Jock" Blair. Blair, who was an armourer/air gunner, flew the Blenheim 350 miles back to Ma'aten Bagush and made a very good landing, earning the DFM. Later he became a pilot and would survive the war as a Flight Lieutenant. It seems that this was one of the bombers attacked by *s. ten.* Notari.

The second engagement started at 13:40, when *serg.* Ernesto Pavan of the 92ª *Sq.* scrambled alone from Derna in a Fiat CR.42 to intercept two Blenheims. The first was downed and crashed near Derna airfield (crew POW) while the second was followed for some miles and finally claimed shot down over the sea. S/Ldr Bax of 211 Sqn flew the first Blenheim. Bax and his crew (Sgt R. A. Bain and Aircraftman 1st Class L. E. C. Wise) force-landed in the desert in enemy territory and reported that the Blenheim Mk.I (L8376/UQ-D named "*The Porpoise*") was shot up while on the ground by fighters. The British crew was taken prisoner shortly after. The other Blenheim was L8471 piloted by F/Sgt Marpole (observer P/O Eric Bevington-Smith, gunner Leading Aircraftman Alcock), which force-landed at Sidi Barrani at 16:25 with an oil leak in the port tank, 7-8 bullet holes in the port wing and damage to the port tailplane tip. The crew was safe and the aircraft was later recovered and repaired only to be finally lost in Greece in the ranks of 84 Sqn. Bax was replaced as CO of 211 Sqn by acting S/Ldr James Richmond Gordon-Finlayson.

Serg. Pavan landed back at base at 14:20. He had expended 1000 rounds of ammunition and his aircraft was damaged by return fire from the Blenheims. In fact, during the furious dogfight, which the returning British crew reported as started at 15:20 and lasted 5 to 8 minutes, they were able to fire some 200 round against the CR.42, some of which found their target.

Apart from the attack on Derna, Tmini, Menelao and Ain El Gazala also suffered air attacks during the day. Damage was however light. Tmini suffered two wounded and three SM 79s lightly damaged (RS) and Menelao had two barracks destroyed, while Ain El Gazala didn't suffer any damage at all.

These attacks on Tmini, Menelao and Ain el Gazala were performed by 55 and 211 Sqns, which during the morning and the early afternoon put up six pairs of Blenheims for "nuisance" high level raids over the Italian airfields. 55 Sqn's Blenheims didn't observe particular results from their bombing and almost all came back to Fuka without incident. Only during the sortie flown over Tmini at 11:50 was an Italian fighter observed, but this didn't attack. The port airscrew of Blenheim L4818, flown by Sgt R. W. Mason, flew off the engine shortly after 09:30 (probably over Tmini) but the bomber was able to fly back to base, landing at 11:35.

Sunderland L5807/R from 228 Sqn, flown by Wing Commander Nicholetts, was attacked twice by unidentified fighter aircraft when on patrol off Kaso strait. The plane returned to Malta without suffering damage.

5 September 1940

At 08:00 in the morning an SM 79, flown by *ten. col.* Umberto Klinger, took off from Derna and, after a stop at Menastir to refuel, made an attack in the Suez area at 13:20. At 18:00 the aircraft was back at Derna.

Ten. col. Klinger was a pre-war flight pioneer who in 1934 was part of the group who created the Italian National flight company Ala Littoria. Blessed with outstanding organisational ability, at the beginning of the war he quickly integrated "Ala Littoria" into the transport branch of the Air Force (the so-called S.A.S., *Servizi Aerei Speciali* or Special Air Service) and then placed himself at V^a *Squadra Aerea*'s disposal, to organise special (mostly night) missions.

The 10° *Stormo* officially ended operations over North Africa with a bombing attack on Mersa Matruh, made by nine SM 79s led by *ten. col.* Unia.

Two SM 79s of 175^a *Sq. R.S.T.* covered the border area from Bardia to Giarabub.

Five SM 79s of 45° *Gr.* under *magg.* Berni attacked troop concentrations near Sollum.

6 September 1940

During the day, a series of operations started with the aim of putting the railway station of Mersa Matruh out of action.

The first formation, 15 bombers in three vics of five, took off from Tmini led by *Generale* Porro himself. The take-off was made under a sand storm and three SM 79s suffered engine failures and were forced to crash-land immediately (they were classified RD), while three others were forced to turn back The rest of the formation, four aircraft of the 60^a *Sq.*, 33° *Gr.*, with Porro and *ten.* Pastorelli and five planes of the 45° *Gr.* under *col.* Attilio Biseo, proceeded to the target. After bomb release, seven Gladiators attacked, damaging slightly the plane of Pastorelli. All SM 79s landed at Tmini at 10:40.

In the meantime 15 SM 79s of the 15° *Stormo* (ten SM 79s of the 47° *Gr.* led by *col.* Napoli and *magg.* Tivegna and five SM 79s of the 21^a *Sq.* led by *cap.* Lualdi) took off from Maraua for the same target. The attack was carried out under heavy AA fire while the Gladiators attacked. This time too the SM 79s were able to defend themselves without suffering losses, the returning crews claimed many hits on the railway and two Gladiators shot down plus two probables.

It seems that the two Italian formations had clashed with Gladiators from 112 Sqn. A patrol composed of F/Lt Lloyd Schwab, P/O Henry Harrison and P/O Peter Wickham, was over Matruh at 15000 feet and reported to have met and driven out to the sea a group of five SM 79s.

Another patrol composed of F/O A. M. Ross, P/O Leonard Bartley and Sgt G. M. Donaldson attacked five SM 79s without results. Ross' Gladiator was damaged by one bullet in the fuselage on the starboard side. It seems that F/O Joseph Fraser claimed an unconfirmed SM 79 on this occasion.

At 09:05, *cap.* Guidorzi of the 20^a *Sq.* flew over Alexandria harbour for the usual daily strategic reconnaissance

During the subsequent days up to 9 September, bombing and reconnaissance missions continued incessantly following this path: strategic bombing mission by formations up to fifteen planes over Mersa Matruh, strategic reconnaissance missions over Alexandria, tactical missions of smaller formations in the border area, night bombing missions by the S.81s of 54° *Gr.* No losses were suffered.

Joseph Fraser remembered:

"During this period as well, we were having to keep two aircraft at readiness all night for night interceptions but the only air the Gladiator had to intercept at night was an indifferent H.F. radio communication with his base. Many attempts were made to intercept at night by the squadron's pilots without success, though F/O Happy Clarke probably came nearest to a night interception. Under the control of the A.O.C., A/Cmdre Collishaw, Happy heard a continuous commentary of the presumed whereabouts of an Italian bomber – "Good show, laddie; bandit over Ma'aten Bagush now, laddie; flying west, laddie; should be over Qasaba now laddie; Go like hell, laddie; Well tried, laddie".

Mersa Matruh, being the enemy's main night target, Gladiators were often sent on night patrols 5 miles south of the port with orders to attack whenever the enemy were illuminated by search lights. But as these searchlights and guns were mostly manned by Egyptians at the time, they were invariably miles behind the target and if you did see an enemy bomber and give chase, the guns were far more likely to shoot you down than the enemy as you came up behind him."

8 September 1940

S. ten. Griffaldi of the 8° *Gr.* flying in a 82ª *Sq.* aircraft crashed on take off. He was unhurt but the plane was written off.

9 September 1940

Operations supporting the planned offensive on Sidi Barrani started during the day.

First the 44° *Gr.* starting from Benina with a formation of ten aircraft attacked Mersa Matruh. The operation was full of problems, and in the end only one aircraft landed back at base; one SM 79 aborted immediately because of engine problems, three aircraft landed at Z1 to develop the photo shots of the objective they had taken during the mission, one aircraft made a forced-landing after running out of fuel (and was probably written off), other aircraft were forced to land in Maraua, Apollonia and Barce after becoming dangerously low on fuel.

At 12:55 another formation of nine SM 79s of the 14° took off, the aircraft of *col.* Coppi being heavily damaged (RD) at the start. The other eight aircraft attacked Sidi Barrani.

The British answer to all these attacks was, as usual, extremely effective. In the afternoon British bombers put up a combined effort by all three operative squadrons, with 55 and 211 Sqns attacking the north foreshore of Tobruk harbour and 113 Sqn attacking Derna harbour and landing ground. The bombers took off at around 13:30 and were back at base at around 16:30.

The raiders of Tobruk succeeded in hitting the cruiser *San Giorgio* with four small calibre bombs, they were not the first bombs to hit the *San Giorgio* but were among the first to explode, although without causing casualties. Sailors fighting on the Italian cruiser's AA batteries had in fact learned, since the beginning of war, to immediately throw away the bombs hitting the bridge, which often were fused for delayed explosion, thus avoiding their detonation on the ship. Italian sailors were also trained to fight the incendiary bombs hitting their positions with sand. From their aircraft British crews were frequently able to appreciate direct hits on *San Giorgio* but then when the reconnaissance returned to document them the Italian ship was always intact and fighting back with all its guns, thus originating the myth of the ship already sunk and beached in shallow waters. Over Derna, 113 Sqn caught the 26° *Gr.*, 9° *Stormo*, which just had arrived. The aircraft of the *Gruppo* Commander was hit by a bomb that destroyed it together with the flag of the *Stormo* and all the personal effects of the occupants (but luckily without causing casualties).

Three Blenheims of 55 Sqn also raided Ain El Gazala and Tmini at dusk. Over Tmini bombs were seen to fall on the target area and in fact one barrack was destroyed with three personnel wounded.

Three Blenheims of 211 Sqn again raided Tobruk harbour.

During the night the 4° *Stormo* started a night alarm service from T3 with pilots from the two *Gruppi* on alerts during cloudless full moon nights. Later the alarm duty was carried on even without the help of moonlight. The equipment for this kind of service was extremely primitive. The aircraft took off with the help of two lamps put at the end of the airstrip, while three lamps signalled its middle. In case of total absence of light, take-offs and landings were done with the headlights of cars and lorries. There was no radio communication, so the presumed direction of enemy aircraft was given to the pilot from the ground using machinegun tracers. The CR.42 only had basic instruments and was without illumination in the cockpit, so the pilots used torchlight to read anemometer, altimeter and variometer, their only help during night flights.

In the 9° *Gr.*, *ten.* Vittorio Pezzè and *serg. magg.* Guglielmo Biffani (both of the 73ª *Sq.*) were two of the few pilots able to do this job. Biffani remembered that the big dimensions of El Adem and the low landing speed of the Fiat were his greatest help during these missions.

10 September 1940

The 9° and 10° *Gruppi* with *magg.* Ernesto Botto and *magg.* Carlo Romagnoli in the lead, protected the movements of the Italian troops preparing to attack Egypt with standing patrols throughout the day.

Ten SM 79s of the 33° *Gr.* (including some borrowed crews of the 33° *Stormo*) attacked Mersa Matruh at 17:00. This time, after some days of ineffective interceptions, the British fighters were up in full strength with twelve Gladiators of 80 Sqn, helped by two Hurricanes of 274 Sqn (F/O John Lapsley and Sgt Clarke, who had flown up from Alexandria on attachment to 112 Sqn) and two Blenheim fighters of 30 Sqn. The Gladiators were from 'B' Flight and recently back from Sidi Haneish.

After the bombing (reportedly scoring direct hits) the SM 79s were intercepted at 5000 metres by the RAF fighters and a running battle began, after which two Italian bombers failed to return. The returning Italian bomber crews claimed two Hurricanes and two Gladiators, which were later downgraded to two fighters confirmed and two probables.

The RAF pilots claimed four SM 79s. F/O John Lapsley claimed two, F/Lt Frank Marlow (Blenheim K7096 with gunner Sgt Lord) claimed one, while the fourth was claimed by P/O 'Heimar' Stuckey of 80 Sqn. The guns of Clarke jammed when he was in a very favourable position. In another combat later in the afternoon, Lapsley's Hurricane got its windscreen completely shattered by return fire from the Italian bombers. Marlow recorded that after having taken off at 12:50, he joined Gladiators and Hurricanes in attacking six SM 79s in two flights of three. The leading aircraft of the second formation was shot down and the other two became stragglers. He attacked the starboard aircraft until he saw it falling into the sea. P/O Stuckey was up with P/O Samuel Cooper and Sgt Donald Gregory when at 15:00, they intercepted a formation of five SM 79s in two sub-Flights of three and two, which was already under attack by a Hurricane. Gregory had to disengage with engine trouble, while Cooper and Stuckey attacked the port aircraft of the sub-section of two SM 79s, which was damaged, seen to lose height steadily and finally ditching at 15:20. Stuckey circled the wreck until it sank 25 minutes later, and saw the five surviving members of the crew in their rubber boat, also giving them a thumbs up sign. During the attack his gun ceased to fire after he had silenced the rear and side gunners, so he tried to hit the Savoia from short distance shooting at it with four Very lights. From the very detailed description given by Stuckey and his wingmen, it seems highly likely that one of Savoias of the 33° *Stormo* fell to his fire (perhaps double-claimed by a Hurricane pilot).

Both lost SM 79s were from the 46ª *Sq.*, 33° *Stormo* (*ten.* Felice Scandone, *s. ten.* Alfonso Colpi, *serg. magg. Radiotelegrafista* Francesco Minicillo, *Primo Aviere Fotografo* Ubaldo Spallone, *Aviere Scelto Motorista* Riccardo Leghissa and *Aviere Scelto Armiere* Ferdinando Muto; *s. ten.* Alfonso Magliacane, *serg. magg.* Manfredo Fucile, *Primo Aviere Motorista* Ugo Rizzotto, *Primo Aviere Armiere* Ubaldo Esposito, *Primo Aviere Radiotelegrafista* Orazio Minotta and *Allievo Aviere Fotografo* Antonio Ferrero –a cadet) with both crews MIA.

According to all existing British Squadron ORBs, the successful interception occurred at around 14:00. This is not consistent with Italian records, which didn't record any action before that just described, which reportedly occurred later, at 17:00. The possibility of a gap in Italian records, however, remains.

Near Ain El Gazala Z1 the eight returning bombers were involved in an air battle between Bristol Blenheims (most likely from 113 Sqn) and 2° *Stormo*'s fighters. In the ensuing confusion CR.42s of the 13° *Gr.* (77ª and 78ª *Squadriglie*) also attacked an SM 79 in error. In one of the first documented cases of "friendly fire" between units of the *Regia Aeronautica*, *s. ten.* Mario Fabbricatore of the 77ª *Sq.* attacked, and before realising his error the 59ª *Sq.*'s SM 79 flown by *s. ten.* Barion (second pilot *serg.* Benvenuti) caught fire. In panic, two members (*Primo Aviere* Luigi Martini and *Allievo Aviere Armiere* Pietro Pinna) baled out of the burning aircraft but, being too low both were killed when they hit the ground. The rest of the crew was able to fight the fire and force-landed fifteen kilometres short of base.

In the end landing at Z1 (badly holed by British bombers) was considered too dangerous by the last aircraft of the formation, and *ten.* Giancandido Pastorelli turned back and brought his aircraft to Tmini.

A board of inquiry was immediately installed by the *Comando di Squadra*, its conclusions are not known, apart from that the finding that the Italian bombers too often had unnecessarily large crews and this increased the losses among the ever difficult to replace personnel.

The British raid over Ain El Gazala caused no additional damage.

Flight Lieutenant Black of 208 Sqn went on an unescorted tactical reconnaissance in the evening, which ended with the interception by a CR.42 that Black evaded by flying very low.

211 and 55 Sqns carried out attacks against T2, Tobruk harbour, Bardia, Tmini, Menelao and Ain El Gazala during the evening with single aircraft. They reportedly encountered no opposition.

11 September 1940

An SM 79 of the 175ª *Sq.* on the usual strategic reconnaissance over Alexandria was intercepted during the morning by a Blenheim fighter and shot down, with the loss of the crew of seven - *ten.* Antonio Bilancia, *serg.* Vittorio Caretti, *ten. di Vascello Osservatore* Giorgio Bosinelli, *Primo Aviere Motorista* Albino Caruso, *Primo Aviere Radiotelegrafista* Guido Venanzi, *Primo Aviere Armiere* Giovanni Silvi, *Primo Aviere Fotografo* Angelo Arabito.

The Italian bomber was shot down by a Blenheim Mk IF of 30 Sqn flown by P/O S. N. Pearce and Sgt Tubberdy, who attacked four times before seeing their opponent go down.

Notwithstanding this loss the missions over Alexandria continued regularly.

From 13:30 to 15:30, 24 fighters from the 8° *Gr.* under *magg.* Vincenzo La Carruba made a protective cruise over Gabr-Saleh - Bir Sheferzen - Sidi Omar.

The 9° and 10° *Gr.* were still employed in standing patrols over the troops. During the second patrol of the day, at 17:45 in the Sidi Omar – Bardia area, a Blenheim was discovered at 6000 metres.

The Italian formation was escorting three CR.32s and was led by *magg.* Carlo Romagnoli. It was composed of seven CR.42s from the 84ª *Sq.* (*cap.* Luigi Monti, *cap.* Vincenzo Vanni, *ten.* Giuseppe Aurili, *s. ten.* Paolo Berti, *serg.* Roberto Steppi, *serg.* Narciso Pillepich and *serg.* Domenico Santonocito), five CR.42s from the 91ª *Sq.* (*cap.* Giuseppe D'Agostinis, *s. ten.* Ruggero Caporali, *serg. magg.* Leonardo Ferrulli, *serg.* Elio Miotto and *serg.* Alessandro Bladelli) and six CR.42s from the 90ª *Sq.* (*ten.* Giovanni Guiducci, *ten.* Franco Lucchini, *s. ten.* Neri De Benedetti, *m. llo.* Omero Alesi, *serg. magg.* Angelo Savini and *serg.* Bruno Bortoletti).

Cap. Vanni, *ten.* Aurili and *serg.* Steppi attacked first, followed by other pilots of the formation. During the combat Vanni's aircraft was hit by return fire, and with the compressed air piping pierced, he was forced to turn back. His wingmen continued the pursuit and claimed the Blenheim shot down.

The bomber however was assigned as a shared kill to all the 10° *Gr.* pilots presents (even if , for example, it is known that 90ª *Sq.* pilots used only 140 rounds of ammunition in total, so possibly only one of them was able to use his guns).

This claim can't be verified from RAF sources, but it is possible that it was a Blenheim from 113 Sqn since this unit's ORB is lacking.

15 kilometres west of Sidi Omar, a large concentration of Italian motor transports was attacked at dusk by nine Blenheims of 211 Sqn led by S/Ldr Gordon-Finlayson. Several large fires were started and the Blenheims were back at base at 21:00.

12 September 1940

From 16:05 to 18:25, 25 fighters from the 8° *Gr.* under *magg.* Vincenzo La Carruba made a protective cruise over Uadi El Mrega-Sidi Omar.

On 12 September S/Ldr William Hickey of 80 Sqn took off at night to intercept a lone bomber attacking Mersa Matruh. As searchlights were illuminating it, he was able to fire a couple of bursts at it but failed to observe any results.

At 19:40, a formation of nine Blenheims of 55 Sqn under S/Ldr R. A. T. Stowell attacked the troops of *Raggruppamento Maletti*. The raid was reported successful, and in fact the Italian unit, which had left behind its AA guns complement at Derna, suffered quite heavily in the air attacks, which resulted in a reduction of its logistic capabilities and its operating range.

13 September 1940

The Italian attack against Egypt (the so-called "*Graziani Offensive*") began. The 9° and 10° *Gruppi* intensified the protective missions over the advancing troops with two big mixed formations of the two *Gruppi* (36 and 38 aircraft respectively). Some sources reported that during the second mission of the day, a Blenheim was attacked and claimed as shared, but this is not confirmed in the available *Squadriglie*'s Diaries.

A 208 Sqn Lysander flown P/O Waymark discovered the Italian Army on the move during a morning tactical reconnaissance. Another reconnaissance was carried out in the evening and both missions were escorted by Gladiators of 'A' Flight 80 Sqn (detached at Sidi Barrani). During the day, possibly when returning from a late evening sortie in K8013, P/O William Vale collided on landing with a barbed wire fence. The fighter was badly damaged but the pilot was uninjured.

The 13° *Gr.*, which had moved to Gambut the day before, performed a free sweep, flying at high altitude (7000 metres) over the border area from 09:50 to 12:00 with 19 fighters under *magg.* Secondo Revetria. They returned without seeing any enemy.

From 09:40 to 12:00, 25 fighters from the 8° *Gr.* under *magg.* Vincenzo La Carruba made a protective cruise over Uadi El Mrega-Sidi Omar.

At 10:20, *ten.* Guido Robone of the 278ª *Sq.* took off from El Adem in SM 79 "278-1" (second pilot *serg.* Corrado Deodato) with the Navy Observer *ten. di Vascello* Giovanni Marazio aboard. This was in response to a message from the Vª Squadra HQ, signalling a British convoy discovered at 09:00 by reconnaissance off Sidi Barrani.

At 12:45, when south-east of Crete, Robone discovered the small convoy (two merchants covered by three escort ships) and attacked under heavy and precise AA fire at 13:05. Unable to aim at the escort ships, Robone launched his torpedo against one of the freighters from a distance of 800 metres and at a height of 100 metres. He then escaped passing over the stern of the attacked ship. He remained around the convoy for half an hour and, although not able to follow the torpedo run because of his disengaging manoeuvres, could appreciate from long distance that his weapon had probably found its mark. He landed back at 14:55 and was credited with the hit that, however, has not been confirmed from Allied sources.

With the start of the offensive, all the bombers were called to maximum effort. Bombing and reconnaissance missions were flown from dawn to dusk with an average up to 90 SM 79s employed each day. Employed units on the first day were 14° *Stormo*, 15° *Stormo*, 33° *Gr.*, 175ª *Sq. R.S.T.* and 54° *Gr.* One plane of 45° *Gr.* was seriously damaged in the late morning during a take off from T2 (RD).

In the evening the aircraft of the 45° *Gr.* were moved from Ain El Gazala to Tmini.

The assault aircraft of the 50° *Stormo* hit the Qabr Abu Fayres area. The assault pilots claimed four tanks and seven armoured cars (all confirmed by the advancing Italian troops that captured the wrecks).

14 September 1940

From 07:50 to 10:00, 19 CR.42s from the 8° *Gr.* under *magg.* Vincenzo La Carruba made a protective sortie over Gabr Abu Fayres – Bir Gib. They didn't encounter any enemy.

Magg. Secondo Revetria led 16 fighters of the 13° *Gr.* in a high-level (6500 metres) sweep over Bardia-Sollum-Sidi Omar. The fighters took off at 08:00 and landed at 10:00 without meeting any enemy.

The 4° *Stormo* continued to protect the ground forces. A mixed formation of 23 CR.42s from the 9° *Gr.* commanded by *magg.* Ernesto Botto with 15 CR.42s from the 10° *Gr.* as high cover, took off at 10:25. At 11:00, over Sollum some 10° *Gr.* pilots discovered a formation of four Blenheims. They attacked and claimed one shot down in flames. The bomber was credited as a shared to the whole formation from the 10° *Gr.* (*ten.* Giovanni Guiducci, *s. ten.* Luigi Prati, *ten.* Franco Lucchini and *serg.* Bruno Bortoletti of the 90ª *Sq.* and *magg.* Carlo Romagnoli, *cap.* Giuseppe D'Agostinis, *s. ten.* Andrea Dalla Pasqua, *s. ten.* Ruggero Caporali, *s. ten.* Carlo Albertini and *serg. magg.* Leonardo Ferrulli of the 91ª *Sq.* and *cap.* Luigi Monti, *cap.* Vincenzo Vanni, *ten.* Giuseppe Aurili, *ten.* Paolo Berti and *serg.* Domenico Santonocito of the 84ª *Sq.*).

This clam can't be verified from RAF records. The only known British actions for the day were a couple of afternoon bomber raids. Four Blenheims of 55 Sqn with others from 211 Sqn were ordered to attack Italian troops in the Sollum area in the afternoon. The 55 Sqn quartet came back at 16:45 without suffering losses. Its pilots reported slight and ineffective AA fire and the presence of Italian fighters (but no interception occurred). Eight machines of 211 Sqn led by Gordon-Finalyson also attacked, claiming many hits in the target area. However no Italian fighters were seen and all the bombers were back at around 17:10.

Six Gladiators from 112 Sqn, which had taken off from 'Z' LG (Flight Lieutenant Charles Fry, F/O Joseph Fraser (K8019), F/Lt R. J. Abrahams, P/O R. H. Clarke, P/O R. J. Bennett and P/O Edwin Banks) in the meantime patrolled over Sollum without seeing any enemy.

From 16:30 to 18:25, 25 fighters from the 8° *Gr.* under *magg.* Vincenzo La Carruba made an uneventful protective flight over Gabr Abu Fayres – Bir Gib.

Coming back from an attack in the Bir El Kreigat area, the 160ª *Sq.*'s *serg. magg.* Corrado Sarti's CR.32 (MM4665) hit a Ba.65/A80 (MM75257) on landing. The two aircraft were written off and the pilot was wounded.

The 14° *Stormo*, 15° *Stormo*, 33° *Gr.*, 175ª *Sq. R.S.T.* and 54° *Gr.* flew many sorties during the day but no losses were suffered.

After approximately one month in North Africa the 7° *Gr. Combattimento* tried its hand in a combat action for the first time, from its bases at Derna and T2.

Taking off from Tobruk two Breda Ba.88s were briefed to attack Sidi Barrani airfield with small calibre bombs. One aircraft was flown by the *Gruppo* commander *magg.* Marcello Fossetta (gunner: *m. llo. Armiere* Cassano) and the second aircraft was flown by *m. llo.* Montanari (gunner: *serg. magg. Motorista* Casciani).

Immediately after take off Fossetta's aircraft, loaded with 119 two kg bombs in a "Nardi" ventral rack, proved impossible to fly. It didn't gain height and whenever the pilot tried to turn, the plane went out of control. Fossetta remained with the only option to fly straight and low, landing at the advanced airstrip of Sidi Rezegh before passing the border. In the meantime Montanari, experiencing the same kind of problems, was able to return to base. Fossetta and Cassano were quickly returned to Tobruk by an aircraft sent to Sidi Rezegh.

A technical inspection was immediately made. It showed that the Nardi bomb rack, protruding from the belly of the Breda, aerodynamically "shaded" the tail and made it impossible to fly. After some attempts to solve the problem together with the Breda's technicians, in a period during which the Ba.88s were used - together with the fighters - in protective missions over Derna, Fossetta was obliged to stop flights for all his aircraft.

15 September 1940

In the morning, ten SM 79s of the 33° *Gr.* led by *ten. col.* Forte were attacked by three Gladiators over Sidi Barrani, but only one bomber suffered slight damage.

The 13° *Gr.* performed the "usual" morning sweep from 08:00 to 10:00 over Sollum-Bardia-Buq-Buq. 19 CR.42s led by *magg.* Secondo Revetria returning without meeting any enemy.

80 Sqn flew both its Flights up to the front to a location simply known as 'Y' landing ground.

The Italian targets of the day were closer to the battlefront and centred in the area of Sidi Barrani. At around 13:00 (the sixth Italian mission of the day) ten SM 79s from the 46° *Gr.*, led by *magg.* Cunteri, were intercepted over Sidi Barrani by Gladiators from 112 Sqn, which were on patrol at 16,000 feet, thirty miles out to sea. The Gladiators were divided into two sub-Flights. In the first were F/Lt Charles Fry, F/Lt R. J. Abrahams and F/O Joseph Fraser (Gladiator K8019). In the second were P/O R. H. Clarke, F/O Edwin Banks and P/O R. J. Bennett.

When the Italian bombers approached, the No 1 sub-Flight took on the first formation of five aircraft and drove them out to sea before they could release their bombs, while No 2 sub-Flight closed on the second five after they had released their bombs. Banks and Clarke chased this formation out to sea and managed to get close enough to open fire. Both claimed damage to one aircraft each. Banks attacked the outside aircraft, but the enemy took evasive action causing his aircraft to be hit by cross fire from the bombers and he was forced to break off the action. It seems that F/O Fraser was able to put a good burst into an SM 79, which was seen losing height but remained unconfirmed.

Two Hurricanes of 274 Sqn and two Blenheims of 30 Sqn, flown by F/Lt Frank Marlow (Blenheim K7096 with gunner Sgt Lord) and P/O Jarvis (Blenheim K7105 with gunner Sgt Sigsworth) got amongst the enemy formation as well. F/Lt John Lapsley (Hurricane P2544/YK-T) and Sgt John Clarke (Hurricane P2641) each claimed one SM 79 in this combat (this was Lapsley's 6th kill of a total of 11 kills). Clarke's Hurricane was hit and a bullet tore the mouthpiece of his flying helmet away. Jarvis and Marlow chased the SM 79s for twenty-five minutes, firing all their ammunition. They damaged two, one of which was later confirmed as destroyed by 202 Group HQ (and possibly credited to F/Lt Marlow).

Meanwhile, ten Gladiators from 80 Sqn had been on patrol on the seaward side of Sidi Barrani. Nothing was seen and the Sqn split up into sections. The section lead by P/O Anthony Hugh Cholmeley came across five of the SM 79s approaching from the northeast. The Gladiators attacked and forced the bombers to turn back, but return fire hit Cholmeley's aircraft (K7916) and it fell into the sea killing the 22-year-old pilot. One SM 79s was damaged by F/Lt 'Pat' Pattle.

The Italian bombers fought back with determination and claimed one Gladiator, one Hurricane and one Blenheim, with a second Gladiator as a probable. Three SM 79s didn't make it back to Maraua while four other SM 79s returned damaged. Two of the three bombers that didn't return were forced to make emergency landings at T2 (one of them was probably written off after landing). On the SM 79 flown by *s. ten.* Di Francesco there were one dead and four wounded, and on the SM 79 flown by *m. llo.* Berghino was *m. llo. Fotografo* Walter Nencini (operator of the *Istituto LUCE*, the propaganda service) killed and two wounded. The third SM 79, flown by *cap.* Masoero of 21ª *Sq.* (co-pilot *serg. magg.* Giovanni Furini), crash-landed at Ponticelli airstrip with two crewmembers dead (*1° Aviere Marconista* Eustachio Masone and *1° Aviere Armiere* Antonio Bordigato) and two wounded (Furini and *serg. magg.* Motorista Mario Macerati). Masoero correctly identified his attackers as two monoplanes that had hit them in the left engine with their first bursts of fire before he was able to release the bombs, then after the bombing his bomber slowing, lagged behind the other machines of his "*arrow*" and once left alone they were wildly attacked by the two monoplanes. Wounded himself in the left arm and with nobody inside his bomber still able to return fire, Masoero started a steep dive with the two remaining engines at full power that possibly seemed "*final*" to his attackers, which in fact broke off the chase. He landed on the right leg of the landing gear only. The wreck had between 600 and 700 bullet holes holes and was most likely abandoned in place.

The 50° *Stormo* suffered heavy losses during an attack three kilometres south-west of Bir el Kraigat. The Ba.65/A80 (MM75258) flown by *ten.* Adriano Visconti of the 159ª *Sq.* was hit by AA fire and he was forced to crash-land in Egyptian territory. Visconti was, however, able to safely reach T2. Two Ba.65/K14s of the 158ª *Sq.*, 16° *Gr.*, were also lost in the same action when they were hit by AA fire. MM75154 was destroyed in a crash-landing near Sidi Omar, breaking the wing and the landing gear leg, while MM75148 flown by *ten.* Burroni came down near the advancing Italian troops and was destroyed to avoid the chance of being captured in an eventual British counter-attack. Apart from the three losses *serg.* Pandini's aircraft was damaged in the engine and forced to land at Gambut, but after a quick repair the plane was able to return to T2.

4° *Stormo* continued its patrols in the Sidi Omar – Buq-Buq – Sidi Barrani area. No enemy planes were encountered and the patrols continued next day.

From 16:20 to 18:25, 24 fighters from the 8° *Gr.* under *magg.* Vincenzo La Carruba made a protective flight over Buq-Buq. The mission was uneventful.

The SM 79s of the 9° and 33° *Stormi* started to take part in the attacks during the day.

In total the SM 79s flew 15 missions during the day.

55 and 211 Sqns put up a couple of Blenheims each, for night bombing raids against Italian troops between Sollum and Buq-Buq. The bombers came back without incident.

16 September 1940

13 CR.42s from the 13° *Gr.* made an uneventful sweep over Sollum-Bardia-Sidi Barrani between 08:55 and 11:00.

From 10:55 to 13:10, 24 fighters from the 8° *Gr.* under *magg.* Vincenzo La Carruba made a protective flight over Sidi Barrani-Ogerin-Gabr Abu. The mission was uneventful.

The 50° *Stormo* attacked British vehicles 15 kilometres east of Sidi Barrani.

During the day the Italian bombers flew many bombing missions. At around 17:00 three SM 79s of the 59ª *Sq.*, 33° *Gr.* and two of the 53ª *Sq.*, 47° *Gr.*, led by *cap.* Guidoni, were attacked by enemy fighters when they were about to attack a concentration of enemy troops near Bir Rabia. The Savoias had to cancel the attack to defend themselves, but returned safely to Benina at 18:00.

In the meantime 33° *Gr.* sent two additional SM 79s over Bir Rabia to hit the same target. The aircraft were from the 60ª *Sq.* and flown by *cap.* Loris Bulgarelli with *ten.* Pastorelli and *ten.* Giovanni Roggero with *serg. magg.* Ilario Busi. At 18:20, south-east of Sollum at 1000 metres the SM 79s crossed a patrol of 15 CR.42s from the 9° *Gr.* (five planes from each *Squadriglie*) led by *magg.* Ernesto Botto that were coming back from an uneventful standing patrol over Italian infantry in Sidi El Barrani. Visibility was poor and the Italian bombers were fired on from the ground and were mistaken for enemy bombers coming back to base. Four of the Italian fighters attacked and immediately shot down Roggero's aircraft with the loss of the whole crew (*serg. magg. Motorista* Rinaldo Guizzardi, *serg. Radiotelegrafista* Vittorio Orgaro, *Aviere Scelto Armiere* Romeo Pettinelli) and damaged heavily Bulgarelli's aircraft, killing a member of the crew (*Primo Aviere Armiere* Luigi Andreani).

The Royal Navy tried to help its land forces with a series of daring attacks against the Italian bases. During the day the heavy cruiser HMS *Kent*, together with the AA cruisers HMS *Coventry* and HMS *Calcutta*, seven destroyers, the new carrier HMS *Illustrious* (on its first sortie from Alexandria) and the battleship HMS *Valiant* left Alexandria to attack Benghazi harbour, the deepest raid into Italian waters to date.

During the night of the 16th and 17th, nine Fairey Swordfish of 815 Sqn armed with bombs and torpedoes (weapons of a new type with magnetic pistols) and six from 819 Sqn armed with mines took off from HMS *Illustrious* and arrived undetected over Benghazi harbour. The AA defences immediately opened fire but were unable to stop the British raiders. The destroyer *Borea* was hit near the ammunition room by a torpedo and sank with the loss of 27 men. The freighters *Gloriastella* (5490t) and *Maria Eugenia* (4702t) were bombed and went down too. The aircraft of 819 Sqn spread their mines over the harbour; one of them caused the subsequent sinking of the destroyer *Aquilone*, which sank with the loss of three men. After the attack all the Swordfish landed back on HMS *Illustrious*.

Bombing operations were carried out by 55 and 211 Sqns, which despatched six aircraft each in night bombing missions against Italian troops on the Buq-Buq - Sollum road. On landing back at 20:50, enemy bombs were seen to fall on the airstrip and this stopped all further landings for a while. Italian units involved were probably the S.81s of the 54° Gr.

Ten. Giuseppe Zuffi of the 368ª Sq., 151° Gr. C.T., took off at 20:00 from Benina and intercepted a British night bomber, expending 130 12.7 mm rounds and 155 7.7 mm rounds on it. From the ground, the British bomber was seen to escape with a red light (as of a small fire) in one of the engines.

Benghazi Benina was attacked by British bombers during the night of 16/17 September. A hangar was hit and the three damaged SM 79s of 33° Stormo inside were completely burnt out.

The attack was by six old Bombays of 216 Sqn, led by S/Ldr Simmons. Originally nine machines had taken off from Fuka, but three were forced to return early due to engine problems or because they were unable to locate the target. The Bombays correctly claimed heavy damage to dispersed planes, hangars and other buildings, with the use of 11,000 lbs of 250 and 20 lb bombs and with a prolonged strafing attack. AA lightly damaged one of the bombers.

Blenheim Mk.IV T2052 from 113 Sqn, piloted by P/O Eric Samuel Roberts, took off from Ma'aten Bagush on a night ferry flight to Ma'aten Bagush Satellite (LG 15) with a full bomb load and fuel, ready for operations the following morning. Approaching the aerodrome from the wrong direction, the aircraft was fired on by the airfield defence, causing the aircraft to crash on landing at 20:30. The pilot was killed and the aircraft was destroyed by fire.

17 September 1940

From 08:40 to 11:15, 23 23 fighters from the 8° Gr. under magg. Vincenzo La Carruba made a protective flight over Sidi Barrani-Bu Matrud-El Bisri with the purpose of also protecting ground-attack CR.32s employed in the same area. The mission was uneventful.

Only five SM 79 missions were carried out during the day, and a reconnaissance SM 79 of the 175ª Sq. flown by ten. Marini was chased unsuccessfully by three Gladiators during a morning mission over the new front line.

A Cant Z.501 flying-boat of the 143ª Sq. R.M. was forced down while shadowing British ships, and the crew (Pilot s. ten. Renato Balestrero and the Navy observer s. ten. di Vascello Walter Giunchi) was captured by a British ship after ditching.

Another Cant Z.501, this time of the recently deployed 145ª Sq. R.M., was lost on this date in North Africa (s. ten. Raniero Cottali di Vignale and s. ten. di Vascello Pericle Colocci MIA).

It seems that one of the two Cants fell victim to a Sunderland, N9020/W flown by S/Ldr G. L. Menzies and F/O Farries of 228 Sqn, who were on a reconnaissance mission from Malta to Aboukir (probably the aircraft of 145ª Sq.). The other was shot down by a patrol of three Fairey Fulmars from White Section, 806 Sqn, commanded by Sub Lieutenant Stanley Orr from HMS *Illustrious*.

Eight Blenheims of 113 Sqn attacked Benghazi Benina at 10:35. They claimed a large fire in a hangar and two aircraft in flames. The bombers didn't encounter any opposition and returned without losses. A Savoia S.81 was written off at Benghazi Benina and a hangar was destroyed.

Two groups of three Blenheims each from 55 Sqn attacked motor transport concentrations at Sidi Barrani at 13:45 and 14:15. They reported medium AA fire and no fighter opposition. Damage was difficult to estimate because of the dust rising after the first bomb bursts.

During the afternoon 25 fighters of the 4° Stormo protected troop movements in the Sollum – Sidi Barrani area.

P/O Henry Harrison of 112 Sqn claimed a CR.32 in the Sidi Barrani area during the day.

The night missions from El Adem intensified, Vittorio Pezzè (73ª Sq.) and Guglielmo Biffani (73ª Sq.) did a night scramble each while s. ten. Riccardo Vaccari (97ª Sq.) flew a night patrol in the Sidi Barrani area. During this mission, thanks to the moonlight, he discovered a British naval formation steaming north-east of Sollum. Returning to El Adem he gave the alarm, and two SM 79 torpedo-bombers flown by ten. Carlo Emanuele Buscaglia ("278-3" with the crew of ten. Carlo

After a night raid on 17 September, Blenheim Mk.IV L6660 of 211 Sqn undershot a night landing at Qotafiya at around 20:40, bounced, struck the CO's car and hit a tent. The crew (Sergeant Hutt with Sergeant Pollard as Observer and Sergeant Munro as Wireless Operator/Air Gunner) were uninjured but the aircraft was destroyed beyond repair.
[via Mike Grierson]

Copello, *Aviere Scelto motorista* Neroni and *Primo Aviere Marconista* Giuseppe Dondi) and *ten*. Guido Robone ("278-1"; with the crew of *serg*. Deodato, *ten. di Vascello Osservatore* Marazio, *Primo Aviere Marconista* Mauri and *Primo Aviere Motorista* Sabatini) of the 278ª *Sq. Autonoma Aerosiluranti* took off at 21:55.

Occupying spare room in the bombers were, in "278-3" *ten*. Giuseppe Aurili (84ª *Sq*.) and *s. ten*. Ezio Viglione (97ª *Sq*.) sharing one parachute, and in "278-1" *s. ten*. Aldo Gon (96ª *Sq*.) without a parachute.

At 22:40, near the coast of Ras Azzaz they discovered the enemy ships, the heavy cruiser HMS *Kent* with its escort, bound to bombard Bardia.

With the moon on the right side, lighting the target, the two SM 79s attacked in single line (Robone after Buscaglia) with an approach of 50 degrees with regard to the course of the ship. At 22:45, they launched their torpedoes from a distance of 700 metres. One of the torpedoes hit HMS *Kent*'s stern near the propellers. It was the first serious damage caused to a British ship by the *Regia Aeronautica*, and indeed HMS *Kent*, towed to Alexandria in two days with great difficulties, was unfit for further service in the Mediterranean. At this time it was the only 8-inch cruiser of the fleet, because the other one assigned to Cunningham's fleet (HMS *York*) was still on its way towards Suez.

Back at base Buscaglia's aircraft was late in landing, and *col*. Grandinetti threatened Gon with imprisonment since he held him responsible for "such a silly thing" and the loss of two pilots of the importance of Aurili and Viglione. After half an hour Buscaglia landed safely and it all ended well for Gon.

55 and 211 Sqns continued their attacks against the Sollum - Buq-Buq road and complemented this with attacks on Sidi Barrani. 55 Sqn participating with eight planes, which took off at 18:30. 211 Sqn carried out two raids, by seven bombers at 12:45 and eight at 18:35.

After the second raid, Blenheim Mk.IV L6660 of 211 Sqn undershot a night landing at Qotafiya at around 20:40, bounced, struck the CO's car and hit a tent. The crew (Sgt S. L. Hutt with Sgt V. Pollard as Observer and Sgt J. Munro as Wireless Operator/Air Gunner) were uninjured, but the aircraft was destroyed beyond repair.

One Bombay (L5821) from 216 Sqn attacked the road Derna-Tobruk-Bardia, claiming at least six lorries damaged.

18 September 1940

From 07:55 to 10:30, 24 fighters from the 13° *Gr*. flew a high-level (7000 metres) sweep as far as Buq-Buq, led by *magg*. Secondo Revetria. They came back without meeting any enemy.

S. ten. Gilberto Cerofolini and *m. llo*. Gastone Calzolai of the 82ª *Sq*. escorted the Caproni Ca.309 of *Generale* Francesco Pricolo, CO-in-Chief of the *Regia Aeronautica*, to Menastir M when he was visiting the African front.

To keep Italian aircraft down while the cruiser HMS *Kent* was rescued, 55 Sqn was ordered to attack with one aircraft each "El Gubbi" (T2), "Menastir", Sidi Azeiz, El Adem and Sidi Barrani. These attacks were repeated on M, T2 and T3 a second time later the same day.

211 Sqn received similar orders and attacked Derna, Tmini, Bomba and Ain El Gazala.

El Adem and Ain El Gazala were thus raided but didn't suffer any damage, and correctly the 55 Sqn pilots didn't claim any. Bombs also fell on T2 and Menastir but even here, damage claimed was nil. At Derna, the Blenheims from 211 Sqn, led by S/Ldr Gordon-Finlayson, wounded three personnel and heavily damaged (RD) an SM 79. Damage suffered at Tmini M2 (probably attacked by P/O Pearsons of 211 Sqn) was quite heavy; three SM 79s of the 14° *Stormo* and one of the 33° *Gr*. were heavily damaged (probably RD).

Over Benghazi, an enemy shadower was discovered at 12:20. A section from the 368ª *Sq*., 151° *Gr*. (*ten*. Giuseppe Zuffi, *serg. magg*. Annibale Ricotti and *serg. magg*. Alvise Andrich) were scrambled. The three pilots identified their opponent as a Blenheim and attacked. The British aircraft started to dive after some bursts from Zuffi and Ricotti. The bomber was followed down for a while by Ricotti and Andrich, who clearly had the impression that their opponent's dive was final.

Meanwhile Zuffi remained at height and after some time discovered another Blenheim and attacked. The enemy dived to ground level and retreated east, fighting back. After some time Zuffi was forced to end his attacks after running low on fuel. He returned to claim this Blenheim as damaged after having spent 300 12.7mm rounds and 450 7.7 mm rounds.

Cap. Bruno Locatelli took a car and started in search of the shot down enemy aircraft, but found nothing. When asking some Bedouins it transpired that the Blenheim was not shot down in the first attack but its dive was only an evasive manoeuvre, while the bomber damaged by Zuffi was probably the same aircraft.

In fact, a 113 Blenheim sent over Benghazi at 13:05 was chased by fighters and obliged to turn back without completing its mission of checking of the damage inflicted upon Benina the day before. The reconnaissance aircraft however was able to discover two ships in flames inside the city's harbour. They were possibly the freighters *Gloriastella* and *Maria Eugenia* sunk previously.

Starting from 12:30, with the last landing at 18:15, the 92ª *Sq.*, 8° *Gr.*, carried out three small patrols of three, two and two aircraft over the El Adem area. All the mission were uneventful.

The readiness section at Tmini M2 (*ten.* Guglielmo Chiarini of the 82ª *Sq.*, *serg. magg.* Leone Basso of the 77ª *Sq.* and *serg.* Franco Porta of the 82ª *Sq.*) were flying to Gambut when they discovered a formation of nine Blenheims at 1500 metres, which was heading towards Tmini. The three CR 42s immediately started in pursuit but were only able to intercept the RAF bombers after they had dropped their bombs over the airfield at 18:20.

The Blenheims were reportedly flying in three vics. The three aircraft in the first vic were the first to be attacked, *ten.* Chiarini claimed the leader, *serg.* Porta one of the wingmen while *serg. magg.* Basso was machine-gunning the other. They then attacked the second vic, which split up with each Blenheim looking for safety on its own. In the meantime, the third vic remained manoeuvring in close formation and departed towards land, while the remaining Blenheims tried to counter-attack the CR.42s and were heavily machine-gunned. Now the three Italian pilots started in pursuit of the fleeing "vic". Flying straight into the Blenheims (because whatever approaching manoeuvre would have meant losing the chance of closing on the fast escaping enemy bombers), Chiarini ran into a shower of return fire and was wounded in the shoulder. He didn't turn back immediately, but when he realized the seriousness of his wound he had to leave the chase and return to home base, but before leaving the combat zone he witnessed a fourth Blenheim machine gunned by Basso and very close to the sea with one engine smoking. Basso himself didn't witness his opponent going down, but estimated that it wouldn't make it back because of the damage suffered, so he turned back home very low on fuel.

When the three Italian pilots landed, it was already dark but the light of the incendiary bombs released on the landing strip guided them. Once on the ground (in three damaged fighters) Chiarini claimed two bombers shot down (by him and Porta), one probable (Basso) and six heavily machine-gunned as shared. The final assessment of the outcome of the combat was made by the HQ of Vª Squadra following the reports of land observers. The HQ fixed the number of enemy planes shot down to five; one each for Chiarini and Porta, two for Basso and a fifth shared. Considering the rather aggressive attitude of the Blenheims over Tmini, it was assumed that they were "*Bristol Blenheim Fighters*". For this action Chiarini, Basso and Porta all were decorated with the *Medaglia d'argento al Valor Militare*.

113 Sqn reported that they attacked at 19:20 with nine aircraft using 72 40lb, 80 20lb and 400 4lb incendiary bombs. All the bombs were seen to fall within the target area, except a single container of incendiary that overshot. Three Italian planes were observed in flames on the south side of the area and two were directly hit. A cement blockhouse was also hit and damaged. Damage suffered at Tmini was quite heavy; three SM 79s of the 14° *Stormo* and one of the 33° *Gr.* were heavily damaged (probably RD). After the first run a reportedly 20 (!) CR.42s attacked the formation, shooting down Blenheim Mk.IV T2048 in flames. S/Ldr Gerald Barnard Keily DFC AFC baled out

and was taken POW, while the observer, 24-year-old P/O John Sisman Cleaver and the wireless operator/air gunner, 27-year-old Sgt James Jobson were killed. 113 Sqn claimed to have destroyed one of their attackers and possibly a second. Two other Blenheims were unserviceable on landing but in fact not seriously damaged (possibly the rest of the first "vic"). F/Lt R. N. Bateson assumed temporary command of the squadron. It seems highly likely that Keily was shot down by *ten.* Chiarini.

Six Bombays from 216 Sqn attacked Derna-Tobruk-Bardia-Capuzzo-Sollum-Barrani, reportedly claiming little or no damage.

Six Gladiators from 80 Sqn operating from Sidi Heneish South carried out a patrol in the Sidi Barrani area but no enemy aircraft were sighted.

This night saw the first active service operations performed by 70 Sqn. Wellingtons T2735 piloted by Sgt Brookes and T2733 piloted by F/O Wells (with S/Ldr Rolfe among the crew), took off at 01:00 and attacked Porto Lago and Leros bay in the Aegean Islands.

Wellingtons T2734 piloted by F/Sgt Mirfin and T2732 piloted by F/O Ridgeway (with Wing Commander Webb among the crew), attacked Maritza aerodrome and Wellington T2731 under F/O Brian attacked Calato. Both targets were on Rhodes. The first two bombers reported good results, while the third experienced difficulties in finding suitable targets but claimed to have caused a large fire. The three planes came back without damage.

On the Italian side, bombing activity tended to decrease after the concentrated effort of the previous days that ended in the occupation of Sidi Barrani. The SM 79s of the 5ª *Squadra Aerea* only flew night bombing missions, and the usual strategic reconnaissance (units involved were 9°, 14°, 15°, 33° *Stormi*, 54° *Gr.* and 175ª *Sq.*). This was to continue during the following days.

19 September 1940

The continuous missions of the previous days forced the 4° *Stormo* to slow down activity, to service and refit its fighters. Operations restarted on 22 September.

Four bombers of 70 Sqn, with Wing Commander Webb aboard T2734 piloted by F/O Ridgeway, moved to Fuka and from there bombed Benghazi harbour, claiming hits on two ships (by T2735 piloted by Sgt Brookes and T2732 piloted by Ridgeway) and damage to the quay. The Wellingtons were all back at Fuka at 02:10. Five personnel of the *Regia Aeronautica* were among the losses.

Two Bombays from 216 Sqn attacked Italian forward positions, reportedly claiming little or no damage.

20 September 1940

The attacks on Benghazi, apart from the damage on military installations, also caused much damage and victims among the civil population (in particular the Muslim community). For this reason a strong retaliation attack was planned for the day with the use of all available bombers.

At 06:40 ten SM 79s of the 47° *Gr.* led by *col.* Napoli took off from Maraua; two of them had to return early due to problems with the landing gear. 20 SM 79s from the 9° *Stormo* led by *col.* Aramu took off from Derna. At 07:05 four SM 79s from the 20ª *Sq.*, 46° *Gr.*, led by *ten.* Recagno took off (one of them failed to take off). At 07:10, the last 15 bombers of the 14° *Stormo* led by *col.* Coppi took off. In total 46 bombers headed towards Mersa Matruh. 37 CR.42s of the 2° *Stormo* (the whole 8° *Gr.* plus twelve fighters from the 13° *Gr.* under *cap.* Domenico Bevilacqua) escorted them.

From 08:58 until 09:15 450 50 and 20 kg bombs rained down over the British base. Enemy fighters failed to appear, and the returning crews reported hits well centred on the railway station, the army base and the town itself.

Almost 50 bombers over the same land target in seventeen minutes was a record for the *Regia Aeronautica* bombing units, probably a record never equalled, and the bulletin gave wide credit to the units involved.

Between 16:45 and 18:00, six Gladiators from 80 Sqn carried out a patrol over Mersa Matruh but no enemy aircraft were sighted.

At 17:30, two CR.42s of the 92ª *Sq.*, 8º *Gr.*, flown by *s. ten.* Vittorio Muratori and *serg.* Ernesto De Bellis took off from Menastir M. *s. ten.* Muratori intercepted a British formation of three Bristol Blenheims, which were out to attack Menastir, and claimed one of them probably shot down. Muratori landed back at 18:10.

In the meantime, *serg.* De Bellis intercepted a group of three planes identified as Sunderlands, and was able to claim one of the enemy aircraft shot down. De Bellis landed back at 18:20. No RAF Sunderland reported any kind of engagement during the day, so most probably these planes were incorrectly identified machines of another type.

The attack on Menastir was performed by three Blenheims from 55 Sqn, commanded by F/Lt H. R. Goodman. The Bristols attacked at 18:30 making two runs; their bombs were seen falling over the landing strip and near dispersed aircraft, but it was difficult to see any results because of the dust raised. Four CR.42s were seen over Menastir and one on the return journey near Sidi Barrani, but in both cases these fighters were left behind and no engagement took place. From Italian reports, no losses were suffered during the raid on Menastir, described as two separate raids made by three aircraft at 17:25 and 17:30 (obviously the two runs of the same 55 Sqn formation). No British losses can be verified on this day, even if it is known that around the same time 211 Sqn made an evening attack on Sidi Barrani.

Six Blenheims of 211 Sqn under S/Ldr Gordon-Finlayson attacked Italian motor transports south-west of Sidi Barrani at dusk. They were all back at 18:30 without suffering any loss.

Six Bombays from 216 Sqn attacked Tobruk-Derna-Bardia-Sollum, reportedly claiming little or no damage.

P/O Roald Dahl was posted to 80 Sqn and during the evening he was ferrying Gladiator K7911 from 102 MU to the unit. However, he was unused to flying aircraft over the desert and he made a forced landing 2 miles west of Mersa Matruh. He crashed and the aircraft burst into flames. The pilot was badly burned, and he was conveyed to an Army Field Ambulance Station. Dahl, who later became a famous writer, remembered that he became lost after having been given wrong directions, and lack of fuel forced him to make an emergency landing between the Italian and British lines. He was badly wounded by the gun sight, with a fractured head, broken nose and some lost teeth, and remaining blind for some days. He managed to scramble from the burning fighter and was rescued by three soldiers from the Suffolk regiment. He was later admitted to a hospital in Alexandria, and did not get back to the unit before it had moved to Greece.

Five Wellingtons from 70 Sqn again attacked Benghazi harbour, at around 03:46 in the morning on 21 September, claiming one direct hit on a ship (by T2730 piloted by Sgt Jenkins) and damage to the jetty. One of the aircraft ran into low clouds and had to turn back, while Jenkins suffered a "hang up" of two bombs, which were subsequently shaken off over Tobruk.

On returning the crew of T2730, piloted by F/O Wells and S/Ldr Rolfe, discovered that the hydraulic system was u/s, as was the emergency hand operated system, so the bomber had to belly-land at base. The machine was sent to Abu Sueir for permanent repair on 27 September.

21 September 1940

The 7º *Gr. Combattimento* suffered its first loss when *serg. magg.* Savoiardo's Ba.88 (a reinforcement machine, which had taken off from Pantelleria) disappeared in the sea off Djerba with its crew.

55 Sqn, helped by three Blenheims from 211 Sqn, made the usual evening attack, this time against Sidi Barrani. Again, it was difficult for the returning crews to judge damage inflicted. 55 Sqn reported that a fighter biplane made a half-hearted quarter attack but didn't appear to fire. The identity of this Italian night fighter remains undiscovered.

An evening raid was reported on Menastir, made at 18:20 by seven enemy bombers. No damage was suffered. It was probably made by 113 Sqn.

Lysander L4710 piloted by F/Lt Legge of 208 Sqn turned on its nose on landing at Siwa. The crew was uninjured.

Night attacks were made on British airports by aircraft of the 9°, 14° and 33° *Stormi*. This kind of nuisance raid, made by single planes in the late afternoon hours or during the night, continued for quite a while. The British response to this was quite laconic. Len Abbs, a photographer of 211 Sqn, recounted that night bombers attacked almost daily, obliging the men of 211 to sweep the runway of El Daba at dawn, to explode booby traps dropped by the Italian aircraft:

"*Usually four airmen walked in front. John drove [...] Knocker exploded the offending missiles of which there were many. Fortunately there were no casualties during these dawn adventures. The Ities ceased dropping them after a month. We endured several bombing raids however. Each tent's occupants dug their own slit trench air raid shelter. They were very effective about 6 feet deep and narrow. The only casualties were if you were in there first and some clown jumped in on top of you. The Ities were not that good. Invariably above 10,000 feet and shit-scared of our Gladiator fighter patrols. We always knew through messages passed along the line when they were coming and our fighters would be waiting. I never did know how this worked. I suspected the Bedouins who roamed the desert respecting no frontiers and were paid by both sides*"

22 September 1940

The serious damage suffered to Benghazi still required a response, and another mission over Mersa Matruh was planned for the day. Eleven SM 79s from 14° *Stormo*, led by *col.* Coppi, 19 bombers from 9° *Stormo* led by *col.* Aramu and ten bomber from 15° *Stormo* led by *magg.* Cunteri, attacked with a total of 357 bombs of 100 and 50 kg. All bombers returned between 17:20 and 17:55. The AA fire was reported as strong, and no enemy fighters were seen.

46 fighters escorted the bombers. 21 CR.42s were from the 2° *Stormo* and additional fighters of the 4° *Stormo*. The 4° *Stormo*'s 25 CR.42s had been deployed to Amseat A3 and Menastir M to reduce the distance to the target.

On taking off the plane of *s. ten.* Paolo Berti of the 84ª *Sq.*, 10° *Gr.*, suffered an accident in bad visibility and was damaged.

Five Ba.65/A80s of the 169ª *Sq.*, six CR.32s of the 160ª *Sq.*, four Ba.65/K14s of the 168ª *Sq.* and six CR.32s of the 167ª *Sq.* flew an armed reconnaissance in the Esc Scegga area. Three aircraft were damaged by AA fire.

British bombers tried to retaliate against the raids on Mersa Matruh by attacking Menastir at dusk. In fact, it was believed that 50 Italian bombers were dispersed at this aerodrome after the attack on Matruh. 55 Sqn provided six bombers, 113 Sqn three others, while the three Blenheims from 211 Sqn were to attack the nearby base of Sollum even if they were finally redirected against Menastir too. The British attack developed at around 19:45 but it was difficult to judge the results, which in fact were nil. No Italian fighter was seen.

The Fairey Swordfish of HMS *Eagle*'s 813 Sqn had again been disembarked. On this night they carried out bombing attacks on Italian defence positions at Bardia.

23 September 1940

Nine bombers of 55 Sqn together with nine others from 211 Sqn attacked Tobruk harbour at 15:00. Bombs were seen to fall in the target area and heavy AA fire was experienced. All the bombers were back at 16:20.

25 September 1940

18 CR.42s from the 13° *Gr.* under *magg.* Secondo Revetria made a free sweep over Bir Enba-Sidi Barrani. After taking off at 08:40, they landed at 10:40 without meeting any enemy.

At 13:15, *s. ten.* Gilberto Cerofolini, *serg.* Franco Porta and *serg.* Luigi Giannotti of the 82ª *Sq.*, 13° *Gr.*, scrambled from Gambut to intercept returning enemy bombers that had just attacked Tobruk. The three pilots headed out over open sea and climbed to 4000 metres where 20 minutes after take off they spotted six enemy bombers heading east, in two vics of three.

The British bombers tried to escape by diving, but the Italian fighters caught up with the second vic. The two wingmen were attacked first, the left one was machine gunned and seen to hit the surface of the sea where the crash raised a high water column, while the right one was seen to dive at sea level with the port engine on fire. Then it was the turn of the leader, which was heavily damaged and was last seen heading towards land with the aircraft trailing thick clouds of smoke.

The three pilots then continued to pursue the bombers of the first vic, but when they were down at 500 metres they were unable to get closer and had to content themselves by emptying their guns from a distance, without effect.

They returned to base with damaged fighters at 14:30. Back at base, it was assessed that the first two aircraft of the first "vic" were to be considered confirmed shot down, and the third one probably shot down. All three were credited as shared. Cerofolini, Porta and Giannotti had scrambled without lifejackets and followed their opponents 100 kilometres over open sea, and back at base they were proposed for an immediate *Medaglia d'argento al Valor Militare* for bravery. For Porta this was the second time during the same week.

The Italian pilots had run across a wing formation of Blenheims, which had taken off at around 12:15 to attack Tobruk. It was composed of nine aircraft from 55 Sqn under F/Lt R. B. Cox (acting as Wing leader), nine aircraft from 113 Sqn led by S/Ldr Bateson and nine from 211 Sqn led by S/Ldr Gordon-Finlayson. The attack developed at 14:20 with the Blenheims arriving in vics. 55 Sqn's bombs fell right across the town to the jetty. Further observation of damage inflicted became soon impossible due to high dust clouds rising. 113 Sqn's crews reported a direct hit on a barrack block. 55 Sqn escaped unscathed, landing back at 15:50, while 113 Sqn was intercepted by one flight of CR.42s during the return flight when 20 miles out to sea. A stern chase continued for 10 minutes, resulting in two aircraft being hit and landing at base unserviceable. It appears that 211 Sqn's aircraft were also intercepted, since Blenheim Mk.I L8523 of this unit crash-landed with the starboard engine on fire at Qasaba. S/Ldr J. Gordon-Finlayson DFC, Sgt Richmond and Sgt Jones escaped uninjured. The aircraft was destroyed beyond repair. Gordon-Finlayson had just been promoted to command the squadron, taking the place of S/Ldr Bax.

The *Regia Aeronautica* suffered two dead and ten wounded during the attack on Tobruk town.

26 September 1940

In the afternoon, three machines of 55 Sqn together with others from 211 Sqn raided Sollum. 55 Sqn's Blenheims attacked a tented camp south of the city, while 211 Sqn targeted the landing ground. One IMAM Ro.37*bis* of the 137ª *Sq.* was destroyed and two others heavily damaged (RD), the hits were confirmed by photographic reconnaissance. They were the only combat ready machines of the Italian unit.

27 September 1940

The 9º *Gr.* was busy during the day covering troop movements towards Giarabub (the extreme outpost of the Italian army near the Sahara region, 240km south of El Adem). The first mission was flown by six CR.42s of 73ª *Sq.* led by *magg.* Ernesto Botto, and the second mission made by aircraft from the 96ª *Sq.* led by *cap.* Roberto Fassi. Both these missions went on uneventfully.

The next mission of the day was flown by six CR.42s from the 97ª *Sq.* (*cap.* Antonio Larsimont Pergameni, *serg.* Franco Sarasino, *s. ten.* Giovanni Barcaro, *ten.* Ezio Viglione Borghese, *ten.* Riccardo Vaccari and *serg.* Angelo Golino) to which a CR.42 of the 366ª *Sq.*, 151º *Gr.* (*ten.* Mario Ferrero on the first mission for this unit over the North African front) was attached.

While circling over El Garn ul Grein (90 km south of Ridotta Maddalena) they spotted 14 bombers 500 meters above them, heading towards the troops. The bombers were eleven Blenheims of 55 Sqn led by F/Lt R.B. Cox (acting S/Ldr), which had taken off from Fuka at 12:00, to raid Italian MT concentrations near Giarabub. The Blenheims crossed the border 30 miles north of Giarabub and then followed the road southwards to this town. Not meeting any enemy, they attacked the fort at 13:45, a direct hit causing a column of black smoke to rise from the building.

After the attack, two aircraft from 'C' Flight lagged behind the rest of the formation. They were L8394/L piloted by F/O Godrich and L8454 piloted by P/O I. Hook. The Blenheims then proceeded up to the border road, and when 40 miles north of Giarabub they discovered some MT resting. At the same moment, seven CR.42s were seen on the port side of the formation. The Fiats immediately attacked the two stragglers. The first four fighters were seen to come up behind L8394 while the other three waited above. The bomber was seen to catch fire and crash, one occupant, thought to be the Air Gunner, was seen to jump from the back and escape by parachute. The bomber fell victim to the first trio from the 97ª *Sq.*, composed of *cap.* Larsimont, *serg.* Sarasino and *s. ten.* Barcaro. These pilots in fact claimed the right wingman of the rear section shot down in flames. Larsimont observed a crew member parachute from the burning bomber, while Barcaro claimed to have set one of the bomber's engines on fire. In total they expended more than 2000 rounds of ammunition. 21-year old pilot F/O Ambrose Sydney Barnard Godrich, 28-year old Observer Sgt William Charles Clarke and 22-year old Wireless Operator/Air Gunner Sgt William Thompson were all killed when L8394 crashed.

Meanwhile, *ten.* Ferrero attacked the front section, joined moments later by Larsimont, Sarasino and Barcaro. Ferrero claimed a probable Blenheim after expending 400 rounds. He was less effective than he believed, returning crews from 55 Sqn reported that, apart from the two stragglers, the main formation was chased rather half-heartedly and no damage was done, while an air gunner claimed one of the Fiats shot down but this was unconfirmed.

Ten. Viglione, *ten.* Vaccari and *serg.* Golino attacked the left wingman of the rear section, which was seen to dive to ground level. They pursued it for 80 kilometres over Egypt, until it reportedly crashed burning into the ground. Viglione and his wingmen then damaged other bombers before being forced to return to base due to lack of fuel. They had in fact chased L8454 (P/O Hook,

Flying Officer Sidney Linnard of 80 Sqn in the cockpit of one of the unit's Gladiators in an official photo taken by Air Ministry on 27 September 1940.
[AMC London]

Observer Sgt W. F. Bowker and Wireless Operator/Air Gunner Sgt J. Rigby). This Blenheim was seen by its comrades to dive to ground level and to continue evasive tactics that in the end made the following fighters break off. The machine however was badly shot up, and the crew was reputedly very lucky not to have been hit. The ten surviving aircraft from 55 Sqn landed at base at 15:40.

The claim by Ferrero was due to a misunderstanding, because once back at base, from a telephone call from the Army, it was reported that after the Italian fighters had left the area another formation of bombers arrived. It was assumed that this was the 55 Sqn formation, less three aircraft, which was back over its intended target and for this reason a third plane was presumed shot down. In fact, it now transpires that 55 Sqn didn't come back for a second raid and the second formation were in fact eight Blenheims of 211 Sqn under the lead of S/Ldr Gordon-Finlayson bound for the same target. Five of the 211 Sqn's bombers overshot while three others claimed hits in the target area.

The loss of L8394 was the first operational loss of 55 Sqn due to fighter opposition. On 30 September, men of an Egyptian Frontier Post found the wreck of L8394 with one body in it (Clarke?), and a pilot's parachute together with helmet marked Godrich, outside the aircraft. Footsteps led away from the aircraft towards an Italian outpost, thus assuming that the pilot survived the crash and now was a POW. This was not the case, and in fact all three had been killed.

A fourth uneventful mission was flown by the 73ª *Sq*.

One Bombay from 216 Sqn attacked the Derna-Tobruk-Bardia road, reportedly claiming little or no damage.

28 September 1940

Three Blenheims from 55 Sqn attacked Sid Barrani, escorted by three Gladiators and two MS.406s from 274 Sqn, which still not had fully equipped with Hurricanes.

During the day, *Generale* Pricolo ordered the Italian Units in North Africa to avoid dangerous missions in order to conserve strength.

The Mediterranean fleet was out for the third time in the same month to escort the cruisers HMS *Liverpool* and HMS *Gloucester*, which were to carry 2000 troops to Malta, (*Operation MB5*). The arrival of HMS *Illustrious* and its fighters had clearly changed the situation in the Central Mediterranean, where the British fleet was now able to roam almost at will. The fleet was back at the beginning of October without having seen too much action. The Italian fleet's only concern was to protect Benghazi and the Italian coast from further British raids.

6 Sqn lost Leading Aircraftman Thomas Arthur McNulty, to unknown reasons.

Wreck of a Fiat CR.42 on the Benina airfield.
[via Przemek Skulski]

Somewhere in North Africa.
[via Stratus]

29 September 1940

Two Lysanders from 'B' Flight 208 Sqn were damaged by A/A fire during two separate reconnaissance missions. L4711, piloted by P/O Waymark, was hit in the morning when over Sidi Barrani and landed unfit for further flying. A replacement machine was requested.

L4729, piloted by F/Lt Black, was less seriously damaged during a morning tactical reconnaissance over Sofafi.

Three 'carrier-Hurricanes' (possibly FAA Fulmars) were claimed shot down by the Italians during combat which probably occurred over the British fleet.

One SM 79 was lost to AA fire north of Sidi Barrani. This was possibly an aircraft from the 9° *Stormo*, piloted by *cap.* Antonio Caprini, which failed to return during a mission in search of the British fleet. The crew included *s. ten.* Libero Bertinelli, *Primo Aviere Motorista* Medardo Falsini, *Primo Aviere Armiere* Mario Scialanca and *serg.* Giulio Zamagna.

At 09:55, aerial reconnaissance discovered the British fleet off Sidi Barrani, and the 278ª *Sq.* received orders to attack with all available aircraft. At 14:25, four SM 79s took off from El Adem, these were "278-6" piloted by *magg.* Vincenzo Dequal, "278-1" piloted by *ten.* Guido Robone, "278-2" piloted by *ten.* Carlo Emanuele Buscaglia and finally "278-3" piloted by *ten.* Carlo Copello.

At 15:33, the British formation was discovered, and in bad visibility the four Savoias attacked a ship variously identified as a Battle Cruiser of the *Renown* class or a Cruiser of the *Southampton* class. The attack was made from a distance of 1200-1400 metres and AA fire was slight. After the attack, from safe distance, *magg.* Dequal estimated that two torpedo trails had passed behind the ship while one had clearly stopped on its stern (nothing was seen of the fourth torpedo). A hit was claimed and credited to the unit. No British account of this action has been found and no losses were noted.

In the Mersa Matruh area two Z.501 shadowers from the 143ª *Sq. R.M.* were shot down a few hours apart, and both crews (*magg.* Nicola Covacovich and *ten. di Vascello* Corrado Viola and *s. ten.* Ugo Leardi and *s. ten. di Vascello* Mario Martina) became MIA.

Including these two losses, the 143ª *Sq.* had lost four out of seven aircraft in just 3½ months. Together with the loss of two other aircraft from other *Squadriglie* over North African waters this raised total losses of the *R.M.* in North Africa up to this moment to six aircraft (in fact all the losses were suffered in the space of just two months). This fact showed clearly the unsuitability of the Z.501 in the role of shadower in the presence of enemy fighter opposition.

It seems that the victors were Fulmars from HMS *Illustrious*, Blue Section under Sub-Lieutenant Hogg claimed one at 11:24. However the Cant had fought back and shot down Sub-Lieutenant Lowe's aircraft (TAG, L/A P. Douet). Lowe and his TAG were rescued after ditching by the destroyer HMS *Stuart*. Three hours later White Section caught another Z.501, which was shot down by Sub-Lieutenant Orr.

30 September 1940

At 09:50, Sunderland L2166/U of 230 Sqn, flown by F/Lt Alington, in a combined attack with the destroyer HMAS *Stuart* and the ASW trawler H22 forced the Italian submarine *Gondar* to the surface and sank it.

Unknown to the British sailors, *Gondar* was coming back to base after the second unsuccessful attempt to attack Alexandria Harbour with frogmen driving SLCs. It had been called back the day before, after receiving the news that the British fleet had left Alexandria. Among the captured Italian sailors was the CO of the unit, *ten. di Vascello* Brunetti (former CO of the submarine *Iride*!) and also *Lieutenant* Elios Toschi of X Flottiglia MAS, one of the inventors of the SLC.

After the sinking of the *Iride* it was the second consecutive time that the Italian frogmen were prevented by the RAF from carrying out their mission.

At 10:30 (11:20 in British documents), seven Blenheims from the 113 Sqn (it is possible that the formation also included two additional Blenheims from 45 Sqn) attacked Maraua, surprising some 15° *Stormo* aircraft, which were taxiing before take-off. The AA defences mistook the Blenheims for Breda Ba.88s and didn't open fire until it was too late. One SM 79 took a direct hit and exploded, another aircraft was destroyed, while two bombers were heavily damaged (RD) and four less seriously (RS). The airstrip remained out of service and many pilots died. *ten.* D'Ignazio, *s. ten.* Costanzo, *serg. magg.* Marcantoni, *serg.* Goggi together with two crewmembers were killed, and six more were wounded. 113 Sqn's crews accurately reported two buildings at the edge of the airport blown up, one Savoia SM 79 in flames and two blown up with several believed damaged.

Ten. Giovanni Beduz, *serg. magg.* Ezio Masenti and *serg.* Rovero Abbarchi of the 78ª *Sq.*, 13° *Gr.* scrambled at 11:05 from Gambut G following an air alarm, and flew in north-westerly direction for 100 kilometres until they intercepted three Blenheims over the sea. *ten.* Beduz was credited with an individual victory, while another bomber was shared among the three pilots. They used 1700 rounds of ammunition and returned to base between 12:30 and 13:00.

In fact, a flight of three Blenheims from 113 Sqn, which had been detached from the other, was intercepted 50 miles north of Tobruk. Two of the Blenheims were damaged and rendered unserviceable, while T2171 was shot down into the sea. Sgt Leslie Cater, Sgt Kenneth Herbert Meadowcroft and 18-year-old Sgt Bernard James Shelton were all killed. The returning crews reported that they were attacked by 15 (!) CR.42s, and the defending gunners claimed two of the attacking fighters shot down and one badly hit.

The 9° *Gr.* flew an uneventful patrol over the new frontline.

19 CR.42s from the 13° *Gr.* under *magg.* Secondo Revetria made a protective flight from 12:30 to 14:30 over the Bir Enba-sidi Barrani area. They encountered no enemy.

During a strategic reconnaissance over the LGs around Mersa Matruh, an SM 79 of 175ª *Sq. R.S.T.* flown by *cap.* Iraci was intercepted by three Gladiators, but escaped without damage.

Six Blenheims of 211 Sqn led by S/Ldr Gordon-Finlayson bombed Tobruk's northern foreshore at dusk.

October 1940

The ground war
On 28 October, Italy attacked Greece from Albania.

Regia Aeronautica

Fighters
On 4 October the 10° *Gr.* was back at Benghazi to refit its fighters. The remaining combat-ready aircraft were in readiness to protect Benghazi, Derna and Ain El Gazala.

Cap. Luigi Monti was ill and was sent back to Italy on 11 October for a period of rest. *cap.* Vincenzo Vanni took temporarily command of the 84ª *Sq.* During the same period *cap.* Renzo Maggini partially recovered from his wounds and returned to the 90ª *Sq.*

At Berka on 15 October some CR.42s of the 10° *Gr.* received radio equipment for the first time.

On 25 October *serg.* Luciano Perdoni was transferred to the 84ª *Sq.*

Ten. Vittorio Pezzè left the command of the 73ª *Sq.*, 9° *Gr.*, on 10 October due to illness to return to Italy, and his place was taken by *ten.* Valerio De Campo. Pezzè never returned to front line duties; his experience was used in the newly formed *Scuola Caccia* (fighter school) at Gorizia.

Cap. Giuseppe Mauriello from the 97ª *Sq.*, returned to Italy because of illness on 11 October, as did Emanuele Annoni from the 96ª *Sq.*, who was ill with typhoid fever. Many health problems during this period were caused by insufficient food and bad water quality, problems that would plague Italian soldiers during the whole African war.

On 25 October *s. ten.* Armando Moresi was transferred to the 96ª *Sq. s. ten.* Giovanni Barcaro and *m. llo.* Vanni Zuliani of the 97ª *Sq.* had to return to Italy due to illness around the same date.

Ten. Alessandro Viotti, an expert pilot of the 96ª *Sq.*, died of septicaemia in Tobruk hospital on 28 October. It was the second non-operational death for the 9° *Gr.* during the month of October. Viotti was considered one of the most brilliant officers of the *Stormo*.

Sergente *Luciano Perdoni of the 84ª* Squadriglia, *10°* Gruppo *seen later in the war (most likely in Sicily 1941).* [Perdoni via Fulvio Chianese – Associazione Culturale 4° Stormo di Gorizia.]

Pilots from the 9º Gruppo C.T. at a wintry airfield in North Africa. (From left to right) Unknown, Franco Sarasino (97ª Squadriglia), Santo Gino (73ª Squadriglia), unknown, Armando Moresi (96ª Squadriglia), Valerio De Campo (73ª Squadriglia) and Antonio Valle (73ª Squadriglia).
[Gino via Fulvio Chianese – Associazione Culturale 4° Stormo di Gorizia]

A Fiat CR.42 taking off somewhere in Libya. Observe the amount of dust generated from the aircraft. The dust caused great wear on the aircraft engines.
[via Italian Air Force]

Sergente Maggiore Guglielmo Biffani of the 73ª Squadriglia at El Adem – Tobruk, 1940
[via talian Air Force]

On 20 October *ten.* Raimondo Sacchetti and *serg.* Ernesto De Bellis of the 92ª *Sq.* were transferred to the 368ª *Sq.*

S. ten. Carlo Albertini returned to the 366ª *Sq.* from the 91ª *Sq.*, 10º *Gr.* on 27 October.

The whole 151º *Gr.* was transferred from El Adem T3 to Amseat A3 on 30 October.

Bombers

During October, the activity of the SM 79 units was mainly daily strategic reconnaissance over Alexandria, tactical reconnaissance missions over the front during the morning and afternoon, and night bombing missions against the RAF airfields at El Daba and Fuka and Alexandria harbour. The wide dispersal of aircraft during the night meant that no losses were suffered by the RAF during these missions. The strategic reconnaissance reported an increasing number of encounters with Hurricanes and Gladiators, however no losses were suffered.

On 3 October the 33º *Stormo* (35º and 36º *Gruppi*) left North Africa when they returned to Viterbo. They left the remaining eight combat-ready SM 79s to other units remaining in the area. The move was completed on the 14 October.

At the beginning of the month the 9º *Stormo* was at Derna/El Ftàiah, 14º *Stormo* at Tmini, 15º *Stormo* at Maraua, 33º *Gr.* at Z1, 54º *Gr.* at Ain El Gazala and the 175ª *Sq. R.S.T.* at T2 and T5.

On 8 October the 15º *Stormo* was withdrawn from the frontline and went to Tripolitania to rebuild its strength. Its surviving combat-ready aircraft went to the 54º *Gr.* (ten) while five others went to other *Squadriglie*. The non-combat-ready aircraft returned with the *Stormo* to Tripoli.

Cap. Massimiliano Erasi took command of 278ª *Sq.* A.S. from *magg.* Vincenzo Dequal on 10 October. A former pilot of the *A.P.C. Gruppi*, the thirty-two year old Erasi had a wide experience of the North African theatre after having been stationed in Libya since 1938.

The Vª *Squadra Aerea* was reinforced by the newly formed 114º *Gr. Aut. Bombardamento Pesante* (BP) on 14 October. This unit included the 272ª and 273ª *Sq.* under command of *ten. col.* Umberto Klinger. The unit was based at Ain El Gazala and equipped with a mixed force of S79s and SM 82s. It was planned to give it a full complement of 27 SM 82s and to use it in deep night penetrations as far as the Suez Canal zone. Such large numbers of SM 82s, however, never arrived.

On 21 October the 41º *Stormo B.T.*, commanded by *col.* Enrico Pezzi, arrived from Gela with 22 SM 79s (the last 10 aircraft arrived on 22 October). The *Stormo* included the 59º (CO *ten. col.* Enrico Draghelli) and 60º (CO *ten. col.* Pasquale D'Ippolito) *Gruppi*. The 59º *Gr.* included the 232ª *Sq.* commanded by *cap.* Piero Padovani and the 233ª *Sq.* commanded by *cap.* Valdo Meille, while the 60º *Gr.* included the 234ª *Sq.* commanded by *cap.* Mario Curto and 235ª *Sq.* commanded by *cap.* Athos Ammannato.

One of the SM 79s was destroyed on landing with the loss of two crewmembers, *Primo Aviere Montatore* Luigi Da Dalt, *Aviere Scelto Motorista* Riccardo Gobbi. The *Stormo* would reach Sidi el Magrum by 30 October, to start operations.

On 28 October, a new major unit was formed, the 9ª *Brigata Aerea* "Leone", commanded by *col.* Attilio Biseo. Initial units of the *Brigata* were the 15º and 41º *Stormo*.

Reconaissance forces

The 127ª *Sq.* replaced the 137ª *Sq.* at Sollum on 10 October.

Ground attack forces

During the first week of October the CR.32s and Ba.65s of the 50º *Stormo* patrolled over Tobruk and Derna harbours and the Gulf of Bomba, to protect the unloading operations of many reinforcements for the Army.

On 9 October *ten.* Guido Pastorelli took command of 159ª *Sq.* after the death of *cap.* Antonio Dell'Oro on 8 October. After the confirmation of the death of Dell'Oro his name was written in gold block letters on the fuselages of the Ba.65s of the 159ª *Sq.*

On 14 October, the 7º *Gr.* only had eleven Ba.88s flyable out of twenty-nine on charge.

Sergente Maggiore Guglielmo Biffani of the 73ª Squadriglia at El Adem – Tobruk, 1940. [Biffani via Fulvio Chianese – Associazione Culturale 4° Stormo di Gorizia]

Royal Air Force

Fighters

Early in October 'A' Flight of 33 Sqn rejoined the unit with their new Hurricanes, and 'B' Flight began receiving these also.

Three fighter Blenheims from 'A' Flight of 30 Sqn were detached to Haifa. The detachment was increased during the month. Two aircraft were lost in accidents during the period.

Bombers

A detached Flight of five Blenheims from 84 Sqn, led by F/Lt Cathill, arrived on attachment to 211 Sqn at 12.00 on 22 October. The rest of 84 Sqn arrived from Iraq around the same period. This unit was equipped with Bristol Blenheim Mk.Is.

For a short period 202 Group had six modern bomber squadrons on strength (30, 55, 84, 113 and 211 Sqns with Blenheims and 70 Sqn with Wellingtons), plus the older Bombays of 216 Sqn for night bombing duties.

On 1 October, Wing Commander Lainé took command of 216 Sqn from Wing Commander Chichester. On the same date S/Ldr Dudgeon was posted to 55 Sqn from 45 Sqn.

Early in October 'A' Flight of 33 Sqn rejoined the unit with their new Hurricanes.
[via Robert Gretzyngier]

Reconnaissance forces

On 28 October, 'C' Flight of 208 Sqn relieved 'A' Flight at Siwa.

During the month, many flying-boats from 230 Sqn flew from Malta on attachment to the depleted 228 Sqn.

Sunderland L5807/R of 228 Sqn flew back to England for major overhaul. The aircraft was back in the Mediterranean on 7 November.

On 18 October, S/Ldr K. V. Garside took over command of 230 Sqn from Wing Commander G. Francis.

Royal Australian Air Force

F/O Wilfred Arthur of 3 Sqn RAAF force-landed Gladiator N5769 on 5 October after the engine cut while practising formation flying with the whole squadron. Arthur was uninjured, but the aircraft was extensively damaged when it hit a drum during the forced landing ¼ mile northwest of Helwan.

F/O Peter Turnbull was evacuated to hospital from the detached flight with 208 Sqn on 6 October. He was replaced by F/Lt Gordon Steege. Turnbull re-joined the unit at Helwan on 14 October.

While performing formation flying on 7 October for an Australian official newsreel, an accident occurred to Gladiator N5764 but F/O John Perrin made a successful forced landing. The pilot was uninjured and the damage to the aircraft was not extensive, repairs being effected within the unit.

On 12 October, F/O s John Perrin and J. M. Davidson of 3 Sqn RAAF, with two Gauntlets, joined the flight attached to 208 Sqn in the Western Desert.

On 16 October, three Lysanders of 3 Sqn RAAF, which had been erected at Ismailia, were flown to Helwan. Two days later three more Lysanders were flown from Ismailia to Helwan. At this time, 3 Sqn RAAF had six Lysanders, 12 Gladiators and six Gauntlets.

The Gauntlets were on detached duty with 208 Sqn. The pilots on this duty were F/Lt Gordon Steege, F/Lt Blake Pelly, F/O L. E. Knowles, F/O Alan Rawlinson, F/O John Perrin and F/O J. M. Davidson.

On 21 October the last personnel of 3 Sqn RAAF moved from Ismailia to Helwan.

British Infantry aims at a Gloster Gladiator from 3 RAAF Sqn during an exercise in October 1940.
[via Australian War Memorial]

Since 3 Sqn RAAF had started to be equipped with single seat fighters complementing the six Lysanders, it was found that the unit had too many air crew. On 22 October it was decided that six Air gunner/Wireless operators were to be attached to 6 Sqn at Ramleh.

The next day two gunner officers and five Air gunner/Wireless operators were attached to 208 Sqn.

The Secretary of State for War, Anthony Eden, accompanied by the C. in C. Middle East Lieutenant Sir Archibald Wavell and the A-O-C in C. Middle East Air Marshal Sir Arthur Longmore, visited 3 Sqn RAAF at Helwan on 25 October.

Westland Lysander R2612 of 3 Sqn RAAF.
[via Stratus]

Capitano *Antonio Dell'Oro*, CO of the 159ª, 12º Gruppo, *who was killed on 8 October 1940 when his Breda Ba.65/A80 was shot down by AA fire. He was subsequently awarded a posthumous Medaglia d'Oro al Valor Militare.*
[Italian Air Force]

On 26 October the commanding Officer of 3 Sqn RAAF received a verbal notification that the squadron, less its Lysander flight, was to move to the Western Desert. During the period from 26 to 31 October the squadron's aircraft were thus thoroughly serviced, stores were packed and the unit was generally preparing for the move.

On 28 October it 14 Air gunner/Wireless operators from 3 Sqn RAAF were attached to 6 Sqn at Ramleh.

An advanced party from 3 Sqn RAAF moved to Gerawla on 29 October to prepare for arrival of the squadron in this area.

Operations

4 October 1940

Benghazi harbour was attacked, but the CR.42s, which scrambled too late due to lack of an alarm, were unable to intercept.

5 October 1940

40 SM 79s raided Mersa Matruh escorted by 40 Fiat CR.42s (29 from the 13° *Gr.* and 22 from the 8° *Gr.* led by the respective *Gruppo* Commanders – the fighters took off at 12:40 and landed at 14:50). The bombers came from the 47° *Gr.* (4 aircraft), 46° *Gr.* (9 aircraft), 14° *Stormo* (15 aircraft), 9° *Stormo* (14 aircraft) and the HQ of Vª *Squadra* (1 aircraft piloted by *Generale* Matriciardi). The three *Stormo* COs were at the head of their formations. Three aircraft aborted before the attack but the others hit the target with good precision. The last wave of bombers (that of the 9° *Stormo*) was attacked by many Gladiators, claiming one probably shot down. These were machines from 80 Sqn, which reported being unable to close to effective distance due to the speed of the bombers. All the bombers were back at base at 15:50 claiming impressive results against the railway station and the railway line.

T7106, a 30 Sqn Blenheim Mk.I of the Palestinian detachment, crashed and overturned on landing at Haifa. The crew (P/O T. Allison, P/O Kirkman and Sgt Branch) was only slightly hurt but the aircraft was destroyed beyond repair.

8 October 1940

A strong group of enemy armoured vehicles was discovered near Bir el Khamsa, south of Sidi Barrani, by the Italian reconnaissance aircraft and an attack was immediately ordered.

At 07:20, a group of four Breda Ba.65/A80s of the 159a *Sq.* and nine CR.32s of the 160a *Sq.* (according with other sources three CR.32s) took off from T2. *cap.* Antonio Dell'Oro lead the Breda formation, which also included *ten.* Barbetta, *serg. magg.* Sacchi and *serg. magg.* Giovanni Bianchelli, while *cap.* Duilio Fanali commanded the Fiat formation.

One hour later, they reached the target and were met by strong AA fire. *cap.* Dell'Oro's Ba.65 (MM75169) was hit by AA fire and was seen diving towards the ground smoking, and after a manoeuvre as if to level the plane, was seen to impact against a concentration of British armoured vehicles. A big explosion followed. The remaining aircraft of the 50° *Stormo* returned at 09:30, many of them were damaged by ground fire.

They had attacked, among other vehicles, a troop of two Rolls-Royce and one Morris CS9/LAC armoured cars of the 11th Hussars led by Sgt Lamb (in the Morris), which were out to explore the area of the Bir Enba gap. Sgt Lamb's Morris was hit and the bottom of the car blown out. The crew however was severely shaken but otherwise unharmed. They returned fire with their Bren gun and reportedly hit Dell'Oro's Ba.65, which crashed 30 yards from the Morris. Lamb and his crew reached the Ba.65 and managed to drag the pilot free from the wreckage before it burst into flames, while the other Italian aircraft overhead had stopped their attack as if they didn't want to interfere with the attempted rescue of their leader. However they found him dead, with two bullets through the head. Papers on him confirmed that he was the CO of the attacking *Squadriglia*.

Dell'Oro was sorrowfully missed. An officer coming from the *Regia Aeronautica* Aviation Academy, he was beloved by his men and highly respected by his colleagues. Always at the head of the small formations of Bredas attacking the British Army, he succeeded in rendering the underpowered and quite outmoded Breda Ba.65 an efficient ground attack weapon, developing

with great professionalism all the search-and-destroy tactics necessary for worthwhile use of the type in the desert.

A CR.32 flown by *cap.* Fanali dropped a message inside the British lines, asking for information about the fate of Dell'Oro. Some days after, the answer arrived with the confirmation of his death and a small photo depicting the ceremony of his burial included.

To honour the memory of this outstanding pilot, it was immediately proposed to give him a posthumous *Medaglia d'Oro al Valor Militare*. His comrades and in particular his close friend Duilio Fanali were sure that he had deliberately aimed his falling aircraft against the enemy vehicles.

At 18:00, Ranieri Piccolomini of the 92^a *Sq.* alone attacked a formation, composed of reportedly three Wellingtons, until he was out of ammunition. He returned with his damaged fighter, which had been hit in the wings and in the fuselage, claiming damage to all three Wellingtons with the use of 618 rounds.

He had met a couple of Blenheims from 55 Sqn that had taken off at 17:00 from Fuka to attack targets in Bardia with small calibre bombs. The returning British pilots reported that after the bomb drop they were unable to see their results because they were immediately attacked by a CR.42, which stayed behind them firing alternatively at both from about 400 yards. After around five minutes, the fighter disengaged, having caused no damage and apparently having suffered none. The British crew noted that heavy but inaccurate AA burst mainly around the pursuing fighter 400 yards behind (probably the damage suffered by Piccolomini was caused by Italian AA).

However, when the British bombers landed at 19:10, Blenheim L8391 hit a lorry after landing, slightly damaging one airscrew and the Vokes filter.

While coming back from a patrol over Sidi Barrani, *s. ten.* Furio Lauri of the 368^a *Sq.* hit the searchlight at the end of the landing strip of El Adem. The aircraft was classified RS.

An SM 79 of the 14º *Stormo* crashed into the ground after an engine breakdown, with the loss of the crew, *ten.* Stefano Pelo, *ten.* Virgilio Marroni, *serg. magg. Motorista* Giuseppe Asperges, *Aviere Scelto Motorista* Guido Forlini, *Aviere Scelto Motorista* Ubaldo Nanni and *Aviere Scelto Montatore* Paolo Italiano.

An air attack by two enemy intruders was recorded on Menastir and two CR.42s were damaged, one was classified RD and the other repairable in S.R.A.M.

9 October 1940

At 15:30, F/O Nigel Cullen (Gladiator K7892) of 80 Sqn was on a lone flight south of Sidi Barrani searching for missing army personnel in the area east of El Khamsa. He met five Breda Ba.65 ground attack aircraft from 159^a *Sq.*, 12º *Gr.* in vee formation. He climbed to 10,000 feet and dived down on them from dead ahead, out of the sun. He fired on the enemy leader, using approximately 400 rounds, and reported that it went down with smoke coming from the engine cowling. The other four aircraft immediately went into a tight left hand bank. Cullen was able to get many deflection shots on them but could not see any results. He reported that the Italian aircraft didn't seem to fire from their rear cockpits at all. They all did one quarter attack on him before disappearing by diving into clouds to the west. He gave chase but was outdistanced.

He then continued his search for the missing army personnel and observed a burnt out wreck by a well in the vicinity. On return, he was credited with a probably destroyed. According to Italian sources, all six aircraft returned to base.

At 16:10, Lysander L4729 piloted by P/O Roberts of 208 Sqn was out for a reconnaissance of the Sofafi-Barrani area when it was attacked by a CR.42, which broke off when Roberts was a few feet off the ground. The Lysander suffered some minor damage when diving away. No aerial activity connected with this action has been possible to find in the Italian records.

Ten. *Giulio Reiner with Gina, the mascot of his unit, in front of a couple of fighters of his Squadriglia at El Adem in autumn 1940.*
[Duma via Gabriele Brancaccio]

10 October 1940

British sources reported that Italian bombers attacked Sidi Haneish, but merely succeeded in hitting the road between 112 and 80 Sqns, and there were no casualties or damage.

One Bombay from 216 Sqn attacked Barrani together with HMS *Ladybird*.

Three Wellingtons of 70 Sqn under F/Lt Wells attacked Benghazi harbour. Large fires were started but no ships were observed in the harbour.

11 October 1940

The Mediterranean Fleet was again at sea for *Operation MB6*, another re-supply operation to Malta.

The newly-arrived AA cruisers with four destroyers went with the four merchant ship convoy, while HMS *Warspite* with three other battleships, the carriers HMS *Eagle* and HMS *Illustrious*, six cruisers and sixteen destroyers made up the covering force.

The convoy arrived at Malta on 11 October, undetected by Italian reconnaissance because of bad weather. The two Australian destroyers HMAS *Stuart* and HMAS *Vendetta* were left to refit. Only the destroyer HMS *Imperial* was damaged, by the explosion of a mine.

During the night, while the Mediterranean Fleet was arriving at Malta, the cruiser HMS *Ajax* was attacked by the 1st Torpedo boat Squadron of *Regia Marina* equipped with the torpedo-boats *Airone*, *Alcione* and *Ariel* and by the 11th Destroyer Squadron composed of the ships *Artigliere*, *Geniere*, *Aviere* and *Camicia Nera*.

In a night action fought at ranges of 4000 yards and less, the British cruiser was able to sink *Airone* and *Alcione* and damaged *Aviere* and *Artigliere*, the last one heavily. In exchange it sustained considerable damage to the bridge and radar equipment, caused by gunfire from *Airone* and *Artigliere*. Thirteen sailors were killed and twenty-two wounded.

Three Bombays from 216 Sqn attacked Benghazi harbour.

Italian night bombers (possibly aircraft from the 54° *Gr. B.T.*) hit Fuka at around 19:40 when three 55 Sqn Blenheims were landing after an evening raid on Bardia. The bombs, estimated to be 100kg, fell very close to the sick quarters, and Leading Aircraftman Harry Hall received a wound in the neck and died the next evening.

12 October 1940

During a routine armed reconnaissance patrol along the Allied frontline in the Tobruk area in the evening, Giulio Reiner of the 73ª *Sq.*, 9° *Gr.*, accompanied his *Gruppo* commander, *magg.* Ernesto Botto.

Having completed an uneventful patrol, the two pilots were approaching their El Adem base when they spotted three Blenheims preparing to bomb the airfield. They immediately attacked and prevented the bombers from releasing their bombs. The Blenheims tried to escape, heading out over the sea. Botto finally downed the first, which dived into the water. At this point the other Blenheims turned back over land, pursued by Reiner, who shot down the leader over the El Hagna area and the wingman near Bir el Hannana; both Bristols was left burning on the ground. With his aircraft out of fuel and some bullet holes in its right wing, Reiner successfully made an emergency landing in the dark in the Buq-Buq area. He was "captured" by a platoon of Askaris (i.e. African native troops of *Regio Esercito*), which initially believed that he was a British pilot. He returned to El Adem during the night, but the following day he was back to recover the aircraft.

It seems that they had been in combat with three Blenheims from 55 Sqn, which had taken off loaded with small bombs at 16:15 from Fuka Main (LG 17), Egypt, to bomb Italian aircraft on El Adem (LG 144), Libya. The formation made out to sea and climbed to a height of about 18,000 ft, reached a point about 30 miles north of Tobruk, when a turn on the target was made.

At 17:50 the attack was carried out from a height of 9,000ft (rather too early, as the sun was still up). During the run in, the formation was attacked by three CR.42s. Bombs fell in the target area and bursts were seen among the aircraft on the north side of the aerodrome. The Italian fighters persisted in their attack, firing 0.5" tracer from about 800 yards and closing in to fire their small caliber guns. The British formation took evasive action but unfortunately split up. No. 2 (Blenheim L1538) flown by F/O K. D. Potter was unable to keep up with the leader. No. 3 (Blenheim L8530) flown by P/O M. S. Singleton was hit in the starboard engine, the fuselage was riddled, wireless and intercommunication unusable, both rudder control badly damage, the tail-wheel shot through and the rudder trim gear also unusable. Although the Blenheim was badly damaged the pilot managed to return to base. The Blenheim was categorized as Damaged Beyond Repair. The observer Sgt B. J. Fox and the wireless operator/air gunner Sgt I. Brownrigg escaped uninjured.

The leader, (Blenheim L6659) flown by F/O G. E. P. Green made for the coast near Ras el Miln, and the fighter following him continued the engagement for about 10 minutes before breaking off the attack. This aircraft then continued back to base, badly hit. Green was wounded under his right arm - a flesh wound - and the observer, F/Sgt W. H. Weller was slightly hurt. The undercarriage was damaged and the turret and W/T set were both rendered U/S. This aircraft was fired on by shore defences at Mersa Matruh but no further damage was done, and it belly-landed at its base with the aid of the observer and the wireless operator/air gunner, Sgt J. McGarry. The pilot was awarded a DFC and the observer and gunner awarded mentions in despatches for the action. L6659 was finally lost with 70 OTU on 27 February 1942 in Kenya, when it burst a tire on take-off and the undercarriage collapsed at Nakuru.

No. 2 aircraft when left by the formation dived to ground level and escaped. This Blenheim suffered only a few holes in the rudder. The observer Sgt Duffy and the wireless operator/air gunner Sgt B. Noble escaped uninjured. This aircraft was finally lost when it crashed in bad visibility near Fuka on 18 October 1940.

This combat was witnessed from the ground by *cap.* Bruno Locatelli at El Adem, who reported that notwithstanding the attack of two 4° *Stormo*'s fighters three Bristol Blenheims succeeded in releasing some small calibre bombs while being hit by the first bursts from the Fiats. The Blenheims turned around and escaped. One of them was seen to leave the formation and steeply lose height. Locatelli presumed it was seriously damaged.

A Savoia Marchetti S.73 of the 148° *Gr.* T (*trasporto* – transport) was intercepted by British carrier fighters while flying from Benghazi to Catania. The pilot, *ten.* Valentino Valentini, was wounded

Fiat CR.32 MM4666 of 160ª Squadriglia on a trailer at Tobruk airfield on 3 October 1940. This kind of trailer was used by the S.R.A.M. (Squadre Riparazioni Automobili e Motori). [via Przemek Skulski]

and died at Catania Hospital two days later. The damaged plane was landed by the co-pilot, *ten.* Emilio Alliata.

The destroyer *Artigliere*, disabled by the fire of HMS *Ajax*, was taken in tow during the night by the destroyer *Camicia Nera*, but after an abortive attack by three Swordfishes of 815 Sqn from HMS *Illustrious*, she was sunk by the cruiser HMS *York*.

The *Regia Aeronautica* was out in strength to attack the Mediterranean Fleet, and a total of 31 SM 79 bombers from Sicily attacked, finding the Fulmars from HMS *Illustrious* up and ready to intercept. The first formation of twelve bombers, from 34º *Stormo*, attacked HMS *Eagle*. The bombs fell so close to the old British carrier that the shock waves were critical in damaging it sufficiently to miss the upcoming Taranto operation for defects in the fuel system. All the bombers came back in damaged condition, caused by AA and possibly by the attacks of Lieutenant Nicolls' Red Section of 806 Sqn. The subsequent formation composed of ten SM 79s of the 36º *Stormo* was also attacked by the Fulmars, which this time shot down two machines of the 108º *Gr.* (*ten.* Alberto Soldati and his crew MIA) and the 109º *Gr.* (*ten.* Francesco Tempra and his crew MIA). These were almost surely victims of Lieutenant Commander Evans and Sub Lieutenants Hogg and Lowe of Blue Section. Another aircraft returned damaged with one dead crew member and two wounded, while another SM 79 of the 109º *Gr.*, flown by *ten.* Giorgio Pieri, crashed on Mount Etna while coming back to base and was reputedly damaged by the British. In general the Italian crews were unable to claim any hits on the British ships because of the heavy opposition experienced.

It is also reported that a Z.501 shadower was shot down at 11:45, victim of Sub Lieutenants Jack Sewell and Roberts of 806 Sqn. They chased it from 3,000 feet down to sea level, where it ditched. They strafed it, but saw no sign of life.

A third formation of seven SM 79s of the 34º *Stormo* attacked in error the Italian ships, luckily without causing damage. The commander of the Italian formation was removed from his position at the end of the mission.

Fourteen Ju87s of the 96º *Gr.* and SM 79s of the 105º *Gr. Aut. B.T.* failed to find their targets.

It is reported that Sunderland L2164 of 228 Sqn, flown by F/Lt McCall, saved the crew of a shot down Italian Cant Z.501 seaplane. It was reported that after a two hour search, three Italian airmen (2nd pilot a Sgt Major, observer a naval officer and the wireless operator) were found in a rubber boat, the pilot and the gunner were unable to escape from the sinking plane and were drowned. The Z.501 was the one claimed by Fulmar pilots (Sub Lieutenants Sewell and Roberts) during the day and although there is little doubt that it was indeed shot down, it is still unidentified.

One Bombay from 216 Sqn attacked Barrani, while three more bombers from the same unit attacked Tobruk harbour.

Three Wellingtons of 70 Sqn, led by S/Ldr Rolfe, attacked Tobruk harbour causing a large fire.

30 Sqn reported the loss of Leading Aircraftman Harold Kenneth Spencer, for unknown reasons.

13 October 1940

Three Bombays from 216 Sqn attacked Benghazi harbour. A direct hit was observed on a moored ship.

Three Wellingtons of 70 Sqn under Wing Commander Webb attacked Benghazi harbour, seeing a very large fire approx. 200 yards long. On returning, Webb's Wellington (T2826) had to belly land at Quotafia (El Daba) owing to failure of the undercarriage actuating gear.

14 October 1940

The Mediterranean Fleet came under attack by Libyan based aircraft.

The 9º *Stormo*, although not claiming any hits, suffered eight damaged SM 79s, caused by British fighters. At 19:00, an SM 79 torpedo bomber ('278-6') flown by Massimiliano Erasi from the 278ª *Sq.* attacked the cruiser HMS *Liverpool* from 700 metres and a height of 70 metres, hitting it with a torpedo in the bow, which broke away just forward of the bridge and remained hanging. The ship was taken in tow by the stern by the cruiser HMS *Orion*. Erasi landed at 20:20 at El Adem. This had been his first torpedo attack, and HMS *Liverpool* was out of operations for twelve months. The British ships finally arrived at Alexandria at 01:00 on 15 October. Admiral Cunningham recorded:

" *The entry of the battle-fleet into Alexandria (…) was most spectacular, (…). We approached during a heavy air raid, and low-flying aircraft, thought to be carrying torpedoes, had been reported. We made for the shallow water of the Great Pass – the entrance to Alexandria Harbour - at high speed, firing a blind barrage on both sides with our guns flashing and the sparkle of bursting shell all over the horizon. These night attacks had now been fully developed by the Italians. They were nerve-racking and dangerous, particularly as they were thrown in at dusk after our aircraft carrier had flown all her fighters for the night (…) However, we realized how lucky we were that they had not started when we were entirely without radar. The Illustrious, so fitted, now picked up the attackers at a good distance and they were met with a heavy barrage at five miles*".

During this operation the *Regia Marina* lost a destroyer and two torpedo-boats, with another destroyer damaged trying to attack a more potent (and superbly manned) British cruiser (HMS *Ajax*). *Regia Aeronautica* lost three bombers and a seaplane, attacking with small unescorted formations in the face of fighter opposition.

Their results were never decisive or impressive, but were not as ineffective as they are generally depicted (in particular by British historians). On the morning of 15 October the Mediterranean Fleet had one cruiser out of action (HMS *Liverpool*), another considerably damaged (HMS *Ajax*), one aircraft carrier damaged (HMS *Eagle*) and one destroyer heavily damaged (HMS *Imperial*).

The British sailors (and Admiral Andrew Cunningham) were particularly impressed by the night attack on 12 October, but the Headquarters in London followed the Official attitude towards the Italians, an attitude that is easily visible in many contemporary action reports (even those of the RAF). The Admiralty in London signalled to Cunningham: "*In view of public feeling here suffering under intensive and ruthless attacks, it might be well to exclude from future communiqués reference to gallantry of enemy (…)*".

Eight SM 79s were slightly damaged (RS) on the ground during a Blenheim raid over Derna. It seems probable that the unit responsible for the attack was 113 Sqn.

The 7° *Gr.* only had 10 or 11 Ba.88s flyable out of 29 on charge. Notwithstanding the low efficiency, another effort was made to use the Bredas of the *Gruppo* operationally, when a three-plane formation of the 98ª *Sq.*, led by *ten.* Saverio Gostini, was ordered to attack enemy armoured vehicles in the general area between Sidi Barrani and Bir Enba. This time the Ba.88s were at least able to reach the target area, but the enemy were not located and they failed to draw first blood.

Benghazi Berka was raided and the Command post of the airbase was damaged.

Three Bombays from 216 Sqn attacked Benghazi harbour.

Three Wellingtons of 70 Sqn, under S/Ldr Kerr, raided Benghazi harbour. Two explosions were observed.

15 October 1940

While on a patrol between 10:50 and 13:25 over Sollum and Giarabub, together with *serg. magg.* Guglielmo Gorgone and *serg.* Nadio Monti, *ten.* Ranieri Piccolomini of the 92ª *Sq.* spotted and shot down a Lysander with the use of 2284 rounds of ammunition.

This was P/O David Mervyn Boughey Druce of 208 Sqn flying a reconnaissance over Giarabub in a lone Lysander (L4714), who reportedly was attacked by the CR.42s and shot down, his aircraft blowing-up on hitting the ground, killing him and his Wireless Operator/Air Gunner Sgt John Felix Muldowney. Before being shot down, however, the Lysander fought back tenaciously, discharging four pans of rear gun ammunition and damaging both Gorgone's and Monti's fighters.

Egyptian soldiers from a frontier post witnessed the action, and later recovered the bodies of the two British pilots. Lysander L4720 was allotted as replacement for L4714.

The Lysander (possibly L4712) of F/Lt Legge of 208 Sqn force-landed near Melfa oasis due to engine failure while conveying Brigadier General Gallaway from Ma'aten Bagush to Siwa. The aircraft suffered no further damage.

A couple of Ba.88s of 98ª *Sq.*, 7° *Gr.* were out for an armed reconnaissance over the front line near Sidi Barrani. The Italian AA was quickly on target and *ten.* Luigi Proner (CO 98ª *Sq.*) was hit, while he was orbiting at 250 metres to permit the flack personnel to better spot his nationality markings and cease fire. His aircraft fell in flames and Proner was killed, while his gunned escaped by parachute.

After this the combat career of the Breda Ba.88s was over, A few days later news arrived that the Bredas would be definitely struck off charge, and they officially left the ranks of Vª *Squadra Aerea* on 16 November. In almost three months of operations they never saw action against the RAF.

A night intruding SM 79 of 59ª *Sq.*, coming back from the usual raid over El Daba, was intercepted by British night fighters, damaged and followed as far as Sollum. *ten.* Pagano was forced to make an emergency landing 35 kilometres east of Tobruk, causing severe damage to his aircraft (RD).

Three Bombays from 216 Sqn attacked Tobruk harbour. Hits were claimed on naval and military barracks. One of the bombers avoided interception by four fighters by diving steeply.

Three Wellingtons of 70 Sqn under F/Lt Wells raided Tobruk. Direct hits on military barracks were observed.

16 October 1940

S/Ldr Patrick Dunn took off from Amiriya at 19:15 in a Gladiator II to intercept an SM 79, which escaped after discovering him. The result of the engagement was inconclusive and Dunn noted: *"In a faster aircraft should have proved an easy victim"*.

17 October 1940

Five Bombays from 216 Sqn attacked Benghazi harbour. Heavy damage was claimed to shipping and installations.

Three Wellingtons of 70 Sqn under S/Ldr Rolfe attacked Maritza aerodrome and Calato landing ground in the Aegean Islands. The attack was reputedly highly successful.

18 October 1940

Blenheim Mk.I L1538 of 55 Sqn returned to Fuka with engine trouble 30 minutes after take-off (15:00) for a raid. The aircraft crash-landed and was destroyed beyond repair. There were no reports on injuries to the crew, Sgt E. Coughlan, Sgt W. F. Bowker and Sgt D. Clayson.

Blenheim Mk.I K7180 of 30 Sqn, piloted by Sgt Childs, was destroyed by fire at Haifa in a landing accident. The crew escaped uninjured.

Seven aircraft of the 33° *Gr.* attacked Siwa Oasis at 10:10 from 4000 metres. This was the first day bombing mission since 5 October.

Siwa Oasis, logistic base for the British raiding teams that operated in the deep desert, was attacked by 50° *Stormo*. A formation of 15 CR.32s from the 160ª and the 167ª *Sq.* together with six Breda Ba.65/K14s of the 168ª *Sq.* took off from the advanced base of El Guasc (at which they had arrived on the evening of 17 October) loaded with 2 kg, 15 kg and "thermos" bombs. The Bredas were forced to return to base due to engine problems (while returning Ba.65 MM75086 was lost in a landing accident), and the attack was carried out only by the CR.32s. The attack was a complete surprise but the small biplanes weren't able to cause much damage. The two raids were noted by 208 Sqn's diarist, who reported a bombing raid at 10:00 with 50 bombs falling in the area and a second attack at 13:30 performed by six biplanes. No damage was suffered.

In the ranks of 50° *Stormo* for this mission there were also many pilots coming from the 76ª *Sq.*, 7° *Gr.* (CO *cap.* Valentino Festa) that, deprived of their useless Breda Ba.88s, continued their African adventure with the 50° *Stormo*.

Three Bombays from 216 Sqn attacked Benghazi harbour. Bombay L5816, which had taken off from Fuka at 19:00, failed to return. The pilots, F/Lt Edward Lionel Cullimore and P/O Lyon Curtis Quick, were lost together with their crew, Leading Aircraftman Rolfe Vivian Minton, Leading Aircraftman William Robert York and Leading Aircraftman John Campbell Perry.

Three Wellingtons of 70 Sqn under F/Lt Brian attacked Benghazi harbour, while three machines under Wing Commander Webb again attacked Maritza and Calato. No particular damage was observed on either operation.

At 17:10, four SM.82s specially equipped for long range bombing operations took off from the airstrip of Gadurrà in Rhodes, *cap.* Paolo Moci leading the formation with *magg.* Ettore Muti (CO of the 41° *Gr.*) acting as second pilot. *cap.* Arturo Mayer-Ziotti, *cap.* Antonio Zanetti and Fortunato Federigi piloted the other bombers. They reached 3000 metres at 18:35, and then proceeded for the target, the oil refinery of Al Manamah on Bahrain Island.

At 02:20, Al Manamah was bombed (each plane carried 100 15kg incendiary bombs) then Moci and his men continued and reached Massaua-Zula airstrip in Italian East Africa at 08:45. The record mission had lasted 15 hours and 35 minutes, with a total distance flown of 4100 km. Moci came back to Benghazi early in the morning of 24 October and then proceeded to Rhodes. He was awarded a *Medaglia d'argento al Valor Militare* and a *Medaglia di bronzo al Valor Militare* for this mission. This remarkable mission covered a record distance, and Al Manamah was possibly the farthest target ever attained by a bombing mission in the European and African theatres. However, as with many others Italian "records", this remained an isolated incident. Apart from its propaganda value, the *Regia Aeronautica* never really posed a serious threat to British oil production.

19 October 1940

During the night, Italian bombers carried out a raid on Cairo, bombs falling on the suburb of Maadi.

Three Bombays from 216 Sqn attacked Tobruk town. A large explosion was observed.

22 October 1940

Twelve fighters from the 13° *Gr.* took off to make a protective cruise over the Italian engineers, who were building a water pipeline between Bardia and Sidi Barrani. During take off, *serg.* Francesco Morana of the 78ª *Sq.* suffered an engine breakdown and crashed. The fighter was written off and the pilot was seriously wounded.

At 11:25, *serg. magg.* Danilo Billi from the 94ª *Sq.*, 8° *Gr.* scrambled from Menastir to intercept a lone reconnaissance aircraft identified as a Wellington. He was soon followed by *ten.* Vittorio Gnudi and *serg.* Alberto Bottazzi (also from the from the 94ª *Sq.*). *serg. magg.* Billi attacked immediately, starting a fire on the British aircraft. The three pilots were back between 12:20 and 12:45 and Billi was credited with the victory after having used 220 rounds of ammunition.

He had intercepted a reconnaissance Blenheim Mk.IV of 113 Sqn (T2063) piloted by Sgt Price, which had taken off at 10:35. The Bristol landed back at base at 13:00 and was rendered U/S by the fire of the intercepting CR.42s.

On 21 October, 819 Sqn had disembarked to Dekheila, where six Swordfishes had been fitted with magnetic mines. Together with six Swordfishes of 815 Sqn and four from 824 Sqn they went to Fuka, where they refuelled and taxied out to take-off position at 23:00 on 22 October. Owing to the sandstorm caused by the 16 aircraft running up their engines on the desert aerodrome, the situation became nothing short of a shambles and the raid was postponed until the next night.

One Bombay from 216 Sqn attacked Italian forward troops together with the Army.

23 October 1940

One Bombay from 216 Sqn attacked Benghazi harbour and El Adem. No results was observed over Benghazi, but a large fire was seen at T3.

At 23:30, the Swordfishes at Fuka took off with long-range tanks and proceeded towards Tobruk, which they reached at about 03:00. The four aircraft of 824 Sqn dropped 250lb bombs from a height of 8,000 feet while 819 and 815 Sqns went down low and dropped their mines at the entrance to Tobruk harbour. They then returned to Fuka after a six-hour flight. The crew of Midshipmen Williams and Bowker of 815 Sqn missed Fuka during the return, and made a forced landing 50 miles east of Ma'aten Bagush, the Swordfish being damaged. After refuelling, the aircraft retuned to Dekheila in the morning on 24 October. No result from this operation is known.

24 October 1940

S. ten. Carlo Battaglia of the 73ª *Sq.* died in a crash during take-off from Berka.

Nine British bombers raided Benghazi Berka where one barrack was destroyed.

Wellington T2735 from 70 Sqn attacked Benghazi harbour alone with unsatisfactory results.

25 October 1940

At 06:00, eight Blenheims, six from 55 Sqn and two from 84 Sqn, took off to take part in a wing raid on Tobruk north foreshore. Two aircraft from 55 Sqn aborted immediately, while the remaining six proceeded alone to the target having missed the rendezvous with nine Bristols from 113 Sqn (that attacked independently). The attack was made at 08:35 and hits on M. T. at the northern edge of Tobruk aerodrome were claimed. Twelve CR.42s were seen climbing towards the formation, but only two of these attacked from astern. The attack lasted 5 minutes, one attacking fighter being believed shot down. L8362 from 84 Sqn, flown by Sgt Gordon, was shot up by CR.42s, being damaged in the starboard engine (rendered U/S), both wings, fuselage and petrol tanks. The Blenheim force-landed among British forward troops, with the observer slightly wounded in the back of the neck. The rest of the formation was back at 10:00. It is reported that the damaged Blenheim was sufficiently repaired next day to fly back to base, but this is not corroborated by existing records.

The Blenheims had been intercepted by three fighters from the 96ª *Sq.*, flown by *cap.* Roberto Fassi, *s. ten.* Carlo Agnelli and *serg.* Bruno Spitzl. Fassi had led them in a scramble following an air alarm and left Spitzl to orbit over El Adem. Together with Agnelli, he attacked six Blenheims, which were flying at 3500 metres over Tobruk, and together they claimed two shared victories (one confirmed and one probable) while the two fighters returned damaged by return fire.

Nine machines from 211 Sqn, together with three of the detached Flight of 84 Sqn, were also to take part in this raid, but instead bombed a perimeter camp south of Sidi Barrani.

27 October 1940

Blenheim Mk.IV T2068 of 113 Sqn took off from LG 68 (Waterloo) as one of three Blenheims detailed to bomb Benghazi. On return in darkness it strayed over Alexandria and was fired on by local flak units. The crew failed to locate their base and bailed out when the fuel was exhausted. The aircraft crashed 20km north-west of Wadi Natrun. The crew, F/O P. Squires, Sgt Durrant and Sgt Hancorn, were safe. The other two machines force-landed short of fuel at Qotaifiya.

At 15:50, three Lysanders of 208 Sqn, piloted by S/Ldr Sprague, F/Lt Wilson and F/O Webber, dive-bombed a lorry concentration on the track between Tummar and Bir Enba. It was not possible to observe damage inflicted.

A couple of Wellingtons of 70 Sqn took off to attack Benghazi, but T2731 collided with a telegraph pole and abandoned operations, while T2813 missed the target in ground haze and bombed Derna harbour.

28 October 1940

S. ten. Neri De Benedetti had a narrow escape when his Fiat overturned at Berka, after he had suddenly been taken ill while steeply descending to land. The plane was heavily damaged but he luckily escaped.

29 October 1940

RAF flew a number of bomber sorties during the day to prevent the *Regia Aeronautica* from attacking Crete. Two RAF bombers raided Menelao, two more raided Ain Gazala and a further two raided Derna but none of them caused any damage. A raid on Tmini caused six wounded. 55 Sqn and the detached Flight of 84 Sqn carried out all these attacks.

Two more bombers from 211 Sqn raided El Adem under the cover of a Ghibli thunderstorm, damaging the base barracks. They also attacked Menastir and T2, while a raid on Sollum (probably made by 113 Sqn) destroyed two IMAM Ro.37bis.

One Bombay from 216 Sqn attacked Tobruk harbour.

30 October 1940

One Bombay from 216 Sqn attacked Tobruk harbour.

31 October 1940

After some days of inactivity due to the incessantly blowing Ghibli wind, a big coordinated Italian action against Mersa Matruh was planned for the day. It was planned to use at least 50 SM 79s from the 9° *Stormo*, 14° *Stormo* and 33° *Gr.* with an escort of 40 CR.42s from the 2° *Stormo* and 151° *Gr.* to attack the British base and its different targets.

At 10:10, Menastir M was attacked by British bombers, reported as ten Armstrong Whitworth Whitleys (in fact seven Blenheims from 55 Sqn and three from 84 Sqn). The bombers arrived from a northerly direction completely undetected, and hit the parking area of the 93ª *Sq.* with many small and medium calibre bombs released from 3000 metres. The *Squadriglia* HQ hut was completely destroyed by a direct hit, while four CR.42s were lightly damaged by splinters (RS) and one was heavily damaged (RD). The heavy damaged CR.42 was immediately taken to the S.R.A.M. of El Adem (according to other sources the RD Fiats were three and the RS Fiats were two). Luckily no losses were suffered by the personnel of 8° *Gr.*

At 10:15 (09:40 according to other sources), while the 9° *Stormo* formation was taxiing on Gambut airstrip, a formation of seven Blenheims from 211 Sqn led by S/Ldr Gordon-Finlayson

The pilots of the 368ª Squadriglia posed around their commander cap. Bruno Locatelli, during the move of the unit to Libya in September 1940. The unit drew first blood on 31 October 1940 when its pilots claimed two Hurricanes and a Gladiator shot down for no losses.
[Giorgio Apostolo]

and two others from 84 Sqn suddenly appeared overhead. The British bombers had managed to approach undetected by gliding down from 3000 metres with their engines off, and bombed with extreme precision, destroying three bombers while three others were RD and many others were less seriously damaged. The losses among 9° *Stormo*'s personnel were also heavy, with two dead from 63ª *Sq.* (*serg. Armiere* Carlo Marchi and *Primo Aviere Radiotelegrafista* Eugenio Bonino).

Three fighters of the resident 82ª *Sq.* scrambled after the bombers had turned on their Mercury engines. They were flown by *s. ten.* Virgilio Vanzan, *serg. magg.* Dante Davico and *serg.* Nino Campanini, but they were unable to intercept.

Three fighters of the 78ª *Sq.* also scrambled at 10:00. These were flown by *ten.* Ippolito Lalatta, *s. ten.* Luigi Cannepele and *serg.* Ernesto Taddia. These were also unsuccessful, and they landed back at base at 10:45.

Serg. magg. Roberto Marchi and *s. ten.* Carlo Albertini of the 366ª *Sq.* scrambled from the nearby Amseat A3 to intercept the British bombers. While in pursuit an enemy fighter, identified as a Hurricane, crossed the path of Albertini, who fired 420 rounds on it. The aircraft escaped smoking heavily and Albertini, who landed at 10:45, was credited with a probable victory.

At 10:25, three CR.42s from 92ª *Sq.*, 8° *Gr.*, scrambled from Menastir M. The three fighters were flown by *s. ten.* Luigi Uguccioni, *serg.* Mario Veronesi and *serg.* Marcello Mosele. Veronesi intercepted a Hurricane which he claimed damaged with 150 rounds of ammunition. The three aircraft returned to base at 10:45.

It seems that both scrambles from 366ª and 92ª *Squadriglie* had been involved in combat with Hurricanes escorting the British bombers, and in fact 80 Sqn had put up eight Gladiators and two Hurricanes between 9.00 and 11.00 to patrol off Bardia at 15,000 feet, to cover bombers attacking Menastir and a target 38 miles west of Bardia (Gambut). The returning pilots didn't report any encounter with Italian aircraft, while returning 211 Sqn crews reported that an Italian CR.42 tried to follow them but, after firing two bursts from 500 yards, was set upon by a Gladiator and a Hurricane and last seen diving towards the ground with smoke trailing from it.

The Italian mission against Mersa Matruh was not cancelled, and at 10:50 only ten SM 79s of 9° *Stormo* (that in the original plan were to constitute the bulk of the formation) took off together with 11 SM 79s of the 14° *Stormo* and five from the 33° *Gr.* The bombers were escorted by 18 CR.42s from the 13° *Gr.*, which flew as close escort, while 19 more from the 151° *Gr.*, which were to fly an indirect support sweep and which replaced the formation from the 8° *Gr.* at the last moment after that the latter unit was unable to take part in the mission because of the damage suffered at Menastir.

At 11:45 two sections with six CR.42s of the 78ª *Sq.* took off from Gambut G, with *cap.* Giuseppe Dall'Aglio leading *s. ten.* Luigi Cannepele (a future posthumous *Medaglia d'Oro al Valor Militare* winner and inspirer of the famous "*Gigi tre osei*" symbol of the 150° *Gr. C.T.*), *serg.* Rovero Abbarchi, *ten.* Ippolito Lalatta (leading the second section), *serg.* Ernesto Taddia and *serg.* Teresio Martinoli. They were followed at 11:55 by two sections from the 82ª *Sq.* The first section included *ten.* Guglielmo Chiarini (section leader), *s. ten.* Giuseppe Timolina and *serg. magg.* Dante Davico while the second section included *ten.* Gianfranco Perversi (section leader), *serg.* Francesco Nanin and *s. ten.* Virgilio Vanzan. Together with these six CR.42s, six more of the 77ª *Sq.* took off with *cap.* Domenico Bevilacqua leading *ten.* Eduardo Sorvillo, *s. ten.* Carmelo Catania, *serg. magg.* Ernesto Scalet, *serg.* Ernesto Paolini and *serg.* Renato Gori. *cap.* Giuseppe Dall'Aglio took command of the whole formation.

For the 151° *Gr.* this was the first long range escort mission since arriving in Libya, and they received the order to move at 11:00. At 12:10 they took off from Amseat A3 to arrive over Mersa Matruh at the same time as the bombers. Participating pilots under command of *magg.* Carlo Calosso in a 367ª *Sq.* fighter were from all three *Squadriglie* - 366ª *Sq.* (*cap.* Bernardino Serafini, *ten.* Mario Ferrero, *ten.* Piero Veneziani, *serg. magg.* Fiorenzo Milella, *serg. magg.* Roberto Marchi and *serg.* Rosario Di Carlo), 367ª *Sq.* (*cap.* Simeone Marsan, *serg. magg.* Renato Mingozzi, *serg.* Maggiorino Soldati, *ten.* Irzio Bozzolan, *serg. magg.* Gino Bogoni and *serg.* Bruno Celotto) and 368ª

Sq. (*cap.* Bruno Locatelli, *serg. magg.* Davide Colauzzi, *serg.* Mario Turchi, *ten.* Giuseppe Zuffi, *serg.* Piero Hosquet and *serg.* Ottorino Ambrosi).

The bombers gathered over Tmimi and then headed east in groups of five in arrow formation. The fighters from the 13° *Gr.* flew in flights of three in echelon right formation at 5000 meters, directed to a rendezvous point 20 kilometres south-west of Mersa Matruh along the road that connected this base with Bir Kenayis, which they reached at 12:56.

After the bombers arrived over Mersa Matruh, each formation went for different targets but was attacked by British fighters while aiming for their targets. At 12:46, the 14° *Stormo*, led by *ten. col.* Lidonici, attacked the airfield of Bir Kenayis, but finding it empty they headed for an alternative target of enemy troops south-west of Mersa Matruh, who were hit at 13:01. In fact, 80 Sqn pilots on the ground noticed Italian bombers attacking the aerodrome of Bir Kenayis at 12:45 and reported that bombs fell to the south-west and some distance away, obviously they thought that the Savoias had missed their intended target by some miles. Gunners of the 14° *Stormo* claimed two Hurricanes and a Gladiator destroyed, and another Gladiator probable. One SM 79 crash-landed near Sidi Barrani and was written off, while a second crash-landed in the desert near Tobruk and was also written off. Three more SM 79s returned at 14:40 so badly damaged that they were classified RD, and another one went to the SRAM for major repairs. Among the crews there were three dead (*s. ten. pilota-puntatore* (pilot aimer) Federico Tonizzo, *Primo Aviere Montatore* Mario Padalino, *Primo Aviere Armiere* Guerino Invorti) and two wounded (*Tenete* Beltramini, another aimer, and *ten.* Martinelli (observer)). Of its 11 SM 79s, by the evening only five were still fit for further operations.

At 12:55 the 9° *Stormo*, led by *ten. col.* Italo Napoleoni, released its bombs on the railway near El Qasaba airfield. The diarist of 6 Sqn noted that Quasaba had been bombed at 13:05 by five Savoia SM 79s, dropping approximately 30-40 100kg bombs, and that no casualties nor damage had been suffered by the squadron's detachment, while the diarist of 208 Sqn reported that around 40 bombs of the 100kg type were dropped by 15 SM 79s and that four of them fell in the camp damaging three lorries and three tents, while the remainder fell around the railway siding. Two SM 79s from the 11ª *Sq.*, 26° *Gr. B.T.* were shot down. The *Squadriglia* flew in a 'V' formation led by *ten.* Giovanni Ruggiero, and it was the two outer SM 79s that were shot down in flames by a Hurricane (*s. ten.* Fulvio Fabiani, *serg.* Arturo Bigliardi, *Primo Aviere Fotografo* Adorno Antonini, *Primo Aviere Motorista* Francesco Farina and *Primo Aviere Armiere* Vincenzo Scarinci; *ten.* Roberto Di Frassineto, *serg. magg.* Armando Zambelli, *Aviere Scelto Motorista* Camillo Caiazzo, *Primo Aviere Armiere* Alfredo Pacifici and *Aviere Scelto Radiotelegrafista* Giuseppe Costa); all but Zambelli (POW) were killed. In an aircraft of the 13ª *Sq.*, *Primo Aviere Motorista* Tommaso Giorgio was killed and *Aviere Scelto RT* Canaponi was wounded by Hurricane bullets. A gunner in the SM 79 to the left of *ten.* Ruggiero, at the time 22-year-old *Aviere Scelto Armiere* Cherubino Mariotti, recalled of this his first combat mission:

"On 31 October 1940 I was on a S79, first left wingmen of a five plane formation that was attacked by British fighters after bombing enemy troops near Mersa Matruh. We, gunners, were returning fire when I noticed that the two end wingmen of our formation were hit and were losing height in flames. Suddenly I centred in my gun sight a Hurricane that was closing to the last three planes shooting continuously at us. Arrived at the distance suitable to start the "famous" turn that permit it to fan with its eight guns its target, I was able to aim at its belly and saw my tracers entering it. Obviously hit, the plane directed towards the ground leaving a thick cloud of black smoke. In this way I avenged the ten dear friends lost in the two planes that fell in flames."

Serg. Pilota Armando Zambelli, who was the only survivor of the SM 79 flown by *ten.* Di Frassineto, recalled:

F/O Joseph Fraser of 112 Sqn, who claimed a damaged SM 79 in the Mersa Matruh area on 31 October.
[via Patricia Molloy]

Richard Acworth of 112 Sqn. Acworth ended the war with seven victories.
[via Ian Acworth]

"It was 31 October 1940, I was hospitalised in Derna infirmary when I heard that we were going to start for an important bombing mission. Today it can seem a bit excessive all the enthusiasm with which we wanted to take part in war missions, but twenty years old and with the high spirit of those days all seemed normal for us. I left the infirmary and reached the Squadriglia. When my Commander cap. Giovanni Ruggiero asked me how I felt I told him: "Perfect and I'm ready to start" [in fact, *ten.* Ruggiero wasn't promoted to *cap.* until 15 November 1940].

My crew was composed of: ten. Di Frassineto, me, Primo Aviere Fotografo Antonini, Primo Aviere Motorista Stramccioni and Aviere Scelto Armiere Costa [Strangely enough, Zambelli here quotes among his crew a member of the crew of *s. ten.* Fabiani and an airman, Stramaccioni, neither is recorded among the casualties of 9º *Stormo* in WWII]. *The action was one of the most important of the war so far and our forces were fifty S 79s with the escort of forty fighters started from an airstrip near Derna* [It appears that the 9º *Stormo* was divided in two formations - one from the 26º *Gr.* (11ª and 13ª *Squadriglie*), which started from Derna and the other from the 29º *Gr.* (62ª and 63ª *Squadriglie*), which was surprised by the Blenheims at Gambut and was prevented from taking part in the action] *and after around an hour of flight we arrived over the airbase of Matruh.*

Our section was composed of five planes disposed in arrow formation under command of cap. Ruggero. We were almost on the target when a hand on my shoulder made me turn my head. It was the Motorista that told me that we were attacked by enemy fighters of which we had already shot down one [the aircraft claimed by Mariotti], *sadly the Hurricanes and Gloster Gladiators from a superior height continued to fire without respite and after a short while I saw the end wingman opposite to my position falling in flames; pilots were ten. Fabiani from Rome and serg. Bigliardi from Bologna. We succeeded in bombing the target but following another enemy burst of fire our plane started to burn and being made of wood and fabric it burned like a wax match.*

I told the members of the crew to bale out but without avail because they tried to fight the fire. Enemy bullets continued to enter the plane and I saw the poor crewmembers hit by the bullets and reached by the flames. We decided to leave the plane, I opened the exit door on the top of the cockpit and immediately air suction threw me against the tail of the plane that was burning; I lost consciousness and I woke up when the parachute opened. I was descending under the area where our CR 42s and the Hurricanes were fighting. Moving my legs I tried to move towards the land to avoid falling into the sea but in that moment I lost consciousness again. When I woke up for the second time I was on a British vehicle between a bearded Sikh driver and an English officer that pointed his gun at me. I was taken to the infirmary because I was burned in the face and in the hands and had a dislocated ankle; there I was left resting for a while. Subsequently I was examined by a General that told me that he was Canadian and that he had fought as our ally during the First World War [Raymond Collishaw!]. *He asked me, in approximate Italian, if in Italy we thought that they killed the aviators that jumped with the parachute. [...]."*

An anonymous crewmember of a 13ª *Sq.* SM 79 (the 13ª *Sq.* composed the second arrow of the 9º *Stormo*) described the combat:

"*Immediately after the bomb release a hard attack of Hurricanes [...] immediately the plane took 116 hits [...] one wing damaged, engines nacelles damaged, flaps and empennages damaged, bomb bay damaged, the three propellers hit, [...] 1º Aviere Motorista Tommaso Giorgio, that was shooting back with the gun in the "hunk" died, [...] his place was taken by Aviere Scelto Marconista Canaponi but after a short while he was wounded too [...] finally Primo Aviere Fotografo Marcucci took the gun [...]."*

In the end the gunners of the SM 79 expended 1337 rounds. Notwithstanding the damage suffered, the aircraft was back at base at around 15:00.

The first formation of five SM 79s from 33º *Gr.*, led by *ten. col.* Ferri Forte, was able to repel the attack by reportedly three Gladiators. At 13:03 they hit with precision the new railway station of Mersa Matruh, built after the old one was definitely put out of action by the last month's bombing attacks.

In total the Italian War Bulletin reported that seven enemy planes were shot down by return fire from the bombers, in exchange for two bombers that failed to return. It is known that the 14° *Stormo* claimed two Hurricanes and a Gladiator, plus another Gladiator as a probable. It seems that 33° *Gr.* didn't claim anything and so the other four claims should be credited to the 9° *Stormo*, one of them by the gunner Mariotti of the 11ª *Sq.* (and following this deductive argument the other three were probably claimed by the gunners of the 13ª *Sq.*).

The Italian escorting fighters arrived over Mersa Matruh at around 13:00 and immediately entered combat with enemy fighters that were already attacking the SM 79s. The formation of the 368ª *Sq.* first attacked three Hurricanes. One of them was claimed shot down in flames by *serg. magg.* Davide Colauzzi while a second one was claimed by *serg.* Mario Turchi. The third one, attacked by *cap.* Bruno Locatelli, was hit by a precise burst in the cockpit area and seen abandoning the fight (the pilot was reputedly wounded). Locatelli then headed towards the sea and encountered a lone Gladiator. He closed in on its tail and from close distance he hit it with a short burst. The Gladiator first emitted a cloud of black smoke and then exploded in mid air. The other section of the *Squadriglia* (Zuffi, Hosquet and Ambrosi) didn't entered the combat since the fighters from the 13° *Gr.* that were flying higher waded in and split the 368ª formation, excluding Zuffi and his men from the ensuing combat. At 14:10, all the CR.42s were back at base.

The formation of the 367ª *Sq.* didn't obtain concrete results in the combat, which they described as started at 5500 metres. All its pilots were back at base at 14:10.

The 366ª *Sq.* were more successful. Immediately after the arrival over Matruh at 13:00, *cap.* Serafini attacked a Gladiator that, damaged, escaped by diving. *serg. magg.* Marchi followed it shooting until they were down at 2000 metres and the British fighter was considered shot down. Then Serafini discovered an "arrow" of five SM 79s with a Hurricane that was following at close distance. He gave full throttle trying to cut the path of the Hurricane but had to witness one of the Savoias being hit and falling in flames. Finally, he managed to overtake the Hurricane and hit it in the side. The RAF fighter went down immediately. AA fire at this moment was extremely intense and Serafini saw another SM 79 of the same formation that suddenly was engulfed by flames and went down. He was unable to understand if the aircraft was previously hit by the Hurricane or if it was hit by flak. Another Hurricane tried to attack the SM 79s but this time Serafini was quick in reacting and hit the Hawker, that dived away smoking. *serg. magg.* Colauzzi also took part in this last attack. In the meantime, *ten.* Ferrero hit and damaged three Hurricanes before being forced to disengage with guns jammed. While coming back he was attacked by another enemy plane but was able to outmanoeuvre it and land safely at base. The 366ª *Sq.* were back at 14:00. It also seems that the 151° *Gr.* claimed a probable Gladiator (possibly recorded as a *Gruppo* claim).

The CR.42s of the 13° *Gr.*, following the road between Bir Kenayis and Mersa Matruh, arrived over the target at 13:00 and discovered the 151° *Gr.* some 500 metres higher and then, at a distance of 4 to 5 kilometres to the west, two formations of Italian bombers heading towards the frontier. The 78ª *Sq.* opened the formation followed by the 77ª *Sq.* and the 82ª *Sq.* A Gloster Gladiator was seen to heading towards the 78ª *Sq.* fighters and was immediately counter-attacked by *cap.* Bevilacqua and his section. In the meantime, the 78ª *Sq.* was crossing the path of the bombers and discovered a Hurricane that was following them, but this aircraft escaped diving before the arrival of the Fiats. Meanwhile more fighters from the 78ª and 82ª *Squadriglie* joined the fight. Those of the 78ª *Sq.* endeavoured to protect their comrade *s. ten.* Luigi Canneppele, who because of problems with his propeller only was able to fly straight and level. *serg.* Taddia was damaged in the process but remained in the fight being credited with a probable Gloster, while *serg.* Martinoli (claimed as a destroyed in his logbook), *ten.* Ippolito Lalatta and *serg.* Abbarchi claimed damaged Gladiators. Bevilacqua in the meantime fought down to ground level, claiming two Gladiators in the process and while pursuing a third British machine witnessed another CR.42 that, while trying to close on the same aircraft, collided with it. It was the Fiat of *ten.* Perversi of the 82ª *Sq.*, who was killed.

Before leaving the area, Bevilacqua saw two British parachutes (bright white in colour and hemispherical in shape) so he argued that Perversi had possibly shot down a British aircraft before colliding with the other. The rest of the 77ª *Sq.* under *ten.* Sorvillo and the 82ª *Sq.* under *ten.* Chiarini remained high and attacked British Hurricanes that were attacking the SM 79s. *serg.* Gori damaged a Hurricane and *serg.* Paolini a Gloster, which he left to other Falcos to finish it off. *ten.* Chiarini and *serg.* Nanin claimed a shared Spitfire that was attacking the SM 79s while *serg. magg.* Davico claimed a second as a damaged. All the pilots were back between 14:05 and 14:20.

The Italian aircraft had been in combat with at least nine Gladiators from 112 Sqn and twelve Hurricanes from 33 Sqn. 112 Sqn's Gladiators from Sidi Haneish carried out many patrols over Mersa Matruh during the morning. Participating pilots were F/Lt R. J. Abrahams, F/O Joseph Fraser (Gladiator K7973), F/O Robert Hugh Clarke, P/O B. B. E. Duff and Second Lieutenant E. R. Smith (SAAF).

At 13:00, P/O Duff sighted a reported ten SM 79s and gave chase However, he failed to see the escorting fighters. Six CR.42s, part of an 18 strong escort formation, dived on him and shot him down. Fortunately, he managed to escape by parachute, suffering only slight burns. The fighters were engaged by F/O Lloyd Schwab, Second Lieutenant Smith and P/O Richard Acworth (who had just joined the patrol, scrambling from readiness). Schwab claimed two CR.42s shot down, after which he reported that his engine failed and he force-landed, later returning to his unit. Acworth claimed a third CR.42. Acworth and Smith then collided, and both had to bale out. Acworth was unhurt and Smith suffering from a dislocated collarbone (possibly after having been engaged by Bevilacqua's and Perversi's sections). F/O s Fraser and Clarke (both also ordered on patrol from readiness) also engaged the bombers, and Fraser managed to put one engine of an SM 79 out of action (from Fraser's logbook it appears that this Savoia was credited to him as a "confirmed" victory). 24-year-old Clarke was posted missing at the end of this engagement. When last seen he was engaging three SM 79s, and he was presumed killed by return fire coming from them. S/Ldr Harry Brown, F/Lt R. J. Abrahams, and F/O Edwin Banks also took off but were unable to intercept.

33 Sqn with its new Hurricanes, which had taken off at 13:15 from Fuka, also encountered the Italian aircraft over Mersa Matruh and they reported meeting SM 79s escorted by 12 CR.42s, which caused the Hurricanes some inconvenience since they were intercepted during the climb up. Three of the bombers were claimed shot down. Two of them were seen to be shot down ("witnessed and confirmed by land troops") by the 26-year-old Canadian F/O Edmond Kidder Leveille, who was then attacked by four CR.42s. Leveille was forced to bale out, but was killed when his parachute failed to deploy completely. The third SM 79 was claimed by F/O Perry St Quintin (Hurricane P3724), who claimed a second as a probable, reportedly with the starboard engine on fire. St Quintin was, however, also shot down by the escort, and he was forced to make a forced landing at Qasaba with a holed fuel tank. These victories were the CR.42's first over Hurricanes in the Western Desert. F/O Frank Holman (Hurricane P3725) claimed a CR.42 between Matruh and Barrani after a running fight (possibly *ten.* Ferrero) and another probable SM 79 was claimed by F/O Henry Starrett (Hurricane P3729). F/O Littler's Hurricane was considerably shot up and forced to turn back during the combat.

The combat was the most important for many weeks and received the press honours. An Egyptian newspaper reported:

Eight Italian Planes Down – Air Battle over Mersa Matruh. Cairo, Saturday.

It was announced from Headquarters, RAF, Middle East on Friday, that a large force of enemy bombers (SM 79s) escorted by a dozen fighters (CR 42s) attempted an attack on targets in the Mersa Matruh area yesterday. Fighter aircraft of the RAF immediately engaged the enemy. In the ensuing battle, four SM 79s were shot down and four CR.42s were destroyed. In addition, four more enemy aircraft were so damaged that it is unlikely that they returned to their base. During the battle, two of our fighter aircraft collided, but the pilots landed safely by parachute. One of our fighters was shot down and one, which was last seen engaging three SM 79s making for home, has so far not returned to its base.

The Italian fighters in total claimed ten victories in this combat (Colauzzi, Turchi, Locatelli, Marchi, Serafini, Bevilacqua (2), Perversi (2) and Chiarini's and Nanin's shared) (post war studies raised this number to eleven, considering the one claimed by Martinoli, which was not credited to him by his unit) while the bombers claimed seven, for the loss of one CR.42 and two SM 79s (two more were write-offs after forced-landings). The British fighters claimed four CR.42s and three SM 79s (and one probable) for the loss of five Gladiators and two Hurricanes. 33 Sqn's ORB in recording the presence of 112's Gladiators claimed that they had shot down three CR.42s and two SM 79s.

The killed *ten.* Di Frassineto was son of a senator, Count Alfredo Di Frassineto, thus the notice of his loss required special care. Therefore, on 21 November 1940 *Generale* Urbani, Chief of cabinet of the Air Ministry, wrote a personal letter to Marquise Pierfranco Citterio, son-in-law of the father of the missing pilot:

"*On 31 October, two S 79s of 11ª Sq. failed to return from a bombing action at 12.57 over enemy positions.*

Crew chief of one of those planes was ten. Di Frassineto.

It seems that coming back from the action the two planes were attacked by numerous enemy planes, together with them other eight planes of the same Gruppo; the two S 79s were seen to fall near Mersa Matruh, one of them presumably hit by the AA fire.

The other crewmembers were serg. magg. Armando Zambelli, Aviere Scelto Motorista Camillo Caiazzo, Primo Aviere Armiere Alfredo Pacifici, Aviere Scelto Radiotelegrafista Giuseppe Costa.

All these personnel until now are considered missing in action.

We already started the procedures on the Red Cross, necessary to know the names of possible prisoners."

The Italian fighters were rightly quite pleased with their performance, the 151° Gr. started well and the 13° Gr. confirmed that it was the best Italian unit in theatre. However, considering the ordeal of the SM 79s their Commander, *Generale* Matricardi, Commander in Chief of Vª

A side view of a 112 Sqn Gladiator K7974/RT-D. The wheels have silver coloured covers to protect them from the searing desert heat.
[via Alfred Thorne]

Squadra Aerea awaiting Felice Porro's return from Italy, wasn't satisfied. In a reserved note regarding the 31 October engagement Matriciardi commented:

"*Indirect protection in the sky over the target was not reliable for the protection of big formations of S79s (…) so, it happened that the S79 had to fight hard (…) while the fighters, in areas far from the fighting, (…) didn't do anything!*".

Looking at RAF losses the judgement of Matriciardi seems to be (undeservedly) too hard. But indeed, such were the losses of the bomber force that for some weeks after the 31 October daylight operations had to be curtailed. On the other hand, Calosso, in his relation of the combat, openly complained about the extreme dilution of the bomber formation whose last aircraft arrived 12 minutes from the first ones thus making the task of the escorting fighters almost impossible.

This remarkable combat was remembered by Joseph Fraser and Richard Acworth with two short poems as follows:

> **MUNKEY – MUNK** *(Apologies to Stanley Holloway)*
> *You've 'eard of 112 per'aps of Western Desert fame*
> *'oo braved the Eastern mysteries to earn their bloody name.*
> *At 'Munkey-Munk' they fought & bled till battle came to stop*
> *And only aircraft left on line were one with busted prop.*
> *Some lost their wings-some lost their tails but 'It is' lost by far*
> *For though we flew to Munkey-Munk, we did come back by car.*
> *By F/O Acworth DFC - Oct.1940*

A 112 Sqn Gladiator undergoes some outdoor maintenance. The oil tank has been removed.
[via Alfred Thorne]

MONKEY MONKEY *(To Kipling's 'IF')*
*The last day of October 1940
was history for the few of 112
And just before the luncheon hour a call came
direct from Operations 202
"Two Austins scramble Monkey Monkey quickly,
12 Bandits flying north, height eighteen thou'"
And once again two clouds of dust departed
And two minds thought their first chance might be now.
Twelve 'It is' in two waves of six approaching,
One can't believe it true, they've come at last –
And down we dived full out in chase of raiders
For all know well a GLAD' is far from fast
Each 'Glad' attacked a wave of 'Seventy Nine S'.
And shot away two thousand rounds of lead
And down came two with engines pouring black smoke
And doubtless all the personnel were dead.
Poor 'Happy' never lived to tell his story
But living still's his famous Happy smile
And then two waves of five fast moving 'bandits'
Twelve 'Forty Twos' escorting all the while.
And then three Hurricanes attacked the last wave
And down came two or three more 'Seventy Nines'.
Two Glads collided and a third shot down but
All pilots landed safely 'hind our lines'
But not before 3 'forty twos' went spinning
To hit the desert sand and burst in flames.
We won the day by Five to Seven airframes
But what is more eighteen to two in names.
And so more blood is spilt by human folly
And sweat just wasted building aeroplanes.*
Written by S/L J. Fraser after the First Victory at Mersa Matruh on 31st October 1940.

In the late 1960's, Acworth wrote an unpublished short story about this combat as seen by him:
The Unfinished Game by Acworth DFC
"Start-up!"……"Start-up!"

The powerful Canadian voice of Sqn Ldr Algy Schwab sent mechanics racing across the arid, Western Desert landing ground at Gerawla towards the four single-seater Gloster Gladiator fighter aircraft of 'A' Flight stand-by Section of 112 Sqn. Deft hands manipulated the throttles and starter-batteries, and almost as one, the engines burst into life.

Schwab, Duff, Smith and myself had been whiling away the time playing 'Pontoon', along with the Station Padre, another Smith, known affectionately as 'Slip-trench'.

We were a mixed bunch: Plt Off Bertie Duff and the Padre hailed from Australia, 2nd Lieut. Smith from South Africa, and myself, a Plt Off from England. We had been playing for about an hour, in the comparative shade of the recreation tent, when our peace was shattered by the hash ring of the 'operations' telephone. Algy had grabbed the 'phone, and learned that our presence was requested at 18,000 feet, some fifty miles away at Mersa Matruh. Apparently, a formation of 25 Italian three-engined Savoia bombers had been reported in that direction from out at sea.

"Stick around Slip-trench! We'll be back to finish", Algy had poked the Padre playfully in the ribs, and addressed us, as he dashed by to alert the ground crews.

"Mersa, fellers!…18,000 feet.!"

We raced towards our waiting aircraft, and climbed gingerly in, for, in spite of the hastily-removed cockpit covers, the sun-baked metal cockpits were about as hot as kitchen stoves in winter, and in our khaki shirts and shorts, we had respect for such heat.

I settled down onto my parachute, already resting in the bucket seat, forming a cushion of sorts, and adjusted the straps. My 'Fitter' flung the Sutton harness straps over my shoulders, helped me to adjust the leg straps, and jumped down, shielding his face from the flying sand.

Waving away the 'chocks', I opened to full throttle, and taxied after Algy, who was almost in position for take-off. I formed up on his right, whilst Smith and Duff took up positions on his left. Algy glanced quickly at us in turn, and receiving the 'thumbs-up" sign lowered his right arm, the signal for take-off. His aircraft moved forward, gathering speed extremely quickly, until the four of us were airborne in loose search formation.

We set course for Mersa Matruh, climbing on nearly full throttles, and could see other Gladiators and Hurricanes taking off from our own, and near-by landing grounds.

To the right, I could see the Mediterranean, blue and pretty as a picture; below, and to my left, nothing but sand, sand and more sand, with just the small Desert 'scrub', growing here and there, in a vain attempt to break the monotony. By the time we had reached 10,000 feet, all heat from the cockpit had long-since dissipated, and I began to wish I had worn flying overalls. However, we were soon at our pre-determined height, with Mersa Matruh beneath us, and suddenly Algy's excited voice comes overt the intercom...

"Bandits approaching from 2 O'clock!" Then, after further inspection, "they're already being engaged by the Hurricanes, blast them!"

We had been so engrossed in watching the bombers out at sea that we failed to notice the pending arrival of 15 C.R. 42's, the Italian counterpart of the Gladiator. They had sneaked up on us from the south, un-reported by the Observer Corps, and I'm ashamed to say, un-noticed by myself, although I should have been concentrating on the sky in that direction.

Without warning, they attacked, and the sky seemed filled with madly twisting aircraft, as we broke formation. It was the first time our squadron had encountered Italian fighters, and I remember thinking they looked rather like angry hornets.

Bertie Duff dived out of the melee with a C.R. 42 on his tail, and another on either side of him, had his engine badly hit, and shortly afterwards baled out of his burning aircraft.

I dived on one of his attackers, and followed the aircraft through a loop, for some unknown reason, a popular Italian 'dog-fight' tactic of the early war days. The loop completed, I managed to get my sights on the C.R. 42, and 'let fly' with my four Brownings. At once, its engine started smoking badly, and the aircraft fell away on one wing; then….it happened!

For a time, I thought my engine had blown up, for during the dive, it had been doing far more 'revs' than the designed had intended. There was an explosion, and the next moment, I was drenched from head to foot with petrol, and suddenly frozen, as it began to evaporate. The 'stick' was knocked smartly forwards, and momentarily trapped my thumb, as it hit the dashboard. My aircraft started a mad spin, and I had a split-second impression of a pair of mainplanes disappearing to my right, downwards twisting and turning like the blades of a lawn mower.

The controls were completely useless, and looking behind me, I soon discovered the reason why; to my dismay, there was only about a yard of fuselage left behind the cockpit, …..my complete tail-unit was missing.

Most Gladiator pilots flew with their cockpit hoods open, as at times, they were difficult to open. I was no exception, and throttling back the engine, I tried to raise myself in my seat to commence the jump I knew was inevitable. I couldn't move! I had often heard tales of pilots who had experienced difficulty in leaving a spinning aircraft, then I realized that during the 'general flap' I had forgotten to remove the pin securing the Sutton harness. By this time, the aircraft was in an inverted spin, and I pulled out the pin, and left the falling aircraft so relatively slowly, that it seemed like 'slow motion'. The Gladiator, or what was left of it, followed me down, and it seemed an age before I was suffi-

ciently far enough away to dare to pull the rip-cord of my parachute, for, to pull it too soon would have meant certain death, with my canopy caught by the crashing aircraft.

I felt no ill effects from the delayed drop, and found I could move my arms and legs quite easily. However, I was taking no chances! I gripped the parachute ring very carefully in my right hand and gave a clean pull. After an anxious second or two, my rapid descent was abruptly checked as the 'chute' opened, and I had the strange feeling of being suspended in space, which, there and then, was not unpleasant, for firing on parachutists, at that time, and theatre of war, was unheard of.

The main battle with the bombers had drifted inland, and dotted over the desert, in the area I was heading for were crashed Savoias, C.R. 42s, together with the odd Hurricane and Gladiator. Most of them were flaming, and in spite of my pity for those who had died, I couldn't help thinking of the swift end I would meet, if the flames caught the silk canopy of my parachute.

I could see two other parachutists in the area, but they were not close enough to recognize friend or enemy.

Luck was with me. By the time I had descended to within about 200 feet from the ground, I was drifting towards open desert. From that point on, the ground seemed to race towards me with increasing speed. With my feet ready for the coming impact with Mother Earth, I pulled up on the shrouds lines of my parachute, to lessen the bump, and I was down, and releasing the billowing canopy.

The two other parachutists landed shortly afterwards, and fairly near, and from across the desert, I could see a Staff car coming in our direction. As it drew nearer, I could make out a soldier standing on the running board, pointing a levelled rifle at us. The car approached the nearest parachutist, who advanced with his hands in the air, and climbed in, shortly followed by the other pilot. I thought it was about time I put my hands up, as the car approached me, and although the driver was a stranger, an Army Officer, I recognized his three passengers. Two of them were the recently collected Duff, and Smith, and the third was Algy Schwab.

2nd Lieut. Smith had been after the same Italian that I was chasing, and had crashed into me, losing his wings in the process; P/O Duff had baled out on fire, as already described, and Sqn Ldr Schwab had had engine failure, but had managed to shoot down two enemy aircraft before he finally forced landed; a noble effort!

So, about 15 minutes after our take-off from Gerawla, we were all four heading back along the road to our base, driven by the obliging Army Officer, when, who should we see but the Padre, who had left shortly after us, to take the mail and cables to Mersa Matruh, a daily task of his. Algy leaned out of the window, and addressed him as both cars pulled up with a squeal of brakes, on the narrow road.

"I thought you were going to stick around to finish the game, Slip-trench!"

The poor Padre went as white as a sheet. Until explained, I think he had a shrewd suspicion that we were four ghosts, recently raised from the remains of four crashed Gladiators.

During the night, one Bombay from 216 Sqn attacked Derna harbour.

November 1940

Regia Aeronautica

Fighters

In the middle of November the 4º *Stormo* received a new adjutant, *cap.* Mario Pluda.

On 12 November, *ten.* Antonio Angeloni of the 93ª *Sq.*, 8º *Gr.*, returned from Benghazi K airfield with a CR.42 on which experimental RT equipment had been mounted.

On 15 November the 92ª *Sq.* had seven combat-ready CR.42s, one being repaired at El Adem and one at Benghazi waiting for an engine.

On 13 November, *serg.* Luciano Perdoni of the 84ª *Sq.*, 10º *Gr.*, destroyed CR.42 MM4332 in a landing accident at Benina.

The fighters from the 13º *Gr.* once again started to suffer from desert wear and in the 77ª *Sq.* (based at Gambut with the rest of the *Gruppo*) on 28 November, five of the CR.42s were considered useable for short distance flights only, while just six aircraft remained completely combat-ready.

Ten. Guglielmo Chiarini was (again) posted to the 366ª *Sq.*, 151º *Gr.* on 27 November.

On 18 November, the 368ª *Sq.* had eight combat-ready CR.42s and one at the SRAM of El Adem.

On 29 November, the 367ª *Sq.* had nine combat-ready CR.42s and one at the SRAM of El Adem.

Pilots of the 4º Stormo at El Adem, Cirenaica in front of a Fiat CR.32. The photo was probably taken between September and November 1940. From left to right: Aldo Gon, Giulio Reiner, Carlo Agnelli, Ezio Viglione Borghese, Armando Moresi and Alvaro Querci. [Gon via Fulvio Chianese – Associazione Culturale 4° Stormo di Gorizia]

Bombers

During November, SM 79 operations were slowed down considerably and practically all the daylight bombing missions were cancelled.

The operations that were flown were strategic reconnaissance operations over Alexandria to check the Mediterranean fleet (these missions were almost daily and sometimes twice a day), reconnaissance missions over the desert to check the movements of O'Connor's Army, and night nuisance bombing incursions by single aircraft operating over the same target (mainly RAF airbases) with around four-five bombers each night. In the night bombing role the SM 79s were supported by the SM 82s of the 114º *Gr. Aut. B.P.* and by the S.81s of the 54º *Gr. Aut. B.T.* The SM 79s also started to visit Suda Bay, Crete, which suddenly become an important Royal Navy base.

The SM 79s of the 41º *Stormo* were sent back to Tripolitania on 6 November after a period of acclimatisation and training in the new desert conditions. Their level of readiness was considered insufficient to confidently start operations.

Ground attack forces

In early November the 7° *Gr.* left their useless Ba.88s in North Africa and returned to Italy to be re-equipped.

On 23 November, the 12° *Gr.* was ordered back from the line for a period of rest and reorganisation.

Mass being conducted in the shadow of a Savoia SM 79.
[Italian Air Force]

A Breda Ba.65/A80 of the 159ª Squadriglia, 12º Gruppo, emerges from the morning mist at Tobruk T2 in November 1940.
[via Istituto Luce]

Colonial forces
The 1º Gr. A.P.C. received one Cant Z.509 in November. It was used to escort S.75s around Libya.

Royal Air Force
After the Italian attack on Greece on 28 October, the British Minister in Athens called for help and Sir Arthur Longmore allocated 30 Sqn for immediate transfer to Greece. This unit was to be followed as swiftly as possible by two more squadrons of Blenheim bombers and one of Gladiators.

The Chiefs of Staff fully appreciated that these moves would leave Egypt dangerously weak, and took action to replace the withdrawals as quickly as possible. They planned to send thirty-four Hurricanes (73 Sqn plus eighteen reserve aircraft) on the carrier HMS *Furious* to Takoradi, whence they would fly to Egypt and begin to arrive there about 2 December and onwards. The squadron ground crews would arrive at about the same time via the Mediterranean. As regards bombers, 32 Wellingtons (37 and 38 Sqns) over and above the current replacement and rearmament programme would be sent to Egypt via Malta; their move and that of their men and stores, and of a station headquarters, would also be completed by about 2 December. Finally, to add weight to the attacks made from Greece, the number of Wellington bombers at Malta was to be increased to 16.

A typical Italian desert airfield.
[Italian Air Force]

Fighters

On 29 November, 33 and 274 Sqns received the following signal from the Air Ministry:
FIGHTER TACTICS – HURRICANE versus C.R.42.

Recommend following tactics Hurricane versus C.R.42 20,000 to 25,000 feet as result tests A.F.D.U. between Hurricane I and Gladiator latter being comparable C.R. 42. 16,000 feet upwards Hurricane used 15 degrees flap climbed 300 feet per minute 20,000 to 25,000 feet constant speed airscrew 2400 r.p.m. Between these heights both aircraft climbed practically identical but Hurricane outdistanced Gladiator. Gladiator or C.R. 42 easily turn inside Hurricane which must therefore deliver straight attacks breaking away when sight comes off C.R. 42 and outdistancing to attack again. Practicable deliver attacks thus when Gladiator same level or lower than Hurricane. If C.R. 42 attacks from above Hurricane should use superior speed to outdistance enemy then turn and attack. On escort duty Hurricane May have to turn to flank to attack C.R. 42 before it reaches escorted aircraft. On offensive patrol May be advantageous Hurricane turn towards C.R. 42. Hurricane should not attempt competitive turning circle manoeuvres with C.R. 42. Gladiator used in tests had not repeat not constant speed airscrew.

80 Sqn was ordered to Greece, and on 18 November the 'B' Flight of 80 Sqn left Egypt and reached Athens with at least nine Gladiator IIs led by S/Ldr William Hickey and including F/Lt 'Pat' Pattle, F/O s Greg Graham and Sidney Linnard, P/O s Samuel Cooper, 'Heimar' Stuckey and William Vale and Sgt Charles Casbolt.

"A" Flight of 80 Sqn, led by F/Lt Edward Jones, left Egypt for Greece on 23 November.

On 23 November, 274 Sqn moved up to the front at Sidi Haneish.

On 29 November, Peter Wykeham-Barnes of 274 Sqn became the first fighter pilot in North Africa to receive a DFC.

On 30 November, Mr. J. J. B. De Sidour, an expert from England, arrived at 274 Sqn's base to change the squadron's Hurricane propellers from two position variable pitch to constant speed, thus considerably increasing their performances.

Bombers

As a response to the Italian attack on Greece on 28 October, 30 Sqn was immediately sent there, the first aircraft arriving at Athens on 3 November when S/Ldr U. Y. Shannon led eight Blenheim IFs to Eleusis airfield, accompanied by four Bristol Bombay transports of 216 Sqn. At this time 30 Sqn operated one flight of Blenheim IFs fighters and one of standard Blenheim I bombers. On 5 November, F/O D. R. Walker departed from Egypt at the head of four Blenheim bombers from 30 Sqn.

70 Sqn wasn't active over Libya during November because it was called to operate over Greece. On 6 November, six Wellingtons left Kabrit for Eleusis in Greece. They were T2731, T2733, T2734, T2816, T2813 and T2826, under the overall command Wing Commander Webb.

The day after they committed the error of raiding the Italian-held harbour of Valona in Albania in full daylight. Attacked by (reportedly) CR.42s and Ba.65s (the latter were G.50s of 154° *Gruppo AUT*), two bombers were shot down (T2731 and T2734), one of them exploding in mid-air, with the loss of the crews and two were very badly damaged (T2826 and T2813). The latter bombers returned to Egypt on 8 November together with the undamaged T2733 and T2816.

Six more Wellingtons (T2735, T2828, T2815, T2814, T2827 and T2829) replaced them the same day, four of them newly arrived aircraft, led by S/Ldr Kerr and S/Ldr Rolfe. Up to 14 November, they were used in night operations against Durazzo and Valona, but also against Bari and Brindisi in Italy, without suffering any losses.

On 13 November, T2733 and T2831 left for Greece and on 14 November, T2815, T2827, T2829 and T2735 came back to Kabrit while T2730 and T2816 arrived.

On 16 November, the six Wellingtons left in Egypt were joined by T2815 and T2827, and on 17 November by T2732, bringing the detachment up to nine bombers.

On the night of 17-18 November, T2827 crashed in the hills of Yugoslavia some 80 miles north of Durazzo with the loss of the crew.

On 19 November, T2828 and T2814 returned from Greece, on 20 November T2733 returned from Greece, on 21 November T2730 returned from Greece and on 24 November T2831, T2816, T2815 and T2732 returned from Greece. The whole 70 Sqn was back at its base. In the meantime, T2891 had joined the squadron from the UK on 19 November.

84 and 211 Sqns were also sent to Greece. On 8 November, 'A' Flight of 84 Sqn with five Blenheim Mk.Is flew in to Eleusis, led by S/Ldr D.G. Lewis, before moving to their allotted base of Menidi. 211 Sqn started to arrive at Menidi on 23 November, led by S/Ldr J. R. Gordon-Finlayson.

45 Sqn returned to Egypt from Sudan on 28 November. During the previous two months, the unit had operated over Italian East Africa, starting with almost daily missions which were then gradually reduced in intensity in what had been its first real "tour of duty". At the beginning of the period (2 October) S/Ldr J. W. Dallamore had been shot down by CR.42s of the 412^a *Sq.* over Gura and killed in the crash of his burning bomber, which he had gallantly tried to control until the end to permit his crewmen to escape by parachute. On 15 October, S/Ldr Ray, who assumed command on 5 November, joined the unit. During the period, heavy losses were suffered at the hands of the Italian CR.42s, especially over the fighter's base of Gura where three more Blenheims were shot down before the middle of October with the loss of the complete crews.

On 5 November, 37 Bomber Sqn, based at Feltwell, UK, was ordered to pack up and move overseas to reinforce the Middle East Command. At 23:00 on 8 November, the first seven Vickers Wellingtons Mk.Ic were scheduled to leave for Malta, but only five arrived (F/L M. J. Baird-Smith, Sgt Thomas, Sgt Gillanders, Sgt Noden and Sgt Spiller) because of various problems that left the remaining two machines at Feltwell. During the flight, F/Lt Baird-Smith's Wellington was attacked and damaged by Italian fighters from the 1° *Stormo* (reportedly near Pantelleria). Two crewmembers were wounded, but the aircraft was able to reach Malta without further problems.

On 13 November, seven more Wellingtons arrived at Malta led by the CO (Wing Commander Merton, S/Ldr Collard, S/Ldr Golding, F/O Currey, P/O Ford, P/O Benbow and Sgt Green).

The next day, on 14 November, the CO flew to Heliopolis with another Wellington, followed by two more planes the day after. On 19 November, three additional machines flew from the UK to Malta (Flight Lieutenant Lenon, P/O Lax and Sgt Elstub). Five Wellingtons left Malta on 21 November and arrived in Egypt. The unit moved first to Kabrit and then reunited at Fayid on 30 November.

After having aborted a raid against Emden, Germany, because of the weather conditions on 2 November, 38 Bomber Sqn, at Marham, was ordered to move overseas on 4 November.

On 22 November, the Wellingtons Mk.Ic of "B" Flight, led by Wing Commander Thomson (CO), took off from Marham at 23:00 and landed at Malta at 08:30 on 23 November. The same night, they were followed by "A" Flight.

On the morning of 24 November, while "A" Flight was arriving from England, "B" Flight departed for Ismailia, which was reached without problems. Finally, on 25 November, "A" Flight reached Egypt minus one aircraft that was destroyed on Malta. In the beginning of December, the unit moved from Ismailia to Fayid.

The Wellingtons of the two units were immediately fitted with tropical installations: Vokes dust filters and Marston oil coolers.

The need to use 216 Sqns Bombays in transporting the British Air contingent to Greece much reduced this unit's bombing operations.

Reconnaissance forces

On 8 November, 'C' Flight of 6 Sqn left Quasaba for Ramleh on conclusion of their attachment to 208 Sqn. 'B' Flight, commanded by F/Lt C. S. F. Wood, and with four Lysander Mk.IIs left Ramleh for Qasaba to replace them. At the end of the month, the strength of 6 Sqn was eleven Lysander Mk.IIs at Ramleh and four detached to Qasaba.

The Lysanders of 208 Sqn in the meantime continued to rotate to 103 MU. where they were fitted with armour plates and Vickers 'K' guns. 'C' Flight returned to Qasaba on 9 November with the only serviceable Lysander left. On 22 November, 'C' Flight left Qasaba for Abu Sueir to collect Hurricanes and hand in five Lysanders.

Royal Australian Air Force

On 2 November Sqn headquarters and ground personnel of 'B' and 'C' Flights of 3 Sqn RAAF moved by road from Helwan to Gerawla. The move started at 08:15 and was completed at 17:15 the next day.

S/Ldr Ian McLachlan, F/O Alan Gatward, F/O M. D. Ellerton, F/O Alan Boyd, F/Lt Charles Gaden, F/O B. L. Bracegirdle, F/O Peter Turnbull and F/O Wilfred Arthur moved from Helwan to Gerawla by air on 3 November. Flight Lieutenant Gordon Steege, F/Lt Blake Pelly and F/O Alan Rawlinson left their attachments to 208 Sqn and rejoined 3 Sqn RAAF at Gerawla, while F/O John Perrin, F/O L. E. Knowles and F/O J. M. Davidson, who also had been attached to 208 Sqn, returned to 'A' Flight at Helwan. 15 Air gunner/Wireless operators from 3 Sqn RAAF were attached to 208 Sqn. After the completion of these movements the disposition of the squadron was as follows. At Gerawla - Officers: 13 pilots, 1 crew, 6 non-flying and 2 (attached) air intelligence liaison.

Airmen: 185 non-flying, 6 (attached) air intelligence liaison and 1 (attached) Royal Corps Signaller.

Aircraft: 10 Gladiators and 4 Gauntlets (two Gauntlets had been left with 208 Sqn at Qasaba, being unserviceable and awaiting spares).

At Helwan ('A' Flight) - Officers: 3 pilots and 1 crew.

Airmen: 5 crews and 32 non-flying. Aircraft: 6 Lysanders and 2 Gladiators (in reserve for 'B' and 'C' Flights).

Attached to 208 Sqn - Officers: 2 crew. Airmen: 5 crew and 15 non-flying.

Attached to 6 Sqn: Airmen: 6 crew and 14 non-flying.

In Hospital - 2 airmen.

At Abu Sueir (on anti-gas course) - 2 airmen.

On 21 November 'A' Flight of 3 Sqn RAAF moved from Helwan to Ikingi Maryut for the purpose of cooperation with the 6th Division A.I.F.

On 28 November 3 Sqn RAAF received orders from 202 Group to have one Gladiator at standby and two more on five minutes' notice from 09:00 to 16:00 daily, to act as fighter patrol when ordered into the air.

On 30 November F/O John Perrin moved from Ikingi Maryut to Gerawla together with four other officers and eight other ranks.

Gladiators from 3 RAAF Sqn returning to a landing ground near Sollum after a patrol over Bardia. The Sqn's mobile operations room can be seen in the left foreground. [via Australian War Memorial]

A Gloster Gladiator of 3 RAAF Sqn. In the background, a Westland Lysander from the Sqn can be seen. [via Australian War Memorial]

Operations

1 November 1940

This was the blackest day of war for 228 Sqn, when Sunderland N9020/W was intercepted and shot down off Sicily by a couple of Macchi MC.200s from the 88ª *Sq.* 6º *Gr. C.T.*, piloted by *ten.* Luigi Armanino and *serg. magg.* Stabile. The experienced crew of the Sunderland disappeared with it (S/Ldr Guy Lambton Menzies, F/O Stuart Maxwell Farries, Sgt Elias Dawes, Sgt Frederick Harris, Sgt George Arthur Stamp, Sgt Edward Louis Setterfield, Leading Aircraftman Benjamin Edwin Nicholas, Leading Aircraftman Leslie Charles Major Hale and Leading Aircraftman Ronald Fletcher).

At 15:30 on the same afternoon, Sunderland L5806/Q, piloted by F/Lt E. M. Ware, was intercepted when only 32 miles from Malta by two more 6º *Gr.* Macchis, piloted by *ten.* Giuseppe Pesola and *ten.* Pio Tomaselli, and a couple of CR.42s of the 75ª *Sq.*, 23º *Gr.* piloted by *ten.* Ezio Monti and *serg.* Francesco Cuscuna. Two of the Sunderland's crew were wounded. Mattresses and clothing in the aircraft were set on fire by the Italian's explosive bullets, and burning articles were thrown out from the rear door. Flame floats and practise bombs (four of each) were set off by explosive bullets and caused the aircraft to fill with smoke, hindering the amidships gunners in their firing. The rear turret was put partially out of action by having the starboard control handle shot away. The Sunderland was badly holed below the waterline, and was taken up slip immediately on return to Kalafrana to avoid it sinking. Despite all this damage the aircraft was back in action on 22 November. The Italian pilots came back reporting that the big flying boat had adsorbed hundreds of rounds, apparently without suffering particular problems, even if *ten.* Tomaselli in one of his attacks had gone so close to it that he had almost collided with its tail. The Sunderland was finally seen to land in Marsaxlokk Bay, without particular problems. Back at base they argued that the plane had been fitted with some sort of special armour.

With these two losses 228 Sqn practically ceased to exist, having no operational plane left. Reinforcement were on their way however, and would soon take the squadron to full strength.

2 November 1940

The 278ª *Sq.* attacked with four SM 79s the British Fleet discovered off the coast between Sidi Barrani and Sollum at 09:40. The attack was made at 13:22 by *cap.* Massimiliano Erasi ("278-6"), *ten.* Guido Robone ("278-1"), *ten.* Carlo Emanuele Buscaglia ("278-2") and *ten.* Carlo Copello ("278-3"). After an approach at very low altitude in close formation, the Savoias were discovered after having released their torpedoes from a distance of 1,300-1,500 metres against a battleship of the *Barham* or *Revenge* type. The AA opened up with great violence, following the escaping torpedo-bombers for up to 20,000 metres. Erasi noted an aircraft carrier that he identified as the HMS *Ark Royal* and a biplane fighter that tried to attack his section, but soon disengaged. Erasi reported that he was unable to estimate any hits because of the heavy AA and the presence of carrier-based planes, but also noted that his crew reported from 7,000 metres a high column of steam rising from the attacked ship as if it had been hit in the boiler room. The day after the Italian Bulettin credited the hit to the 278ª *Sq.* In fact British sources don't corroborate this.

3 November 1940

At 07:55, three Gladiators from 80 Sqn were sent out to attack a motor transport concentration near Garn. Two of the aircraft, S/Ldr William Hickey in N5823 and F/O George Kettlewell in N5858, attacked whilst P/O P. T. Dowding (N5854) stayed above. The attack was most successful and much damage was done. F/O Kettlewell reported that he suffered stoppages to two guns. The three pilots returned to base between 09:20 and 09:35.

5 November 1940

Nine Blenheims of 211 Sqn under S/Ldr Gordon-Finlayson raided a perimeter camp south-east of Fort Maddalena during the morning. This was the last mission of the campaign for the unit, and it ended indecisively.

6 November 1940

Around this date, Royal Navy started under the codename of Operation *MB 8* a series of complicated manoeuvres in the central Mediterranean that would end in the famous Taranto raid. First of all from Gibraltar a reinforcement operation codenamed *Coat* would bring to the Alexandria Fleet (Force F) the battleship HMS *Barham*, the cruisers HMS *Berwick* and HMS *Glasgow*, and three destroyers. Force F would be escorted by Force H, which included the carrier HMS *Ark Royal*, the cruiser HMS *Sheffield* and five destroyers. Then from Malta two convoys (*M3* and *AN3*) of four and six empty freighters respectively, plus the monitor HMS *Terror* and one Australian destroyer, would be sent back to Egypt and from Greece convoy *AS5* would steam for Alexandria with some empty freighters. From Alexandria two convoys would start, one codenamed *AN6* with three merchant ships bound for Suda Bay and one codenamed *MW3* with five freighters full of troops and ammunition bound for Malta. The Mediterranean fleet with its Forces A, B, C and D under Admiral Andrew Cunningham and including four battleships (HMS *Warspite*, HMS *Valiant*, HMS *Malaya* and HMS *Ramilles*), the carrier HMS *Illustrious*, seven cruisers (HMS *Ajax*, HMS *Sidney*, HMS *Orion*, HMS *Gloucester*, HMS *York*, HMS *Coventry* and HMS *Calcutta*) and 26 destroyers would escort them and then, after rendezvousing with Force F, concentrate on the attack on the Italian fleet based at Taranto (Operation *Judgment*). In addition, a raid against Italian shipping in the Adriatic Sea was also planned.

Initially it had been intended that both HMS *Illustrious* and HMS *Eagle* would take part in the operation, but two days before sailing HMS *Eagle* developed defects in her fuelsystem, probably caused by the many near misses she had sustained during a number of heavy bombing attacks, the last one suffered on 2 November, possibly by aircraft from the 9° *Stormo*. The aviation fuel tanks inside the old hull of the carrier were contaminated by leaks caused by these internal concussions and it was stated that they would require a week to clean. The only thing that could be done was to embark five of her 16 Swordfish on HMS *Illustrious*, which sailed with 24 bombers ready for the coming action.

Sunderland N9029/V of 230 Sqn (on attachment to 228 Sqn) was strafed by a CR.42 when moored in Marsaxlokk Bay in Malta. The aircraft had to be taken up the slip for repairs.

7 November 1940

Six Breda Ba.65/A80s of the 159ª *Sq.* left for the El Guasc airstrip together with 18 Fiat CR.32Qs, nine from the 160ª *Sq.* in ground attack configuration and nine from the 167ª *Sq.* with escort duties.

Once refuelled, five Ba.65s took off at 11:55 together with the Fiats (one aircraft was left behind due to lack of fuel). The participating pilots were *ten.* Adriano Visconti, *serg. magg.* Paolo Perno, *serg. magg.* Gianni Pappalepore and *serg.* Zardini.

At 13:00 they attacked the Siwa Oasis, and the Bredas expended 2400 round of 12.7mm and 7.7mm ammunition, six 50-kg bombs and 420 2-kg bombs. In the meantime eight SM 79s of the 14º *Stormo* under *col.* Coppi and five of the 33º *Gr.* led by *cap.* Guidoni bombed the oasis from medium height.

The mission over Siwa Oasis was the only action when the SM 79s were able to operate in daylight without escort. Such a precaution was dictated by the heavy losses suffered by the unescorted Savoia formations, particularly when confronted by Hurricanes, and the Siwa Oasis area was presumed free from these fighters.

In the meantime, six SM 79s of the 9º *Stormo* led by *col.* Aramu hit the nearby Quars Zeitun. All aircraft returned without losses, the assault aircraft arriving at T2 at around 16:45.

Operating from the Siwa Oasis was 'C' Flight 208 Sqn, which suffered one Lysander destroyed on the ground.

Over Force H in the western Mediterranean one of three Skuas from HMS Ark Royal's 800 Sqn, flown by Lieutenant Spurway and P/O (A) Hart, caught a Z.506B, claiming it shot down. The identity of the Italian aircraft has not been discovered.

8 November 1940

On HMS *Illustrious*, the fighter component was increased with two or three Sea Gladiators from HMS *Eagle*'s Fighter Flight.

At 12:30, Lieutenant O. J. Roger Nicolls and Sub Lieutenant Jack Sewell, flying two Sea Gladiators caught and shot down a Cant Z.501 of the 186ª *Sq. R.M.*, flown by *ten.* Paolo Primatesta (observer *s. ten. di Vascello* Paolo Bacchione), which had left its base at Augusta at 09:00. Three of the crew were rescued by a Sunderland while Primatesta and the engineer Salvatore Calafiore died.

Early in the afternoon, 806 Sqn's Fulmars repulsed the attack by six SM 79s from the Sicilian based 34º *Stormo*. The British pilots claimed one of the Savoias shot down, even though they all made it back (three of them were damaged).

Over the western Mediterranean, Lieutenant Rupert Tillard of 808 Sqn claimed a lone SM 79 destroyed. The identity of the Italian aircraft remains unknown.

9 November 1940

806 Sqn continued its string of successes when, at 16:40, Sub Lieutenant Stanley Orr shot down another Italian shadower, this time a Z.506B from the 170ª *Sq.* piloted by *s. ten.* Toaldo Furia. Killed together with him were the observer *ten. di Vascello* Emilio Nacher and the rest of the crew; *serg.* Pietro Raiteri, *m. llo. Radiotelegrafista* Giuseppe Bardellini, *serg. magg. Motorista* Giuseppe Di Gianpaolo, *Primo Aviere Armiere* Biagio Sole.

Over the western Mediterranean, fighters from HMS *Ark Royal* were up several times and effectively protected the fleet. At 09:50 a Fulmar from 808 Sqn, flown by Lieutenant Rupert Tillard, shot down a 196ª *Sq.* Z.506B flown by *ten.* Silvano Donda (Italian sources speak of the loss of the aircraft with observer *s. ten. di Vascello* Oscar Carli aboard, but Carli was recorded as part of the 287ª *Sq.*). The Italian shadower was able to launch the discovery signal to its Sardinian base prior to its demise, and at 11:00, SM 79 bombers started to attack. They were intercepted by three Fulmars from 808 Sqn and six Skuas from 803 Sqn, and eighteen out of the twenty bombers attacking were damaged, even if none were lost. One of the FAA victories was claimed by Lieutenant Tillard. The Italians claimed two enemy fighters shot down (two Skuas were lightly damaged), and hits on a carrier and a cruiser (it seems that no hits were in fact obtained).

Helwan was attacked by a single Italian aircraft on 9 November. The pilot made three good runs across the station and dropped a stick of bombs across the south-east corner, but since the bombs didn't explode no harm was done.

10 November 1940

806 Sqn continued their good work, shooting down unescorted Italian shadowers and bombers. At 12:20 a Z.501 from the 144ª *Sq. R.M.* at Stagnone (pilot *s. ten.* Alfio Ferri and observer *s. ten. di vascello* Umberto Gabrielli) was shot down by Lieutenant Barnes and Sub Lieutenant Jack Sewell, after chasing it down from 4,000 feet to sea level. It was then strafed.

At 13:30, nine SM 79s from the 90º *Gr.*, 30º *Stormo* attacked the fleet. Barnes's Yellow Section of 806 Sqn again attacked one, which started losing height after being hit in the starboard engine, and claimed it as a shared damaged. They had in fact shot down the bomber of *ten.* Raffaele Brandi (crew: *s. ten.* Luciano Giorchino, 1º *Aviere Motorista* Ludovico Talanca, 1º *Aviere Radiotelegrafista* Ambrogio Caroppi, 1º *Aviere Armiere* Alfonso Dittadi, 1º *Aviere Motorista* Alessandro Ghezzi, all MIA), which failed to return.

Valentia K5605 from 216 Sqn, flown by F/O Baker, attacked enemy concentrations at Barrani. 80 20lb bombs were dropped but no effects were observed due to low clouds. No AA or fighters were encountered. On return the aircraft landed at Ma'aten Bagush. This was the first operational use of this type by 216 Sqn and RAF's sole raid with the type.

11 November 1940

Helwan was attacked during the night. AA fire opened up and the two bombs dropped fell wide.

During the same night, further north in the Mediterranean, HMS *Illustrious* launched 21 Swordfishes against the Italian fleet at her Taranto moorings. The RN intruders were divided in two separate waves, the first from 815 Sqn and the second from 819 Sqn.

Over Taranto, the attack started at 22:50 on 11 November, and by 03:00 on 12 November the 19 surviving aircraft were all back on HMS *Illustrious*. With five torpedo and two bomb hits, it was an unprecedented success that started a period of British advantage in the Mediterranean war.

A night raid on Benghazi Berka burned out one S.75 (604-1/I-TULE) (two S.75 or two SM 79s according to other Italian sources) and slightly damaged two Ro.37*bis*.

12 November 1940

Ten. Riccardo Vaccari, flying a CR.42 from the 96ª *Sq.*, took off from a forward airfield at Amseat, and performed a reconnaissance mission over the enemy airfield of Ma'aten Bagush.

Over the British fleet, heading at full speed towards Alexandria, the Fulmars of 806 Sqn continued to keep a steady patrol and claiming three shadowers. Sub Lieutenant Stanley Orr and Sub Lieutenant W. H. Clisby claimed a Z.501 at 11:55, ten minutes later Lieutenant Commander Evans and Sub Lieutenant Lowe shared another, and finally after another half an hour Evans claimed a Z.506B.

It seems that two Italian aircraft were lost, a Z.501 of the 184ª *Sq.* flown by *ten.* Enrico Pelosi (Observer *s. ten. di Vascello* Angelo Agnelli, *serg.* Sebastiano Romeo, *Primo Aviere Motorista* Colombo Corradeghini and *Primo Aviere Radiotelegrafista* Salvatore Golino) and a Z.506B of the 170ª *Sq.* (*ten.* Aldo Salvaneschi, *s. ten. di Vascello* Giuseppe Carmenati, *serg.* Sebastiano Causa, *Primo Aviere Radiotelegrafista* Mario Tedesco, *Primo Aviere Armiere* Piero Guerci and *Primo Aviere motorista* Giuseppe Gamna). The second was most probably Evans' victim.

F/O Joseph Fraser (Gladiator L7622) of 112 Sqn reported an interception on an SM 79 during the day. He fired one burst in a quarter attack and saw strikes on the enemy bomber, but did not make any claim.

13 November 1940

Ten. Riccardo Vaccari took off (in the same aircraft as the previous day) at sunset and strafed the same airfield at Ma'aten Bagush, claiming a bomber and three fighters burnt on the ground before returning home in darkness.

The bomber was Valentia K5605, which was destroyed (the loss is recorded as on 12 November in 216 Sqn's ORB), while the fighters were most probably from 33 Sqn even if the squadron didn't record any losses, nor the attack, on this date. The lost Valentia was one of the only three ground losses admitted by the RAF in the Western Desert during 1940 (the others were Lysanders). 208 Sqn's personnel at Qasaba recorded that at 17:45 a CR.42 made three strafing runs against the refuse dump to the east of the camp. It had been burnt out during the day and was still smouldering slightly.

The aircraft used by Vaccari in these sorties was CR.42 96-11/MM4383, which was field-modified with an additional fuel tank behind the pilot's seat. The tank was installed through a door in the right side of the fuselage (45 cm wide). Later the tank was removed and an AC 81 vertical camera was installed.

Sqn Leader Ian McLachlan, CO of 3 RAAF Sqn in the cockpit of a Gloster Gladiator at Helwan on 11 November 1940. [via Australian War Memorial]

Gloster Gladiators from 3 RAAF Sqn at Helwan on 11 November 1940. [via Australian War Memorial]

Two Gladiators from 3 Sqn RAAF flew a tactical reconnaissance of enemy positions at Sofafi-Rabia-Bir Enba-Helegat-Nebiewa between 14:20 and 16:20. The mission was flown by F/Lt Gordon Steege (N5777) escorted by F/Lt Charles Gaden (N5780). Steege had received instructions to land at Minquar Quaim and report the details of his observations to the Air Intelligence Liaison Officer at HQ, Armoured Division. Steege mistook the landing ground, which bore no distinguishing marks, and in landing the aircraft was damaged. The pilot was uninjured. The aircraft was salvaged by No. 53 Repair & Salvage Unit, to which it was allotted for repair.

At 13:20, two SM 79s of the 278ª *Sq.* ("278-1" and "278-3") respectively piloted by *ten.* Carlo Emanuele Buscaglia and *ten.* Carlo Copello attacked a convoy of 13 freighters discovered by reconnaissance during the morning. The escort was far away and two torpedoes were launched from 800 metres and a height of 100 metres, and a hit was clearly seen during the escape route. Buscaglia and Copello landed at El Adem at 15:45. A Z.506 later confirmed the sinking of the ship, however no confirmation of this is found in British documents.

At 15:30, Sub Lieutenants Orr and Hogg of 806 Sqn claimed a Z.506B that was later confirmed shot down. It is known that during the day, a Z.501 of the Menelao-based 143ª *Sq.* was lost while transferring from Taranto to Menelao, and this was Maybe the victim of Orr and Hogg. *ten.* Sereno Ghiotti and the observer *Guardiamarina* Domenico Cassone were lost with the aircraft.

Now the action over the fleet was over, and the three Fleet Air Arm Squadrons on HMS *Illustrious* and HMS *Ark Royal* protecting the British fleets had performed very well. Radar directed the Sea Gladiators, Fulmars and Skuas of 800, 806 and 808 Sqns towards the Italian shadowers, and the FAA fighters were able to shot down at least seven Cant seaplanes (they actually claimed nine), preventing in this way the intervention of the Italian bombers that remained without information and often wasted their efforts. The few times that the SM 79s were able to reach their intended targets they were violently attacked by the FAA fighters and were unable to obtain hits or near misses on the British ships, and also losing one of their number (FAA fighters claimed three). Apart from the Taranto attack, this week of November showed the supremacy of the British carrier-based fighters over the Italian shadowers and unescorted bombers.

During the night, four Wellingtons of 37 Sqn attacked Taranto from Malta, claiming hits in the target area. All aircraft returned safely to base.

15 November 1940

25 CR.42s of the 9° *Gr.*, led by *magg.* Ernesto Botto, attacked Mersa Matruh airfield at dawn. The strafing run of the Italian fighters produced no results because there were no planes present on the gorund. Again bad intelligence led to the waste of an intrepid and well conducted action.

At 09:00, two Gladiators from 3 Sqn RAAF flew a tactical reconnaissance of enemy positions at Sofafi-Rabia-Bir Enba-Helegat. The mission was flown by F/Lt Blake Pelly (N5753) escorted by F/O Wilfred Arthur. Accurate AA fire was encountered over Rabia. The two Gladiators landed back at base at 11:15.

At 10:25 two Gladiators from 3 Sqn RAAF flew another tactical reconnaissance. The mission was flown by S/Ldr P. R. Heath (N5764) escorted by F/O Alan Boyd (N5752). The intention was to cover the Dignaish-Bir Khamsa areas but the pilot, being unfamiliar with the territory, actually made a reconnaissance of Fort Maddalena. Moderate but inaccurate AA fire was encountered. The two Gladiators landed back at base at 12:50.

Three British bombers attacked Menastir M at 12:45, damaging a CR.42 of the 92ª *Sq.* with bomb splinters. The fighter was sent to El Adem SRAM. The S.81 hack of the 93ª *Sq.* was damaged too (RS).

A Z.501 of the 143ª *Sq.* was lost while ditching off Mersa Matruh. *ten.* Virgilio Lorenzoni and *serg.* Guerrino Granci were lost. It seems probable that a Wellington flown by P/O Benbow of 37 Sqn, who claimed one such victory while transferring from Malta to Kabrit, shot down this seaplane.

16 November 1940

208 Sqn lost another Lysander to the CR.42s when F/O Benson was shot down, although his gunner claimed one of the attackers shot down. The Lysander (L4686) had taken off from Qasaba at 13:30 and was making a photographic reconnaissance of Maktila camp from 18,000 feet when at approximately 15:00 six CR.42s appeared. Three caught up astern and the gunner, Sgt Phillips, was hit in the leg, but kept firing until his gun jammed. The engine stopped at 100 feet and the Lysander crash-landed at the same moment as a CR.42 hit the ground. Benson was slightly wounded in the thigh, while Phillips suffered a broken leg and was attended by the Medical Officer of the 11th Hussars. Both were evacuated to No. 31 M. R. S. at Fuka.

The six CR 42s were three aircraft from the 366ª *Sq.* (*ten.* Mario Ferrero, *serg. magg.* Cesare Chiarmetta and *serg.* Rosario Di Carlo) and three from the 368ª *Sq.* (*ten.* Raimondo Sacchetti, *serg.* Ernesto De Bellis and *serg. magg.* Annibale Ricotti). The two sections had taken off from Amseat A3 at 13:10 to make a protective flight over Italian infantry in the Buq-Buq - Sidi Barrani area and to escort a Ro.37*bis* over the Bir El Khraigat area.

Returning from Bir El Khraigat and 30 kilometres south-east of Sidi Barrani, *serg.* Di Carlo discovered an enemy aircraft being fired on by the AA 2000 metres higher. The CR.42s started in pursuit and identified their opponent as a Lysander. The British spotter dived at full throttle towards its lines but it was easily followed by the faster Italian biplanes. *ten.* Ferrero and *serg. magg.* Chiarmetta hit it with 1,950 rounds until they saw it crash-landing 30 kilometres inside British lines. Immediately after this, *ten.* Sacchetti's aircraft (MM5580), which was flying at very low altitude and still firing at the Lysander, was seen to suddenly nose up and then crash near the wreck of the RAF machine and burn, as if the pilot had been hit by enemy return fire. Even if a radio intercept that night suggested that Saccheti was found wounded by the British troops, it seems that in fact he died. It was the first loss of the campaign for the 151° *Gr.*

During the usual air attacks against Alexandria, *ten.* Sergio Sartof was forced to turn back after being intercepted by enemy fighters identified as Blenheims.

17 November 1940

At 00:50, an SM 79 flown by *s. ten.* Carabini from 13ª *Sq.*, 9° *Stormo* took off from Ain El Gazala to attack Alexandria. When it returned at 04:25, it tried to force land at T5 but the Savoia hit a radio mast and crashed with the loss of the complete crew (*s. ten.* Angelo Carabini, *s. ten.* Gregorio Tommaso Salvetti, *serg. magg.* Danilo Marangoni, *Primo Aviere Radiotelegrafista* Antonio Lioi, *Primo Aviere Armiere* Mario Ramberto and *Aviere Scelto Elettricista* Aldo Casadei).

There were no British claims or interceptions recorded, so the reason for this loss (the only one suffered by the SM 79 units during November) remains a mystery. It is however necessary to point out that at unknown hour during the day, F/O Joseph Fraser (Gladiator L7621) of 112 Sqn reported an interception on an SM 79. He fired two bursts at long range but his aircraft was too slow and he made no claims.

At 10:00, four Gladiators from 3 Sqn RAAF flew a tactical reconnaissance of enemy positions at Tummar-Barrani-Nebeiwa-Maktila. The mission was flown by F/O B. L. Bracegirdle (N5750) escorted by F/Lt Gordon Steege (N5764), F/Lt Charles Gaden (N5752) and F/O M. D. Ellerton (N5765). Inaccurate AA fire was encountered over Tummar West. The four Gladiators landed back at base at 12:25.

During the night, Italian bombers were again off to attack Alexandria and a machine of the 62ª *Sq.*, piloted by *cap.* Tedeschi, reported a hit on a ship from 3500 metres with a 100kg bomb. Small nuisance raids of this kind, made by single SM 79s or S.81s, continued during the moonlit periods and were much more effective than they presumed, according to Andrew Cunningham:

"Probably in revenge for Taranto the Italian aircraft were keeping up continuous attacks upon Alexandria harbour. It did not much matter when the fleet was present, for the Italians would face the heavy barrage put up by the ships. While we had been away, however, they had been doing pretty much as they liked, even flying low over the harbour in broad daylight. The destroyer Decoy had

a bomb in her wardroom, fortunately without much damage; but what was really serious was that they dropped a number of time bombs round the floating dock which went off at intervals three days later. The dock, our only means of repairing underwater damage to large ships, was seriously endangered, and a Destroyer being undocked had a narrow shave. But luck was with us in the larger issues…"

18 November 1940

Flight Lieutenant Lloyd Schwab intercepted a lone SM 79 during the day and shot it down.

Ten. Riccardo Vaccari was awarded a *Medaglia di Bronzo al Valor Militare* for the mission on 13 November.

19 November 1940

After the capture of Sidi Barrani on 16 September, the Italian Army formed a defensive line composed of big outposts separated by wide desert areas. From north to south there were the 1ª *Divisione Libica* (1st Libyan infantry division) at Maktila, near the sea east of Sidi Barrani and the 4ª *Divisione Camice Nere* (4th Black Shirts Division) at Sidi Barrani. South of these were the 2ª *Divisione Libica* (2nd Libyan infantry division) in three strong points called Alam El Tummar East, Alam El Tummar West and Point 90 (also called Ras El Dai). South of this were the motorised "Maletti Group" in the entrenched camp of Nibeiwa (strong points: Alam Nibeiwa and Alam El Iktufa). Then there was a gap of around thirty kilometres (called the Bir Enba gap) and at the extreme south of the Italian front the 63ª *Divisione di Fanteria* (Italian Infantry division "Cirene") in four strong points around the rocky hill of Bir Sofafi; Alam El Rabia, the crossroads at height 236, the crossroads at Qabe el Mahdi and Height 226 at Bir Sofafi.

This deployment was clearly inadequate, in particular the worst error seemed to be the wide gap between "Maletti" and "Cirene", a distance that allowed for encirclement of the forces south of Sidi Barrani and north of Bir Sofafi.

On 19 November General O'Connor ordered a fully motorised support group to enter the gap and stay there to mark the British supremacy over the important area (in fact he had already planned to use this zone to pass his troops through and attack Nibeiwa). Reconnaissance units of the "Maletti" Group signalled the dangerous presence of British armoured cars and a combined action was planned for the day after.

During the early morning, a formation of 17 fighters of the 151° *Gr.* escorted a formation of Bredas attacking enemy troops in the Bir Enba area and a Ro.37*bis* reconnoitring in the same general area. The mission was uneventful and the 366ª *Sq.* went down after the Bredas to strafe enemy vehicles.

Then an armoured column of the "Maletti" Group (420 troopers and 27 officers on 37 trucks with a six anti-tank and six medium calibre guns and twenty seven M11/39 medium tanks) left Nibeiwa and a column of the 2ª *Divisione Libica* (256 troopers and 17 officers on 29 trucks with four anti-tank and eight medium calibre guns) left Tummar. They had to rendezvous and then explore the Bir Enba gap. British forces opposing them are not known, but Italian Intelligence estimated an armoured group of 60 to 70 tanks and armoured cars (Italian Intelligence generally overestimated the actual force of the Commonwealth troops by a factor of between two and ten).

At 12:40, the "Maletti" group was attacked by the British and forced to do battle. Around half an hour later at 13:00 the 2ª Libyan contingent arrived and together they forced the British forces to retreat. While they were coming back to base, the British returned and attacked again, starting a dangerous rearguard action.

At 13:00, 18 CR.42s from the 13° *Gr.* were ordered off from Gambut G to patrol the Bir Enba area. After take-off a first group of 12 aircraft led by the newly promoted *ten. col.* Secondo Revetria stayed at 3000 meters while a second group led by *ten.* Guglielmo Chiarini covered them 2000 meters higher. Revetria's formation included pilots from the 77ª *Squadriglie* (*cap.* Domenico Bevilacqua, *ten.* Eduardo Sorvillo, *s. ten.* Mario Nicoloso, *serg.* Enrico Botti, *serg.* Vincenzo Campolo and an unrecorded pilot), 78ª (*s. ten.* Natale Cima, *serg. magg.* Salvatore Mechelli, *serg.* Cassio Poggi and *serg.* Teresio Martinoli) and 82ª (*s. ten.* Virgilio Vanzan).

When they arrived over Bir Enba, Revetria made a first pass to better spot targets and observed an artillery duel between Italian guns and British tanks. Immediately the British vehicles that were encircling the right flank of the Italian troops stopped firing and dispersed. Revetria and his eleven pilots attacked in single file causing a lot of damage among the enemy. After the strafing attack, the twelve 13° *Gr.* pilots returned undamaged to base, where they landed 14:50 after having fired 2,200 rounds of 12.7 and 7.7 calibre ammunition.

In the meantime, Chiarini's formation was down to 4000 meters when they spotted a formation of a reported eight Gladiators that looked as if they were trying to attack Revetria's formation. Chiarini immediately attacked with height advantage and surprised the Gladiators. The first pass only managed to break the Gladiator formation without causing losses, and then a long dogfight started (Chiarini recorded that it lasted for 25 minutes) after which six British Gladiators were claimed shot down in flames, all shared by the six pilots of the Italian formation - *ten.* Chiarini, *s. ten.* Gilberto Cerofolini, *s. ten.* Giuseppe Bottà, *s. ten.* Giuseppe Timolina, *serg.* Nino Campanini and *serg.* Francesco Nanin. A seventh Gladiator was claimed as seriously damaged and was last seen flying low towards Matruh smoking and without taking evasive action, being claimed as a shared probable, and the last Gladiator was also claimed as a shared probable. It was reported that all the victories were confirmed by the Libyan land forces (Chiarini also reported that the wreck of one of the Gladiators was noted on the ground by his pilots). The six Italian fighters came back almost without any fuel left, they had used 1,595 rounds 12.7 calibre and 2,330 rounds of 7.7 calibre ammunition. Only four of them were slightly damaged. The heaviest damage was suffered by Timolina's aircraft, which landed at an advanced airbase (probably Sollum) and was flown back to base the next day. His aircraft was still not operational at the beginning of Operation "*Compass*", much more because of the inadequacy of the Italian repair organisation than because of the damage actually suffered.

It seems that the "eight Gladiators" were in fact a formation of four Gladiators from 3 Sqn RAAF. F/Lt Blake Pelly (N5753), had been ordered to undertake a reconnaissance over enemy positions in the Sofafi-Rabia-Bir Enba areas. S/Ldr Peter Ronald Heath (N5750), and F/O s Alan Rawlinson

(Left to right) Flying Officer Alan Rawlinson, Flight Lieutenant Blake Pelly and Flying Officer Alan Boyd of 3 RAAF Sqn on 24 November 1940 during a photo session following the successful combat on 19 November. In the background, Gloster Gladiator N5752/NW-G. This aircraft was received from 33 RAF Sqn in September 1940 and flown by Flying Officer Boyd on 19 November. The aircraft was lost on 13 December 1940 when it was shot down by Fiat CR.42s near Sollum. Flying Officer Wilfred Arthur parachuted safely. [via Australian War Memorial]

(L9044) and Alan Boyd (N5752) provided his escort. The aircraft took off from Gerawla at 13:40. Flying at about 5,500 feet and with Pelly some 200 yards in front of the escort, they headed for their objective. After about half an hour and about seven miles east of Rabia, 18 CR.42s were spotted below strafing British troops. In accordance to orders, the reconnaissance flight turned around and headed for home. They had barely turned around when they were attacked by the CR.42s. Pelly out in the lead found himself at the centre of attention from nine Fiats. His escort were likewise engaged with a similar number.

Boyd found himself being attacked from astern by three aircraft. By twisting and diving he found himself behind one of them and fired off a long burst into the cockpit area. The Fiat rolled over and dived towards the ground. Pulling up into a tight turn he was able to bring his sights to bear on another enemy fighter. Coming in for a quarter attack the Fiat fell into an uncontrollable spin with thick black smoke pouring from the engine. With barely a pause Boyd pulled round and went after a third fighter, which was attacking one of the Gladiators. After hitting it with a short burst it fell away. As he was watching it fall away he was attacked from behind by yet another Fiat. Hauling hard back on the stick, he went straight up, with the engine on full power. This caused the enemy fighter to overshoot him. Rolling over, Boyd came down and fired directly into the engine and cockpit area, the Fiat then spun down towards the ground. Looking round, he saw another fighter and set off in pursuit. The Italian saw him and pulled up into a climb, Boyd followed but his engine stalled and he entered a spin, only pulling out when he was within 30 feet of the ground. As he pulled out he was attacked by yet another Fiat. To complicate matters further Boyd's guns had jammed and he struggled with the mechanisms trying desperately to free them, all the while being pursued a few feet off the ground by an enemy fighter. At last he freed up the two fuselage guns and in a desperate measure he yanked back the stick and went up into a loop. Coming over the top, he saw the Fiat below him and at a range of less than 30 yards he let fly with his remaining guns. The cockpit of the Fiat erupted with bullet strikes and it fell away to the desert floor.

With no more enemy aircraft in the vicinity, Boyd took stock of his situation. He had very little ammo left and only two working guns. In the distance, he saw one aircraft being pursued by two more. Turning in their direction he gained some altitude and closed in. He soon recognised Pelly's Gladiator coming under attack from two Fiats. He immediately attack one which was firing on Pelly, who was about to land with a faltering engine, this aircraft rolled over and dived towards the ground which was only 30 feet away. It seems unlikely that it could have pulled out. Pelly's engine had picked up again and he started to climb away from the area. The remaining Fiat turned on Boyd, whose guns had jammed again, and chased him at low level for about a mile before giving up and turning away. Boyd rejoined Pelly and both pilots made their way home. Along the way Pelly had to land at Minqar Qaim at 14:45 when his engine gave out. It was discovered that his oil tank had been hit and all the oil had drained out (the aircraft was flown back to Gerawla the next day). Boyd continued on his own back to base where he landed at 14:50.

During this combat 26-year-old S/Ldr Heath was shot down in flames and killed. He was later buried beside his aircraft.

Boyd was credited with three CR.42s shot down and one probable, Pelly claimed one shot down and one damaged, while Rawlinson claimed a damaged.

Of the dogfight, Pelly wrote:

"*While proceeding on reconnaissance to Sofafi area in company with an escort of 3 other Gladiators, I encountered two formations of CR42 aircraft, consisting of eight and nine respectively.*

The formation of eight attacked my escort and the other formation cut me off and drove me southwards. The interception occurred at 1400 when I was 7 miles east of Rabia, and my escort were two miles NE of me. I was at 4,000 feet and my escort at 5,000 feet.

I could not get back to my escort, and the repeated attacks of the nine CR42s forced me southwards, and I worked eastwards.

Shortly after the commencement of the battle I found myself meeting one EA head on at 50 feet. We both opened fire and he dived under me and crashed into the ground.

About five EA must have broken off, but at least 3 pursued me and attacked determinedly until 1425 when I worked northwards and rejoined on of my escort (F/O A H Boyd). These three then broke off.

During the battle at approximately 1405 I turned at two EA who were attacking me from rear and got in one good burst. This aircraft issued black smoke, which increased in intensity until he finally broke away. I saw him flying away in a cloud of black smoke."

After the war, Pelly also added that he was also shot at by his own escort during this hectic 25 minute battle. He also recalls being picked up by a Lysander and flown back to base. This was 3 Sqn RAAF's first combat.

At 13:35, three Gladiators from 3 Sqn RAAF took off from Gerawla for another tactical reconnaissance. The mission was flown by F/Lt Gordon Steege (N5780), F/O East (N5765) and F/O Alan Gatward (N5766), and intended to cover the Bir Dignaish area. At about 14:10 the three Gladiators encountered F/O Alan Rawlinson returning to base. The reconnaissance was then abandoned and the four Gladiators returned to base in company and landed at 14:40.

Nine CR.32s of the 160ª *Sq.* also took part in the attacks in the Bir Enba area at different hours of the day and didn't suffer any losses.

At the end of the day the Italian Army losses were twelve dead, 52 wounded and 16 missing, five tanks (the M11/39 in this combat showed for the first time its unsuitability in the role of main battle tank, in particular because its main armament, a 37 mm gun, was in fixed position inside the hull so it was unable to deploy against fast moving targets) and two medium calibre guns destroyed. British losses are not known but the Italians, left in possession of the field, counted ten destroyed armoured cars.

F/O Webber of 208 Sqn crashed on landing at LG 62, he was uninjured and the aircraft was collected by No. 51 Rescue Salvage Unit and taken to Fuka.

20 November 1940

208 Sqn despatched two Lysanders to reconnoitre an area bounded by Sollum, Sofali and Buq-Buq. They were L4724 piloted by F/Lt Burnard and L4728 piloted by P/O Waymark, and took off from Qasaba at 14:20 and 14:15 landing back at 16:35 and 16:20 respectively (another Lysander, possibly L6874, an attached 6 Sqn aircraft piloted by F/O T. H. Davison, was out in the same area).

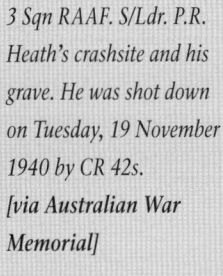

3 Sqn RAAF. S/Ldr. P.R. Heath's crashsite and his grave. He was shot down on Tuesday, 19 November 1940 by CR 42s.
[via Australian War Memorial]

Two members of 3 RAAF Sqn prepare a cross for the grave of Squadron Leader Peter Ronald Heath, who was shot down and killed by Fiat CR.42s from 13º Gruppo C.T. east of Rabia on 19 November 1940. [via Australian War Memorial]

33 Sqn provided nine Hurricanes (including F/O Vernon Woodward (N2498), F/Lt Ernest Dean (P 3818), F/O John Mackie (P3724), S/Ldr Charles Ryley (P3970), F/Sgt Harry Goodchild (N2640), F/O Frank Holman (P3724) and P/O Charles Dyson (N2640)) as escort. It is possible that the unaccounted pilots were one or two pilots from 274 Sqn, since a quartet of Hurricanes from this squadron, piloted by F/Lt Evers-Swindell, P/O Ernest Mason, P/O Thomas Patterson and Second Lieutenant Frederick Johannes Joubert, together with P/O Strange and Second Lieutenant Bester (who followed with the ground party), were on attachment to 33 Sqn on 14 November. On 21 November, Evers-Swindell flew back from Fuka to have repairs on his fighter, reportedly damaged in a running fight with CR.42s. It seems almost sure that the "running fight" was the action described below, so it is possible that Evers-Swindell was present.

The escort took off from Fuka Satellite airfield at 14:15, with one section of three protecting each Lysander while a third section provided top cover. At the same time, a formation of six Gladiators from 112 Sqn would sweep the same general area.

East of Sidi Barrani, 18 CR.42s intercepted them and one Fiat half-rolled and dived away after being fired on by a Hurricane. It is possible that this aircraft was later credited as a destroyed to F/O Mackie, who in a letter sent home to Canada on 4 December recalled:

"Just before I went on leave we had one of two bits of fun up here. On one occasion, you May have heard about it on the radio, fifteen of us got mixed up with sixty wop fighters. We lost none, and got at least eight of them. I got one of these, although not in a very convincing way from my point of view, as I didn't see it go in. Another pilot saw the start and the finish of it. Anyhow, it sure was a mix-up. I have never seen so many machines milling around in such a small amount of sky."

However, after this both sides started to guard each other without giving battle, with the Italians unwilling to tangle with the faster Hurricanes and the British finding it difficult to close in on their more manoeuvrable opponents.

The Hurricanes of the two sections dealing with the direct escort of the Lysanders now started to break off since they were being out-manoeuvred by their opponents and at this moment a huge formation of a reportedly 25-30 Italian fighters was seen above them. The top cover section of 33 Sqn climbed to engage but reportedly to no avail, because the Italian turned back towards Libya without engaging.

The Italian formation was composed of 18 aircraft from all three *Squadriglie* of the 9º *Gr.* led by *magg.* Ernesto Botto (at the head of the 73ª *Sq.*). Six of the CR.42s were from the 96ª *Sq.* (*cap.* Roberto Fassi leading *ten.* Aldo Gon, *s. ten.* Carlo Agnelli, *s. ten.* Armando Moresi and *serg.* Vittorio Pozzati together with 4º *Stormo*'s adjutant, *cap.* Mario Pluda), five were from the 73ª *Sq.* (*ten.* Valerio De Campo, *ten.* Pietro Bonfatti, *m. llo.* Mario Ruffilli, *serg. magg.* Antonio Valle and *serg.* Santo Gino) and six were from the 97ª *Sq.* (*cap.* Antonio Larsimont Pergameni, *ten.* Ezio Viglione Borghese, *s. ten.* Jacopo Frigerio, *m. llo.* Rinaldo Damiani, *serg.* Francesco Putzu and *serg.* Franco Sarasino). They had taken off from El Adem at 14:40 to cover Italian troops in the Bir Enba area (and probably indirectly escorting a reconnaissance plane) when Botto discovered a Bristol Blenheim escorted by several Hurricanes flying lower, and attacked.

At this moment, with the 9º *Gr.*'s attention focused elsewhere, the 112 Sqn Gladiators intervened and managed to surprise the Italian formation over Sidi Barrani. They claimed eight of the Fiats without losses. All of the six pilots made claims, and F/Lt R. J. Abrahams claimed one and one shared with P/O Richard Acworth, who also claimed one additional. F/O R. J. Bennett claimed one, P/O Alfred Costello claimed one, P/O Leonard Bartley claimed two and Sgt 'Paddy' Donaldson finally claimed one. 112 Sqn didn't record any losses in this combat, even if P/O Acworth in his memories spoke of a couple of aircraft obliged to force-land, and the unit's aircraft retuned to Fuka between 16:20 and 17:25. For this one-sided action, they were noted in the press for the first time.

Acworth remembered this combat in a short story written in the 1960's but never published.

"The Lysanders were to be 'covered' against enemy air attacks by six Gladiators from my squadron… three flying at 12,000 feet, and three, led by myself, at 15,000 feet. 'Top cover' was to be provided by six Hurricanes, flying at 20,000 feet. The Hurricanes had strict orders to beat a hasty retreat if they met with enemy aircraft in large numbers, as it was thought at that time that they would be 'easy meat' for the move manoeuvrable C.R. 42's, the single-seater Italian opposite number of the Gladiator.

We had been patrolling for about 10 minutes, when I reported forty CR 42s, in eight sections of five, flying from the direction of Libya, at approximately 25,000 feet, 5,000 feet higher that the Hurricane 'top-cover'. To my dismay, the Hurricanes were soon speeding home, with a CR 42 sitting neatly on each tail. Our six Gladiators were left to finish the fight, for the Lysanders, their task completed, were heading for home, too.

There was not a friendly cloud in the sky, and the powerful desert sun made the enemy aircraft very difficult to see. Forthwith, they carried out the German tactics of remaining aloft, and sending down their more experienced men to finish us off one by one….but it was not to be!

With the first attacks, we broke formation, and it was every man for himself. I soon found myself very much alone, until unfriendly tracer bullets from behind, passed through the space between my right wings. I immediately steep-turned to the left, and caught sight of my attacker as he completed his dive and prepared to re-join his pals up higher, by means of a roll off the top of a loop.

A Fiat CR.42 of the 90ª Squadriglia in front of the hangars at Benina on 20 November 1940.
[Historical Office Italian Air Force]

Seizing my chance, I opened full throttle and followed him to the top of his loop, half rolled in formation with him, and was just about to open fire, when my aircraft stalled and flicked into a spin....not enough speed! I decided my best means of survival was to continue the spin, in the hope that he would think I had been badly hit. This was a fighter tactic from World War I, and it worked! Whilst I was spinning, I looked upwards and caught a glimpse of my adversary circling at his original height, waiting for me to crash into the desert. I came out of the spin at about 8,000 feet, no doubt much to his surprise, and didn't have to wait long for him to dive down to finish me off.

So started a long tail-chasing session. At first, my mouth became rather dry, but after a second or two, my mind became crystal clear, and I was determined to turn the tables on him. Slowly I began to gain ground, and soon part of his tail was in my sights, but I realized it would not have been great enough. When his engine came into my sights, I pressed the firing button, and was immediately cheered to see pieces of fabric or metal ripping off his fuselage, just behind the cockpit.

The Italian pilot turned so quickly in his mad effort to escape, that he pulled his aircraft into a spin, following a 'high-speed stall'. I followed him down, and fired at him as he tried to recover, and he promptly went into another one. On recovering from his second spin, he must have pulled an emergency boost control to give him extra speed, for he left my Gladiator 'standing'.

However, my opponent was not easily scared, and turned about a mile away to come back at me like a bull at a gate. We both opened fire, and when it seemed that a head-on collision was inevitable, he pulled out to my left in a climbing turn. For a second, I was able to fire at his exposed fuselage, and then, with throttle fully open, I climbed into the sun, into an advantageous position. To my horror, my engine stalled near the top of the climb, and I had to carry out the usual drill of closing the throttle and opening it again, slowly. Full power came back, and looking down, I could see my opponent looking for me. This time, I had the advantage of height, and I was nicely lining him up in my sights when he saw me, and tried to turn in underneath me.

Slowly twisting, and with the right deflection, I raked him with bullets from nose to tail, at almost point-blank range. I pulled out of my dive, to regain height, and saw him commence another spin from which he did not recover. I felt immensely relieved, somewhat shaken, and eventually joined up with two stray Gladiators, and returned to Mersa Matruh. I was pleased to learn later that seven aircraft had been shot down in the engagement, and that all the Gladiator pilots had survived the fight, although two had made forced landings.

I shall never forget that day. It was my first one-against-one air battle, and the longest time I had engaged a single enemy aircraft..."

The 9° *Gr.* actually lost only three shot down and four damaged, but two pilots were killed. The three shot down pilots were *s. ten.* Carlo Agnelli of the 96ª *Sq.*, who was killed, *serg.* Francesco Putzu of the 97ª *Sq.*, who was killed, and *ten.* Gon (who usually flew CR.42 MM5605/96-2), who recalled:

"This day [strangely enough he recorded it as on 1 November but this is for certain an error] *I lost the dearest of all my wingmen* [Carlo Agnelli]. *We were up with all the Gruppo and the three Squadriglie were stepped at different heights. The lowest escorting a reconnaissance plane, mine (96ª Squadriglia) at 3000 metres while the third stay higher. The highest group had already engaged the enemy when I saw one of our planes diving almost vertically followed by a Gloster. I made a violent overturning that my wingmen were unable to follow* [again without radio equipment the Italian formation was broken at the beginning of the combat and whatever numerical advantage was impossible to put into full use] *when I reach a distance suitable to open fire I had to wait because there was the risk of hitting my comrade* [with the same burst aimed at the fighter that was following him] *I had to concentrate only on the aim* [the wingmen were far away] *so I couldn't look around and was attacked by two Glosters. With the first burst of fire they shot away my propeller, so without propulsion I could only manoeuvre to avoid further damage. All the height lost I force-landed and the English pilots that had already stopped firing while I was gliding down for my final approach flew past me waving their hands.*

[Gon tried to burn his plane without success and reached an Italian outpost the day after]

Back at base, I discovered that information about the missing pilots (we were three) was lacking.

A sergeant [serg. Francesco Putzu] was seen to jump with parachute and another of our planes was seen to crash after a hard fight, all believed it was mine because the other missing pilot (my dear wingman) was too "green" to be able to fight against three enemies as the pilot of the crashed plane did.

The encounter with Botto was tragicomic. I went to his room and he was waiting for me near the door and as just as he saw me he threw himself right into my arms through the three steps that divided us. But I was too weak and was unable to sustain him so we fell embraced on the ground."

According to the official records of the 4° *Stormo*, however, it seems that during the dive Gon's guns went out of synchronisation and when opening fire he cut his own propeller with the first shots.

Seven confirmed and two probable victories were credited to the pilots of the *Gruppo* after they landed at 16:30. This overclaiming was a result of the *Stormo*'s records being re-recorded in 1941 after they had been lost. This re-recording was done by *ten.* Giulio Reiner, who was then adjutant of the *Gruppo*. Obviously Reiner's reconstruction was not as accurate as a complete debriefing immediately after the battle could be.

Roberto Fassi was credited with a Blenheim, a probable Gladiator and two damaged Gladiators. Pozzati, who was wounded in the right foot, was credited with a Gladiator, while Gon was credited with a Gladiator (a victory that he didn't mention at all in his memoires). Pluda claimed another Gladiator and Moresi one probable Gladiator. The 73ª and 97ª *Squadriglie* claimed one Gladiator and two Hurricanes shot down and four fighters damaged, all shared. Final assessment of the combat was four Gladiators, two Hurricanes and a Blenheim confirmed and two Gladiators probably destroyed (the actual number of confirmed claims varies between the reconstructed Diari of the involved *Squadriglia*s to seven or eight destroyed).

The alarm section of the 90ª Squadriglia having fun in front of the camera at Benina on 20 November 1940. [Historical Office Italian Air Force]

21 November 1940

A raid on Benina slightly damaged one CR.42.

22 November 1940

A raid on Menelao destroyed one Z.501.

Lysander L6880 of 6 Sqn crashed on landing at an ALG after a tyre burst. No casualties were suffered and the aircraft was later recovered and sent to 103 MU at Aboukir, while Lysander P9197 replaced it.

23 November 1940

A raid on Menastir by a single British bomber at 06:40 caused no damage.

Serg. Aldo Rosa and *serg.* Alessandro Bladelli of the 91ª *Sq.* took off from T4 and claimed a damaged Wellington bomber.

Well aware that the Italian Navy was in a critical situation after the losses suffered at Taranto on 11 November, the Admiralty planned another ambitious operation in the Mediterranean.

From Alexandria Convoy *MW4*, composed of four merchant vessels (*Breconshire*, *Memnon*, *Clan Fergusson* and *Clan Maculay*), sailed bound for Malta and escorted by Force "D" (the cruisers HMS *Calcutta* and HMS *Coventry* and four destroyers) and Force "C" (the battleships HMS *Ramillies* and HMS *Malaya*, the carrier HMS *Eagle* - just back on operations - the cruisers HMS *Berwick*, HMS *Sidney* and HMS *Ajax* and eight destroyers).

Another battle group called Force "A" and composed of the battleships HMS *Warspite* and HMS *Valiant*, the carrier HMS *Illustrious* and nine destroyers sailed as indirect support. They were met by the III Cruiser Division already at sea, composed of the cruisers HMS *Glasgow*, HMS *Gloucester* and HMS *York*.

It was intended that after rendezvousing with the "*Collar*" Convoy coming from Gibraltar, HMS *Ramillies*, HMS *Berwick* and the Malta-resident cruiser HMS *Newcastle* would leave the Mediterranean fleet due to the decreased threat posed by the *Regia Marina*.

On 25 November, the light cruisers HMS *Manchester* and HMS *Southampton* steamed from Gibraltar packed with 1370 RAF personnel (among them the complete ground parties of 37 and 73 Sqns aboard HMS *Manchester* and the ground party of 38 Sqn aboard HMS *Southampton*), the freighters *Clan Forbes* and *Clan Fraser* bound for Malta, and the liner *New Zealand Star* bound for Alexandria. They were escorted by Force "H" composed of the battlecruiser HMS *Renown*, the carrier HMS *Ark Royal*, the cruisers HMS *Sheffield* and HMS *Despatch* and nine destroyers (HMS *Faulknor*, HMS *Firedrake*, HMS *Forester*, HMS *Fury*, HMS *Encounter*, HMS *Duncan*, HMS *Wishrt*, HMS *Kelvin* and HMS *Jaguar*) and Force "F" composed of the destroyer HMS *Hotspur* and four Flower class corvettes (HMS *Peony*, HMS *Salvia*, HMS *Gloxinia* and HMS *Hyacinty*) that were heading for Suda Bay. These ships comprised the "*Collar*" group. All the combined operations took the name of Operation *MB 9*.

24 November 1940

At 06:30, *s. ten.* Amedeo Guidi of the 366ª *Sq.* took off from Amseat A3 to patrol over Bardia.

After twenty minutes, when at 3000 metres over the town he saw the AA of Bardia and Menastir firing. Looking in the direction of the AA fire, he discovered an enemy aircraft 1000 metres below and immediately attacked. The enemy plane, a short nosed Blenheim, started a shallow dive towards the sea, returning fire from the dorsal turret. Guidi followed it, firing for twenty minutes and after exhausting his ammunition (1200 rounds) turned back. The Blenheim was smoking heavily from the right engine and was claimed as a probable. Guidi landed at 07:20.

S. ten. Guidi had been in combat with a Blenheim Mk.I from 55 Sqn. A machine from this unit took off at 05:00 and attacked Bardia from 10,000 feet at 06:25. Results of the attack were impossible to appreciate because immediately after the bomb release an Italian fighter, believed to be a CR.32, with exceptional speed attacked the Blenheim. The fighter kept up with the Blenheim for 30 minutes, once passing it and allowing the British pilot to get in a frontal gun attack. Other separate attacks were carried out from astern and lasted two minutes each. Then the Italian pilot waggled his wings and broke away. The Blenheim (L8531 flown by F/O K. H. E. Ellis or perhaps L8514 flown by Sgt E. P. Vignaux) landed at 07:40 and was slightly damaged without suffering any casualties. The Italian opponent was believed damaged by return fire.

At sunset, six CR.42s of the 23º *Gr. C.T.* from Comiso attacked the airfield of Luqa (called Mikabba by the Italians) on Malta. The pilots participating in the attack had been selected among the best of the unit (*magg.* Tito Falconi (*Gruppo* CO), *ten.* Claudio Solaro, *cap.* Guido Bobba (CO 74ª *Sq.*), *cap.* Ottorino Fargnoli (CO 70ª *Sq.*), *ten.* Ezio Maria Monti and *s. ten.* Domenico Tessera).

They strafed from very low altitude, claiming one plane in flames for sure and additional damage. Back at base, the Italian War Bulletin credited them with three ground victories. They had in fact managed to burn Wellington "F" of 38 Sqn (the machine of P/O Timmins) in transit from Marham to Egypt, and according to post war British studies, they had possibly destroyed an additional machine of 148 Sqn. During the return journey, *ten.* Monti became disoriented while escaping the attentions of a British night fighter and used all his fuel before reaching Comiso, being obliged to bale out over Stagnone di Marsala. P/O Timmins was immediately sent back to England to collect a replacement machine.

It is also interesting to note that the same morning, *ten.* Monti and *serg.* Germano Gasperoni had claimed an additional Wellington intercepted when flying alone 40-50 kilometres from Malta. The machine seemed possibly a bomber from 38 Sqn that during the day was transferring its "B" Flight to Egypt while "A" Flight was arriving from England, but the British unit's records don't report any engagement with enemy fighters.

25 November 1940

On the night of 25/26 November, Tripoli's port was dive-bombed by six Swordfish from 813 and 824 Sqns. Carrying a mixed load of 500lb SAP bombs, 250lb SAP bombs, 250lb GP bombs and flares, they flew 60 miles, encountering moderate flak on arrival but returning safely after observing bomb hits and fires in the target area.

26 November 1940

Blenheim Mk.IV T2067 of 113 Sqn took off from Ma'aten Bagush at 07:10 as one of two Blenheims detailed for a sortie towards Bir Sofafi. It was shot down during the sortie, killing the crew, Pilot 28-year-old F/O Donald Stanley Anderson, Observer 23-year-old Sgt George Herbert Lee and 24-year-old Wireless Operator/Air Gunner Sgt Ernest Seath Young.

En route for Malta, Swordfish from HMS *Illustrious*' 819 Sqn attacked the Italian island of Leros, losing the plane of Lieutenant Walter V. Hamilton (a Taranto veteran), who was buried on the island together with his crew.

Giuseppe Oblach (73ª *Sq.*) flew a photo-reconnaissance sortie at 400 meters over the road Sidi Barrani - Mersa Matruh together with *ten.* Pietro Bonfatti (73ª *Sq.*). On their way back to base they strafed some enemy AA sites.

During the sortie Oblach flew CR.42 MM4383/96-11, which was the aircraft field-modified for reconnaissance duties.

Giuseppe Oblach of the 73ª Squadriglia, 9º Gruppo C.T. in front of a Fiat CR.42. [Oblach via Fulvio Chianese – Associazione Culturale 4° Stormo di Gorizia]

27 November 1940

With the British ships of Operation *MB 9* close to their rendezvous point and the convoys reaching Malta, a day of heavy operations started.

Over the western Mediterranean fighters from HMS *Ark Royal* opened the day at 07:55 when a Fulmar section of 808 Sqn, led by Lieutenant Taylour, shot down a Cant Z.506 of the 196ª *Sq.* (*ten.* Manlio Ravasini, *ten. di Vascello* Guido Terconi) ten miles north of Bone off the Algerian coast. The seaplane was probably that identified ditched in the sea off "*Bosa*" (Bona?) at 12:25 by a CR.32 of the 155ª *Sq.*, 3º *Gr.*

At around midday the opposing fleets clashed (as often quite inconclusively) in what was later called the *Battle of Cape Spartivento*. Eleven Swordfish from 810 Sqn, led by Lieutenant Commander M. Johnstone, attacked at around 12:40, claiming a hit on the battleship *Vittorio Veneto* (in fact, they all missed).

In the early afternoon, nine Swordfish from 820 Sqn, led by Lieutenant Commander J. A. Stuart-Moore, attacked the Italian cruisers, claiming two hits (none achieved). Three CR.42s of 154ª *Sq.* piloted by *cap.* Giuseppe Tovazzi, *ten.* Giovanni Giannini and *serg. magg.* Bortolani intercepted a British plane identified as a "Blackburn" during a cruise over the Italian fleet and Giannini claimed it shot down. Ten SM 79s of the 32º *Stormo*, escorted by CR.42s of the 3º *Gr. Aut.* then arrived over Force "H" and seven Fulmars of 808 Sqn, which were up, intercepted at 14:30 claiming two or three victories without being able to stop them. Green Section's Lieutenant Rupert Tillard claimed one SM 79 shot down but then he and the men of his section were bounced by the CR.42s. A formation of five CR.42s of the 153ª *Sq.* led by *cap.* Giorgio Tugnoli and including *ten.* Alfonso Mattei, *s. ten.* Alfonso Ciapetti (154ª *Sq.*), *serg. magg.* Vittorio Visconti and *serg.* Sergio Lucato (154ª *Sq.*) reported a combat against seven British fighters, probably "Hurricanes", over the sea 200 km south-west of Cagliari. They claimed five victories with the use of 1080 rounds, one of the victories was claimed individually by Ciapetti while Lucato failed to return. In fact, unable to fight back because they were low on ammunition and after having mistaken the Fiats for Sea Gladiators, Fulmar N1941 (pilot Sub Lieutenant Richard Maurice Scott Martin and TAG L/A Alexander Laird Milne Noble) was shot down into the sea with the loss of the crew. The FAA pilots were unable to claim anything and the missing CR.42 probably ran out of fuel after the combat and disappeared in the sea with its pilot.

All the SM 79s from the 32º *Stormo* returned to base, even if eight out of ten were damaged by the Fulmars and the AA, two of them seriously. However, a transit Vichy French Farman 223 was involved in the combat and shot down, most likely by the Fulmars.

One hour later, seven Skuas of 800 Sqn led by Lieutenant Smeeton dive bombed the Italian ships without success, but while coming back to HMS *Ark Royal* they run across the Ro.43 seaplane spotter of *Vittorio Veneto* (piloted by *cap.* Violante with observer *s. ten. di Vascello* Davide Sovrano). Four of the Skuas shot it down into the sea (Lieutenant Rooper/Sub Lieutenant Woolston in L3015, P/O (A) Sabey/L/A Cooles in L2009, P/O (A) Burston/N/A Holmes in L3007 and P/O (A) Jopling/N/A Glen in L3017).

Later during the day, three CR.42s of the 153ª *Sq.* piloted by *ten.* Giorgio Pellicioli, *ten.* Falconi and *serg. magg.* Faliero Gelli scrambled and intercepted a British aircraft identified as a "Blackburn Roc" (probably a Skua) and Gelli claimed it probably shot down off the Tunisian coast.

At 16:45, the last Italian attack arrived when ten SM 79s without escort attacked HMS *Ark Royal* achieving some very near misses. Skuas and Fulmars were up but were unable to stop them and the fighters only claimed some damage. In fact, nine of the bombers came back damaged by AA and fighters.

The 73 Sqn ground personnel aboard the cruiser HMS *Manchester* witnessed the air attack, seeing the HMS *Ark Royal* covered by a flurry of near misses. Only later they were informed that the ship was not hit.

28 November 1940

The British ships of Operation *MB 9* arrived off Malta and this brought a response from the *Regia Aeronautica*.

The first recorded mission was a visual reconnaissance carried out by two SM 79s of 34° *Stormo* in the Sicilian narrows.

Later during the morning, eight CR.42s of 23° *Gr.* took off to reconnoitre the harbours of Malta in search of the British ships. *serg. magg.* Arnaldo Sala of 74ª *Sq.* was hit by AA when over the island and he tried to nurse home his damaged fighter, finally falling into open sea, 40 kilometres from Sicily. He and his plane were never found. Italian sources are quite clear in excluding any involvement of enemy fighters in the action, but it is however possible that two machines of 261 Sqn were present, directed by radar against a group of CR.42s that they attacked at 09:30. The reconnaissance however revealed the presence of enemy ships in harbour and consequently offensive missions were planned.

Six Ju87Rs of the 97° *Gr.* B.a'T. (a unit which had recently replaced the 96° *Gr.* in Sicily) (four crews from the 238ª *Sq.* and two from the 239ª *Sq.*, among them Giuseppe Cenni) headed out towards Malta and the ships. The dive-bombers were covered by sixteen CR.42s of the 23° *Gr.* under the command of the unit's Commander, *magg.* Tito Falconi.

The Stukas attacked a Royal Navy formation off Malta, reporting that they were intercepted by Hurricanes, which were immediately counterattacked and dispersed by the escort, and that while the first "kette" didn't obtain hits the second probably hit the enemy's ships. In fact, they had attacked the cruiser HMS *Glasgow* without success, and were all back home without losses at 12:55.

The intercepting "Hurricanes" were in fact a group of six Fulmars from the HMS *Illustrious*' squadrons, three planes from 805 Sqn and three from 806 Sqn. The two Fulmar sections attacked but the operationally inexperienced 805 Sqn trio were unable to make contact. Even though the leader, Sub Lieutenant R. F. Bryant, expended some 3200 rounds in four bursts, he found the Fiats far too manoeuvrable to gain any hits. His observer, Lieutenant John Shuttleworth, recalls:

"During the engagement I fired 'smoke puffs' from the rear cockpit whenever CR.42s got on our tail…I certainly saw one if not two parachutes floating down."

Fiat CR.42s of the 23° Gruppo in close formation are crossing the Sicilian coast during an escort mission to Malta in autumn 1940.
[Maria Teresa Bobba]

In the meantime, the more experienced 806 Sqn's trio was fighting the CR.42s more successfully. Sub Lieutenant S. G. Orr claimed one CR.42 while Sub Lieutenant G. R. Golden and Sub Lieutenant W. H. Clisby claimed damage to two more. Clisby's Fulmar (N1935) was hit in the fight, his TAG, Leading Aircraftman H. Phillips being wounded in the leg, hand and face by an explosive bullet, although not seriously hurt.

(Left to right) F/O Alan Rawlinson, F/Lt Blake Pelly and F/O Alan Boyd (in the cockpit of Gladiator N5752/NW-G) of 3 RAAF Sqn on 24 November 1940 during a photo session following the successful combat on 19 November. [via Australian War Memorial]

The CR.42s claimed four Hurricanes shot down, two confirmed and two probables. Six pilots of the 70ª *Sq.* claimed the former jointly, while the other was claimed by *serg. magg.* Raffaele Marzocca of the 74ª *Sq.*, the two probables being credited to *cap.* Guido Bobba and *ten.* Lorenzo Lorenzoni of this unit. The Fiats returned without losses.

Early in the afternoon nine SM 79s from the 30° *Stormo* attacked the British ships, this time escorted by twelve CR.42s of the 23° *Gr.*, again under the command of Tito Falconi, while ten MC.200s of the 6° *Gr.* made a sweep in the same area. For once Malta's Hurricanes were up in time and were able to dive from 5,000 feet above, through the Italian fighter escort and on to the bombers, of which one was shot down (by Sgt Robertson) and another damaged. It is also believed that F/Lt John Greenhalgh claimed a CR.42 shot down during this combat, while two more were claimed damaged by other 261 Sqn pilots, though possibly the first claim related to *serg. magg.* Arnaldo Sala's aircraft on the earlier sortie. On this occasion only one Hurricane was claimed shot down by the 23° *Gr.*, *serg. magg.* Raffaele Marzocca of the 74ª *Sq.* making the claim, while a second was claimed by the gunners of the 30° *Stormo*'s bombers. Two more Hurricanes were claimed as 'probables' by the pilots of the 23° *Gr.* jointly. It seems that no British fighters were actually lost or damaged on this occasion. The 23° *Gr.* suffered no losses in this occasion while the 30° *Stormo* lost the plane of *s. ten.* Gaio Del Cerro (crew: *serg.* Giovanni Lazzari, *Primo Aviere Motorista* Vasco Ventura, *Primo Aviere Marconista* Italo De Rui, *Aviere Scelto Armiere* Luigi Conti, *Aviere Scelto Armiere* Ovidio Venanzi – the body of Venanzi was found later and buried in St. Andrew's Cemetery), clearly the victim of Robertson, and another plane was obliged to force-land on the volcanic island of Linosa (and presumably written off after landing).

29 November 1940

Menastir M was bombed at 07:00 and a CR.42 of the 94ª *Sq.* was slightly damaged by splinters (RS).

ITALO - BRITISH BATTLES
13 Sept 1940 - 9 Feb 1941

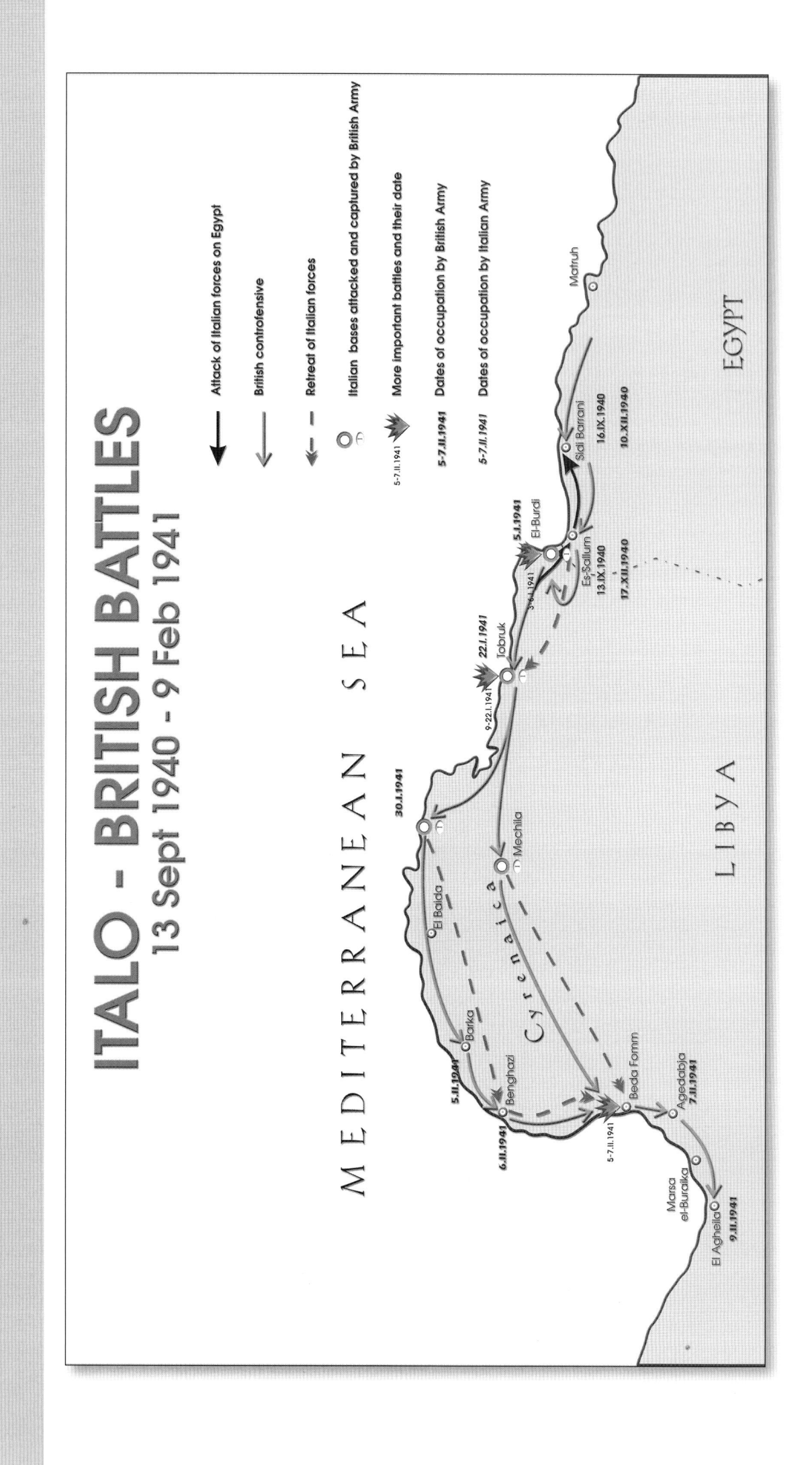

Index

A

Abbarchi, Rovero 5, 84, 87, 152, 168, 171
Abbs, Len 147
Abrahams, R. J 138, 139, 172, 196
Abu Rabia, Muhammed Ibrahim 24
Accorsi, Giovanni 124
Acworth, Richard 2, 14, 76, 114, 170, 172, 174, 175, 196
Agnelli, Angelo 187
Agnelli, Carlo 58, 166, 178, 196, 197
Albertini, Carlo 123, 138, 155, 168
Alcock 121, 132
Aldis 84, 88, 89
Alesi, Omero 7, 85, 136
Alington 45, 152
Alliata, Emilio 162
Allison, John William 29
Allison, T. 158
Ambrosi, Ottorino 124, 169, 171
Ammannato, Athos 155
Anderson, Donald Stanley 200
Andreani, Luigi 140
Andrich, Alvise 124, 143, 144
Angelini, Armando 4
Angelin, Piero 76
Angeloni, Antonio 178
Annoni, Emanuele 58, 153
Antonicelli, Orazio 4
Antonini, Adorno 169, 170
Arabito, Angelo 136
Aramu, Mario 125, 145, 147, 186
Archbell 38, 43
Argenton, Alberto 4, 5, 19, 28, 45
Armanino, Luigi 184
Arnaud 66, 67
Arrabito, Guglielmo 5, 51, 84, 85
Arragona, Raffaele 111
Arthur, Wilfred 97, 130, 156, 183, 189, 192
Asperges, Giuseppe 159
Atti 46
Aurili, Giuseppe 59, 84, 85, 86, 90, 98, 99, 136, 138, 143
Azzarone, Edoardo 4, 37, 38

B

Baccara, Marcello 34
Bacchilega, Salvo 77
Bacchione, Paolo 186
Bacich, Mario 4, 19, 60
Bacon, J.C. 45
Baculo, Calcedonio 10
Bagatta, Aristide 10
Bain, R.A. 132
Bainville, Rougevin 65
Baird-Smith, M.J. 182
Baker 187
Baker, Benjamin Thomas Morgan 43
Balbo, Italo 29, 33, 43, 44, 45, 46, 51, 52, 53, 55, 56, 72, 127, 220
Baldin, Filippo 6, 35, 51
Balestrero, Renato 141
Balistro, Alessandro 52

Ballan, Mario 78
Ballatore, André 20
Bandini, Mario 6, 39
Banks, Edwin 76, 138, 139, 172
Baptizet, Georges 25
Barba, Giuseppe 34
Barber, James Douglas 54
Barbetta 158
Barbieri 11
Barcaro, Giovanni 59, 98, 148, 149, 153
Bardellini, Giuseppe 186
Barioglio 33
Barion 135
Barker, George 14
Baron, Georges 16, 48
Bartin, Danilo 86
Bartley, Leonard 133, 196
Basoli, Pietro 111
Basso, Leone 5, 87, 144
Bateson, R.N. 145, 148
Battaglia, Carlo 58, 104, 166
Battaini, Luigi 59
Bax, A. R. G. 14, 22, 63, 99, 111, 117, 132, 148
Baxter, H. J. 103
Beauclair, D. 30
Beccaria, Francesco 9
Beduz, Giovanni 5, 87, 152
Bellando 17
Bellotto, Mario 11
Beltramini 169
Beluche 49
Benati, Amedeo 5
Benbow 182, 189
Benco, Rodolfo 124
Benedetti, Giovanni 7, 10, 38, 40, 77, 84, 90, 112, 136, 166
Bennett 29
Bennett, R. J. 14, 63, 69, 138, 139, 196
Benson 30, 73, 190
Benvenuti 135
Berghino 139
Bernardi, Duilio 4, 28
Bernardiello, Mario 121
Berni, Ezio 10, 133
Bertelli, Erminio 10, 75
Bertinelli, Italo 4, 19, 28, 32, 45, 82
Bertinelli, Libero 151
Berti, Paolo 94, 136, 138, 147
Bertoli, Giovanni 112
Bester 195
Bevan-John, D. R. S. 44, 103
Bevilacqua, Domenico 5, 57, 69, 70, 91, 145, 168, 171, 172, 173, 191
Bevington-Smith, Eric 28, 132
Biagini, Bruno 59
Bianchelli, Giovanni 98, 158
Biffani, Guglielmo 58, 134, 141, 154, 155
Biggins, George Kenneth 54
Bigliardi, Arturo 169, 170

Bilancia, Antonio 136
Billi, Danilo 4, 19, 27, 64, 68, 165
Biseo, Attilio 77, 133, 155
Bissoli, Gioacchino 4, 19, 28, 30, 37, 64
Black 23, 49, 51
Bladelli, Alessandro 7, 39, 84, 85, 103, 136, 199
Blain 48
Blair, Ian "Jock" 132
Bobba, Guido 199, 202, 203
Bocking, Alfred 79, 128
Bogoni, Gino 124, 168
Boldi, Massimo 77
Bolingbroke, Hale Winter 13, 39
Bonfanti, Clemente 4
Bonfatti, Pietro 58, 196, 200
Bonino, Eugenio 168
Bonoli, Riccardo 6
Bonuti, Aldo 124
Bordigato, Antonio 139
Borello, Mario 51
Borgonovo, Pierino 121
Bortolani 201
Bortoletti, Bruno 7, 84, 97, 136, 138
Bosinelli, Giorgio 136
Bottà, Giuseppe 5, 35, 192
Bottazzi, Alberto 165
Botti, Enrico 5, 191
Botto, Ernesto 3, 57, 59, 60, 92, 98, 99, 111, 135, 138, 140, 148, 160, 189, 196, 198, 218
Boudier 66, 67
Boulton 13
Bouyer 49
Bower, Peter 28, 29
Bowker 166
Bowker, W. F. 150, 164
Boyd, Alan 97, 130, 131, 183, 189, 192, 193, 194
Bozzolan, Irzio 124, 168
Bracco 55
Bracegirdle, B. L. 97, 131, 183, 190
Bradde 47
Branch 158
Brandi, Raffaele 187
Brescianini, Venanzio 10, 33
Bressanelli, Luigi 10, 78
Brian 145, 165
Brigadue, Dario 88, 89
Broganelli, Vittorio 41
Brokensha 67, 68
Brookes 145
Brooks 24
Brown 13, 69
Brown, Harry 128, 172
Browne, G. R. 83
Browning 29
Brownrigg, I. 161
Bruen 67, 68, 120
Brunetti 152
Bruschi, Ottorino 47
Bryant, R. F. 202
Buisson 33

Bulgarelli, Loris 140
Buri, Arduino 33, 43
Burnard 194
Burroni, Mario 7, 140
Burston 201
Burt, Christopher Frederick 79
Burwell 97, 100
Buscaglia, Carlo Emanuele 95, 112, 118, 141, 143, 151, 184, 189
Busi, Ilario 140
Butcher 14

C

Cabassi, Giulio Cesare 32, 83
Cagna, Stefano 33, 40, 46
Caiazzo, Camillo 169, 173
Calafiore, Salvatore 186
Calmel 49
Calorbe, J-B 20
Calosso, Carlo 123, 124, 168, 174
Calzolai, Gastone 143
Cambon 16
Camedda, Antonio 76
Camerini, Antonio 124
Campanini, Nino 123, 168, 192
Campbell, D. A. 89
Campbell 80, 96
Campbell, "Willy" 51, 55
Campione, Fortunato 131
Campolo, Vincenzo 5, 191
Canaponi 169, 170
Canè 46
Cannaviello, Vittorio 70, 71
Cannepele, Luigi 123, 168
Cantarella 61
Cantelli, Romolo 98, 100
Capellini 47
Caporali, Ruggero 7, 98, 136, 138
Cappelletti, Pietro 52
Caprini, Antonio 151
Carabini, Angelo 190
Carapezza, Enrico 78
Cardano, Arturo 4, 27, 53, 68
Cardascia, Martino 52
Caretti, Vittorio 136
Carli 186
Carli, Oscar 186
Carlone, Francesco 47
Carmenati, Giuseppe 187
Carminati, Angelo 34
Caroppi, Ambrogio 187
Carta, Dino 123
Carter 21
Caruso, Albino 136
Casadei, Aldo 190
Casbolt, Charles 14, 181
Casciani 138
Casero, Giovanni 94
Cassano 138
Cassinelli, Guglielmo 18, 69
Cassone, Domenico 189
Castellani, Bruno 124
Catania, Carmelo 48, 123, 161, 162, 168
Cater, Leslie 152
Cathill 156
Causa, Sebastiano 187
Cèard, Vittorio 115
Cecchi, Trento 4, 19, 27, 64, 68, 69, 70

Celotto, Bruno 124, 168
Cenni, Giuseppe 202
Ceoletta, Giovanni Battista 7, 19, 35, 88
Cerne, Bruno 10, 53, 71
Cerofolini, Gilberto 2, 6, 51, 143, 147, 148, 192
Cerutti, Marziale 46
Cesare, Giulio 83, 113, 123, 190
Chaïla, L. 20
Chalandre 72
Chapman 14
Chatterley, Horace Turner 67
Chauby 48
Cheesman, N. A. F. 117
Cherry 29, 35
Chessa 39
Chianese, Raffaele 2, 3, 4, 5, 6, 7, 8, 56, 58, 59, 60, 61, 90, 91, 106, 107, 153, 154, 155, 178, 200
Chiarini, Guglielmo 5, 19, 50, 51, 84, 85, 144, 145, 168, 172, 173, 178, 191, 192
Chiarmetta, Cesare 123, 190
Chichester 156
Childs 164
Cholmeley, Anthony Hugh 14, 105, 139
Chopin 49
Christian 73
Ciapetti, Alfonso 201
Cibrario 76
Cicognani, Eugenio 124
Cima 76
Cima, Natale 5, 82, 83, 87, 192
Cirillo, Angelo 20
Civale, Giovanni 11
Clarke 29
Clarke, John 14, 135, 139
Clarke, Robert Hugh 14, 99, 133, 138, 139, 172
Clarke, William Charles 149, 150
Clayson, D. 164
Cleaver, John Sisman 145
Clisby, W. H. 187, 203
Clostre, Daniel 64, 128
Cocchia, Enzo 12
Cochrane, Homer 14, 99
Coco, Matteo 121
Colauzzi, Davide 124, 169, 171, 173
Colavolpe, Giuseppe 61, 95
Collard 182
Colli, Egisto 121
Collins 11, 21, 35
Collishaw, Raymond 13, 27, 32, 62, 117, 133, 170
Colocci, Pericle 141
Colpi, Alfonso 135
Como, Cesare 113
Contarini, Luigi 123
Conti, Luigi 203
Cooles 201
Cooper, Samuel 135, 181
Cooper, S. G. 84
Copeland, John King 36
Copello, Carlo 95, 112, 143, 151, 184, 189
Copersino, Vito 4, 45
Coppi, Giovanni 10, 134, 145, 147, 186

Coppola, Sante 111
Corbia, Raffaele 77
Corda, Virgilio 38
Corradeghini, Colombo 187
Corsi, Ugo 6, 41, 42, 49
Costa, Giuseppe 169, 170, 173
Costa, Umberto 47
Costantini, Giuseppe 124
Costanzo 152
Costello 13, 35, 45, 86, 87, 196
Costello, Alfred 45
Cottali di Vignale, Raniero 141
Cottingham, Leonard 2, 13, 68, 69
Couchman, R. A 13, 35, 45
Coudray, Christian 20
Coughlan, E. 120, 164
Couppel de Saint-Front, Durand 17
Couturier, L. 20
Covacovich, Nicola 151
Cowlishaw, John George 80
Cox, R. B 29, 45, 52, 148
Craig, J. 13, 36, 37, 45, 54
Craven 24
Cremona, Giacomo 34
Crestani, Onorino 123
Crociati, Silvio 7, 52
Crohill, Alfred Francis 43
Crosara, 33
Cucchi 76
Cudugnello, Bruno 7, 49, 55, 88, 89
Cullen, Nigel 159
Cullimore, Edward Lionel 39, 165
Cunningham, Andrew 72, 83, 116, 119, 120, 143, 163, 185, 190
Cunteri 139, 147
Currey 182
Curto, Mario 155
Cuscuna, Francesco 184

D

Da Dalt, Luigi 155
Dadone 46
D'Agostinis, Giuseppe 7, 42, 51, 59, 90, 98, 103, 104, 136, 138
Dahl, Roald 146
Dall'Aglio, Giuseppe 5, 64, 84, 85, 168
Dallamore, J. W. 13, 28, 35, 129, 182
Dalla Pasqua, Andrea 34, 138
Dallari, Enrico 58, 104, 110, 111
Damiani, Rinaldo 196
Davico, Dante 6, 168, 172
Davidson, J. M. 97, 157, 183
Davies, John Scott 36
Davies, P. F. O. 103
Davison 14, 29
Davison, T. H. 194
Davy 15, 24
Dawes, Elias 184
Day 29
Dean, Ernest 2, 13, 35, 36, 37, 45, 54, 55, 86, 87, 195
Dearnley 73
De Barbieri 51
De Bellis, Ernesto 146, 155, 190
De Benedetti, Neri 7, 84, 90, 136, 166
De Campo, Valerio 58, 104, 111, 153, 154, 196
De Cosa 54, 55
De Fazio, Vincenzo 86

De Fraia, Nunzio 4, 42, 53, 68, 69, 70
de la Hoyde 14
de La Salle, Legrix 15
De Lauzières de Themines, Flotard 43
Del Cerro, Gaio 203
Della Minerva, Enrico Maramaldo 10
Della Rovere, Marcello 5
Dell'Oro, Antonio 7, 43, 55, 98, 100, 155, 158, 159
Del Zotto 94
De Martis, Ottavio 131
De Mattia, Pietro 10
De Mongolfier 67
Deodato, Corrado 137, 143
De Place 24
Dequal, Vicenzo 95, 112, 151, 155
De Rui, Italo 203
De Sidour, J. J. B 181
de Soras, Veyre 16
De Tecini 49
De Vivo, Francesco 43
Dews 29
Di Carlo, Rosario 168, 190
Di Donna, Nunzio 111
Di Francesco 139
Di Gianpaolo, Giuseppe 186
Di Giglio, Nicola 83
Di Giulio, Giorgio 123
D'Ignazio 152
Di Lorenzo, Luigi 4, 28
Di Nardo, Giuseppe 121
D'Ippolito, Pasquale 155
Di Trapani, Antonio 119
Dittadi, Alfonso 187
Di Tullio, Armando 71
Dobson, J. 30
Dodsworth, R. 29
Domenici, Adolfo 11
Donaldson, George Millar 14, 133, 196
Donda, Silvano 186
Dondi, Giuseppe 143
Donelly, N. P. 43
Doolin, E. 80
Dorance, Michel 25
D'Orazio, Paolo 111
Douet, P. 152
Dowding, P. T. 14, 105, 107, 109, 113, 185
Draghelli, Enrico 155
Drago, Carlo 34
Dragone, Vincenzo 70
Drougue 49
Druce, David Mervyn Boughey 163
Dudgeon 129, 156
Duff, B. B. E. 14, 99, 172, 175, 176, 177
Duffy 161
Dugoujon 66, 73
Dundas 86
Dunn, Patrick 62, 95, 104, 105, 106, 109, 110, 164
Dunod 66
Durand, Renè 16, 17
Durrant 166
Duval 68
Dyson, Charles 195

E
Easton 73

East, V. 97
Ellerton, M. D. 97, 131, 183, 190
Ellis, K. H. E. 199
Elstub 182
Erasi, Massimiliano 10, 155, 162, 184
Ercolani, Ercolano 131
Erzetti, Mirko 98
Esposito, Ubaldo 135
Evans, Charles 119, 131, 162, 187
Evers-Swindell, Ralph 14, 21, 47, 95, 105, 106, 107, 109, 195

F
Fabbricatore, Mario 5, 135
Fabiani, Fulvio 169, 170
Fabozzi 83
Fabre 66
Falasco, Albino 6
Falconi, Tito 199, 201, 202, 203
Fallavena 47
Falsini, Medardo 151
Falzoni 115
Fanali, Duilio 7, 9, 20, 41, 46, 60, 94, 98, 99, 100, 158, 159
Fargnoli, Ottorino 199
Farina, Francesco 169
Farries, Stuart Maxwell 141, 184
Fasce 115
Fassi, Roberto 58, 103, 148, 166, 196, 198
Fattoretto 64
Fausti, Agostino 5, 53, 54, 57, 68, 69, 70, 71
Fedele, Mario 5, 53, 84
Federici, Angelo 4, 5, 69, 70
Federigi, Fortunato 165
Feldman, Bernard Alfred 29
Feldon 78
Ferguson, M. S. 29
Ferrandi, Attilio 112
Ferrario, Luigi 7, 85, 86
Ferrero, Antonio 135
Ferrero, Francesco 83
Ferrero, Mario 123, 148, 149, 150, 168, 171, 172, 190
Ferri, Alfio 61, 170, 187
Ferrulli, Leonardo 7, 136, 138
Festa, Valentino 94, 164
Finch 23, 28, 29
Fiorani, Fausto 34
Fioravante, Nicola 86, 98
Fiore, Stefano 124
Fiorito, Natale 7
Fisher 29
Fisher, Herbert Paul Greenwood 88
Fletcher, Ronald 184
Floreani, Ciro 77
Flower, Wanklyn 14, 47, 105, 107, 109, 199
Fogliata, Paolo 86
Folinea, Riccardo 10
Ford 43, 116, 182
Forlini, Guido 159
Forte, Ferri 61, 138, 170
Foschi 46
Fossetta, Marcello 94, 138
Fox, B. J. 161
Fox, Michael Frederick Henry 29, 39, 80
Fox, Stanley George 29

Francis, G. 14, 43, 44, 63, 80, 156
Franco, 40
Franco, Guido 112
Fraser, Joseph 14, 62, 69, 81, 82, 114, 133, 138, 139, 169, 172, 174, 175, 187, 190, 199
Frigerio, Jacopo 59, 98, 196
Frigo, Giuseppe 5
Fry, Charles 14, 114, 138, 139
Fucile, Manfredo 135
Fugaroli, Giuseppe 71
Fuini, Nando 52
Furia, Toaldo 114
Furini, Giovanni 139
Fusco, Enrico 95, 112

G
Gabrielli, Umberto 187
Gaden, Charles 97, 130, 131, 183, 189, 190
Galimberti, Rinaldo 126
Gallaway 164
Gallerani, Giovanni 58
Gallina 43
Galvino 58
Gamna, Giuseppe 187
Gardanne 48
Garrand-Cole, E. 80
Garretto, Gustavo 34
Garrisi, Stefano 38
Garside 75
Garside, K. V. 44, 89, 156
Gasperoni, Germano 200
Gatti 94
Gatward, Alan 97, 131, 183, 194
Geiger, R. 20
Gelli, Faliero 201
Gensoul, Marcel-Bruno 64, 65, 67
Gerrett 67
Gherardelli, Narciso 121
Ghezzi, Alessandro 187
Ghidini, Giuseppe 78
Ghiotti, Sereno 189
Giannini, Giovanni 201
Giannotti, Luigi 147, 148
Giansante, Renato 6, 35
Giardini 94
Gibbs 28, 36
Giglioli 116
Gillanders 182
Gino, Santo 8, 58, 104, 110, 154, 196
Giorchino, Luciano 187
Giorgio, Tommaso 169, 170
Giovacchini 88, 103
Girolami, Victor Hugo 126
Gisbert 68
Gisclon 73
Giuliani, Giuliano 78
Giunchi, Walter 141
Glen 21, 201
Glover, Harry 67
Gnudi, Vittorio 123, 165
Gobbi, Riccardo 155
Godfroy-Fausset 73
Godrich, Ambrose Sydney Barnard 29, 149, 150
Goggi 152
Golden, G. R. 203
Golding 182
Golino, Angelo 59, 98, 148, 149

Golino, Salvatore 187
Gon, Aldo 58, 60, 61, 143, 178, 196, 197, 198
Goodchild, Harry 13, 195
Goodman, H. R. 29, 146
Gordon 2, 86, 97, 118, 132, 136, 138, 143, 146, 148, 150, 152, 156, 157, 166, 167, 182, 183, 185, 189, 190, 194
Gordon-Finlayson, James Richmond 86, 118, 132, 136, 143, 146, 148, 150, 152, 167, 182, 185
Gorgone, Guglielmo 4, 42, 45, 163
Gori, Renato 123, 168
Gostini, Saverio 94, 163
Graham, Greg 2, 14, 70, 105, 108, 109, 181
Granci, Guerrino 189
Grandinetti, Michele 59, 92, 143
Grandjacquet, Guglielmo 126
Grant 31
Gras 67
Gray-Worcester, Anthony 14, 63, 69, 81
Graziani, Rodolfo 53, 56, 220
Green 182
Green, Roy Leslie 13, 41, 42
Green, G. E. P. 161
Greenhalgh, John 203
Gregnanin, Gregorio 111
Gregory, Donald 14, 105, 135
Grieve 119
Grieve, K. C. 83
Griffaldi 134
Griffith 73
Grundy, Thomas Albert 80
Guerci, Mario 58
Guerci, Piero 187
Guidi, Amedeo 123, 199
Guidoni 140, 186
Guidozzi 116
Guiducci, Giovanni 7, 35, 43, 52, 84, 85, 86, 90, 104, 110, 116, 136, 138
Guillaume, Edmond 25
Guillet, Paolo 7
Guilloux 48
Guizzardi, Rinaldo 140
Gullà, Giuseppe 34
Gulli, Mario 10

H

Hale, Leslie Charles Major 39, 184
Hall, Harry 160
Hamilton, Walter V. 200
Hancorn 166
Harris, Frederick 184
Harrison, G. W. 121
Harrison, Henry 14, 54, 133, 141
Hart 11, 186, 205
Harvey 27
Hawkins, G. E. 13, 41
Hayter, F. E. G. 129
Hazlitt 80
Heath, P. R. 97, 131, 189, 192, 193, 195
Hébrard 67
Helfield, J. E. 112
Heme 66
Hewett, Edward 14

Hickey, William 95, 137, 181, 185
Hogg 152, 162, 189
Hohler, C. G 22, 128
Holman, Frank 172, 195
Holmes 201
Hook, I. 149
Hosquet, Piero 124, 169, 171
How, H. A. W. 29
Howarth, T. S. M. 46, 51
Hulbert, J. C. 14
Humpries 67
Hunter 67
Hutchinson 132
Hutt, S. L. 142, 143
Huvet 66

I

Iannaci, Aldo 7, 18, 217
Innes-Smith 88
Innocenti 115
Invernici 55
Invorti, Guerino 169
Italiano, Paolo 159

J

Jacquier, Paul 20, 96, 128
Jarvis 139
Jenkins 146
Jobson, James 145
Johnson, D. V 13, 36, 41
Johnstone, M. 201
Jolivet 68
Jonas, R. C 14, 62
Jones 148
Jones, Colin James Cambell 103
Jones, Edward „Tap" 14, 22, 181
Jones, G. D. 99
Jopling 201
Joubert, Frederick Johannes 195
Judge, J. W. B. 13, 63, 76
Juggins, James George 54

K

Kavanagh 29
Keighly-Peach, Charles 76, 77, 78, 114, 119, 120
Keily, Gerald Barnard 144, 145
Keith, Kenneth 76, 77, 78, 89, 113, 114
Keller, Ernesto 7
Kerr 163, 181
Kettlewell, George 14, 185
Kilroy, Robin 131
King 35, 36, 51, 55, 84
Kirkman 158
Kirton, J. H. 78, 118
Klines, Maurice 29, 39, 80
Klinger, Umberto 133, 155
Knott, Ralph Harry 54
Knowles, L. E. 97, 131, 157, 183

L

Labanti 58
Labanti, Dante 58
Labit 17
Lacampagne 49
La Carruba, Vincenzo 4, 53, 136, 137, 138, 140, 141
Lachaux 66
Lacoste 16

Lainé 156
Lalatta, Ippolito 5, 82, 83, 168, 171
Lallier 72
Lamb 158
La Meslée, Marin 25
Lamiot 26
Lamour-Zevacco, Albert 64
Lampugnani, Giovanni 47
Lancaster, Johnny 14, 97, 98, 100
Lancia, Ottorino 4
Landolfi, Antonio 55
Lanfranco, Aldo 6, 51, 85, 86
Lapsley, John 14, 47, 95, 113, 114, 115, 135, 139
Larsimont Pergameni, Antonio 59, 98, 99, 148, 196
Lauchard, Arturo 114, 115
Lauri, Furio 124, 159
Lavelli, Franco 4, 27, 42, 53, 57, 68, 69, 70
Lax 182
Lay, D. J. H. 129
Lazzari, Giovanni 203
Lea, Derryk Austin 79
Leardi, Ugo 151
Leatham 119
Leatherbarrow 76
Lebois 64
Lebois, Marcel 64
Le Dieu 79
Lee, George Herbert 200
Legge 63, 85, 146, 164
Leghissa, Riccardo 135
Le Gloan, Pierre 25
Legrand 67
Le Moal 26
Lendaro, Roberto 4, 19, 37, 45, 64, 82
Le Nigen, Edouard 25
Lenon 182
Lenzi 55
Leonardi, Giuseppe 10, 77
Leoni, Alcide 59, 109
Le Saint 50
Le Stum 67
Leveille, Edmond Kidder 13, 172
Lidonici 169
Lidstone, R. 53
Li Greci, Aldo 34
Linnard, Sidney 14, 105, 108, 109, 110, 111, 149, 181
Lioi, Antonio 190
Lisardi, Luigi 7, 9
Littler, John 13, 172
Locatelli, Bruno 124, 144, 161, 167, 169, 171, 173
Lockyer, T. M. 21
Loioli, Aldo 5
Longmore, Arthur 32, 55, 62, 95, 130, 157, 180
Lord 135, 139
Lorenzoni, Lorenzo 203
Lorenzoni, Virgilio 189
Lovato, Bruno 47
Lowe 131, 152, 162, 187
Lowe, Leslie 121
Lualdi, Angelo 10, 133
Lucato, Sergio 201
Lucchini, Franco 7, 35, 44, 45, 85, 86, 88, 97, 98, 99, 103, 136, 138
Ludrini, Carlo 51

Lulan 32
Luthereau 16
Lylian, J. C. J 64
Lynch, A. H. 41
Lywood 89

M
Macadre 72
MacBride, T. 45
Macchetti, Vittorio 51
Macerati, Mario 139
Macina, Francesco 52
Mackie, John 195
Madon, Michel 24
Madri, Rocco 52
Maggi, Giacomo 4, 32, 42
Maggini, Renzo 7, 35, 52, 153
Magliacane, Alfonso 135
Magnabosco, Dario 5, 85
Magrì, Giuseppe 10, 75, 116
Mainardis, Fausto 52
Mandolini, Orlando 57, 64, 82, 83
Manfroi, Alfredo 119
Mannu, Augusto 4
Marangoni, Danilo 190
Marazio, Giovanni 137, 143
Marcantoni 152
Marchi, Carlo 168
Marchi, Roberto 123, 168, 171, 173
Marcovich, Riccardo 4, 28, 53
Marcucci 170
Marden, R. A. 84
Marinelli, Vincenzo 86
Mariotti, Cherubino 169, 170, 171
Marlow, Frank 135, 139
Marpole 132
Marroni, Virgilio 159
Marsan, Simeone 124, 168
Marshall, John Roy 121
Martina, Mario 151
Martinelli 33, 169
Martinelli, Ludovico 51
Martinoli, Teresio 3, 34, 123, 168, 171, 173, 192
Martin, Richard Maurice Scott 201
Martire, Elio 94
Marzocca, Raffaele 2, 203
Masenti, Ezio 152
Masoero 71, 139
Masone, Eustachio 139
Mason, Ernest 14, 195
Mason, R. W. 132
Mason, Walter Ronald Price Knight 54
Masserini 46
Massy, Patrick 89
Matacena, Armando 58
Matriciardi 158, 174
Mattei, Alfonso 201
Maurer, Sergio 94
Mauri 143
Mauriello, Giuseppe 59, 153
Mayer-Ziotti, 10
Mayer-Ziotti, Arturo 165
Mazzotti 34
McCall 162
McCue 88
McGarry 29
McGarry, J. 161
McGinn, B. J. 128

McIntosh, J. 99
McKechnie, W. N. 129
McKinley, D. C. 64
McLachlan, Ian 97, 183, 188
McNulty, Thomas Arthur 150
McWhinnie, A. 103
Meadowcroft, Kenneth Herbert 152
Meadows, A. C. 71
Mechelli, Salvatore 5, 82, 83, 84, 192
Méhault 26
Méheut 26
Meille, Valdo 155
Melchiorri 39
Melley, Franco 95
Menzies, Guy Lambton 24, 78, 103, 141, 184
Merton 182
Metcalfe, E. M 121
Meyer 75
Mezzatesta, Giuseppe 98
Migliorato, Lorenzo 7, 19, 85, 98
Milella, Fiorenzo 123, 168
Mills 31
Minelli, Gustavo 59
Mingozzi, Renato 124, 168
Minicillo, Francesco 135
Minotta, Orazio 135
Minton, Rolfe Vivian 165
Miotto, Elio 7, 39, 84, 85, 136
Mirfin 145
Mittelhauser 20
Moci, Paolo 165
Molino, Pietro 7, 94
Molteni 46
Monk 13
Monraisse 67, 68
Monselesan, Renzo 113
Montanari 138
Montanari, Alberto 58
Montanari, Fioravante 98
Monterumici, Amleto 7, 52, 98, 103, 116
Monti, Nadio 4, 42, 45, 132, 163
Monti, Ezio 6, 18, 41, 51, 84, 85, 98, 103, 104, 136, 138, 153, 184
Monti, Luigi 6, 18, 41, 51, 84, 85, 98, 103, 104, 136, 138, 153
Moran 46
Morana, Francesco 123, 165
Moresco, Alberto 94
Moresi, Armando 153, 154, 178, 196, 198
Moretti, Luigi 40
Moroso, Luigi 36
Morris, T. C. 14, 43, 46, 158
Mosele, Marcello 168
Mouliérac 17
Muldowney, John Felix 163
Munro, J. 142, 143
Muratori, Vittorio 146
Murray, Thomas 80
Musch, Gerardo 6, 18, 41, 51, 84, 85, 98, 103, 104, 136, 138, 153
Mussi 115
Musumeci, Mario 10

Muti, Ettore 165
Muto, Ferdinando 135

N
Nacher, Emilio 186
Nanin, Francesco 6, 85, 168, 172, 173, 192
Nanni, Ubaldo 159
Nante, Ugo 52
Napoleoni, Italo 125, 169
Napoli, Silvio 9, 38, 75, 94, 133, 145
Negus, Geoffrey Edward 36
Nencini, Walter 139
Neroni 143
Nicholas Benjamin Edwin 184
Nicholas, Harry Francis Alfred 29, 39, 80
Nicholetts, G. E. 15, 51, 132
Nicola, Emiro 2, 6, 20, 83, 86, 103, 151
Nicolai, Nicola 20
Nicolls, O. J. Roger 162, 186
Nicoloso, Mario 123, 191
Nicolson, R. H. 29
Niggi, Maurizio 10
Nioi, Clizio 49
Niven, George 80
Noble 29
Noble, Alexander Laird Milne 201
Noble, B. 161
Noden 182
Notari, Alfonso 4, 132
Novelli, Raffaello 59, 98

O
Oakley, S. 116
Oblach, Giuseppe 56, 58, 59, 91, 200
Oliphant, R. H. H. L. 119
Ongaro 75
Organo 39, 117
Orgaro, Vittorio 140
Ornani 79
Orofino, Giovanni 94
Orr, Stanley 141, 152, 186, 187, 189, 203
Osborne, Ralph Paul Joseph 38, 80
Owen, H. J. 14, 30, 63, 69, 70, 82

P
Pacifici, Alfredo 169, 173
Padalino, Mario 169
Padovani, Piero 155
Padovano, Giuseppe 83
Pagano 164
Pagliacci, Giuseppe 10, 104
Pandini 140
Paolazzi, Bruno 58, 112, 113
Paolini, Ernesto 5, 19, 84, 121, 168, 172
Paparatti, Guido 124
Pappalepore, Gianni 98, 186
Paroli, Orfeo 124
Pascali, Giuseppe 38
Pastorelli, Giancandido 133, 136, 140
Pastorelli, Guido 155
Pastorelli, Roberto 46, 51
Patch, Oliver 117
Patellani 63
Patrizi, Corrado 6, 39, 45
Patterson, Thomas 195

Pattle, Thomas 3, 11, 12, 14, 22, 47, 62, 97, 98, 100, 102, 103, 105, 106, 108, 109, 115, 139, 181
Pavan, Ernesto 4, 37, 38, 42, 45, 132
Peacock 73
Pearce, S. N 88, 136
Pearsons 143
Pecoraro, Gregorio 55
Pellicioli, Giorgio 201
Pelly, Blake 97, 130, 131, 157, 183, 189, 192, 193, 194
Pelosi, Enrico 187
Pelo, Stefano 159, 187
Pendleton 67
Perdoni, Luciano 153, 178
Perno, Paolo 98, 100, 186
Péronne, Antoine 20
Perotti, Otello 59, 98
Perrin, John 97, 131, 157, 183
Perry, John Campbell 13, 120, 165, 172
Perversi, Gianfranco 123, 168, 171, 172, 173
Pesola, Giuseppe 184
Pettinelli, Romeo 140
Pezzè, Vittorio 56, 58, 103, 104, 111, 134, 141, 153
Pezzi, Enrico 155
Phillips 190
Phillips, H. 203
Pian 115
Piazza, Guido 4
Piccolomini, Ranieri 4, 32, 37, 38, 42, 44, 45, 92, 93, 159, 163
Pieri, Giorgio 162
Pike, D. 53
Pillepich, Narciso 6, 41, 42, 136
Pinna, Pietro 135
Piragino, Armando 6, 7, 41, 42, 49
Pitt, W. J. 103
Piva, Antonio 77
Pluda, Mario 178, 196, 198
Plumbeau, Camille 25
Poggi 34
Poggi, Casio 5, 192
Poli, Lido 58, 104, 108, 110
Politi, Bruno 94
Pollard, V. 142, 143
Pompéi, Jean 64
Porro, Felice 4, 9, 52, 133, 174
Porta 55
Porta, Franco 6, 84, 144, 147, 148
Portalis 66, 67, 73
Potter, K. D. 161
Powning, Richard John Redfern 84
Pozzati, Mario 10
Pozzati, Vittorio 58, 196, 198
Pozza, Ugo 70, 71
Pozzo, Mariuccio 118
Prati, Luigi 123, 138
Preston 13, 45, 85
Price 165
Price, W. D. 103
Price-Owen, W. B. 14, 63, 69, 70, 82
Pricolo, Francesco 33, 122, 143, 150
Primatesta, Paolo 186
Profumi, Fortunato 10
Proner, Luigi 164
Pucci, Edvige 125

Pugnali, Silvio 10
Pulzetti 82
Putzu, Francesco 59, 196, 197, 198

Q
Querci, Alvaro 58, 104, 110, 178
Quick, Lyon Curtis 165

R
Radice, Alberto 4
Raiteri, Pietro 186
Ramberto, Mario 190
Ranieri, Corrado 4, 32, 37, 42, 44, 45, 58, 92, 93, 159, 163
Ranzi, Timo 77
Raspini, Domenico 110
Rawlinson, Alan 97, 130, 131, 157, 183, 192, 193, 194
Ray 182
Recagno, Diego 4, 10, 71, 145
Redfern 29, 84
Regoli 47
Reiner, Giulio 58, 160, 178, 198
Remorino, Alberto 10, 71
Renzi, Norino 58, 104, 106, 110, 111
Revetria, Secondo 4, 5, 84, 137, 138, 139, 143, 147, 152, 191, 192
Rew, Kenneth Russell 14, 97, 100
Reynolds, John Harry 132
Richens, Sidney 14, 105, 109
Richmond 132, 148
Ricotti, Annibale 124, 143, 144, 190
Riddler, Thomas Frank 67
Ridgeway 145
Rigby, J. 150
Rinaldi, Vito 2, 5
Riosa, Giovanni 119
Rixson 28, 31
Rizzati, Graziadio 58, 103
Rizzotto, Ugo 135
Roberts 159, 162
Roberts, Eric Samuel 141
Robertson 203, 208
Robinson, Henry 29
Robone, Guido 95, 112, 117, 137, 143, 151, 184
Roggero, Giovanni 140
Rolfc 145, 146, 162, 164, 165, 181
Romagnoli, Carlo 42, 59, 78, 85, 87, 90, 92, 98, 104, 110, 135, 136, 138
Romandini, Vittorio 7, 39, 106
Romeo, Sebastiano 126, 140, 187, 220
Ronzan, Ferruccio 111
Rooper 201
Rosa, Aldo 7, 90, 104, 110, 199
Ross, A. M. 2, 14, 63, 133
Rossi, Giuseppe 10, 77, 98, 99, 100
Rossi, Pasquale 58
Rousseauu-Dumarcet 15
Roux 49
Royle, William Charles 43
Ruchoux 67
Ruffilli, Mario 58, 196
Ruggieri, Luigi 75
Ruggiero, Giovanni 125, 169, 170
Rusconi, Alessandro 7
Ruzzene, Alessandro 4, 19, 27, 53
Ryley, Charles 21, 63, 83, 96, 195

S
Sabatini 143
Sabey 201
Sacchetti, Raimondo 44, 155, 190
Sacchi 158
Sagliaschi, Enio 51
Sala, Arnaldo 202, 203
Salès 67
Saleun 35
Salvaneschi, Aldo 187
Salvatore, Massimo 58, 59, 98
Salvetti, Gregorio Tommaso 190
Salvi, Bruno 4
Sansone, Vincenzo 4
Santavacca, Italo 5, 50, 51
Santonocito, Domenico 6, 136, 138
Santucci, Aldo 55
Sarasino, Franco 59, 98, 99, 148, 149, 154, 196
Sarti, Corrado 46, 98, 138
Sartof, Sergio 190
Sartore 115
Savage 14
Saville, D. T. 21
Savini, Angelo 4, 7, 90, 104, 116, 136
Savoia, Giorgio 4, 42, 44
Savoiardo 146
Scaglioni, Giuseppe 2, 6, 39, 41, 42, 45, 88
Scalamonti, Cavicchia 51
Scalet, Ernesto 5, 85, 168
Scandone, Felice 135
Scarabellotto, Valerio 40
Scaramucci, Pietro 42
Scarinci, Vincenzo 169
Scattaglia, Michele 10
Schwab, Lloyd 63, 113, 114, 133, 172, 175, 177, 191
Scialanca, Mario 151
Sclavo, Alfredo 7, 97
Scodellari, Raoul 5
Scozzoli, Guido 7
Sella, Spartaco 7
Serafini, Bernardino 123, 168, 171, 173
Sessa, Giovanni 4
Setterfield, Edward Louis 184
Scwell, George Aidan 84
Sewell Jack 162, 186, 187
Shannon, U. Y. 15, 112, 181
Sharrat, John Gerard 36
Shaw 13, 36, 45, 86, 87
Shelton, Bernard James 152
Shuttleworth, John 202
Sigsworth 139
Silvestri, Corrado 2, 119
Silvi, Giovanni 136
Simmons 38, 141
Simonazzi, Ugo 119
Simonini 46
Singleton, M. S. 161
Slater, Ronald 86, 87
Smeeton 201
Smith 29, 67
Smith, E. R. 172, 175, 176, 177
Smith, George Bartle 84
Smith, R. H. 14, 63, 69, 175
Smith, Robert Alwyn 121
Smith, T. M. W. 44, 103
Smith, W. 80

Smither 14
Snowden, Peter Douglas 80
Soffiantino 116
Solaro, Claudio 199
Soldati, Alberto 162
Soldati, Maggiorino 124, 168
Sole, Biagio 186
Somerville, D. M. 14, 22, 64, 65, 67, 73, 114, 119, 128
Soprana, Stefano 59, 122
Sorvillo, Eduardo 5, 85, 168, 172, 191
Sovrano, Davide 201
Spadaccini 32, 51
Spada, Mario 77, 82
Spallone, Ubaldo 135
Spencer, Harold Kenneth 162
Speranza, Oreste 36
Spiller 182
Spitzl, Bruno 58, 166
Sprague, R. A. 14, 63, 119, 166
Spurway 120, 186
Squires, P. 166
Stabile 184
Stamp, George Arthur 184
Starrett, Henry 13, 172
Stauble, Sergio 58
Steege, Gordon 97, 156, 157, 183, 189, 190, 194
Steele, Reginald Alfred 84
Steppi, Roberto 6, 19, 44, 45, 136
Stewart, I. T. G. 103
Stowell, R. A. T. 13, 49, 111, 137
St Quintin, Perry 172
Strahan, Peter 14, 87
Stramccioni 170
Strange 195
Stuart-Moore, J. A. 201
Stubbs, Frankie 14, 113
Stuckey, Vincent 'Heimar' 14, 47, 104, 105, 106, 108, 109, 111, 135, 181
Sugden, John Leonard 121
Swann, Ian Cheesman 88
Sykes, Harold 14, 105, 108, 109, 110, 111

T
Taddia, Ernesto 5, 87, 168, 171
Tadini, Giovanni 4, 27, 64, 68
Talanca, Ludovico 187
Taylor 80
Taylor, J. 53
Taylor, John Frederick 71
Tedeschi, Vincenzo 126, 190
Tedesco, Mario 187
Tempra, Francesco 162
Tessera, Domenico 199
Teste 16, 64
Teucci, Virginio 57
Thomas 182
Thompson 29
Thompson, William 149
Thomson 182
Thurlow, Maurice Cresswell 28, 29
Tillard, Rupert 186, 201
Timmins 200

Timolina, Giuseppe 5, 168, 192
Tivegna, Angelo 71, 133
Tomaselli, Pio 184
Tomasi, Giuseppe 34, 123
Toner, James Patrick 54
Toni 63, 84
Tonizzo, Federico 169
Torelli, Renato 75
Torresi, Giulio 5, 53, 54, 84, 85, 86
Toschi, Elios 152
Tovazzi, Giuseppe 201
Tovey 45, 72
Travaglini, Eduardo 122
Trebbi 55
Trémolet 67
Trevigni, Antonio 114
Trevisan, Giovanbattista 38
Trocca, Bruno 11
Troughton-Smith 28, 35, 63, 129
Tugnoli, Giorgio 201
Turchi, Mario 124, 169, 171, 173
Turnbull, Peter 97, 131, 156, 183
Tyler, "Ginger" 119

U
Ubaldi, Alfio 38
Uguccioni, Luigi 168
Unia, Carlo 10, 77, 97, 117, 133

V
Vaccari, Riccardo 59, 92, 98, 141, 148, 149, 187, 188, 191
Valentini, Valentino 34, 44, 161
Vale, William 13, 45, 63, 80, 137, 181
Valle, Antonio 58, 70, 104, 110, 154, 196
Van der Heijden, P. R. M. 14, 63
Vanelli, Renato 112
Vanni, Ivano 55
Vanni, Vincenzo 6, 39, 84, 85, 90, 136, 138, 153
Vanzan, Virgilio 5, 168, 192
Vaughan, Trevor Martin 14, 105, 106, 107, 109, 110
Venanzi, Guido 136
Venanzi, Ovidio 203
Veneziani, Piero 124, 168
Venosta 115
Ventura, Vasco 203
Veronesi, Mario 168
Vezely 40
Vicoli 76
Vieillard 68
Viglione Borghese, Ezio 59, 148, 178, 196
Vignaux, E. P. 86, 199
Villacèque 66
Viola, Corrado 151
Violante 201
Viotti, Alessandro 58, 153
Visconti, Adriano 20, 32, 33, 36, 55, 98, 100, 139, 186, 215
Visconti, Vittorio 201
Visentin 115
Vitolo 115

W
Wagstaff 29
Walker, D. R. 88, 181
Walker, T. O. 29, 99
Wallace-Tarry 42
Ware, E. M. 131, 184
Watkins 36, 80
Waymark 137, 151, 194
Webb, E. B. 15, 145, 162, 165, 181
Webber 23, 40, 68, 166, 194
Webber, Kenneth Edward 80
Weiss, Antonio 54, 63
Weld, R. E. 129
Weller, Arthur 14, 70, 95
Weller, W. H. 161
Wellham, J. W. G. 117
Wells 145, 146, 160, 164
Wells, R. J. 128
Wentworth-Smith, John Basil 43
Whitaker 42
Wickham, Peter 14, 36, 54, 55, 82, 113, 133
Wiles, 29
Williams 13, 21, 28, 67, 80, 114, 166
Williams, J. 75
Williams, W. C. 14
Wilson, J. R. 96, 166
Winship, Matthew Hetherington 80
Wise, L. E. C. 132
Wood, C. S. F. 182
Woodroffe 31
Woods, Eric 13, 68, 69
Woodward 76
Woodward, Vernon 13, 35, 36, 37, 45, 54, 62, 81, 86, 195
Woolston 201
Worcester, H. C. 14, 63, 69, 81, 82
Wykeham-Barnes, Peter 14, 22, 41, 95, 97, 100, 104, 106, 109, 113, 181
Wynn, Rowland John William 83

Y
York, William Robert 165
Young, Anthony 113
Young, Ernest Seath 200
Young, John 88
Yoyotte-Husson 35

Z
Zamagna, Giulio 151
Zambelli, Armando 169, 170, 173
Zanardi, Alfredo 7, 9
Zanarini, Tolmino 124
Zanetti, Antonio 165
Zannier, Martino ,Nino' 4, 27, 29, 37, 42, 45
Zannini, Romano 83
Zardini 186
Zelè 47
Zimmermann 49
Zirioli, Dante 70
Zolesi, Umberto 36, 43
Zuccarini, Gianmario 5, 53, 54
Zuffi, Giuseppe 124, 141, 143, 144, 169, 171
Zuliani, Vanni 59, 98, 153

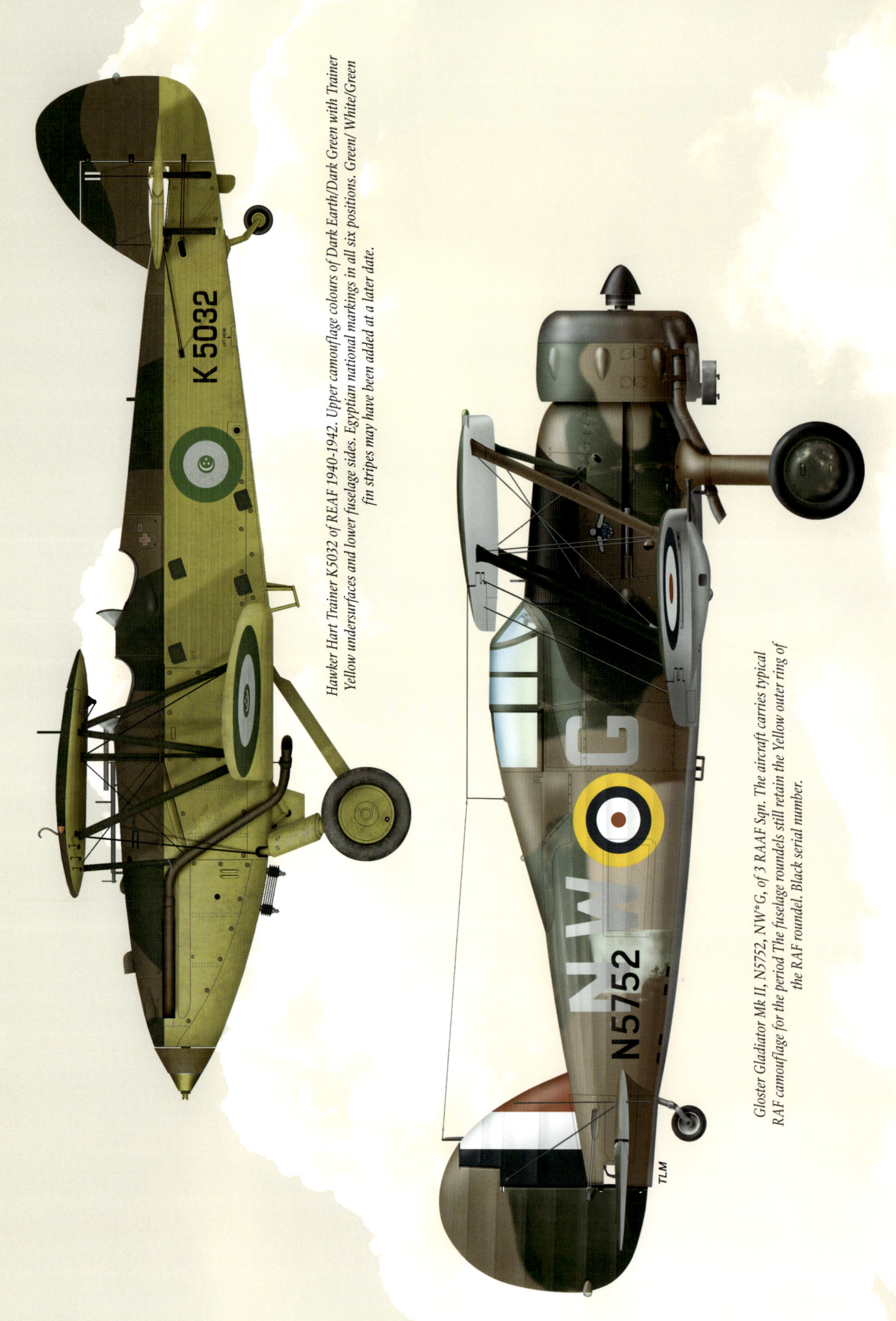

Hawker Hart Trainer K5032 of REAF 1940-1942. Upper camouflage colours of Dark Earth/Dark Green with Trainer Yellow undersurfaces and lower fuselage sides. Egyptian national markings in all six positions. Green/White/Green fin stripes may have been added at a later date.

Gloster Gladiator Mk II, N5752, NW*G, of 3 RAAF Sqn. The aircraft carries typical RAF camouflage for the period The fuselage roundels still retain the Yellow outer ring of the RAF roundel. Black serial number.

212

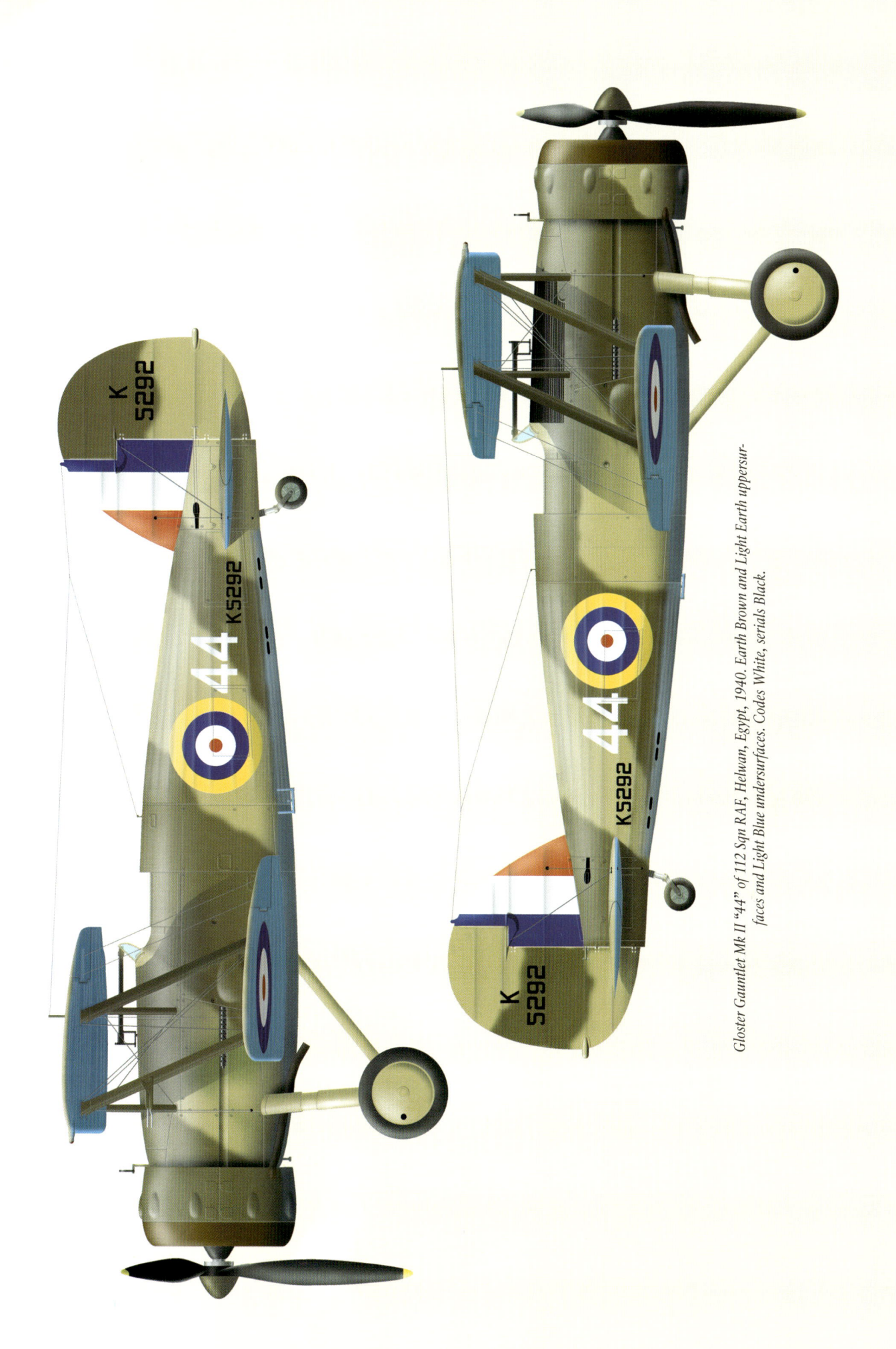

Gloster Gauntlet Mk II "44" of 112 Sqn RAF, Helwan, Egypt, 1940. Earth Brown and Light Earth uppersurfaces and Light Blue undersurfaces. Codes White, serials Black.

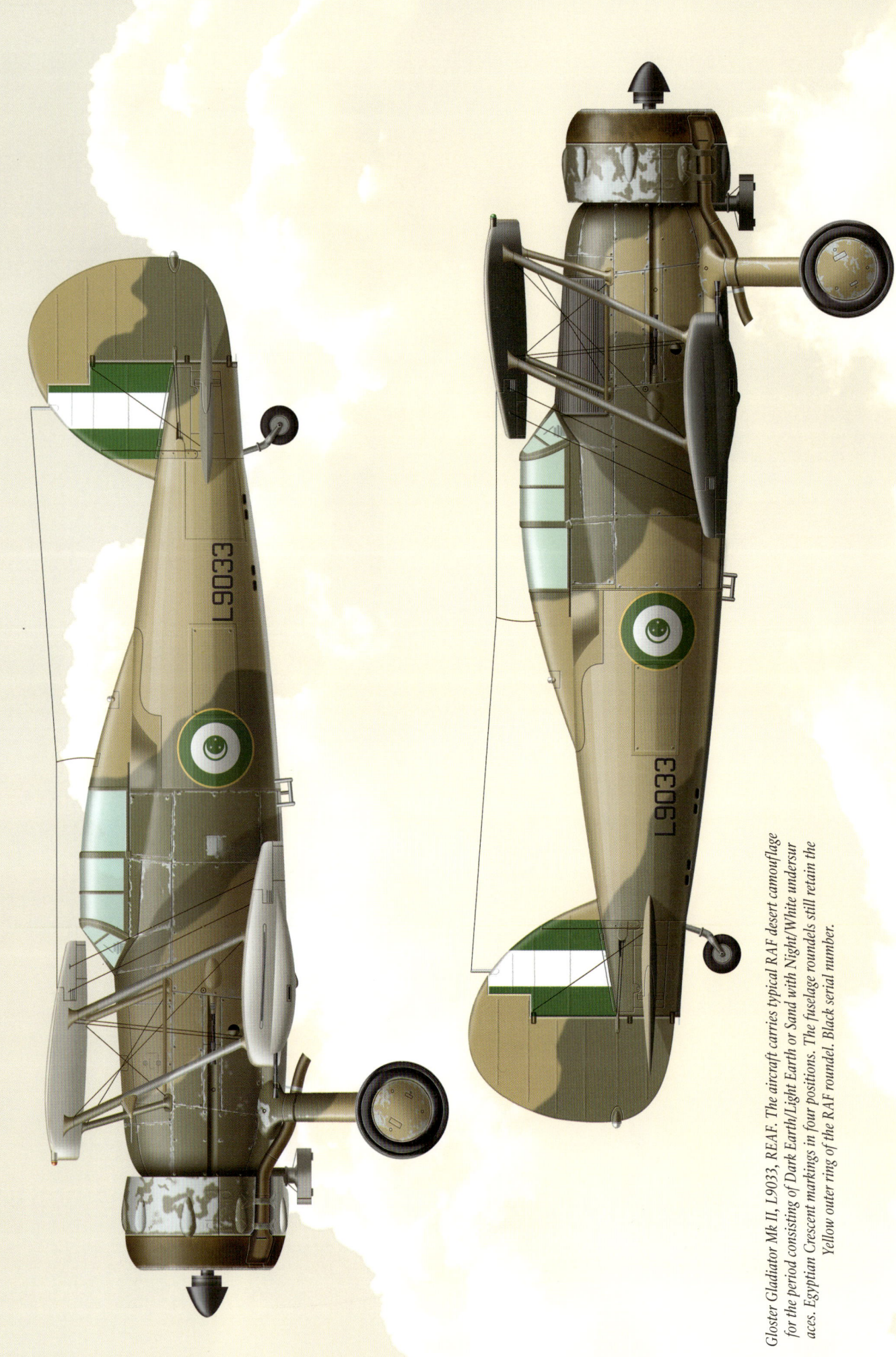

Gloster Gladiator Mk II, L9033, REAF. The aircraft carries typical RAF desert camouflage for the period consisting of Dark Earth/Light Earth or Sand with Night/White undersurfaces. Egyptian Crescent markings in four positions. The fuselage roundels still retain the Yellow outer ring of the RAF roundel. Black serial number.

215

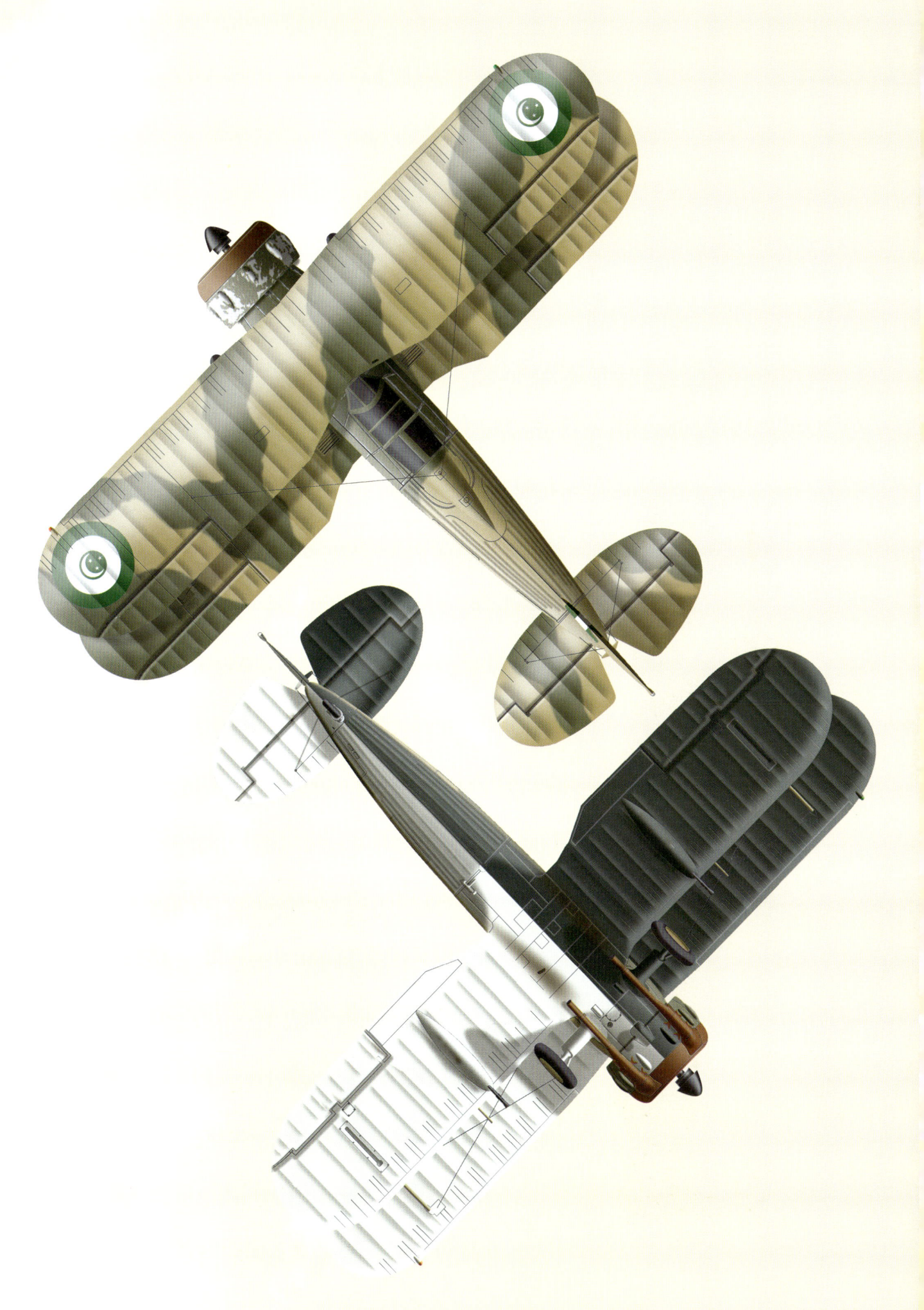

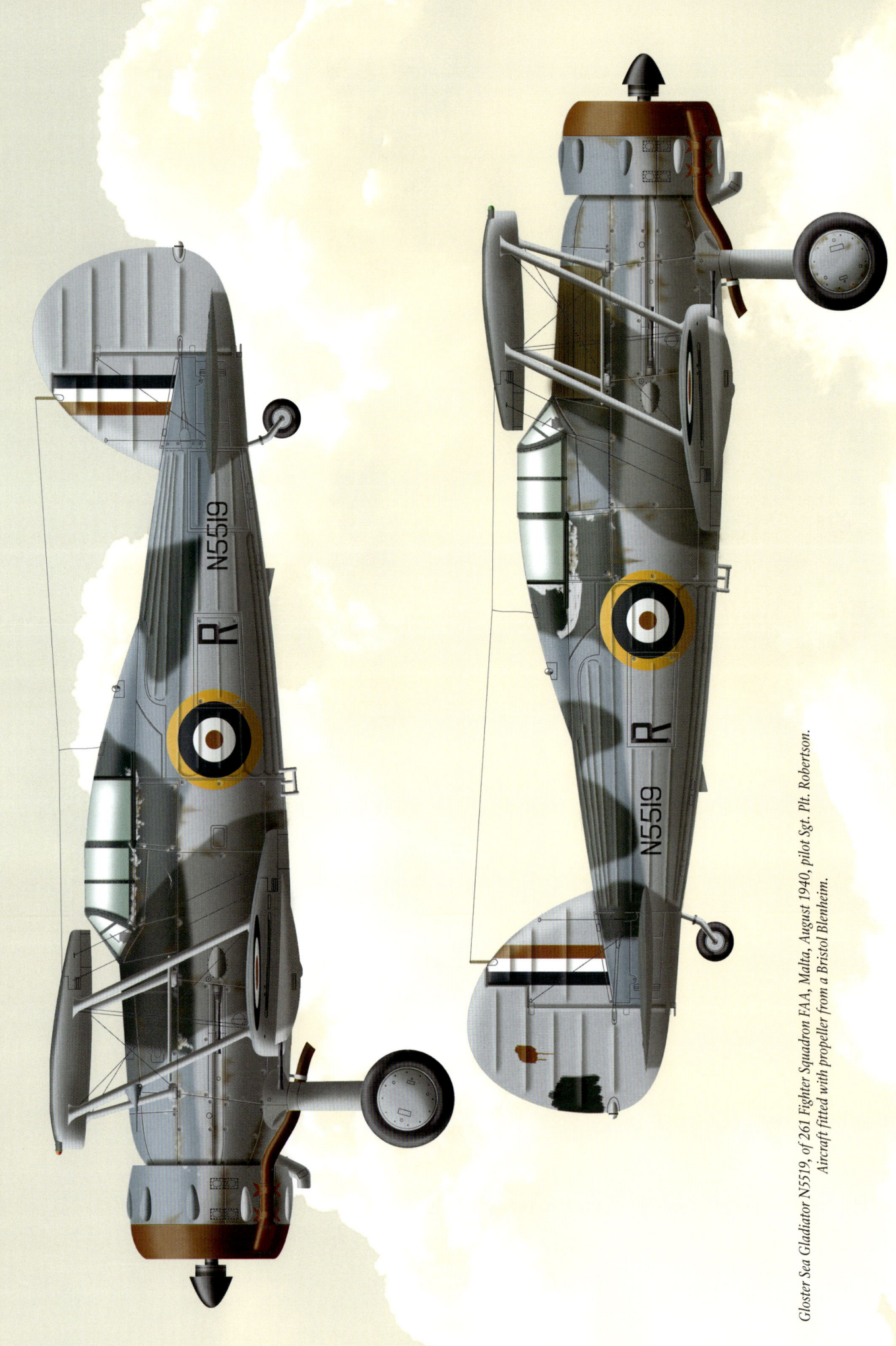

Gloster Sea Gladiator N5519, of 261 Fighter Squadron FAA, Malta, August 1940, pilot Sgt. Plt. Robertson. Aircraft fitted with propeller from a Bristol Blenheim.

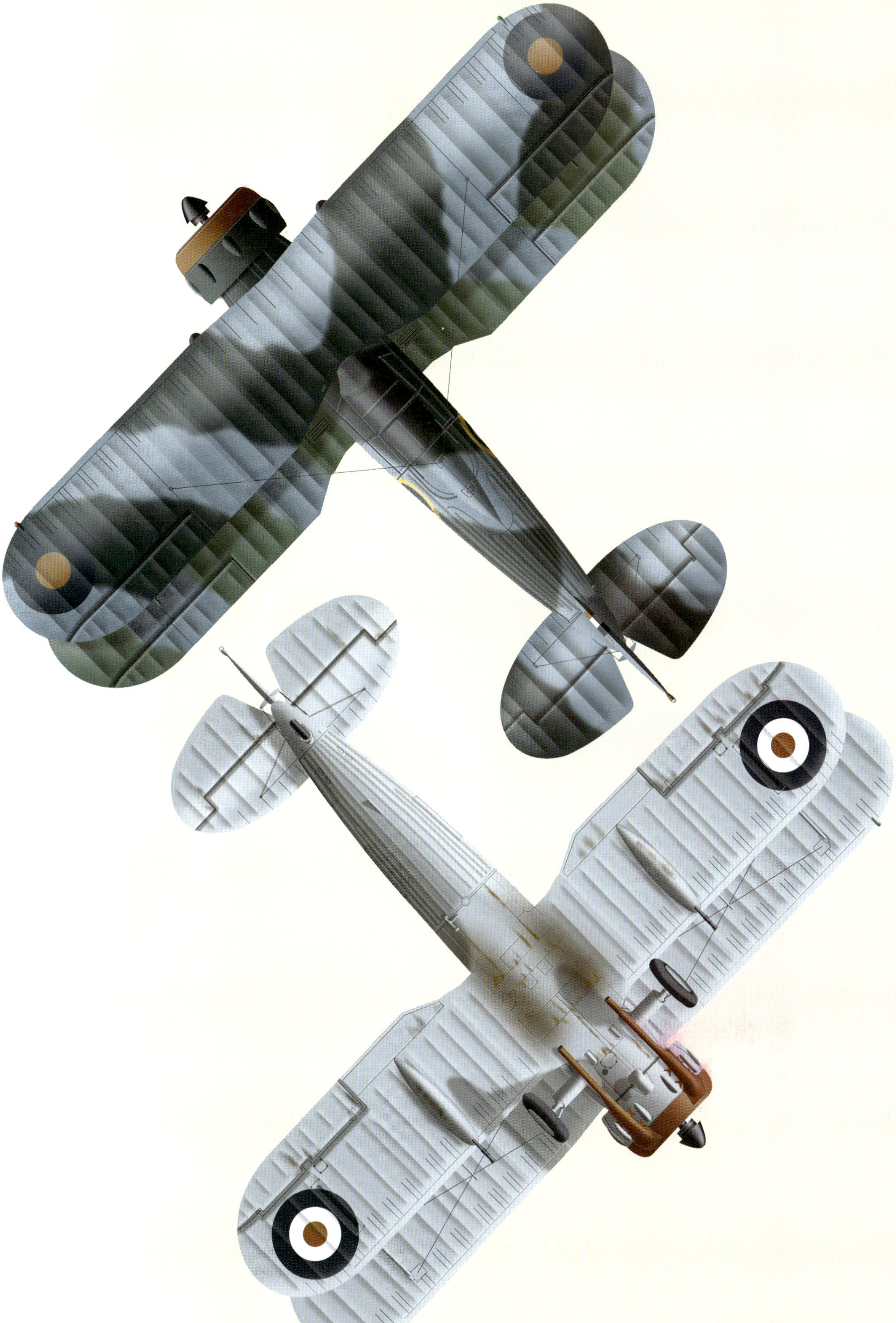

Blenheim Mk.IF (L1336).

Blenheim Mk.I (L1490), LJ*R, of 211. Sqn, El Dabba, Egypt, June 1940.

Breda Ba.65 A-80, of 159ª Sq. (12° Gr., 50° St.) Libya, October 1940.

Breda Ba.65 A-80, MM75244 of 159ª Sq. (12° Gr., 50° St.) Libya, October 1940. Aircraft piloted by Sottotenente Adriano Visconti (1915-1945), one of the most famous Italian pilots.

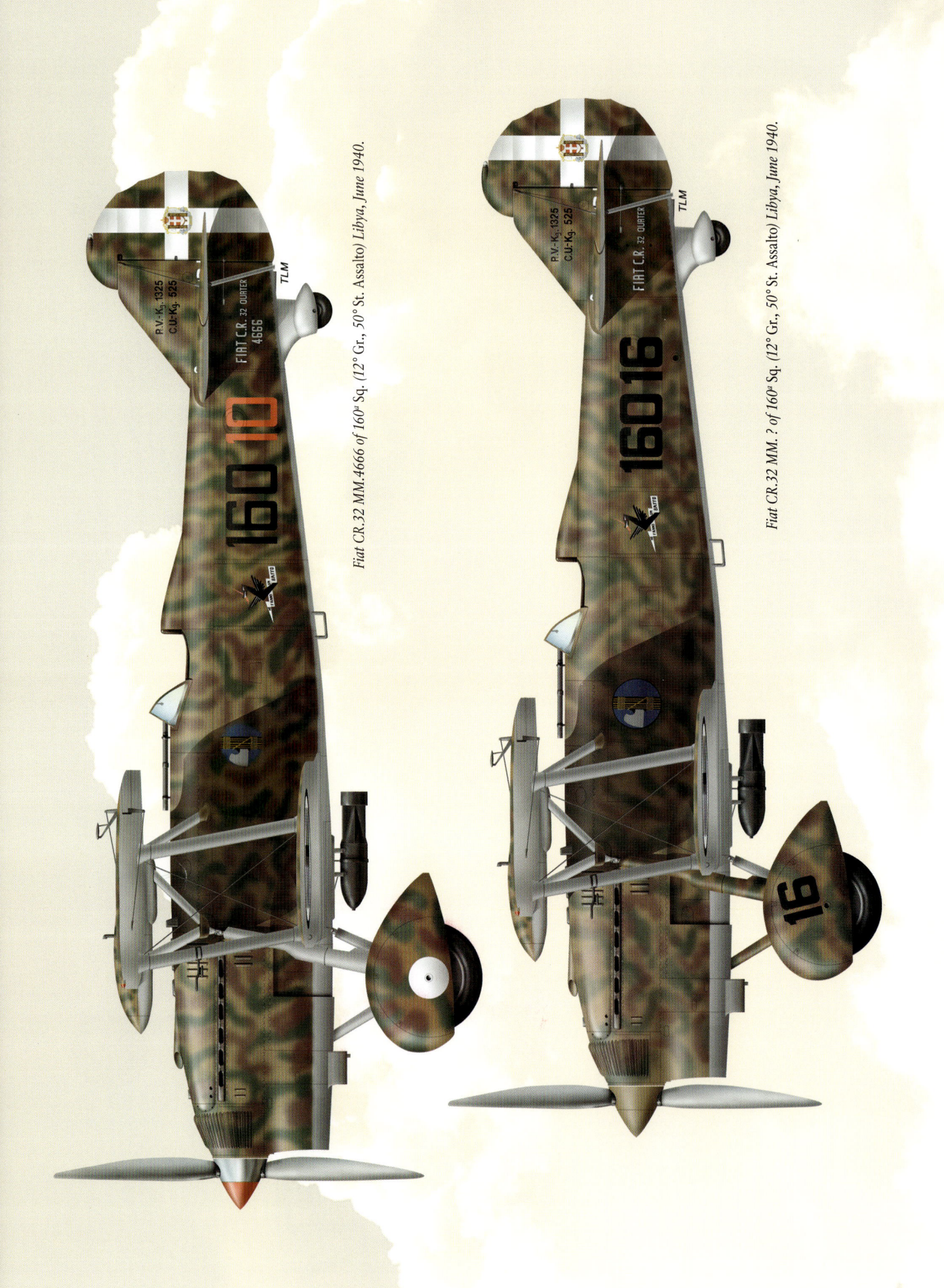

Fiat CR.32 MM.4666 of 160ª Sq. (12º Gr., 50º St. Assalto) Libya, June 1940.

Fiat CR.32 MM. ? of 160ª Sq. (12º Gr., 50º St. Assalto) Libya, June 1940.

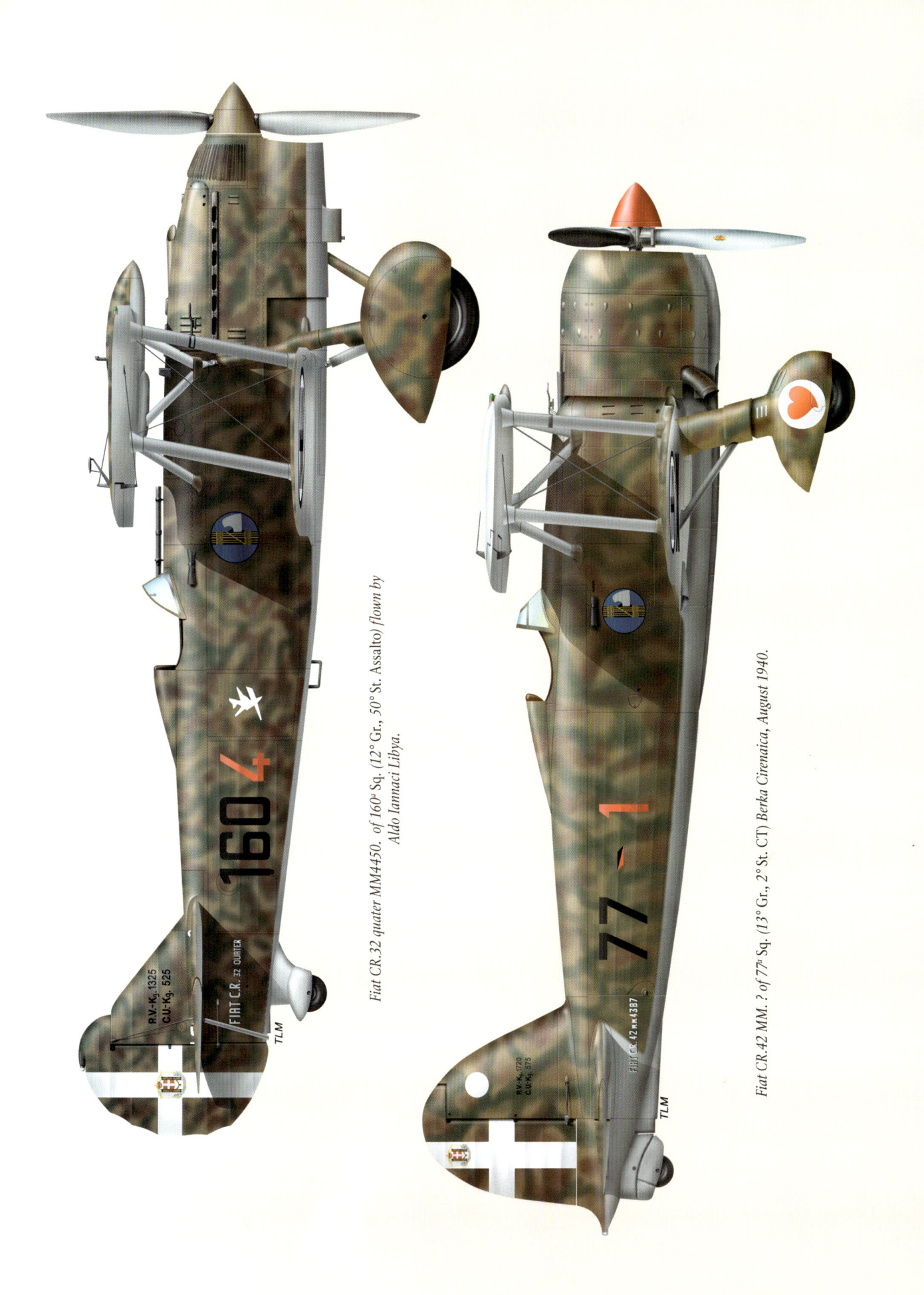

Fiat CR.32 quater MM4450. of 160ª Sq. (12° Gr., 50° St. Assalto) flown by Aldo Iannaci Libya.

Fiat CR.42 MM. ? of 77ª Sq. (13° Gr., 2° St. CT) Berka Cirenaica, August 1940.

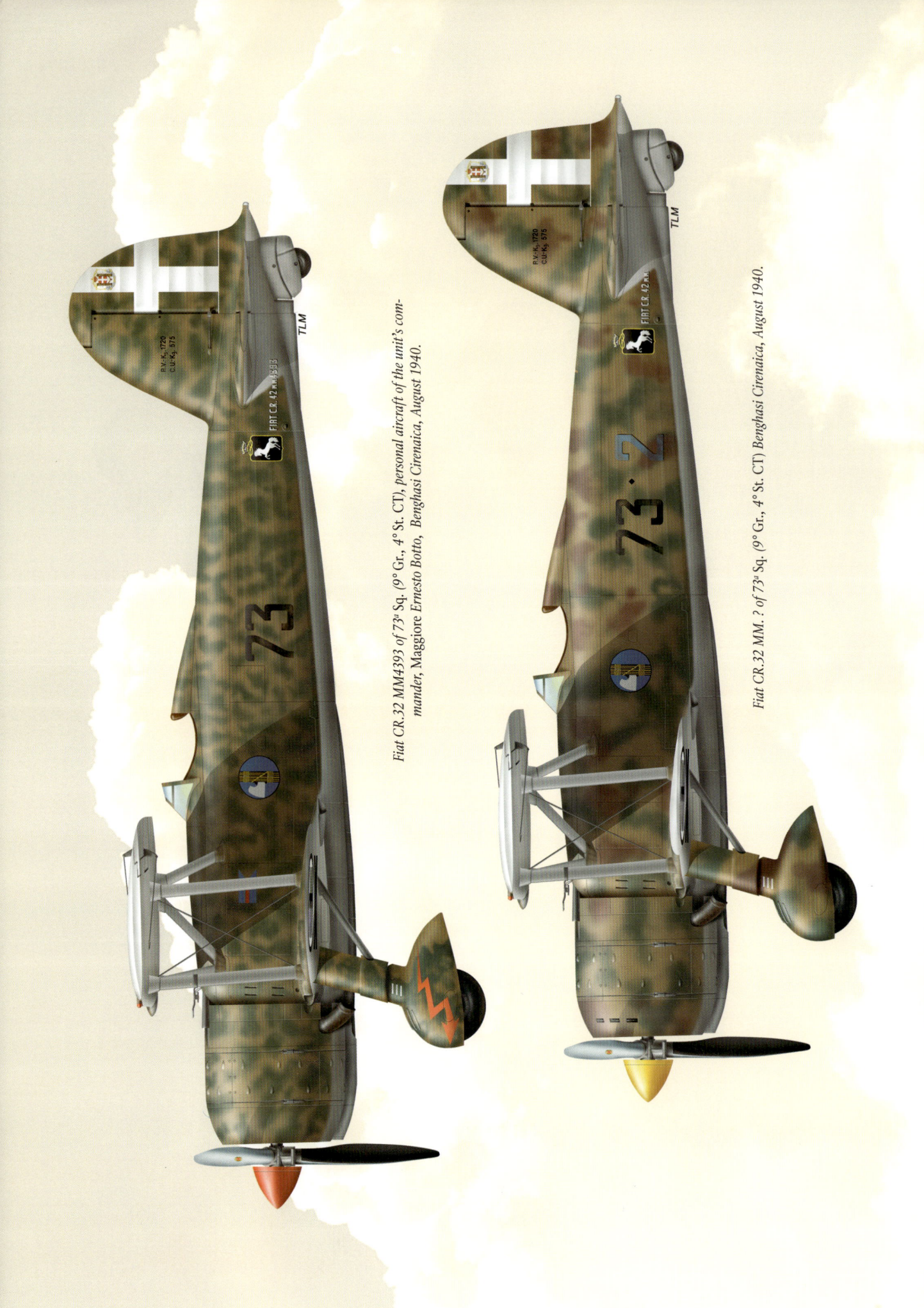

Fiat CR.32 MM4393 of 73ª Sq. (9° Gr., 4° St. CT), personal aircraft of the unit's commander, Maggiore Ernesto Botto, Benghasi Cirenaica, August 1940.

Fiat CR.32 MM. ? of 73ª Sq. (9° Gr., 4° St. CT) Benghasi Cirenaica, August 1940.

Fiat CR.42 MM. ? of 78ª Sq. (13° Gr, 2° St. CT) Tmimi Cirenaica, September 1940.

Fiat CR.42 MM4306 The plane was originally 91-6 the mount of ten. Enzo Martissa. After being damaged and obliged to force land on August the 8th, the plane was recovered, repaired and given these codes by the SRAM of El Adem. In fact the plane never saw service with 84a Squadriglia. It was instead assigned to another unit, possibly of 2° Stormo.

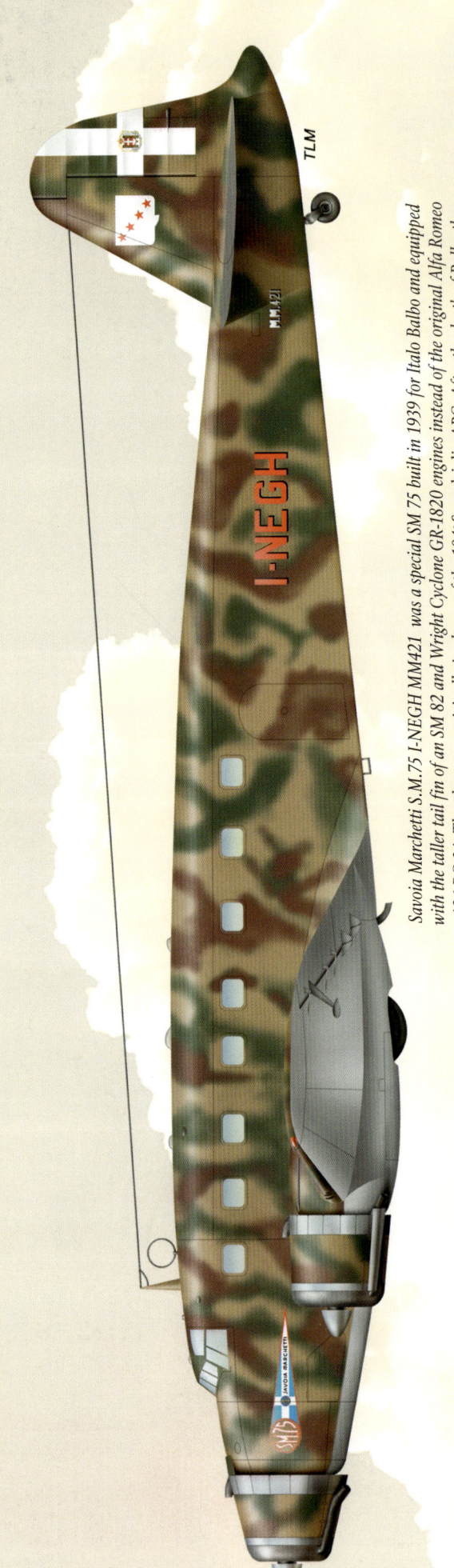

Savoia Marchetti S.M.75 I-NEGH MM421 was a special SM 75 built in 1939 for Italo Balbo and equipped with the taller tail fin of an SM 82 and Wright Cyclone GR-1820 engines instead of the original Alfa Romeo 126 RC.34. The plane was originally in charge of the 104ª Squadriglia APC. After the death of Balbo the plane was given to the new CO in Chief Marshal Rodolfo Graziani and marked I-NEGH. The pennant of an Army Marshal (White flag with red stars in it) was also applied on the tail fin.

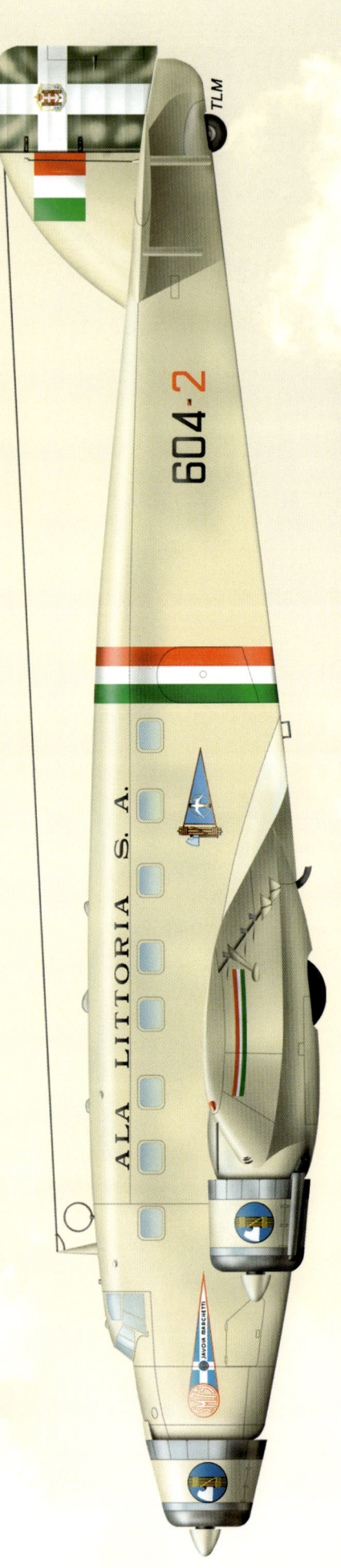

Savoia Marchetti S.M.75, 604ª Squadriglia was formed on 9 June 1940 with six SM 75 previously part of Ala Littoria. These planes were gradually camouflaged but during Summer 1940 had only the tail fin with military colours while the rest of the machine retained those of Ala Littoria.